DAVID SKERNICK

BACK ROADS *of Maine*

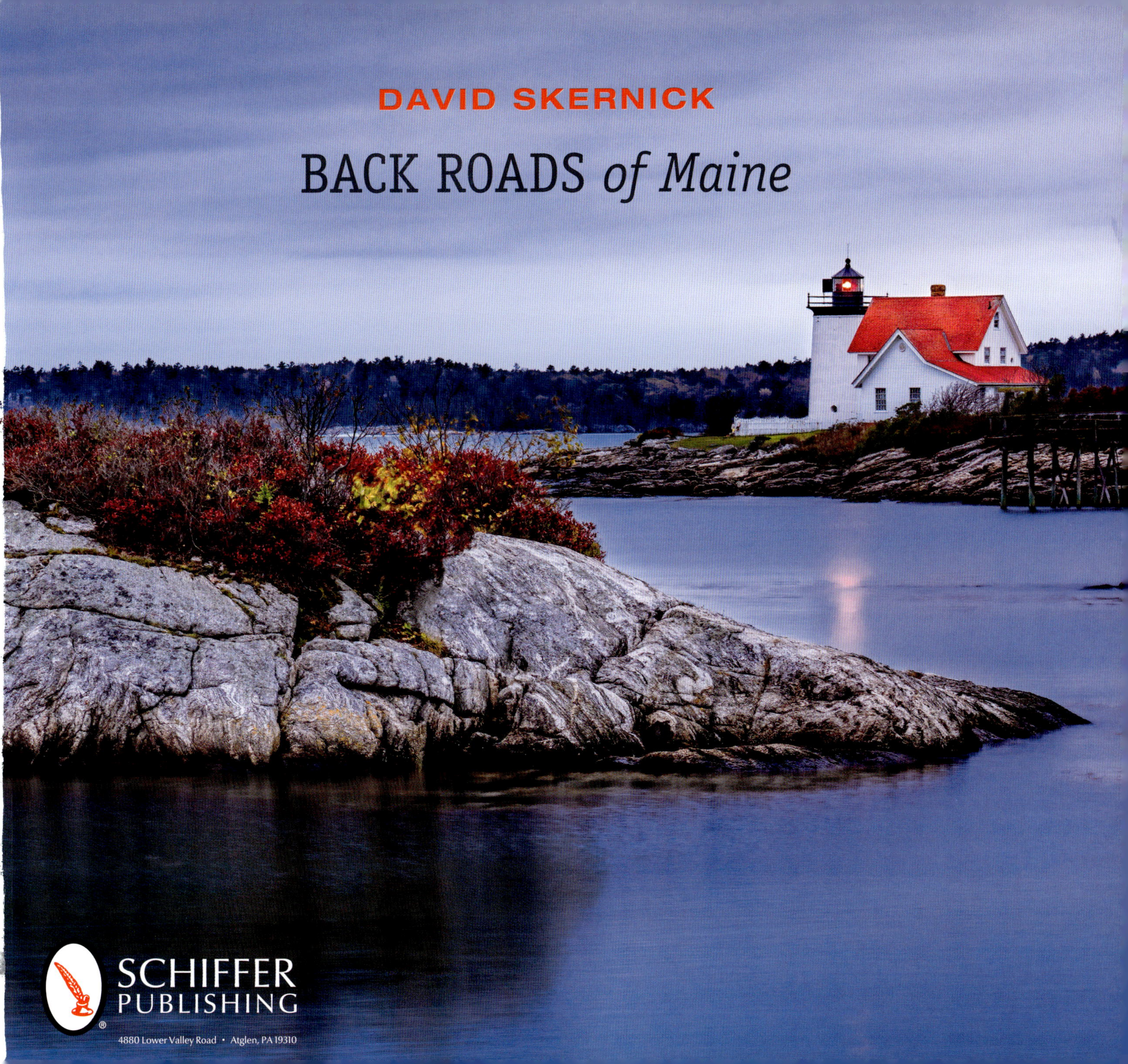

SCHIFFER PUBLISHING

4880 Lower Valley Road • Atglen, PA 19310

Other Schiffer Books by the Author:

Back Roads of Northern California, ISBN 978-0-7643-5762-6

Back Roads of Southern California, ISBN 978-0-7643-5763-3

Back Roads of the Southwest, ISBN 978-0-7643-5858-6

Back Roads of the Great Plains, ISBN 978-0-7643-6186-9

Back Roads of the Pacific Northwest, ISBN 978-0-7643-6290-3

Back Roads of the Midwest, ISBN 978-0-7643-6483-9

How Did You Get That Shot?, ISBN 978-0-7643-5728-2

Easy Astrophotography, ISBN 978-0-7643-6684-0

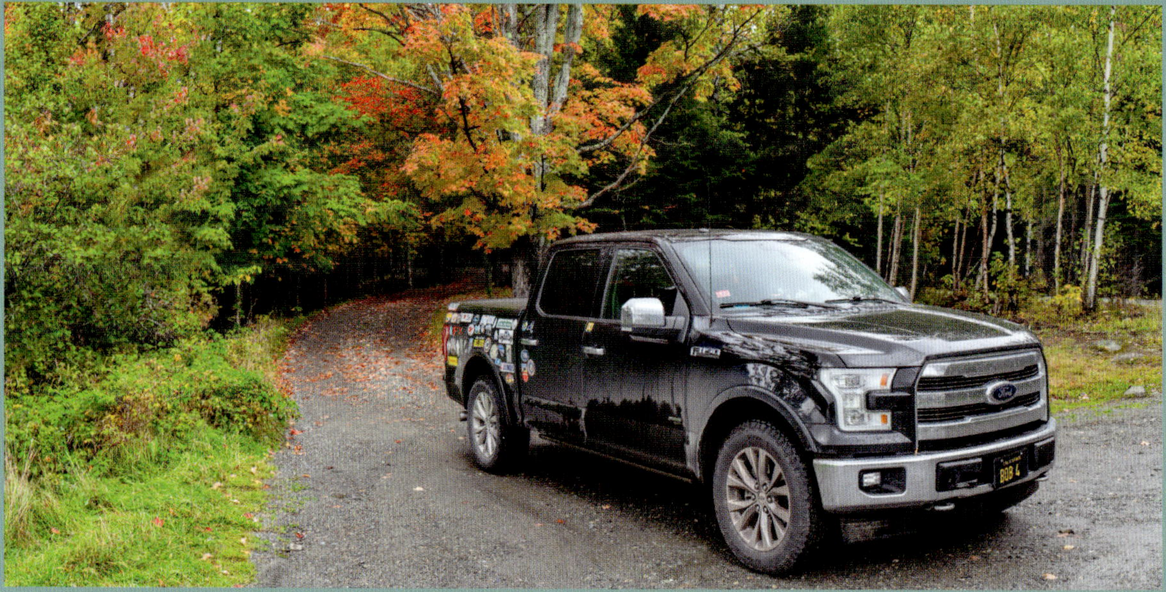

Library of Congress Control Number: 2024941497

Edited by Ian Robertson
Type set in Proxima Nova

ISBN: 978-0-7643-6747-2
ePub: 978-1-5073-0553-9
Printed in China

Published by Schiffer Publishing, Ltd.
4880 Lower Valley Road
Atglen, PA 19310
Phone: (610) 593-1777; Fax: (610) 593-2002
Email: info@schifferbooks.com
Web: www.schifferbooks.com

For our complete selection of fine books on this and related subjects, please visit our website at www.schifferbooks.com. You may also write for a free catalog.

Schiffer Publishing's titles are available at special discounts for bulk purchases for sales promotions or premiums. Special editions, including personalized covers, corporate imprints, and excerpts, can be created in large quantities for special needs. For more information, contact the publisher.

FSC
www.fsc.org
MIX
Paper | Supporting responsible forestry
FSC® C104723

THE PEACE OF WILD THINGS

When despair for the world grows in me and I wake in the
night at the least sound in fear of what my life and my
children's lives may be,
I go and lie down where the wood drake rests in his beauty
on the water, and the great heron feeds.
I come into the peace of wild things who do not tax their lives
with forethought of grief. I come to the presence of still water.
And I feel above me the day-blind stars waiting with their
light. For a time, I rest in the grace of the world, and am free.

—Wendell Berry, *The Selected Poems of Wendell Berry*

ACKNOWLEDGMENTS

I can never say enough about all the people who have helped me make these books. To my wife, friends, and all the people at Schiffer Publishing, I remain grateful beyond words. I truly hope you all know the massive contributions you make and how much you mean to me.

An acknowledgement can also be a confession. I want to take this opportunity . . . .

Like so many photographers, when we switched from film to digital, I made the pledge to only do in post processing what I could have done in a darkroom. Yeah . . .what were we thinking? Just creating the panoramic images that are now my passion goes way beyond anything I could have done with film. Still, most of the time I try to render, as close as possible, what I saw, rather than what I wished I saw. Sure, I clean up the occasional bright rock or dead tree branch, I enhance here and there, but I try to stay true to what was there.

I went a little crazy in one of the following images and I feel I owe it to the reader to come clean (as it were). I spent a total of 18 hours over several months to remove every wire and pole in the panorama of Stonington, Maine. No kidding—you find a wire in there I'll give you free lessons. I'm not sure what got into me. I hope you think it "works" and that the people of Stonington like it.

Most of my photographs reveal another kind of freedom: panoramic photographs. As a photographer, I was trained in the art of seeing things through the confined dimensions of a 35 mm piece of film—approximately 3:2, slightly wider than tall. As all photographers have done, I have worked within these boundaries, using wide-angle lenses to capture more of the scene than would otherwise be possible, but the resulting distortion of distance and perspective never felt quite right. I found myself secretly envious of painters, who could select any shape of canvas on which to create art. When I found panoramic photography, I realized I had discovered my unrestrained canvas. Panorama photographs are carefully crafted from multiple photographs that are combined to form one large image. With panoramas I can photograph without traditional framing limitations. This is immensely satisfying for me, since I feel that panoramas are best able to convey what you would have seen had you been standing there beside me when I took the picture.

Grab your lobster bib and let's go for a ride. We'll start from the southern coast, follow that up, and then work our way inland and just wander around. Let's go to Maine!!

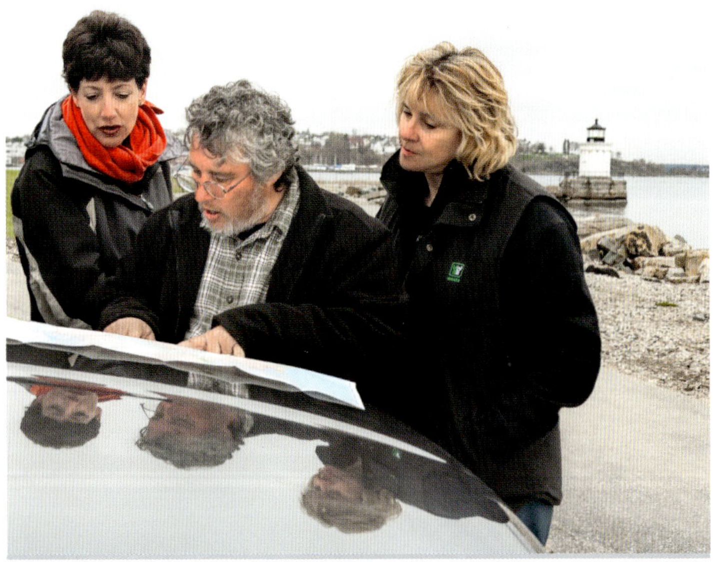

Photo by Carol Zulman

INTRODUCTION

The motel has a screen door. When I opened it this morning it made a long S-Q-U-O-I-N-K sound. Sliding behind the wheel of Bob the Truck, I glance at my map and think, "I could check out 3 lighthouses before lunch." Lunch . . . lobster roll? I'm in Maine.

Every time I go to Maine I fall in love with it. I dream of living there until I remember the cold winters. Then I run home to Los Angeles and spend most of the time wishing I was back in Maine. One of these days I might just give in. I love snow, and I could get a warmer coat. The scenery is stupendous, the people are interesting and friendly, and the food? Well, if you like lobster . . .

There are 65 lighthouses along the Maine coast. No, I haven't found them all yet, but you have to know I'm working on it. The general coastline of Maine measures only 228 miles, but if you include all the inlets and bays the new measurement is 3,478 miles. I have driven and photographed most of those miles, and that's just the coast. Each time I go to Maine I seem to find more roads and more cool stuff.

Inland Maine is a tapestry of lakes, mountains, trees, farms, and moose. I guess there is a lot more to it than that, but that is more than enough to keep this little old camera bug happy. Although Oregon is the number one state for lumber production, Maine contributes about 12 million tons per year. About one-third of the state is only accessible along "unimproved" roads meant for lumber trucks. I traveled many of them searching for just the right tree, stream, and the elusive moose. You want some alone time? Try driving hundreds of miles along narrow dirt roads with few signs or landmarks. Bring your GPS and a compass and watch out for those huge trucks; they have the right of way.

My books are not meant to be exhaustive collections of photographs from each region. They are more a collection of places and things I see as I drive along. I travel 50,000 miles or so every year along the back roads of the United States. Cities and freeways hold little interest for me. I call this getting lost on "gray roads."

As I crisscross the back roads of this amazing country I find little gems and prizes everywhere. If you are looking for your favorite spot or road I may not have found it yet. I will keep looking and you are, of course, welcome to contact me and make suggestions. I would love to hear from you. Lots of my favorite places were found when I asked someone at a gas station or restaurant, "What's good to see around here?"

Grab your lobster bib and let's go for a ride. We'll start from the southern coast, follow that up, and then work our way inland and just wander around. Let's go to Maine!!

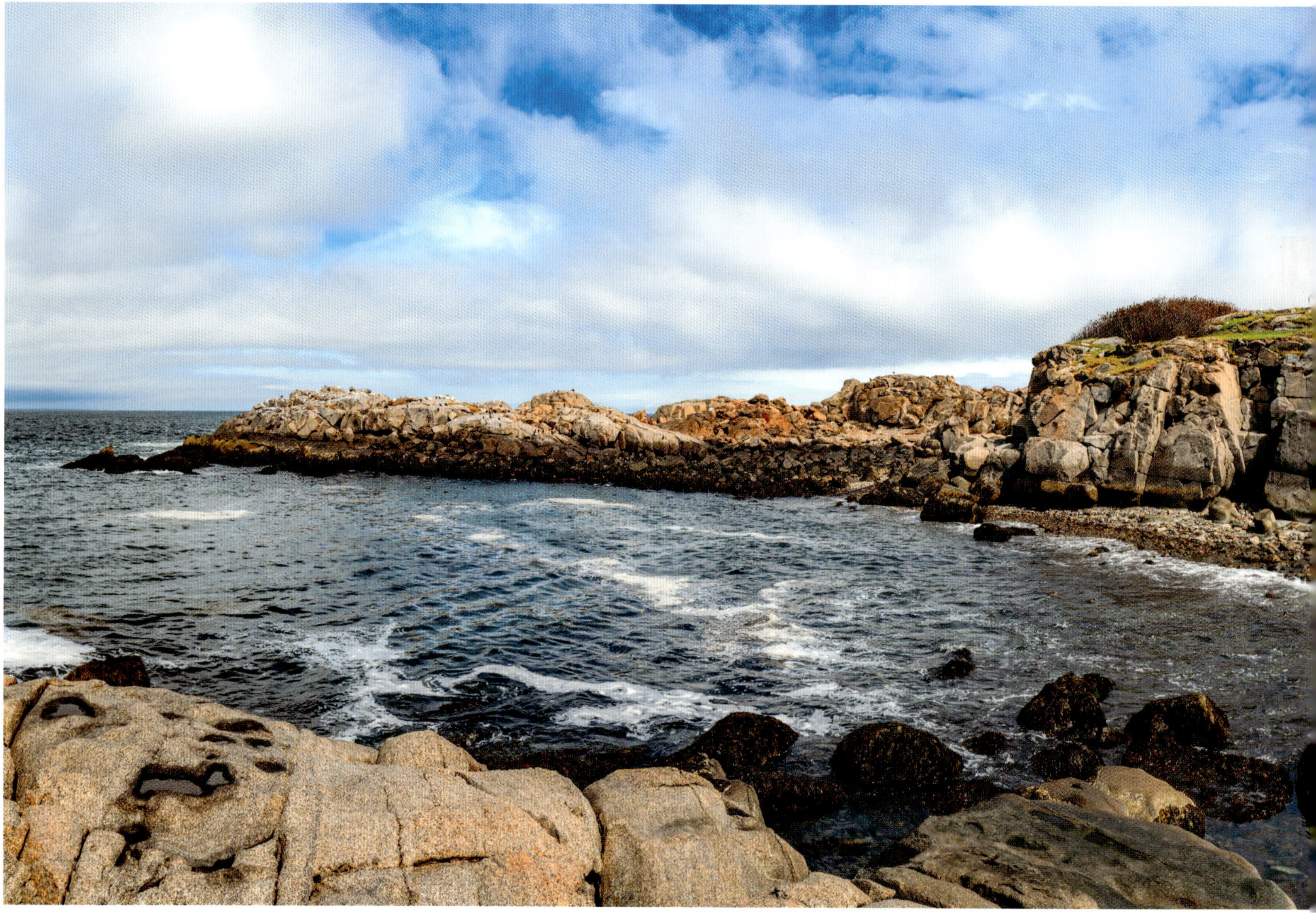

Cape Neddick Lighthouse or "Nubble Light" (1879), York Harbor, Maine

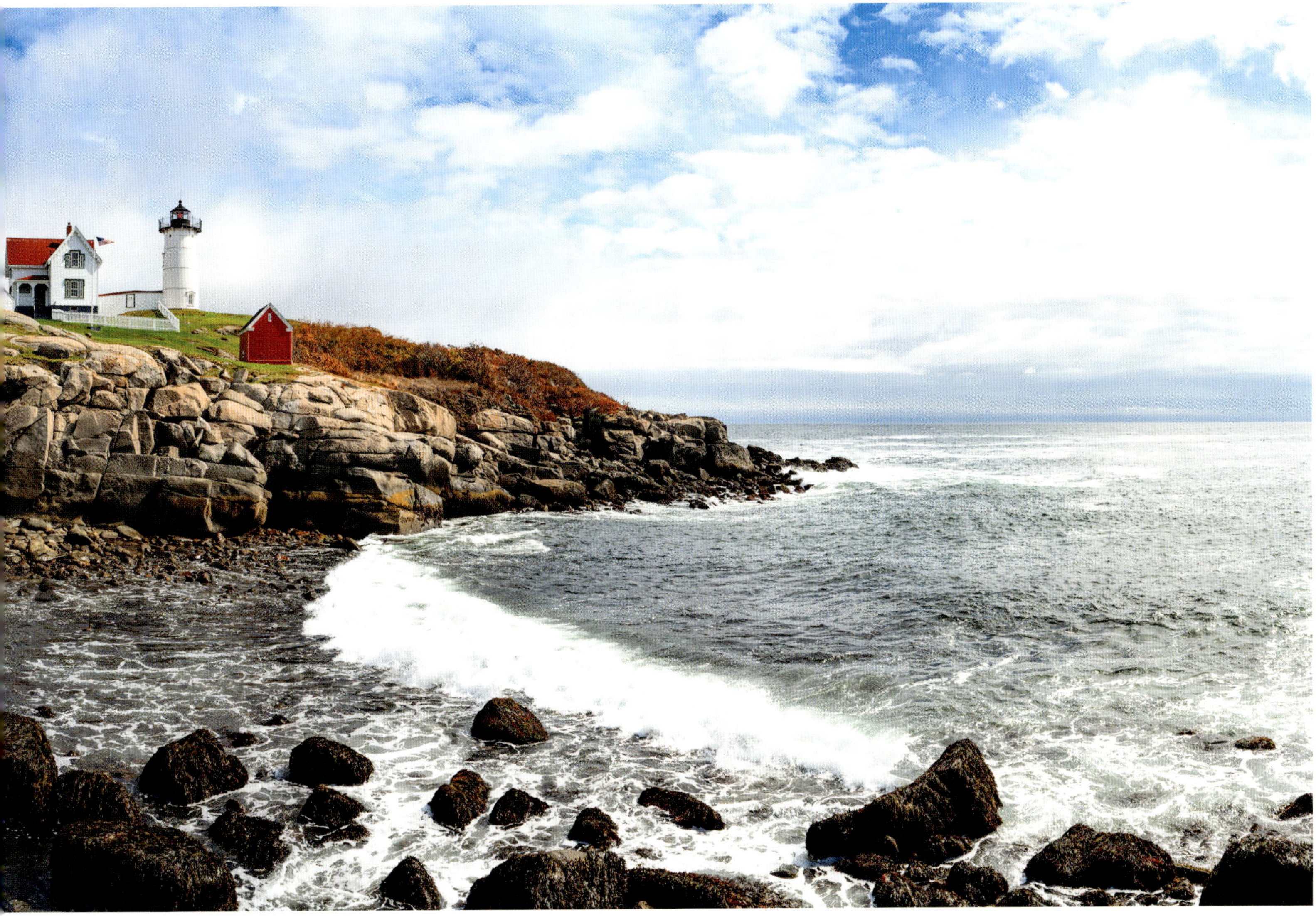

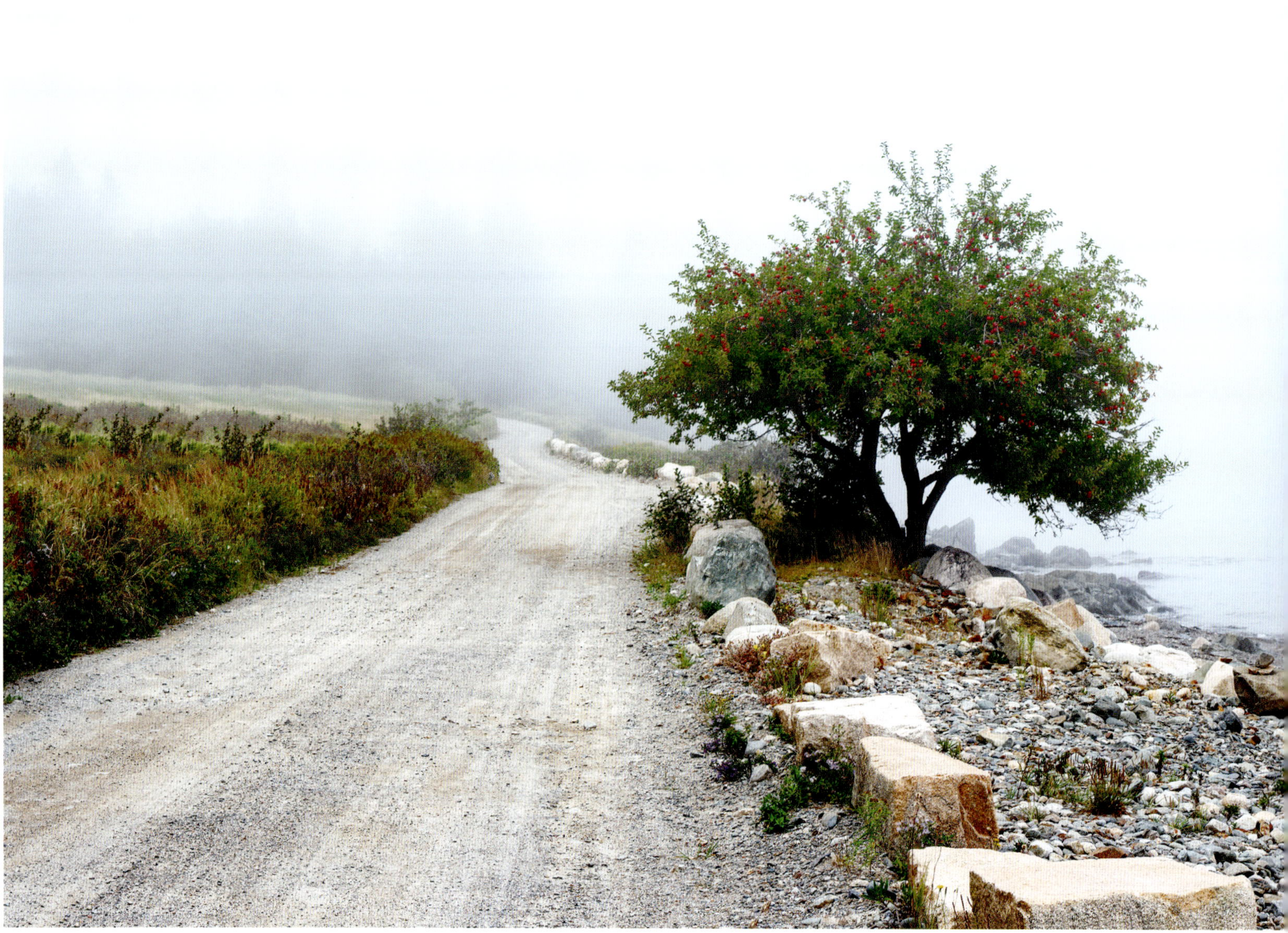

Land's End Road, Porpoise Cove, Maine

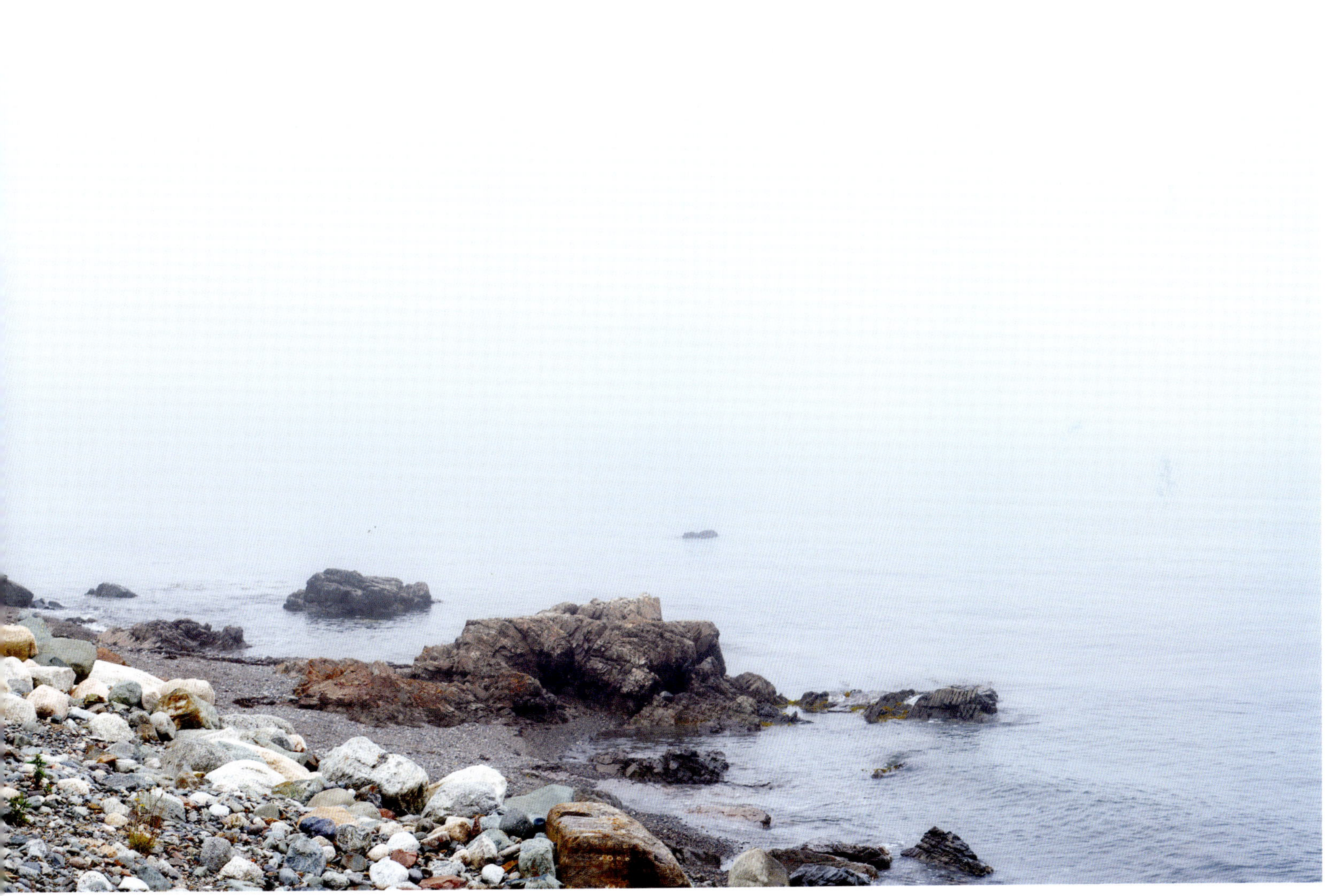

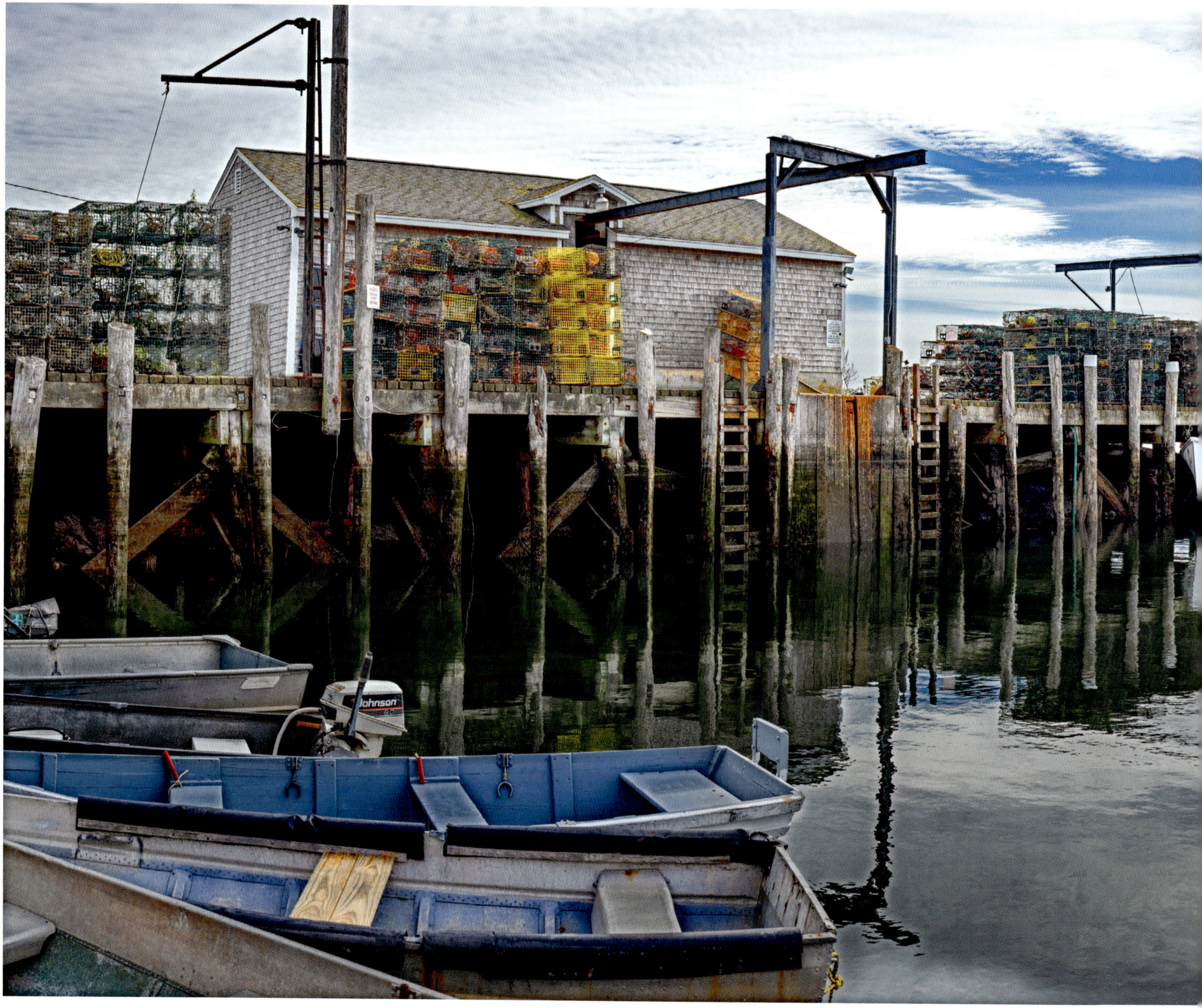

Wood Island Harbor, Biddeford Pool, Maine

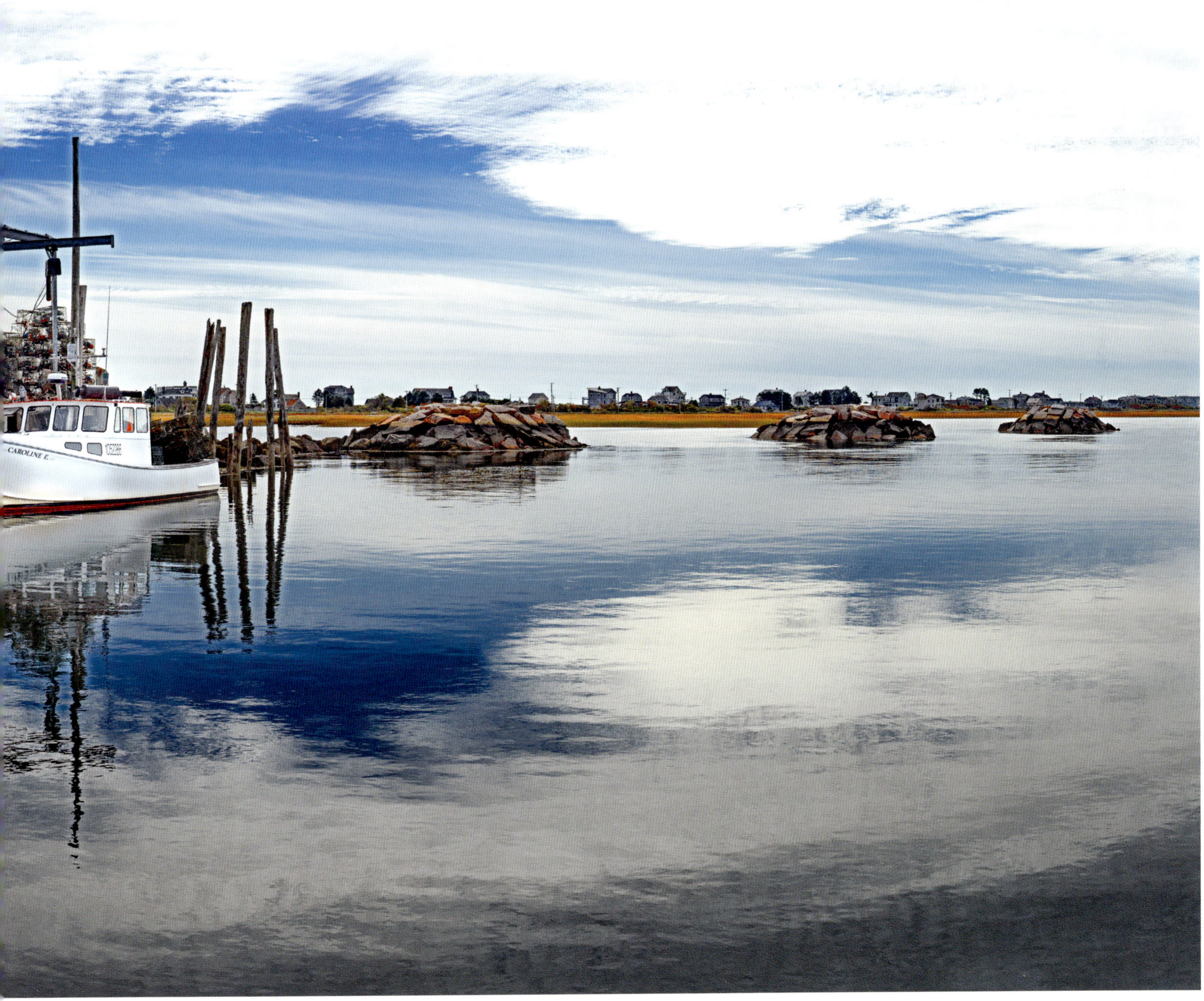

I waited for the clouds to line up. Lucky for me, they did!

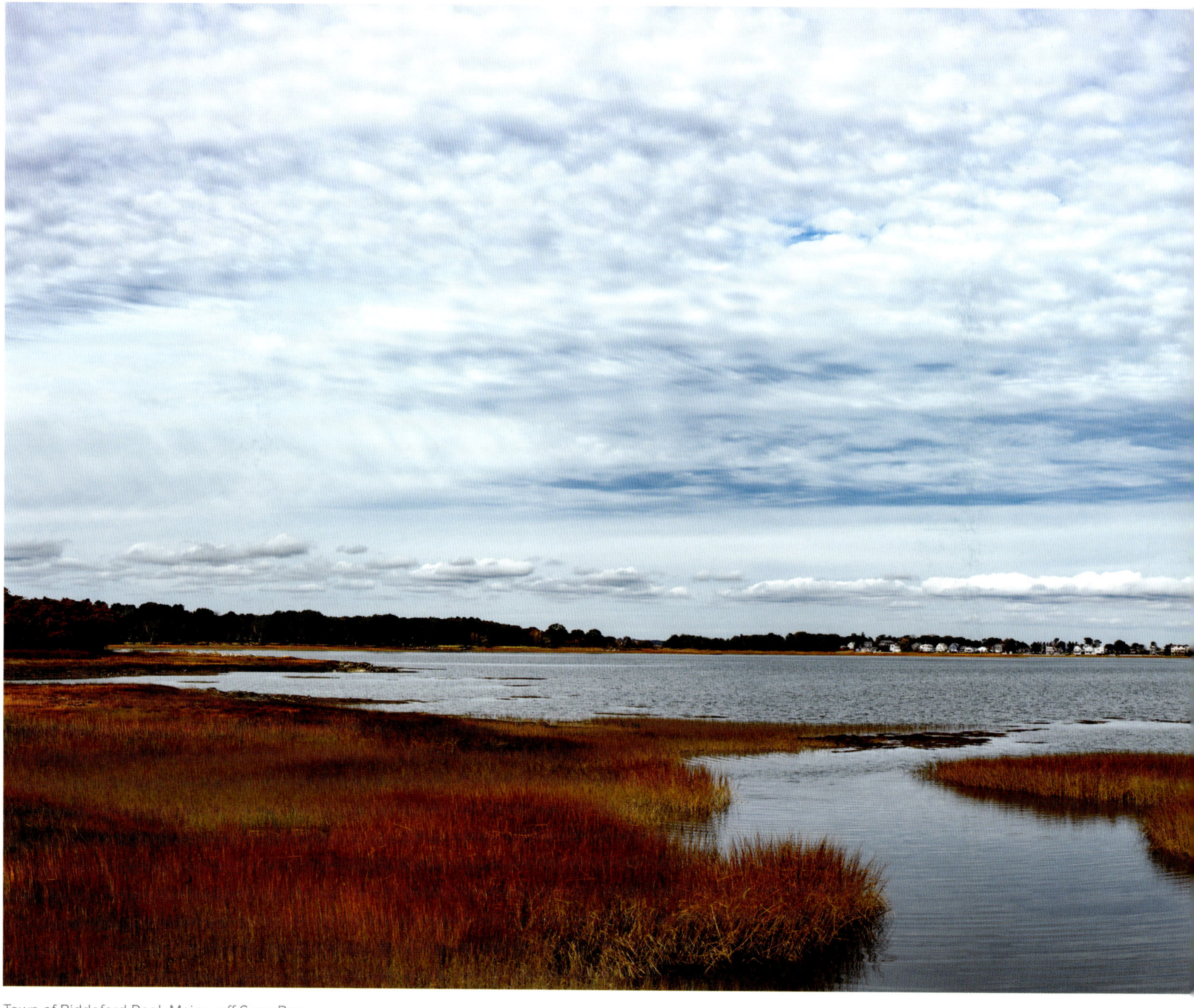

Town of Biddeford Pool, Maine, off Saco Bay

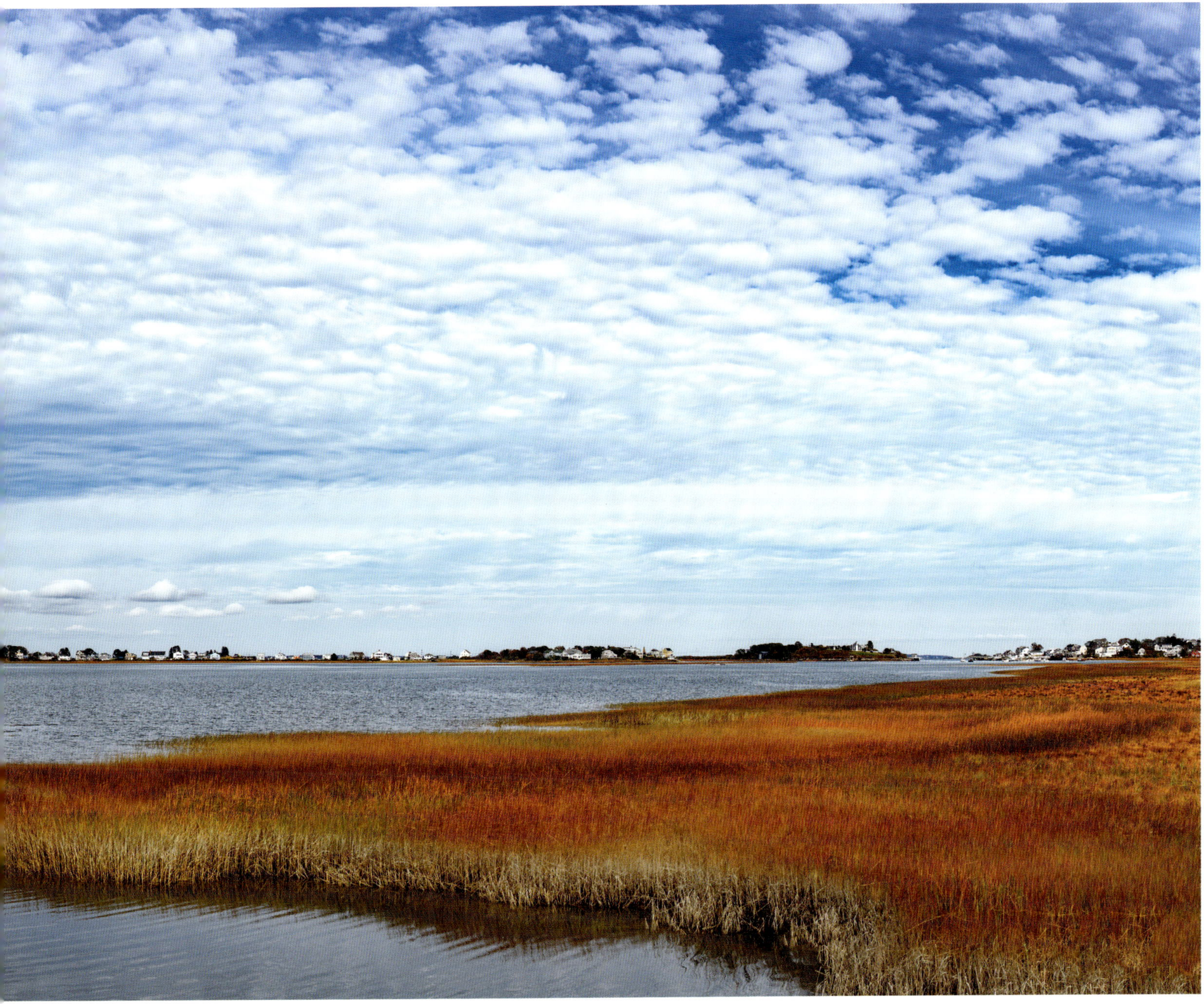

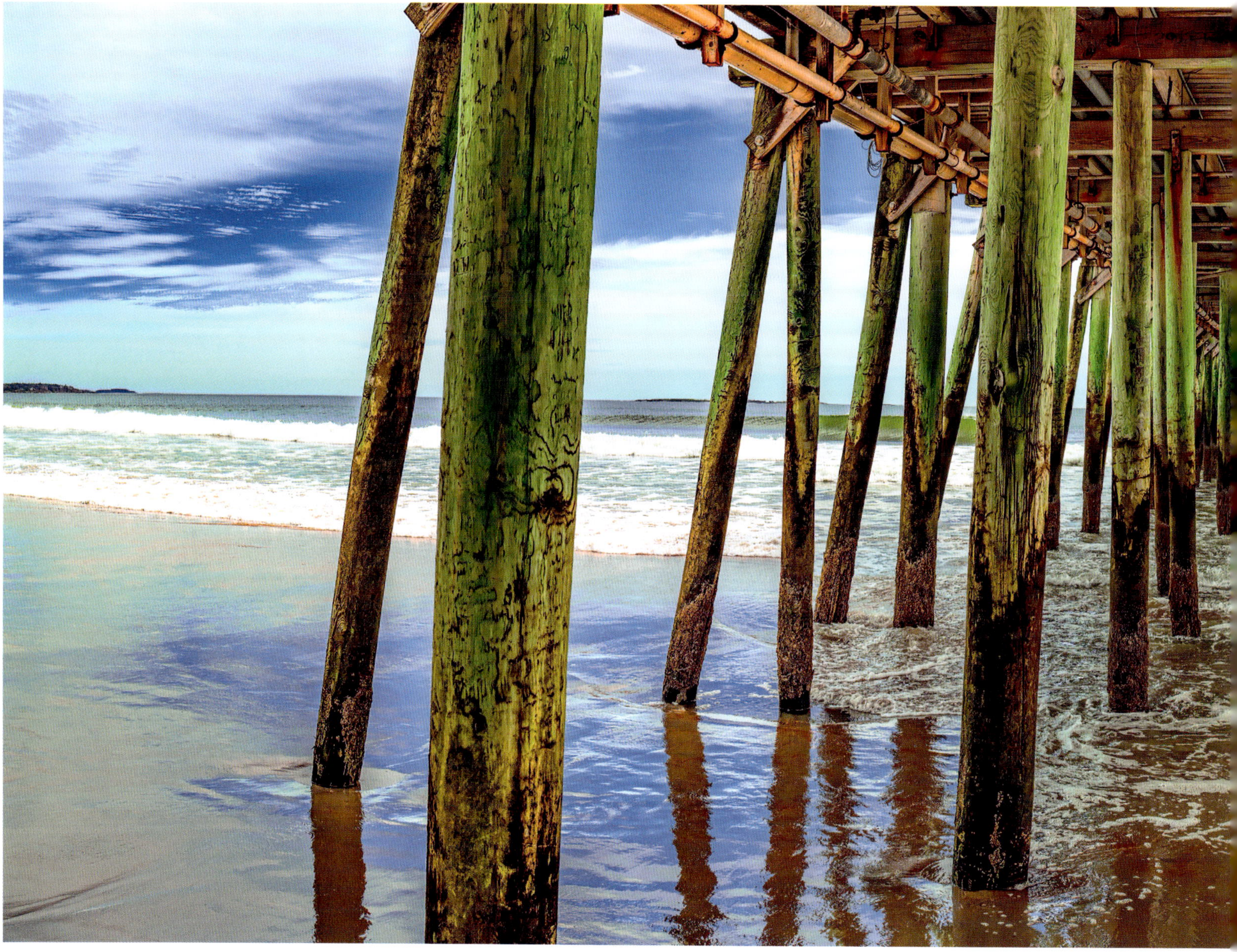

Under the boardwalk, Old Orchard Beach, Maine

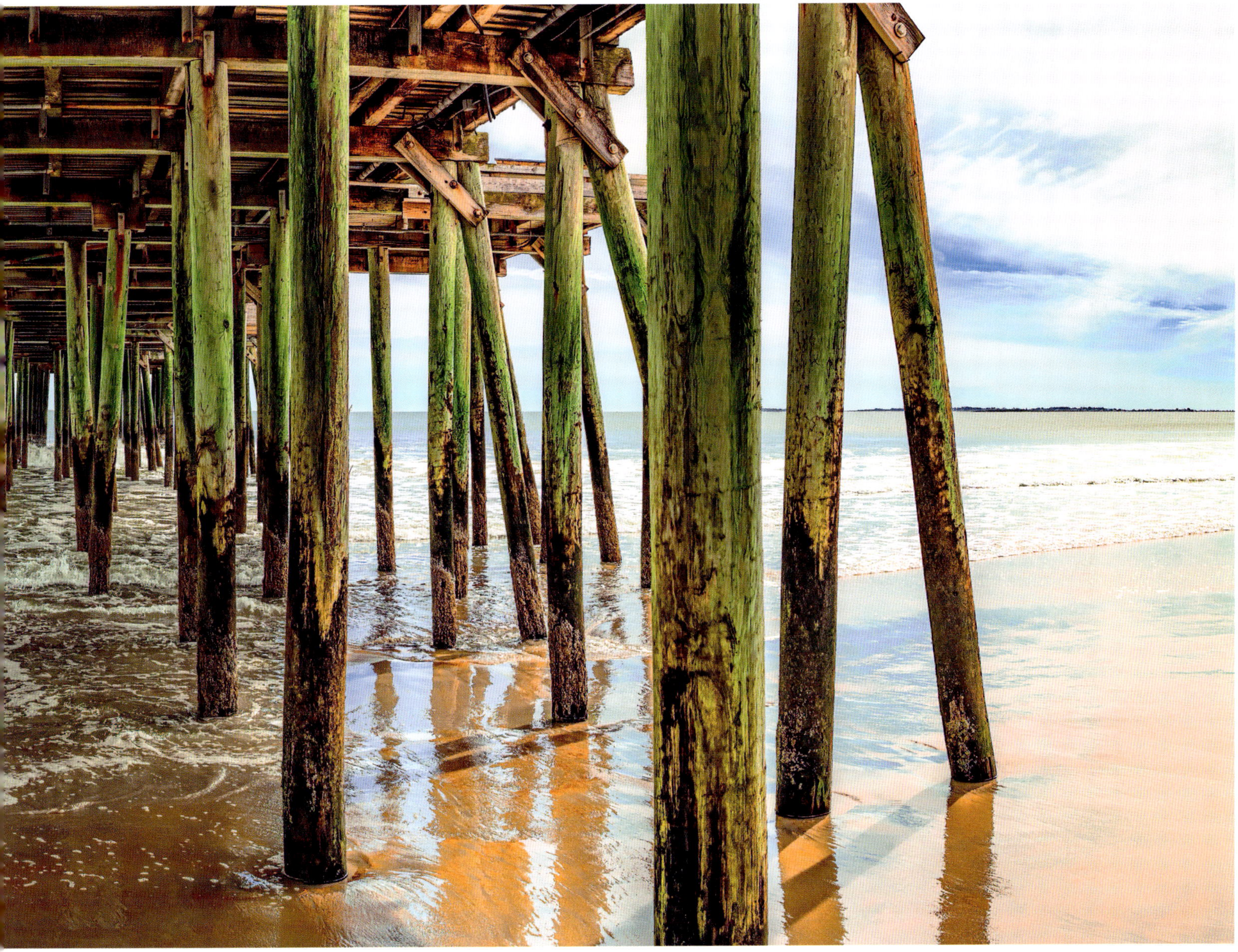

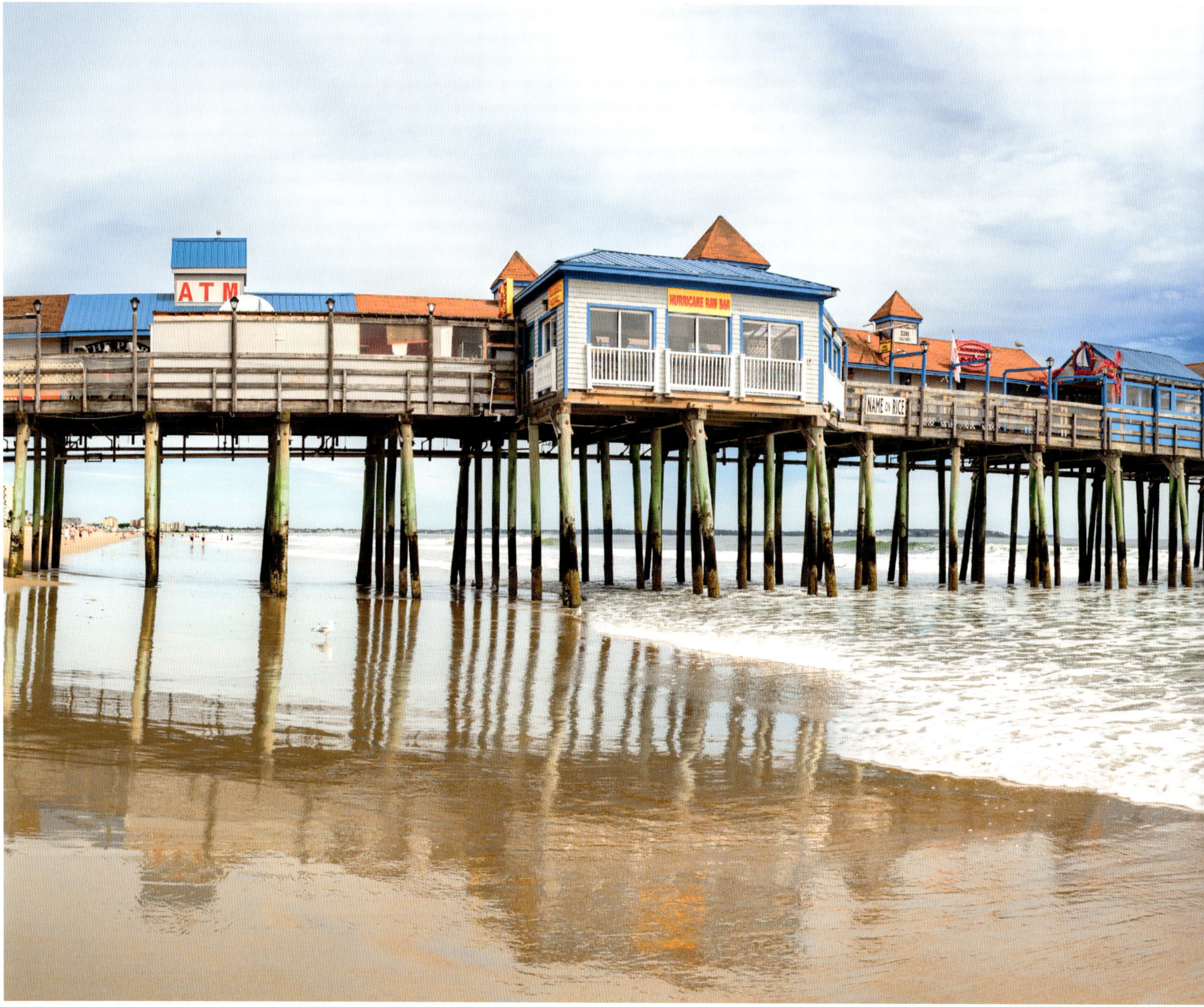

The Pier, Old Orchard Beach, Maine

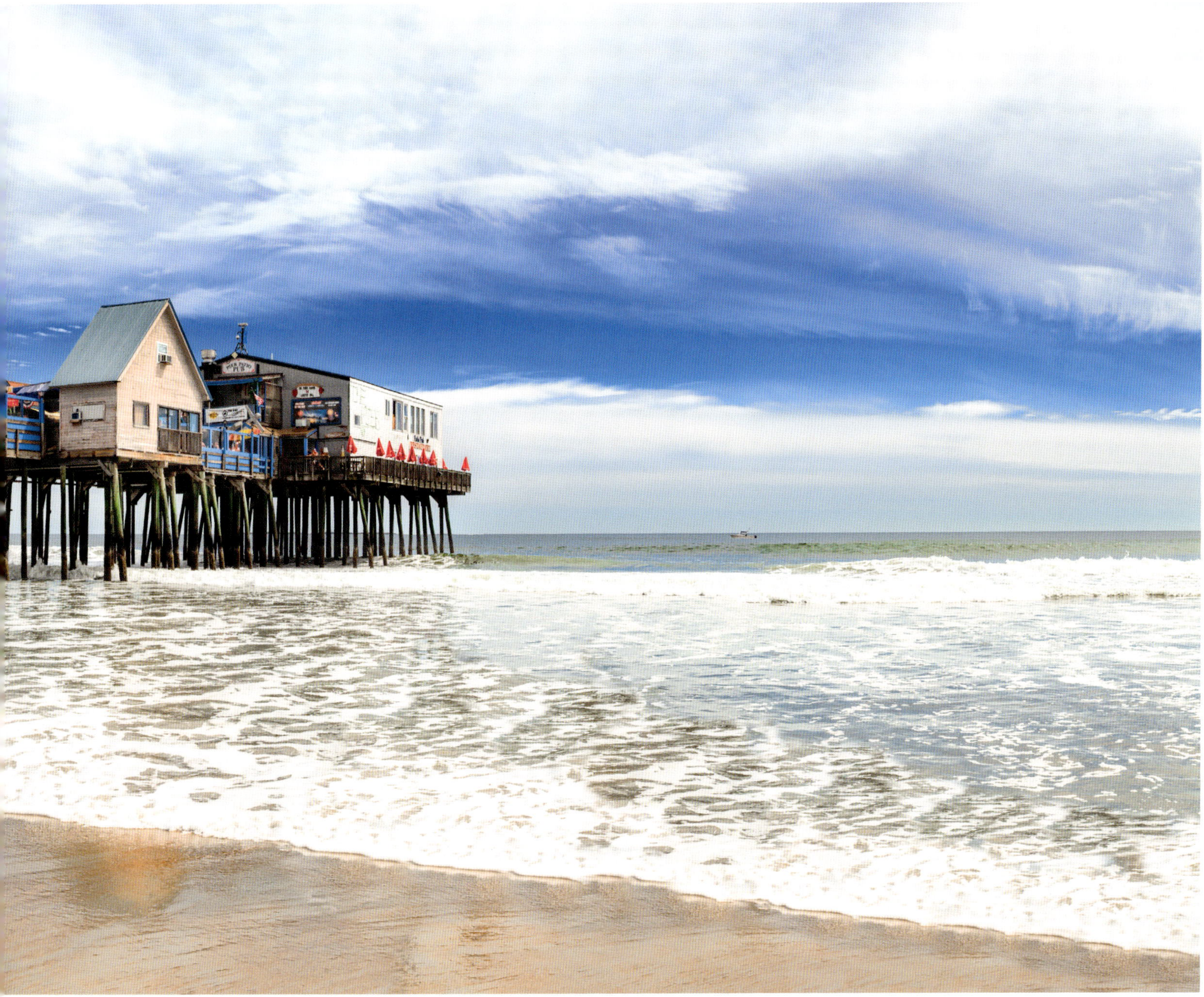

In the summer this is one huge party. I was there in the fall and had it mostly to myself.

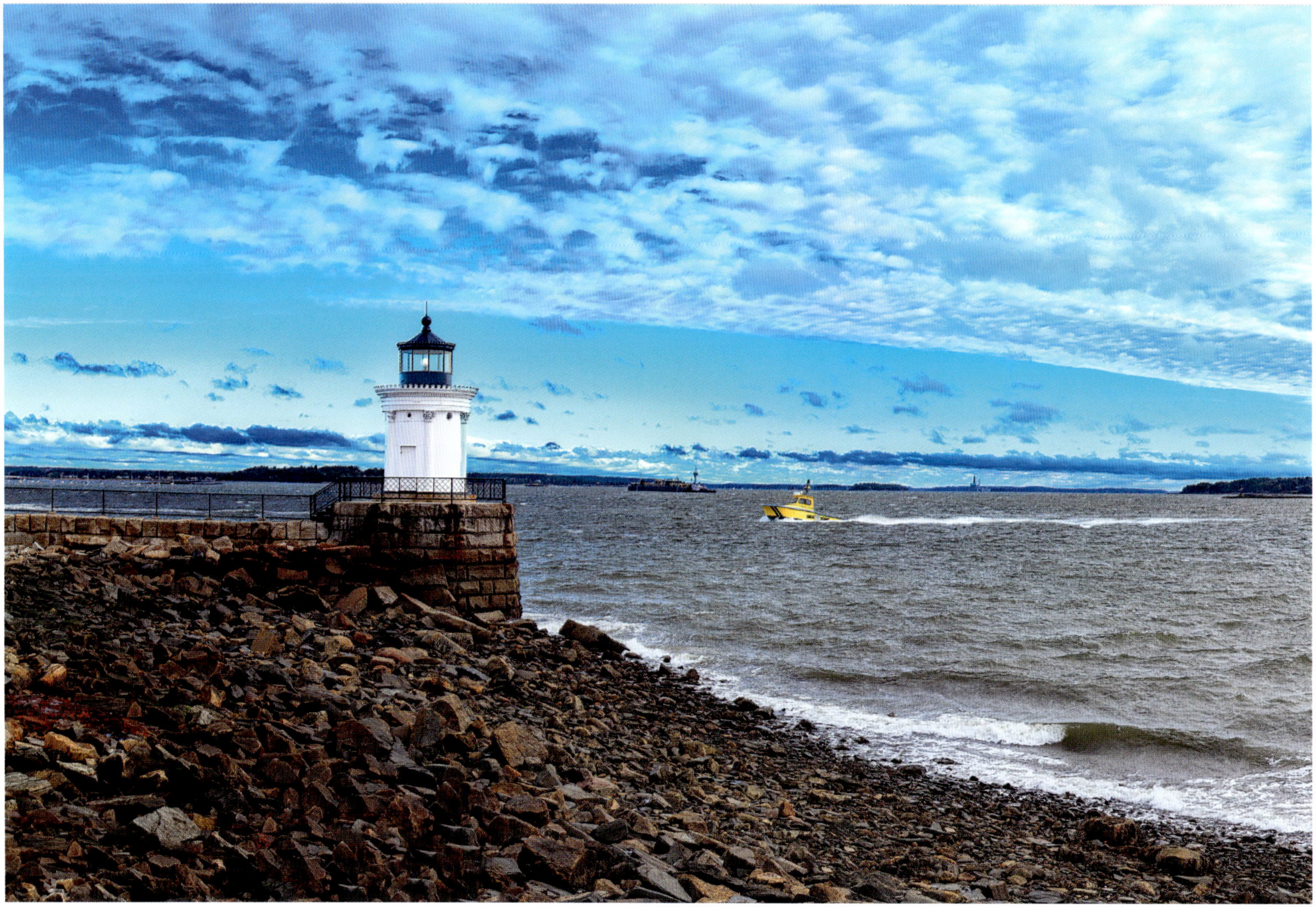

Bug Light (1855), South Portland, Maine

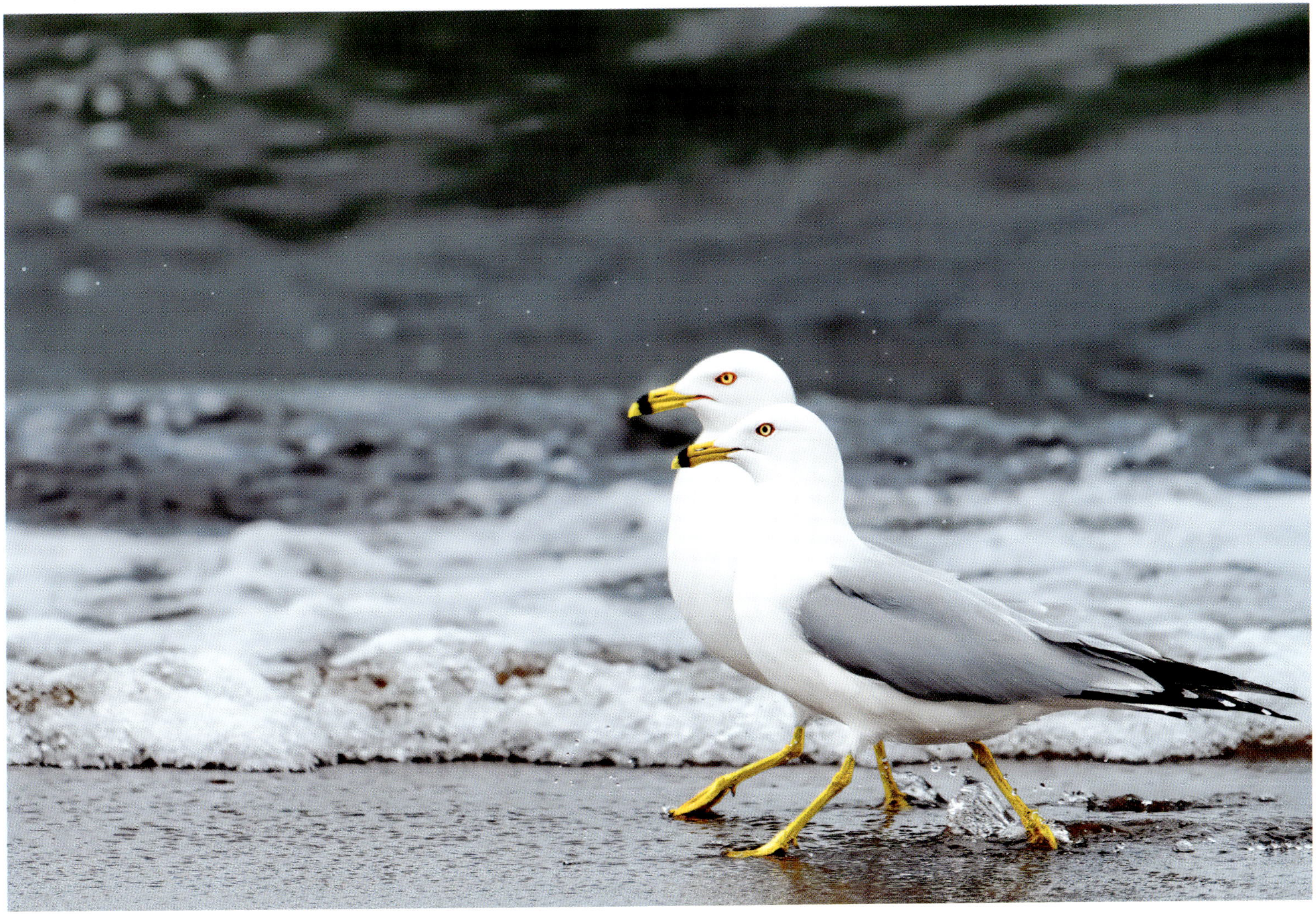

Strutting seagulls, Maine coast

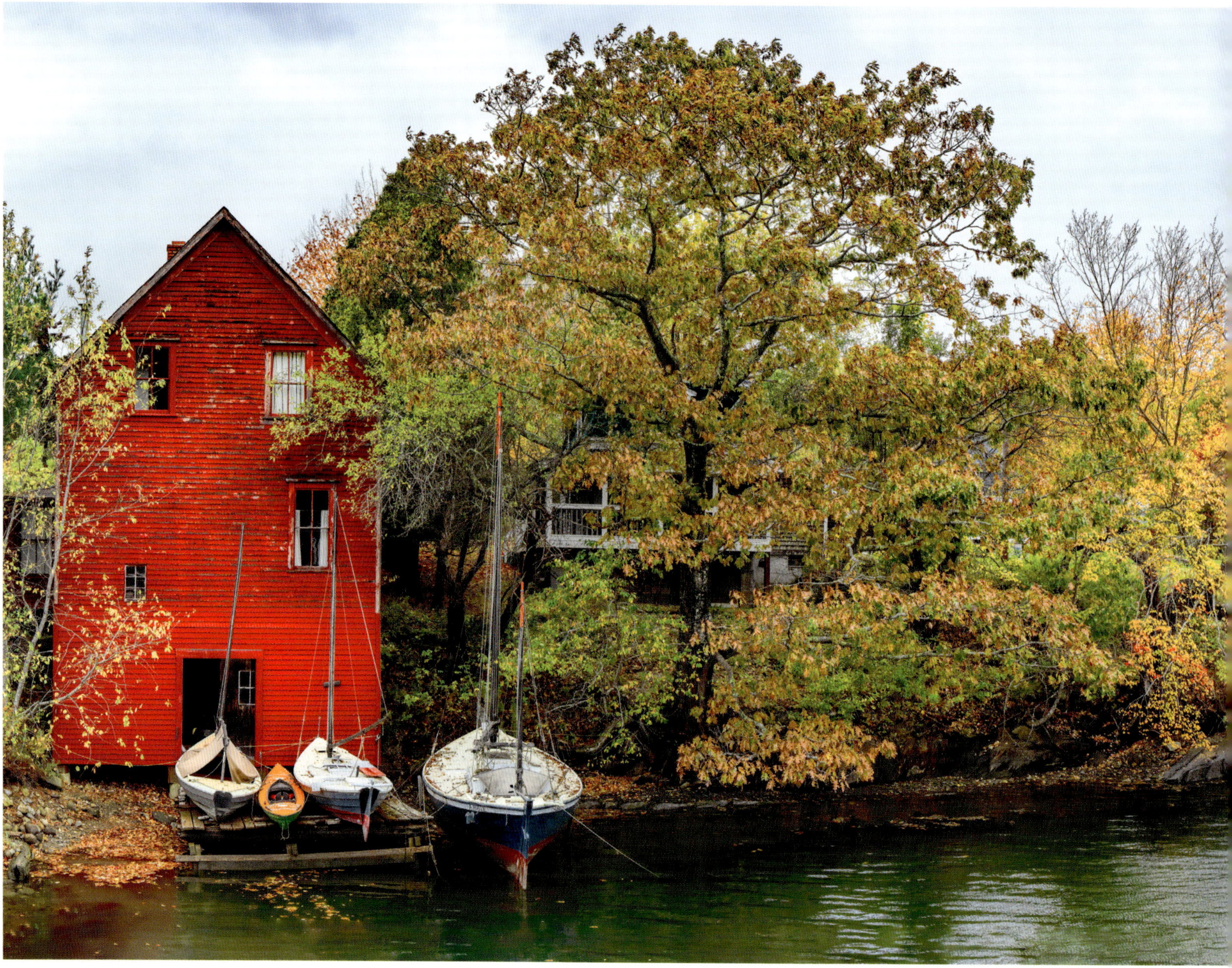

Knubble Bay, near Georgetown, Maine

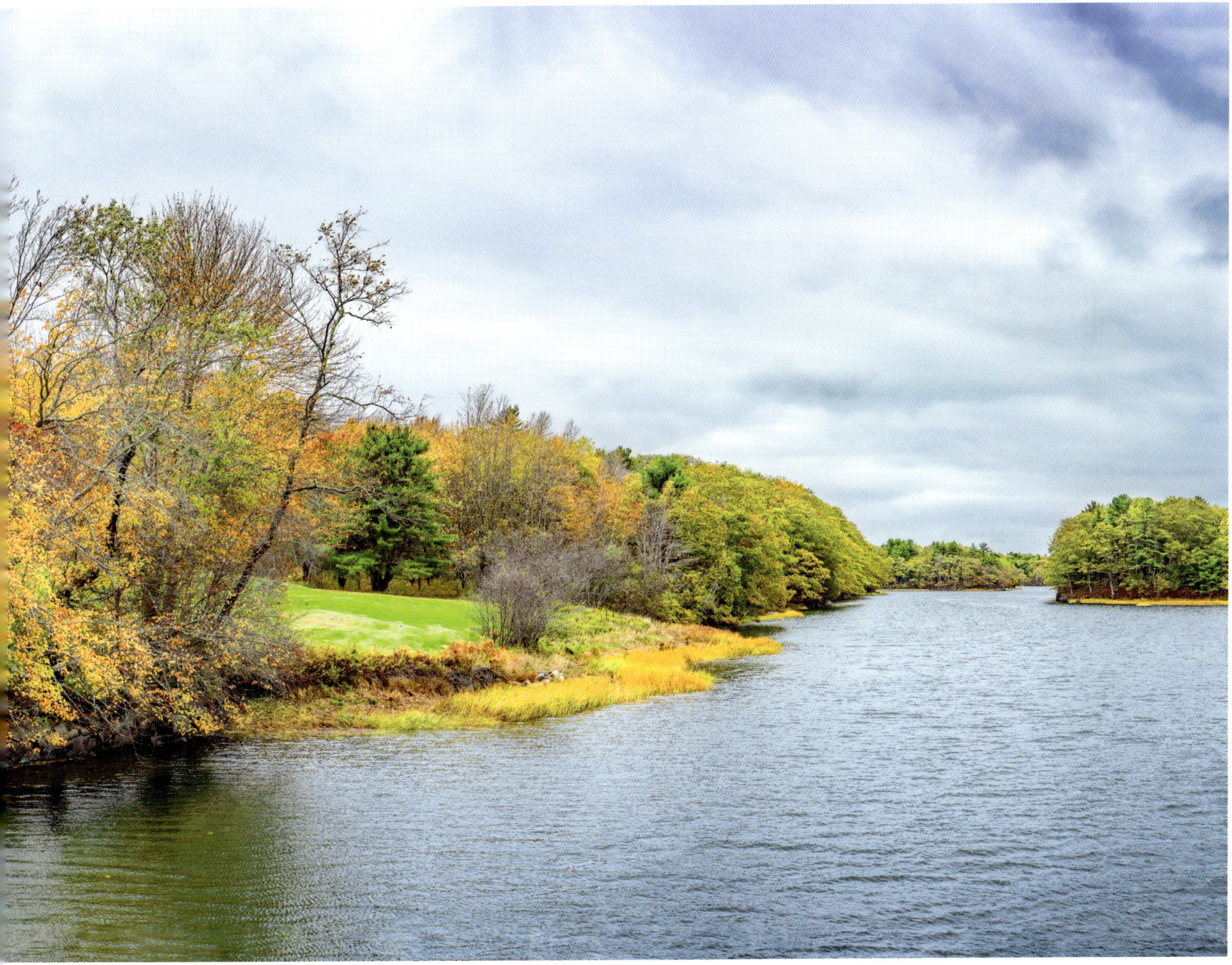

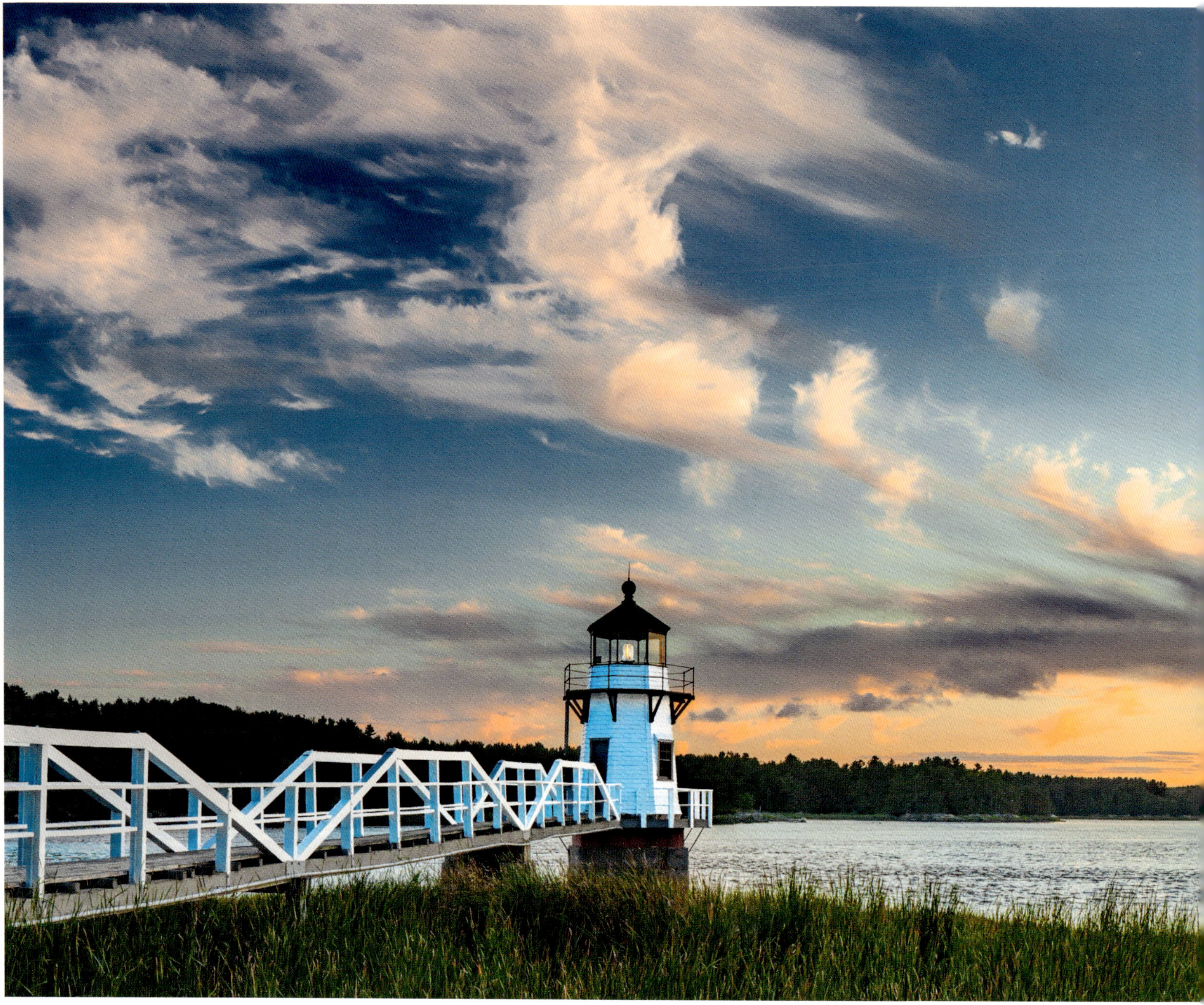

Doubling Point Light (1898), Kennebec River, Arrowsic, Maine

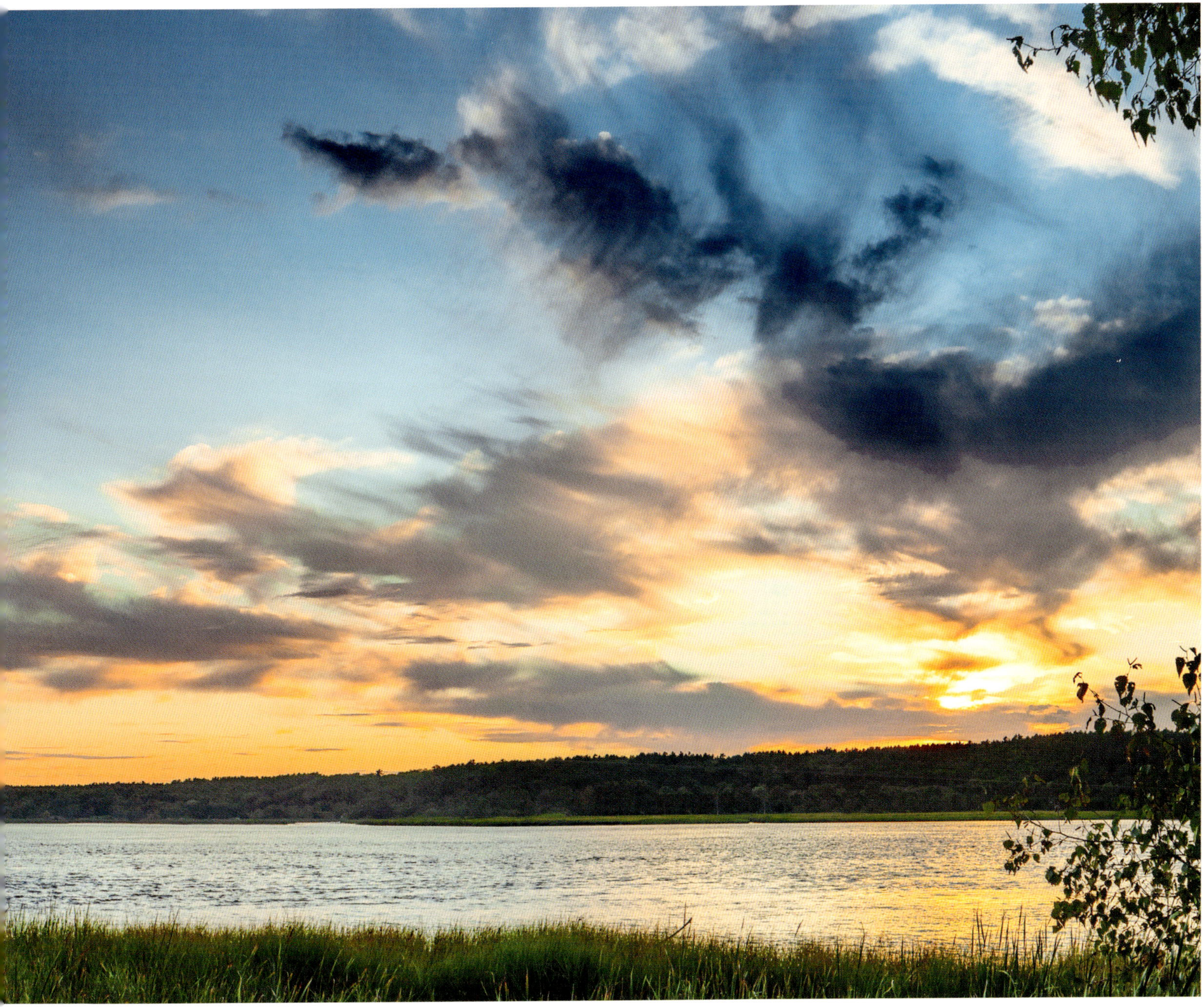

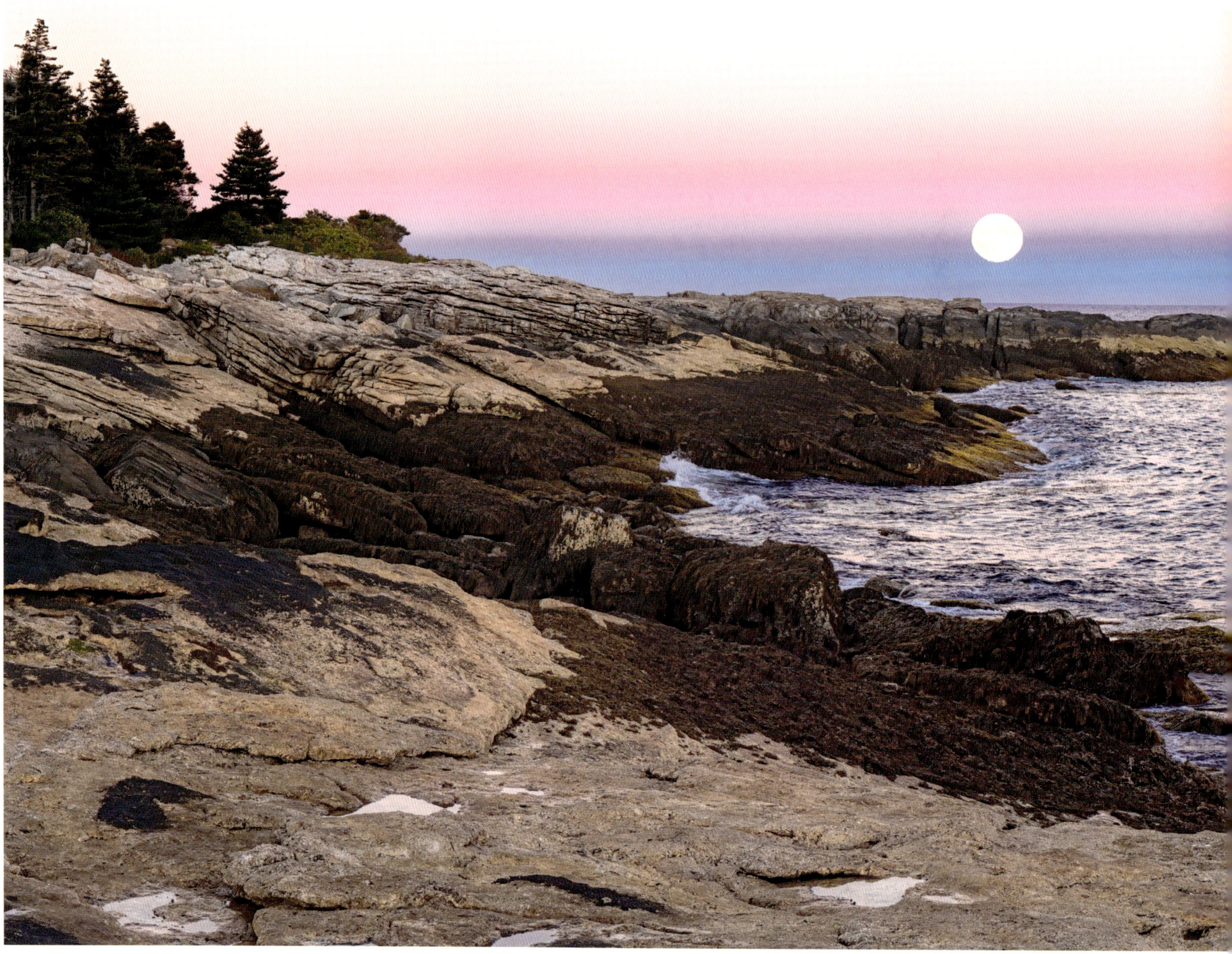

Ocean Point, Boothbay, Maine, with Supermoon

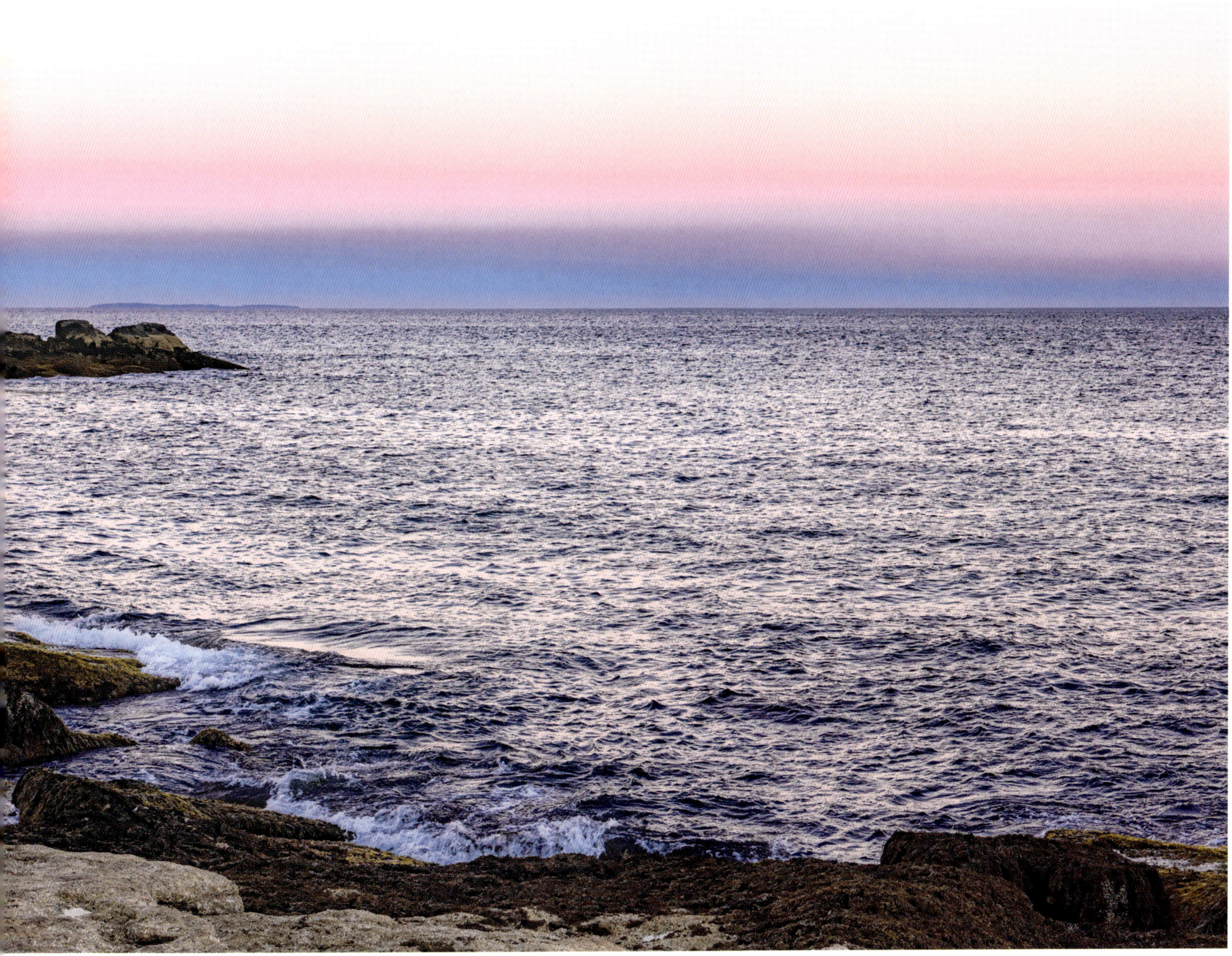

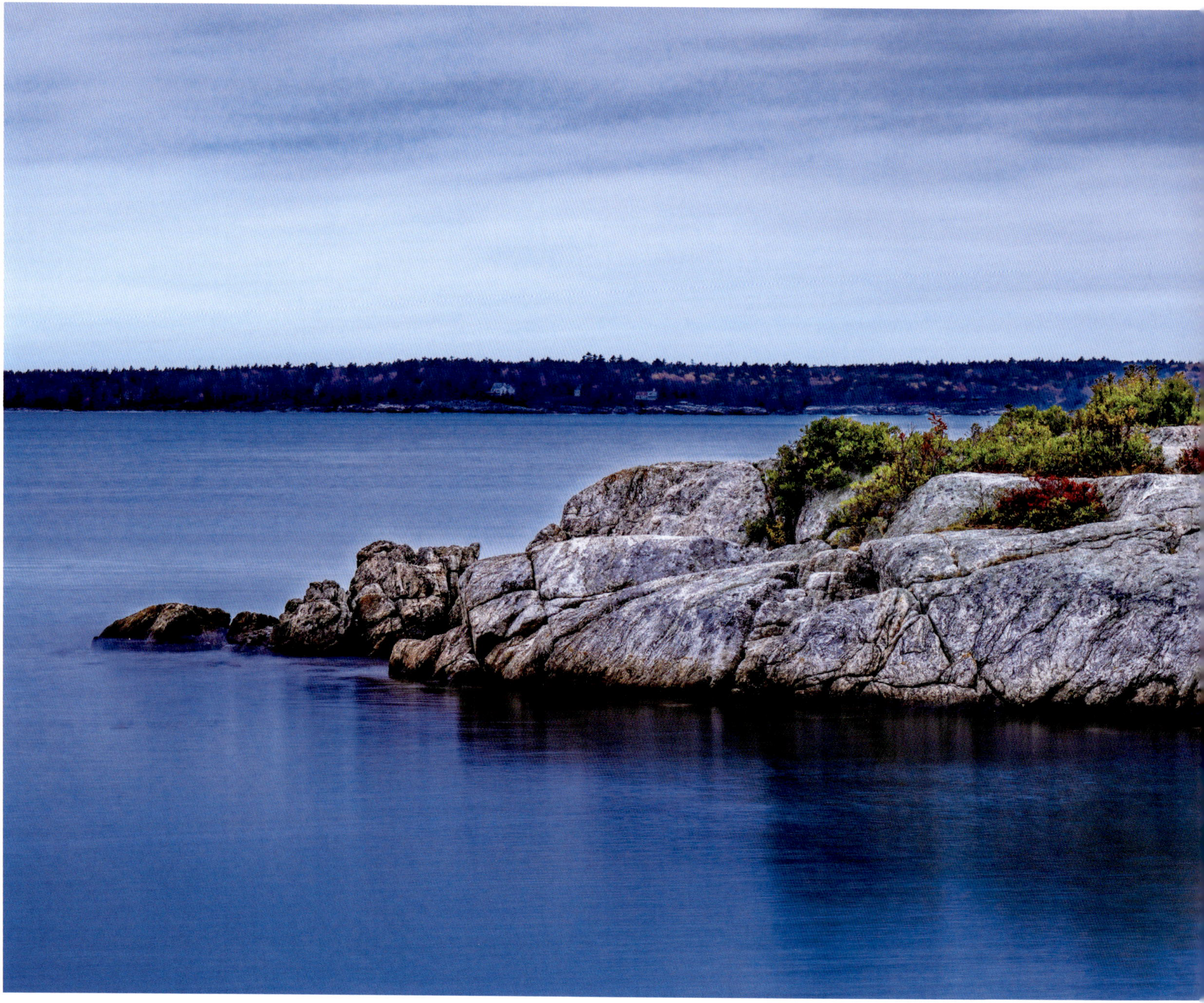

Hendricks Head Light (1829), Boothbay Harbor, Maine

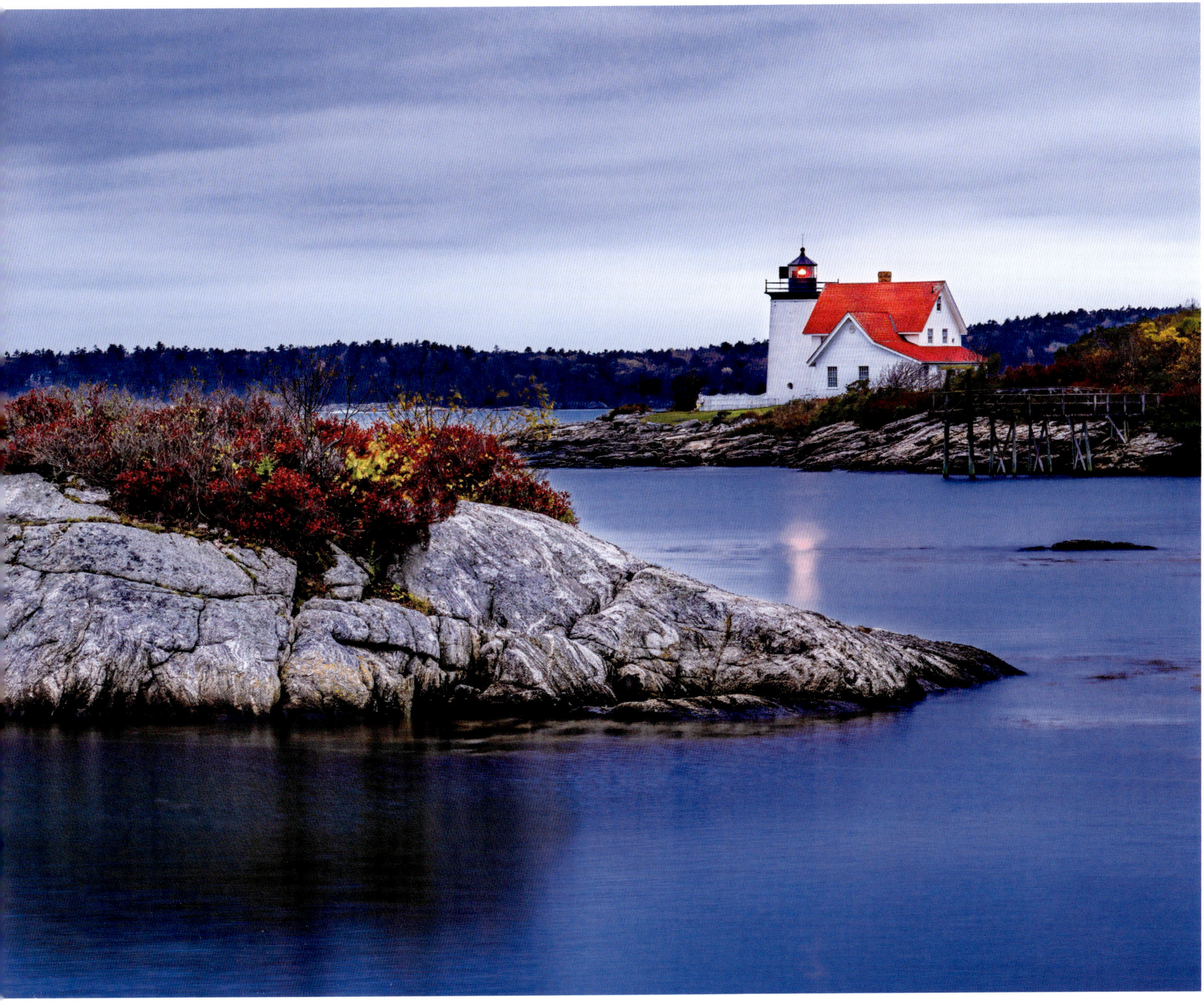

Sometimes waiting for that last bit of light is a really good idea.

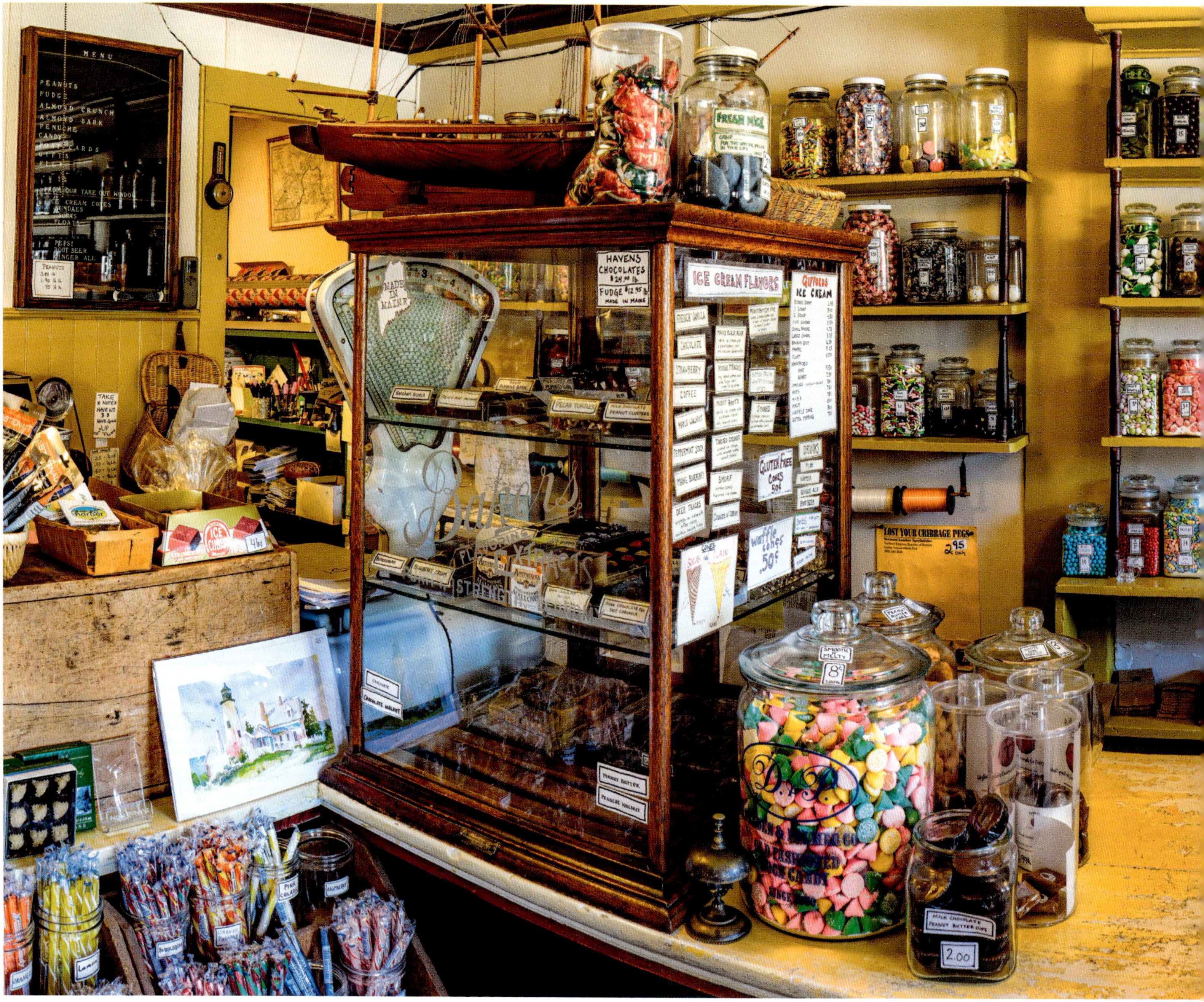

Granite Hall store, Round Pond, Maine

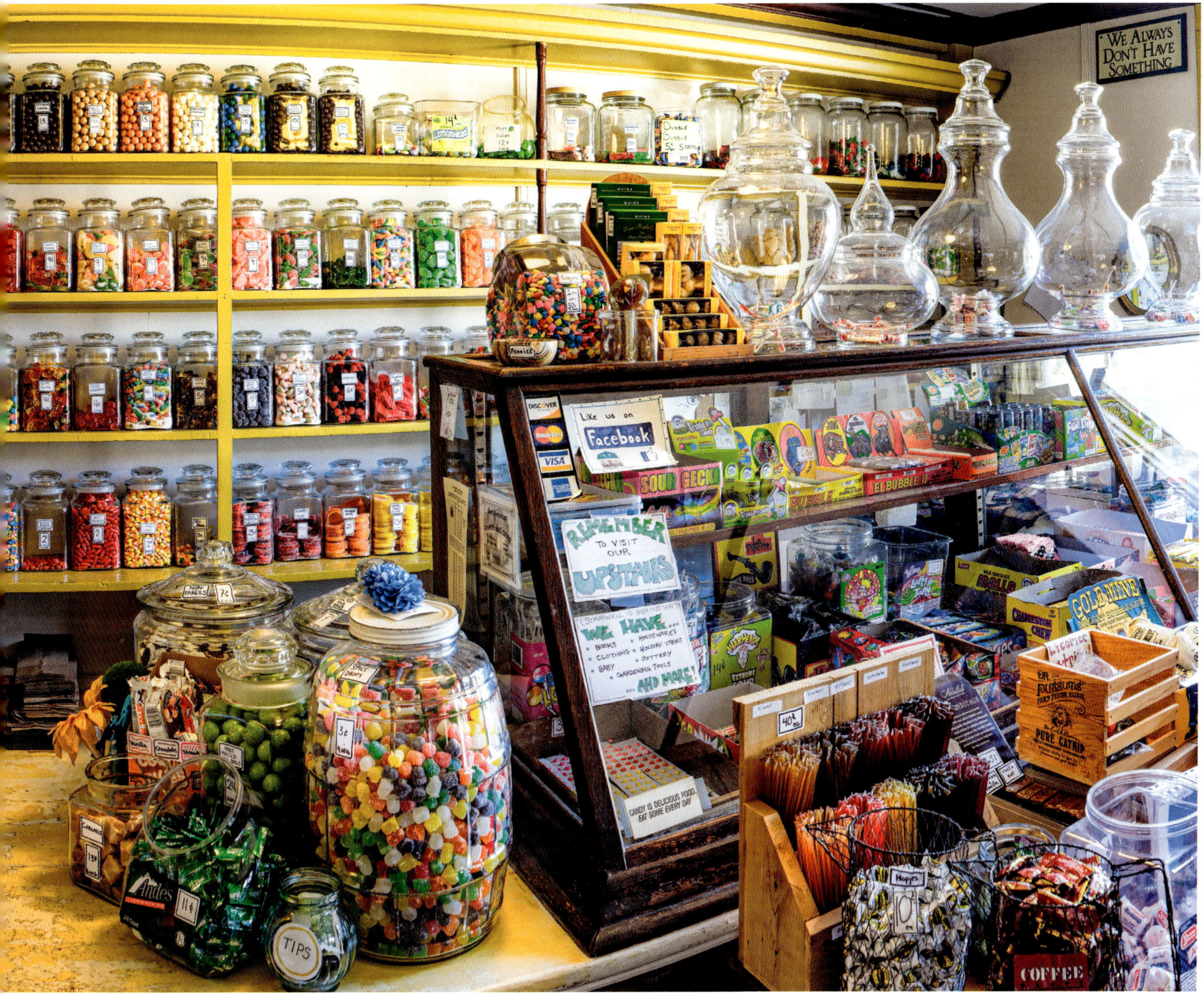

I had some gummy lobsters. They tasted like cinnamon. Look for them on the second shelf.

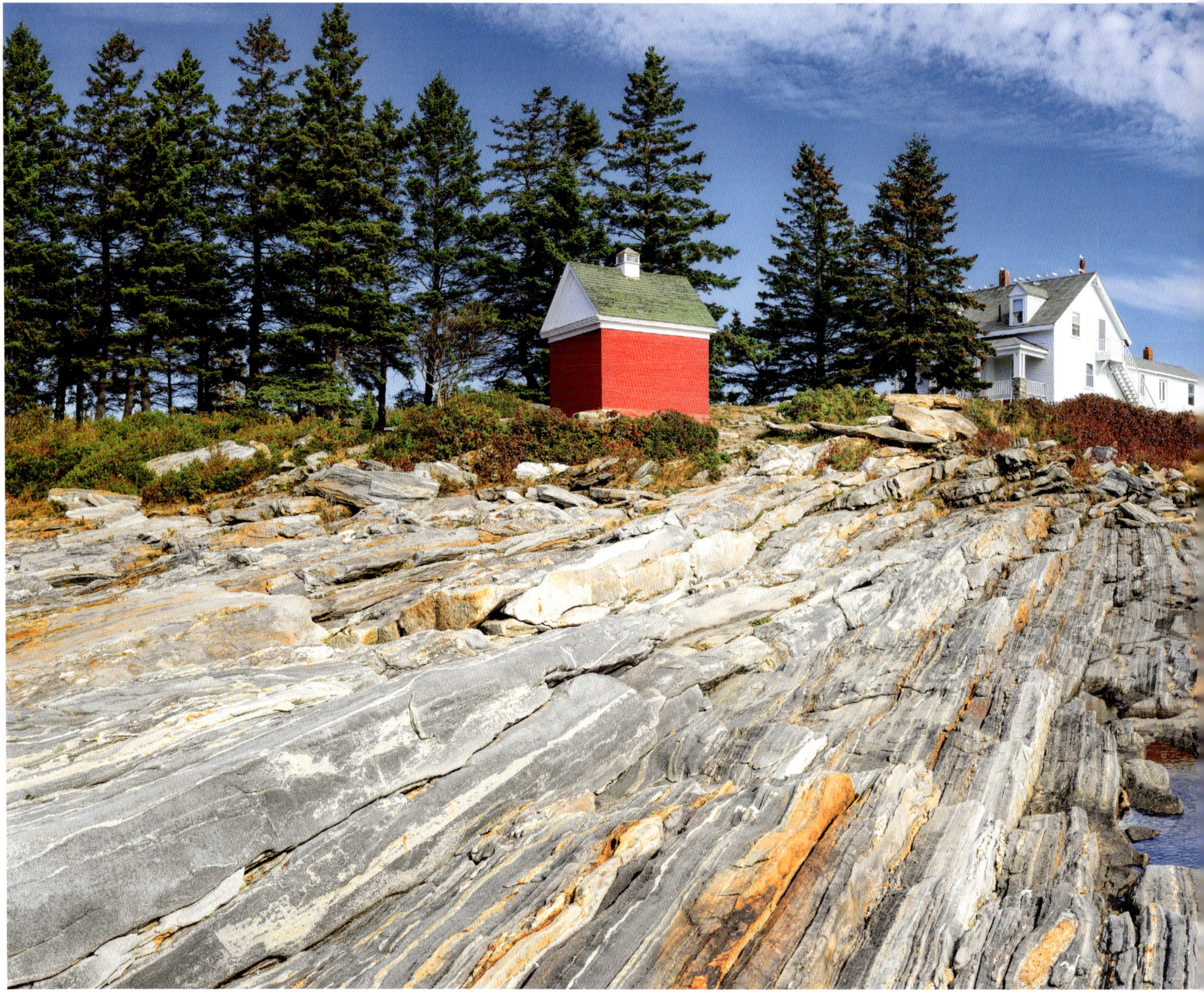

Pemaquid Point Lighthouse (1827), Bristol, Maine

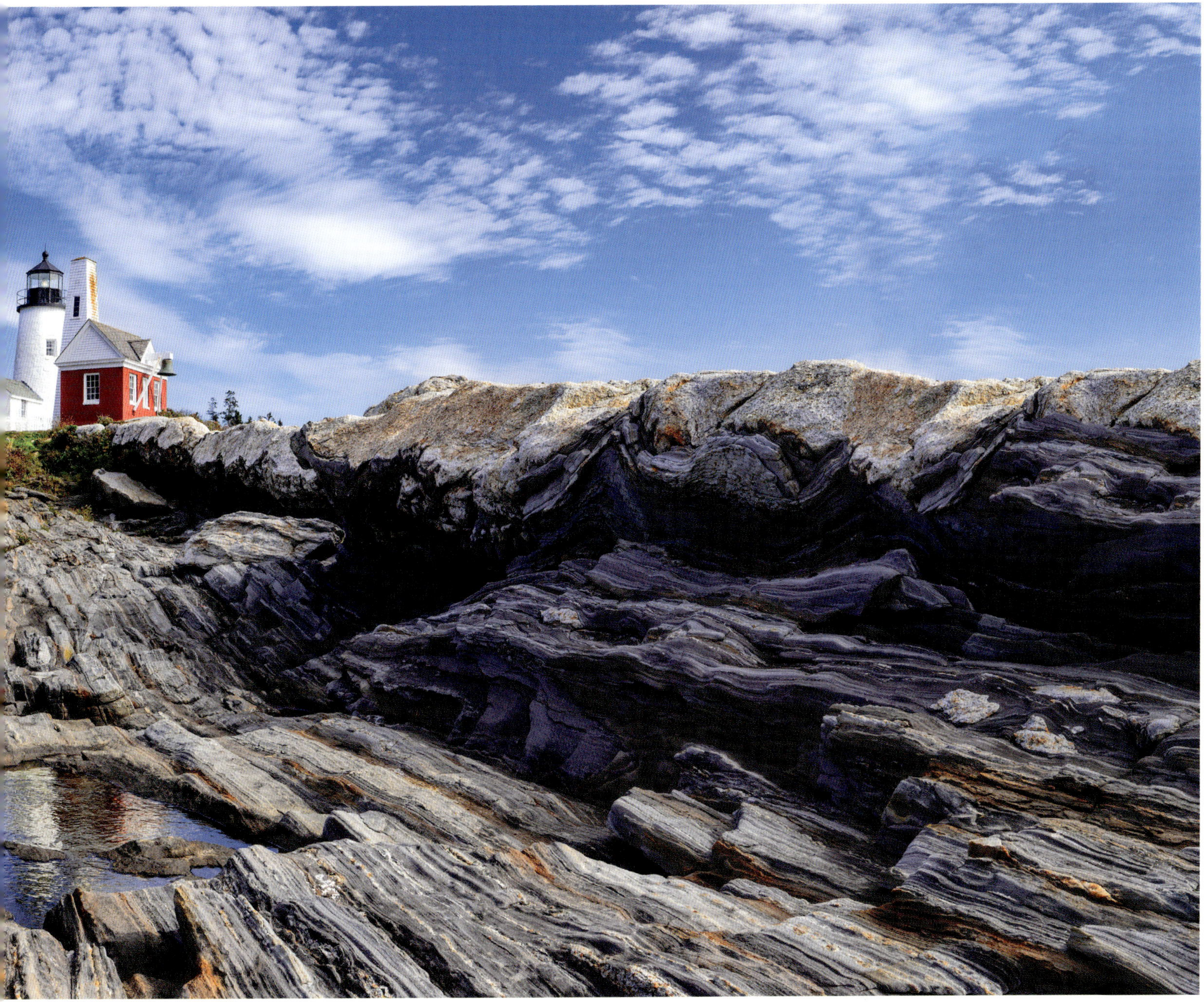

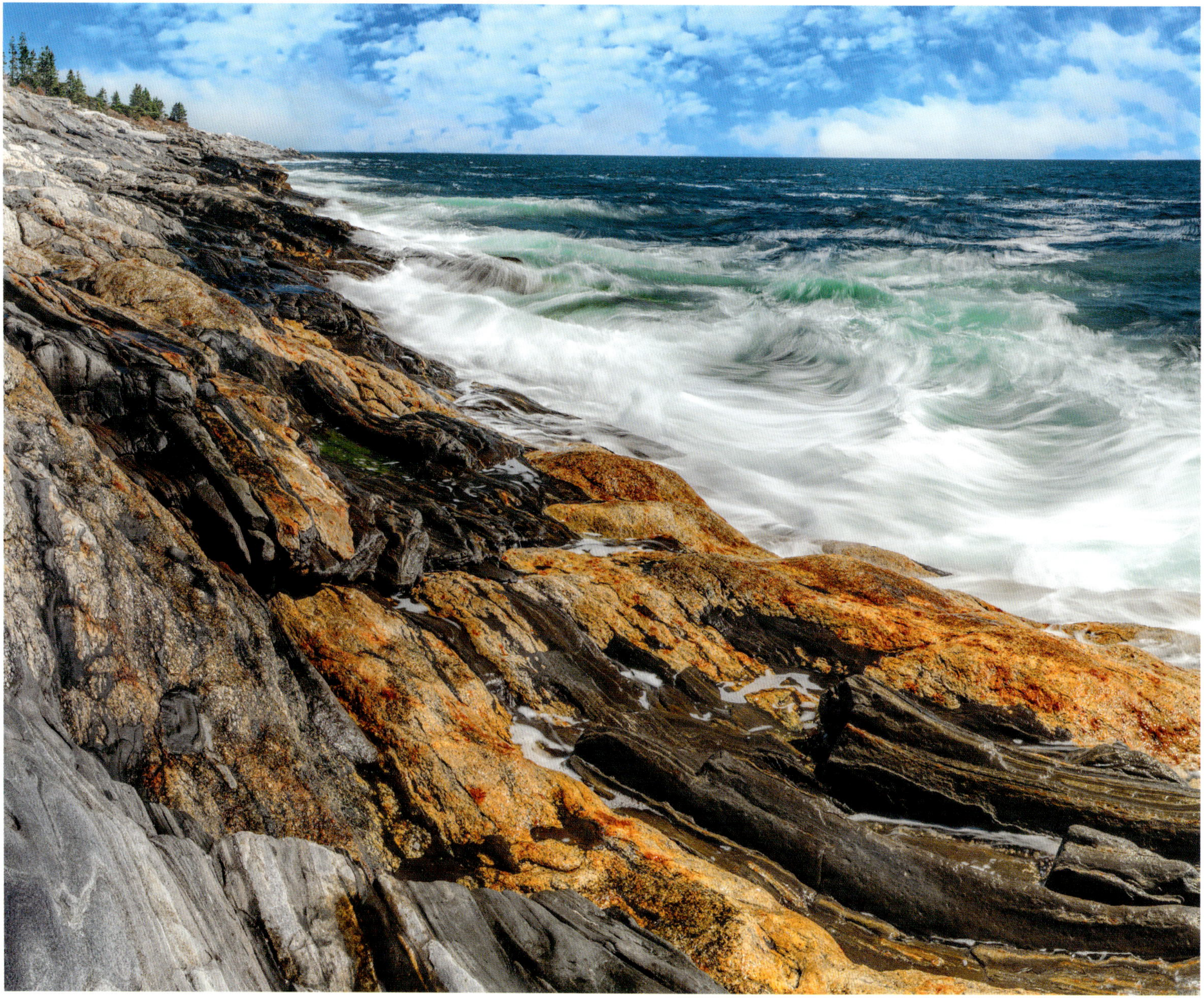

Maine coastline at Pemaquid Point

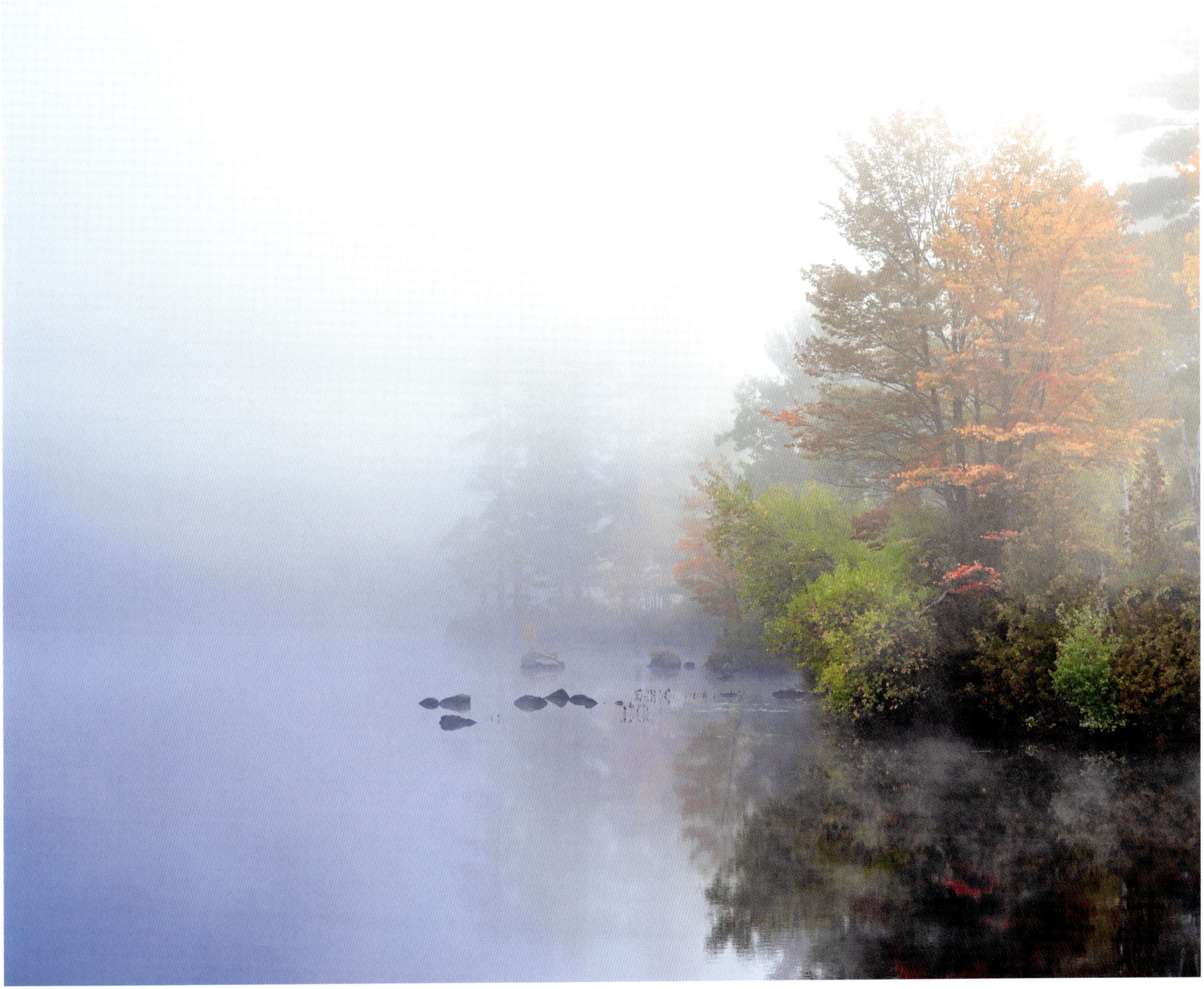

Morning fog on Moose Pond, Bridgton, Maine

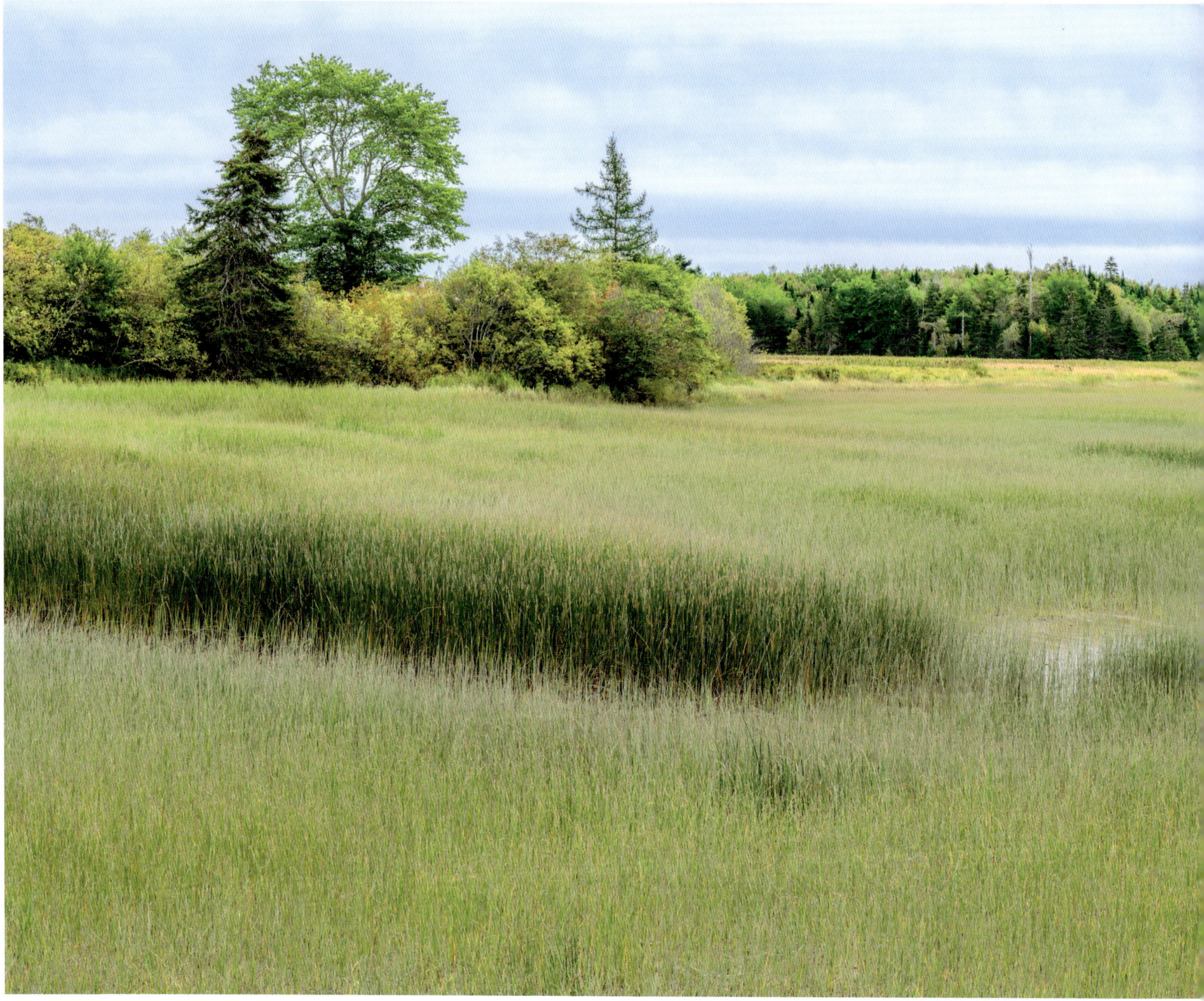

Rowboat along the Pleasant River near Columbia Falls, Maine

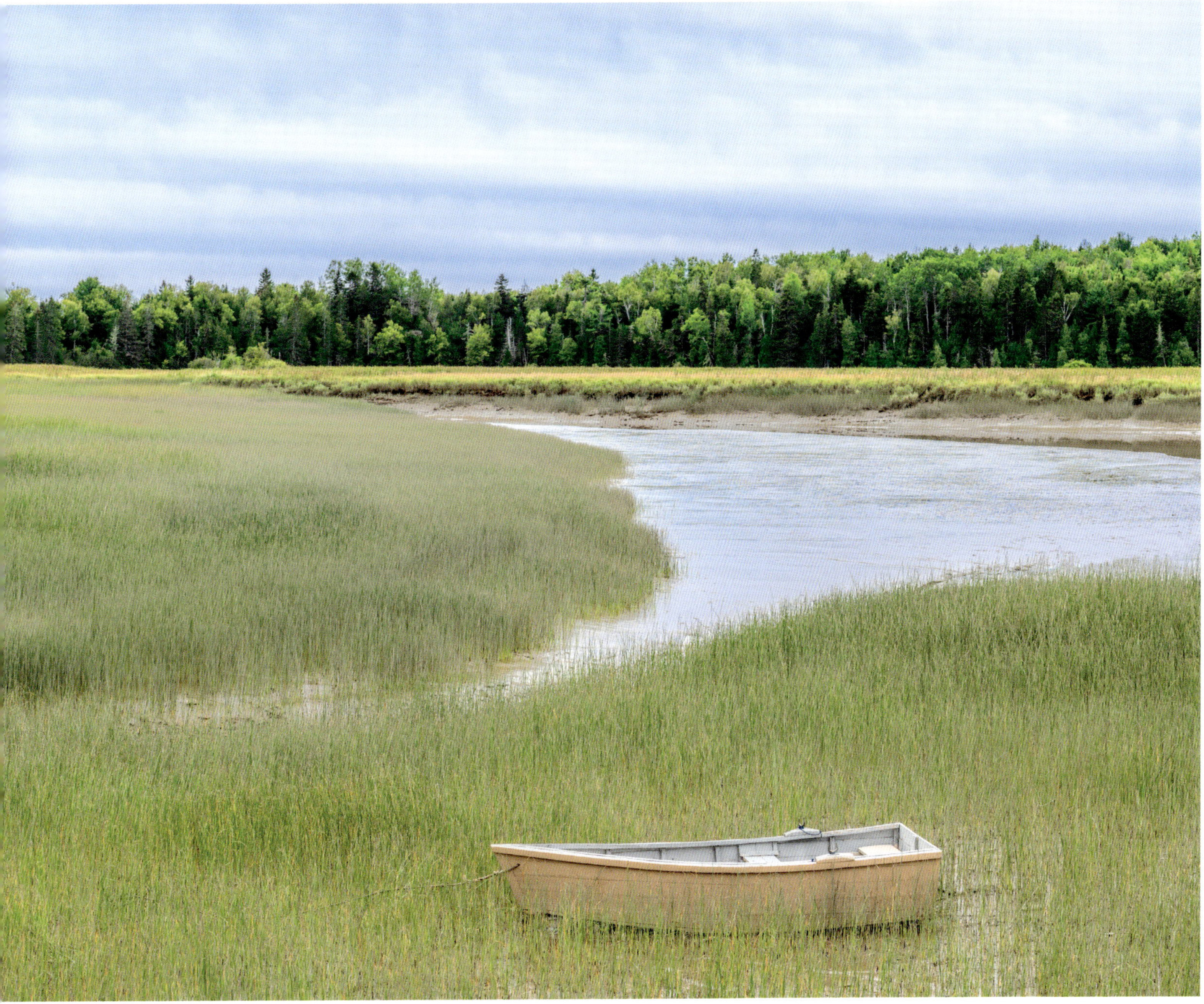

I felt like I walked into a painting.

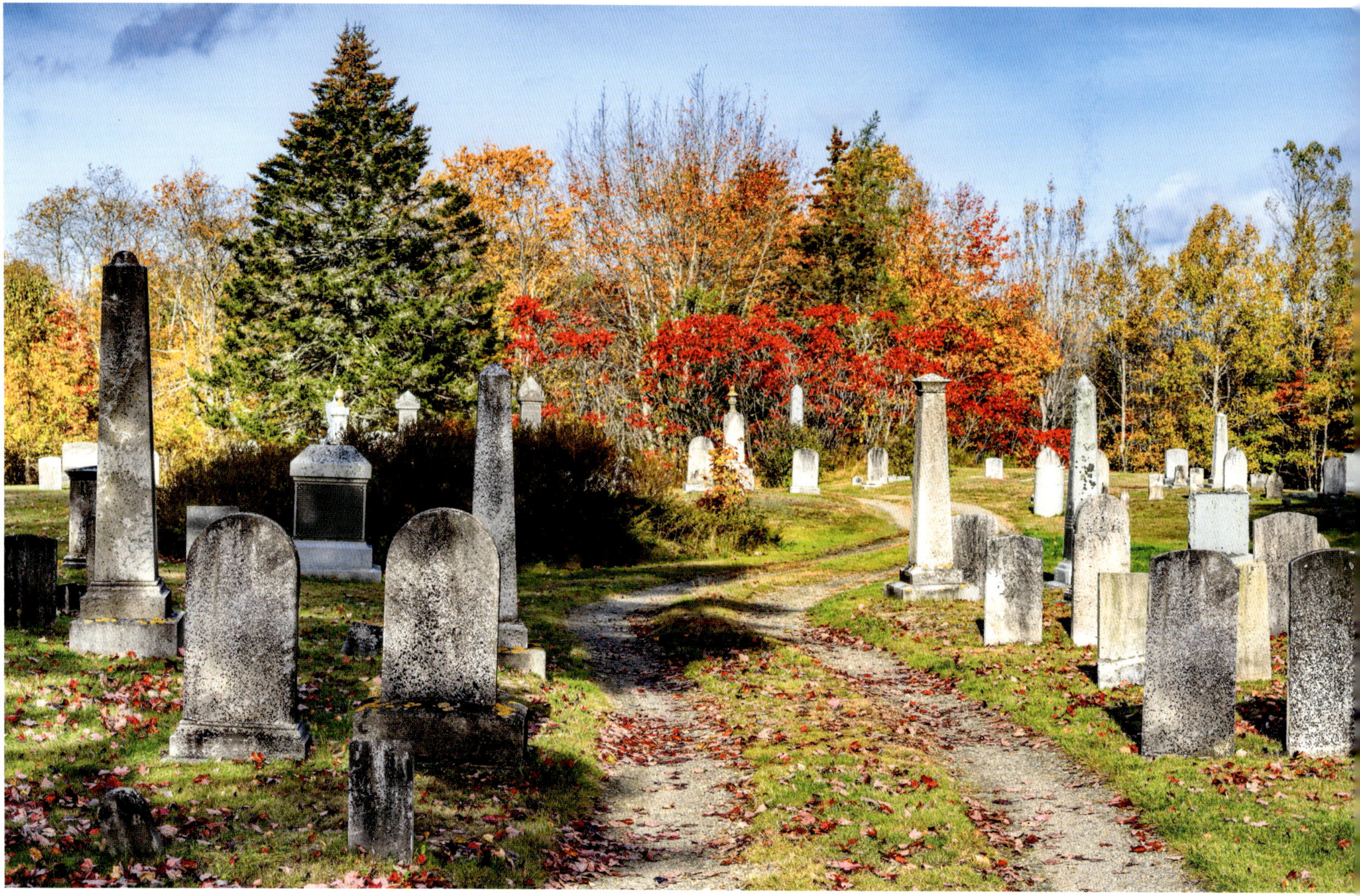

Harbor Cemetery, Friendship, Maine

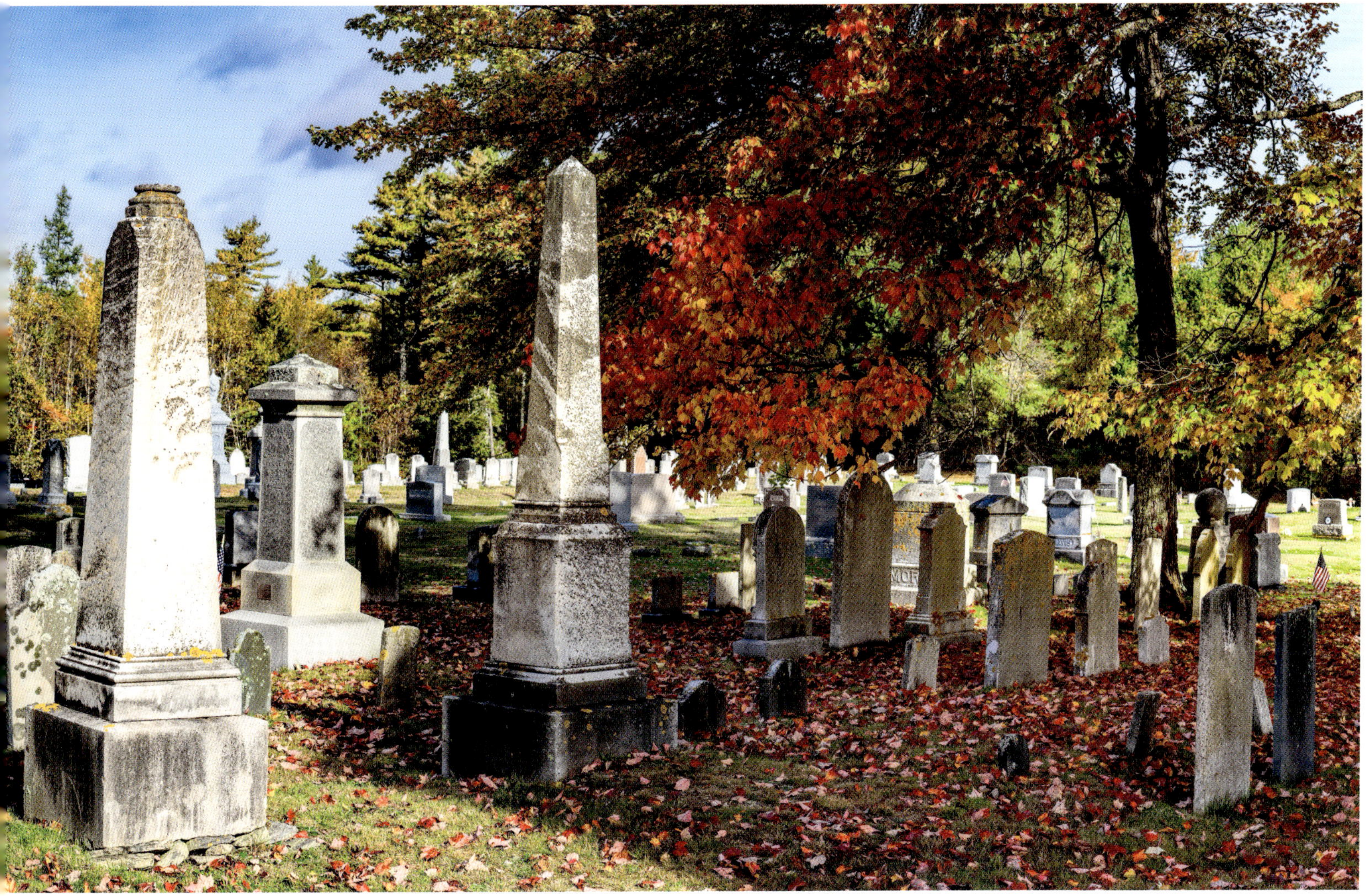

I looked it up. There are more than 7,000 cemeteries in Maine. I chose this one for the leaves.

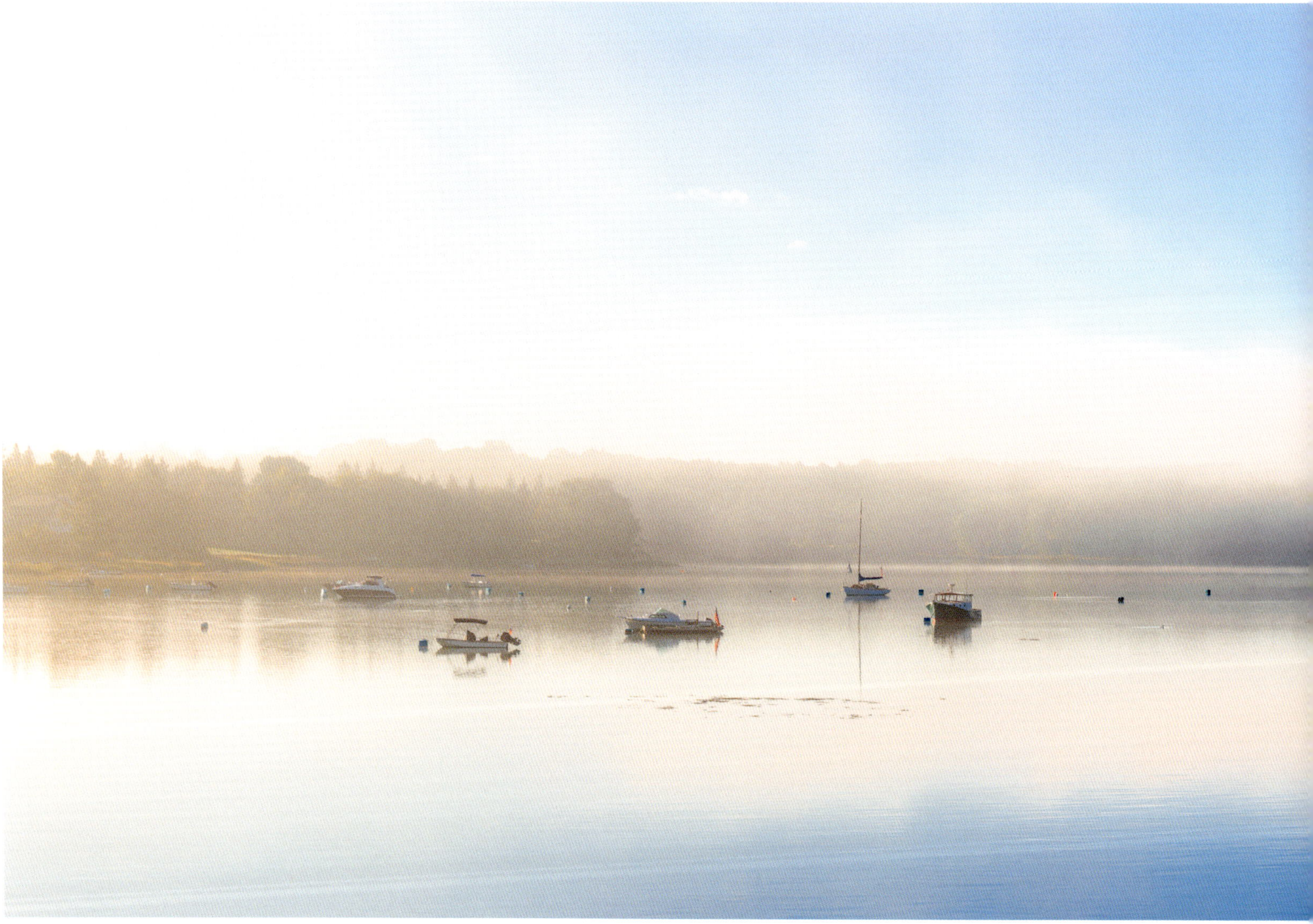

Damariscotta River, Newcastle, Maine

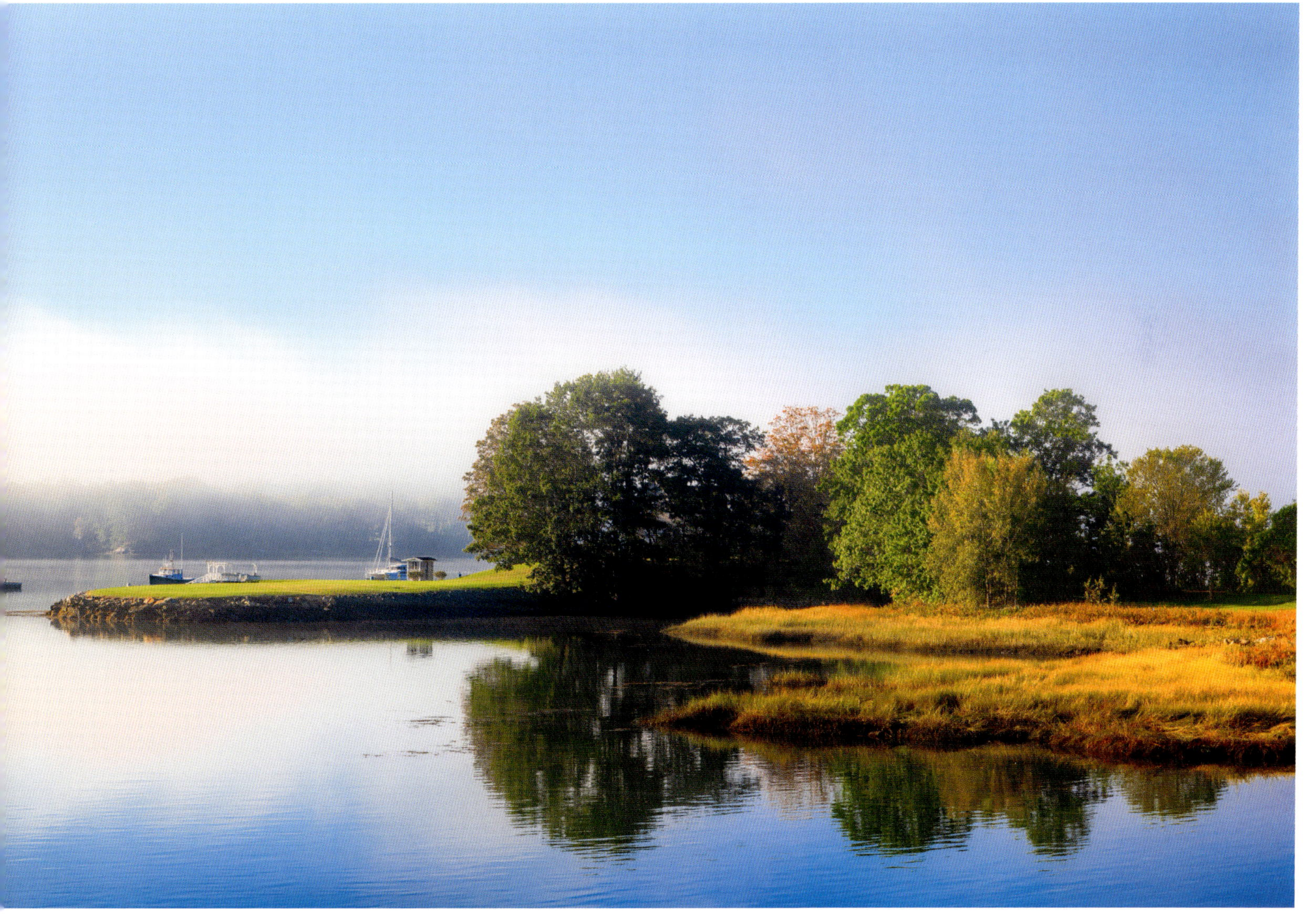

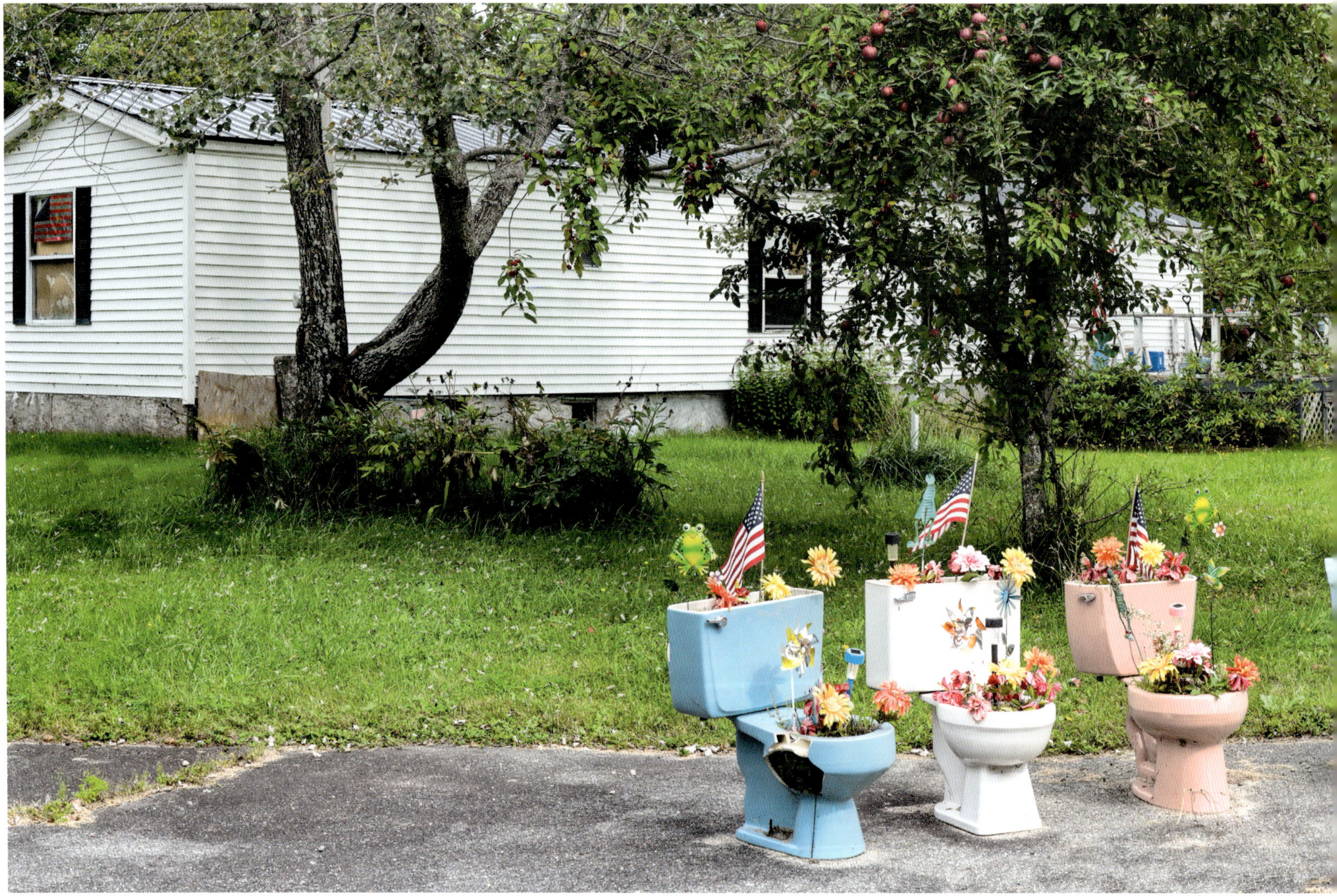

Lawn display, Maine State Route 186

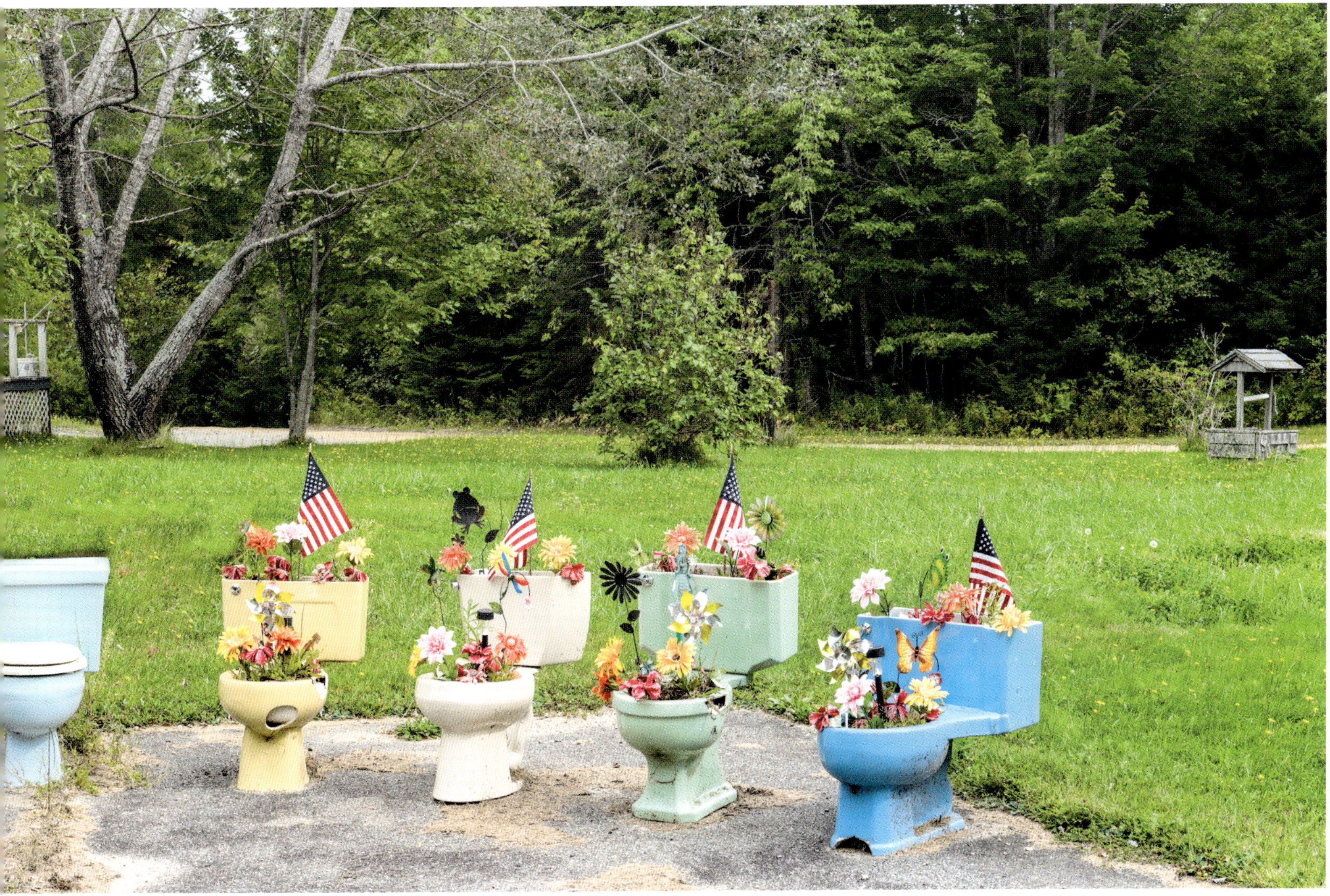

If you follow my books, you know I love to find what I call "lawn collections." This one is . . . well . . . special.

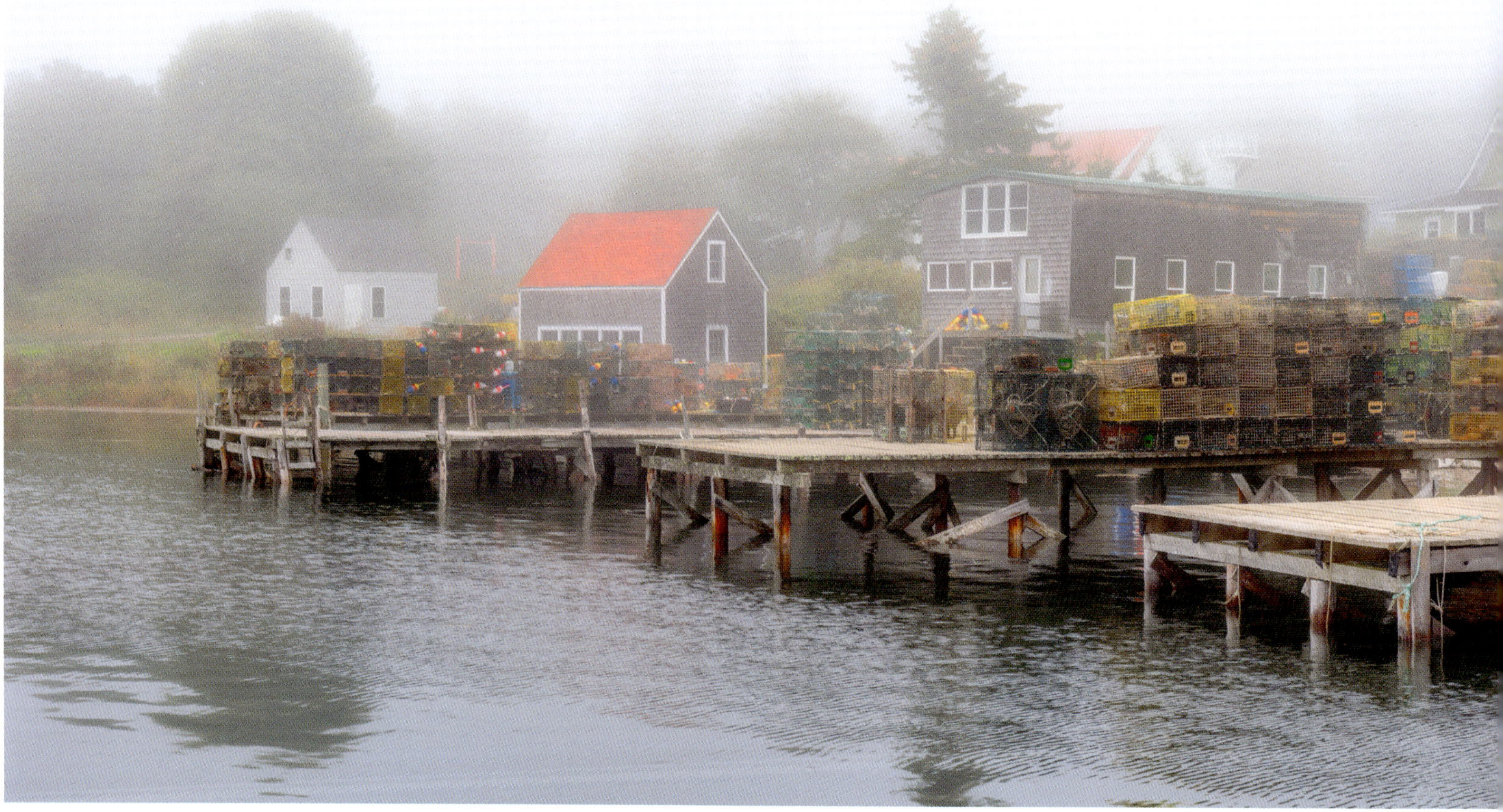

Port Clyde Harbor, Maine

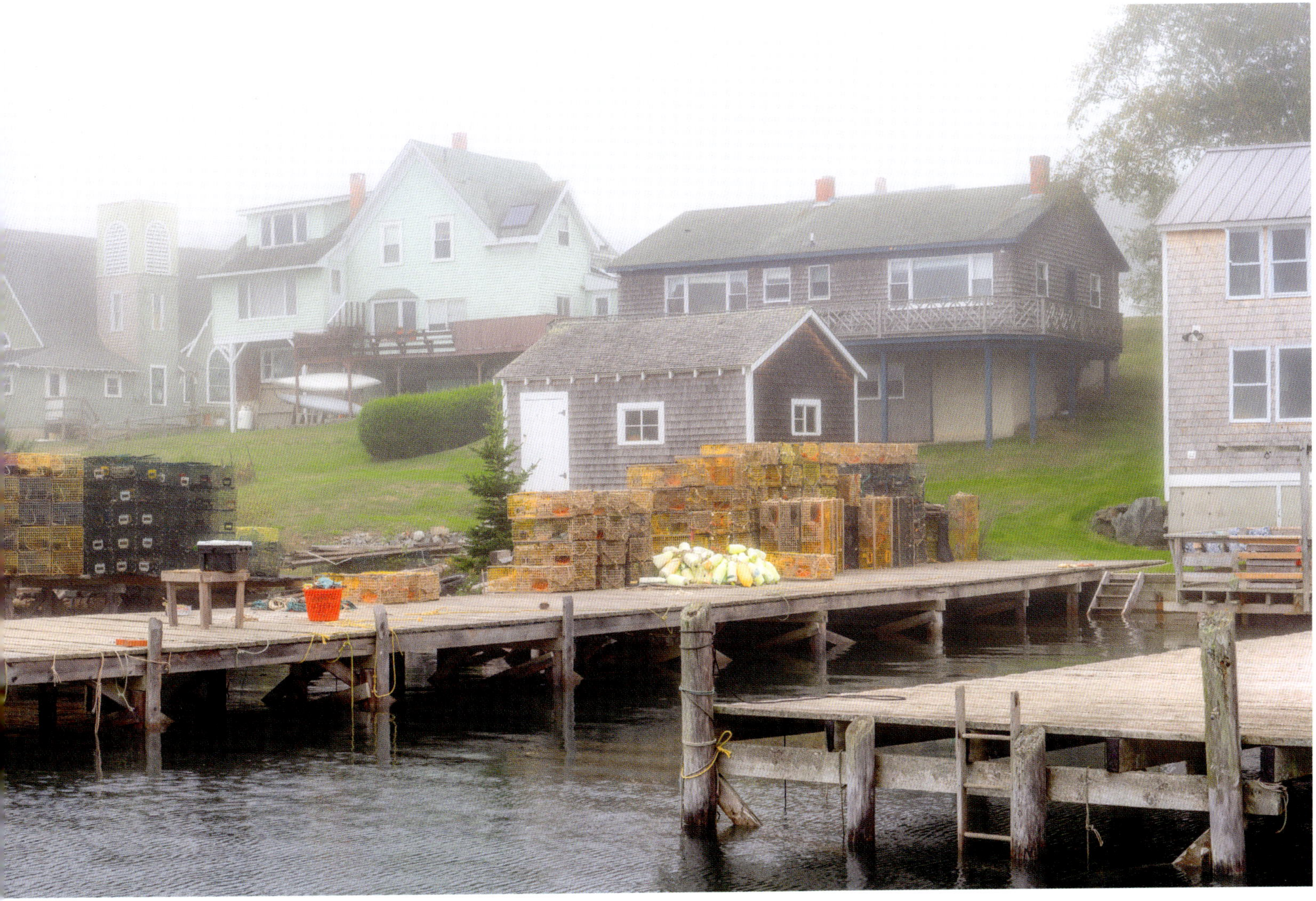

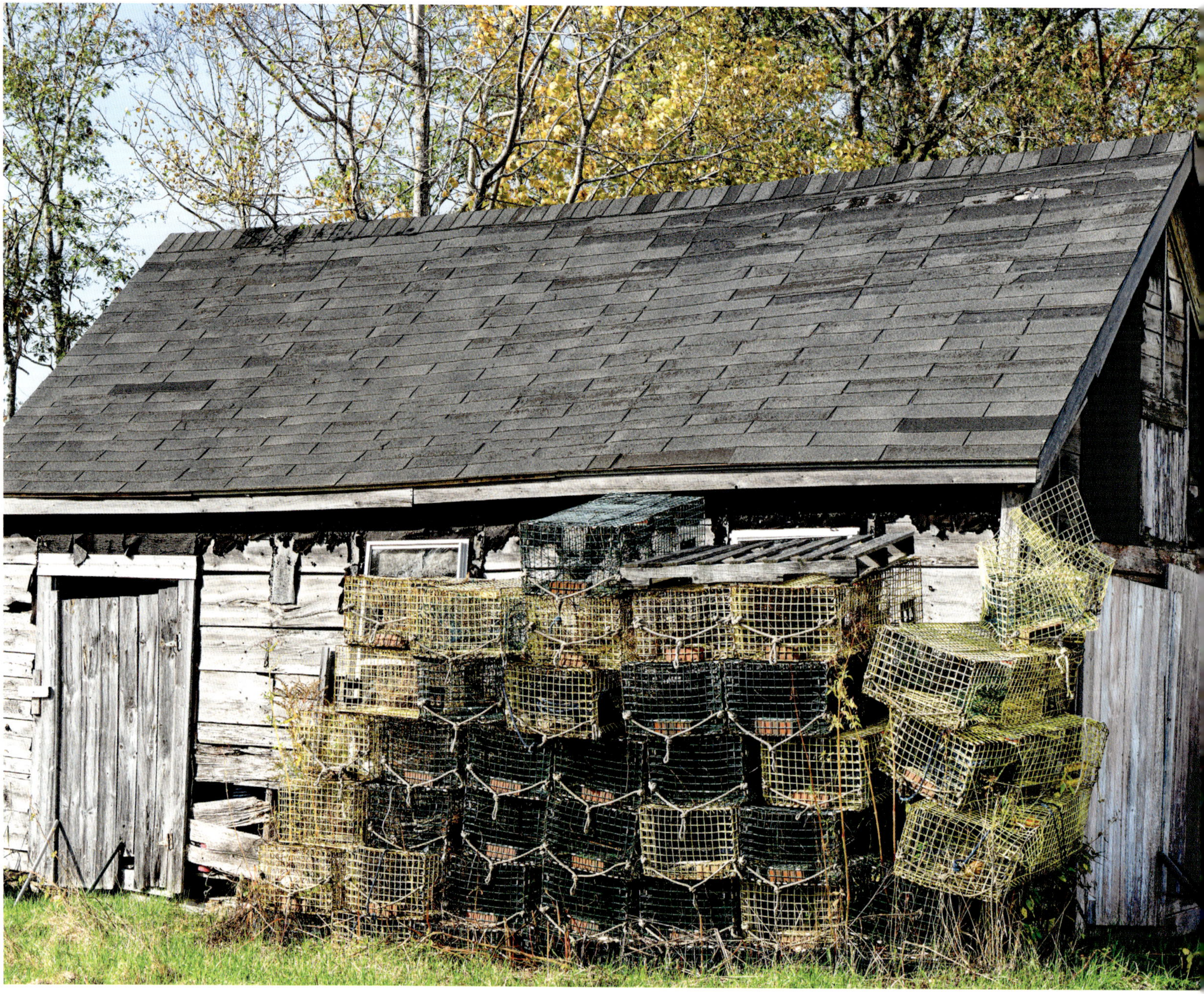

Shack and lobster traps, Waldoboro, Maine

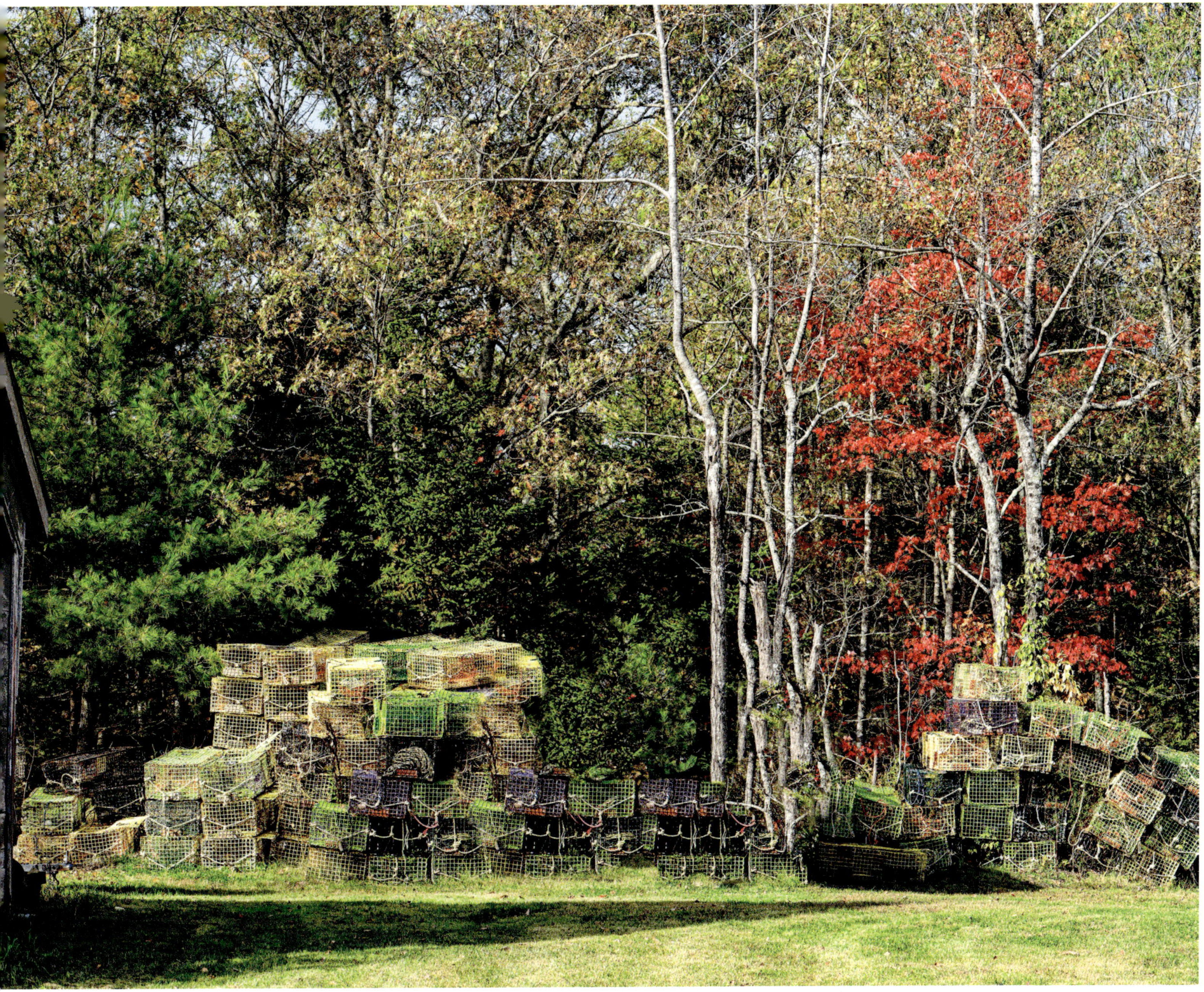

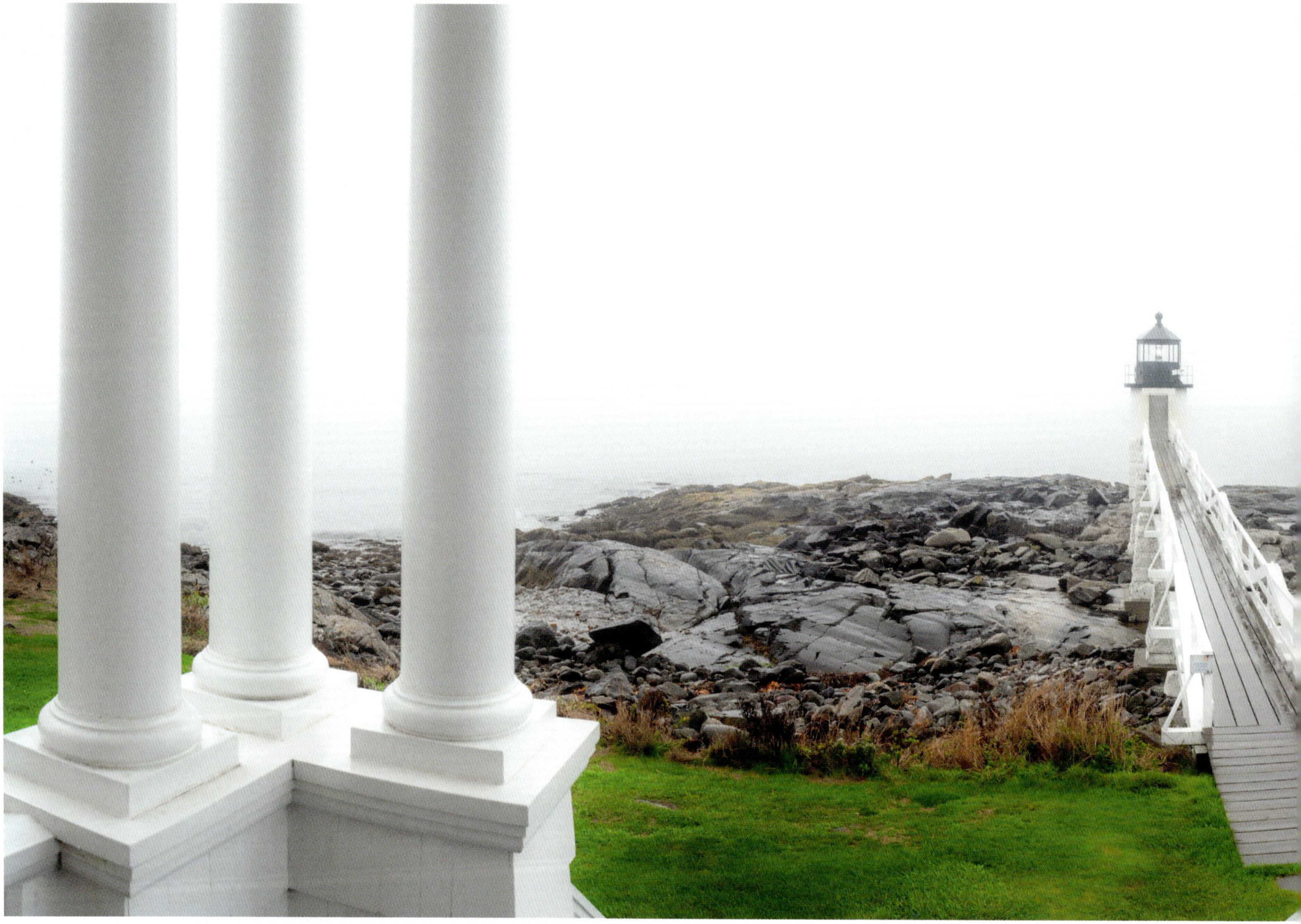

Marshall Point Light (1832), Port Clyde, Maine

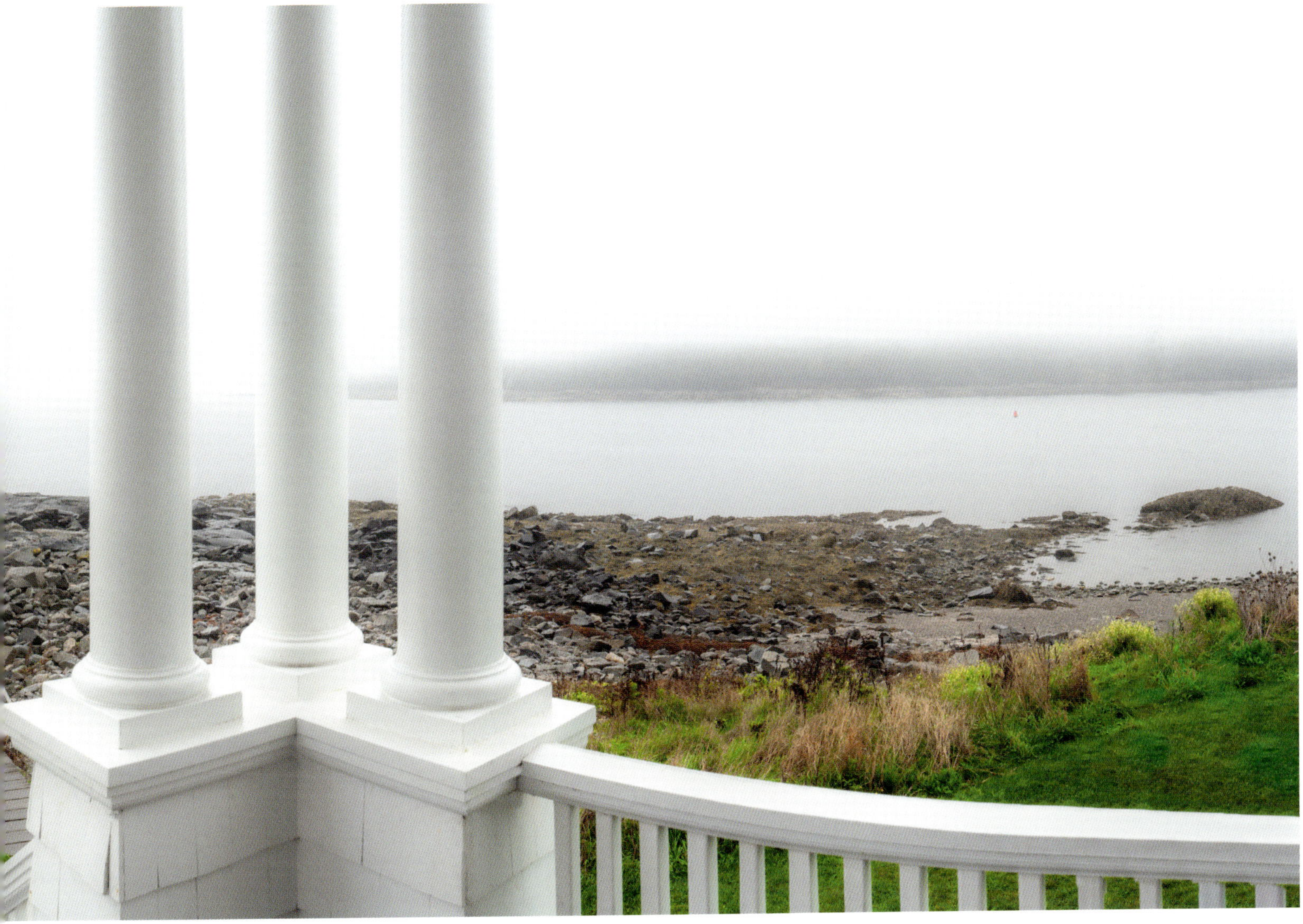

You might remember this lighthouse as the one Forrest Gump ran to in the movie.

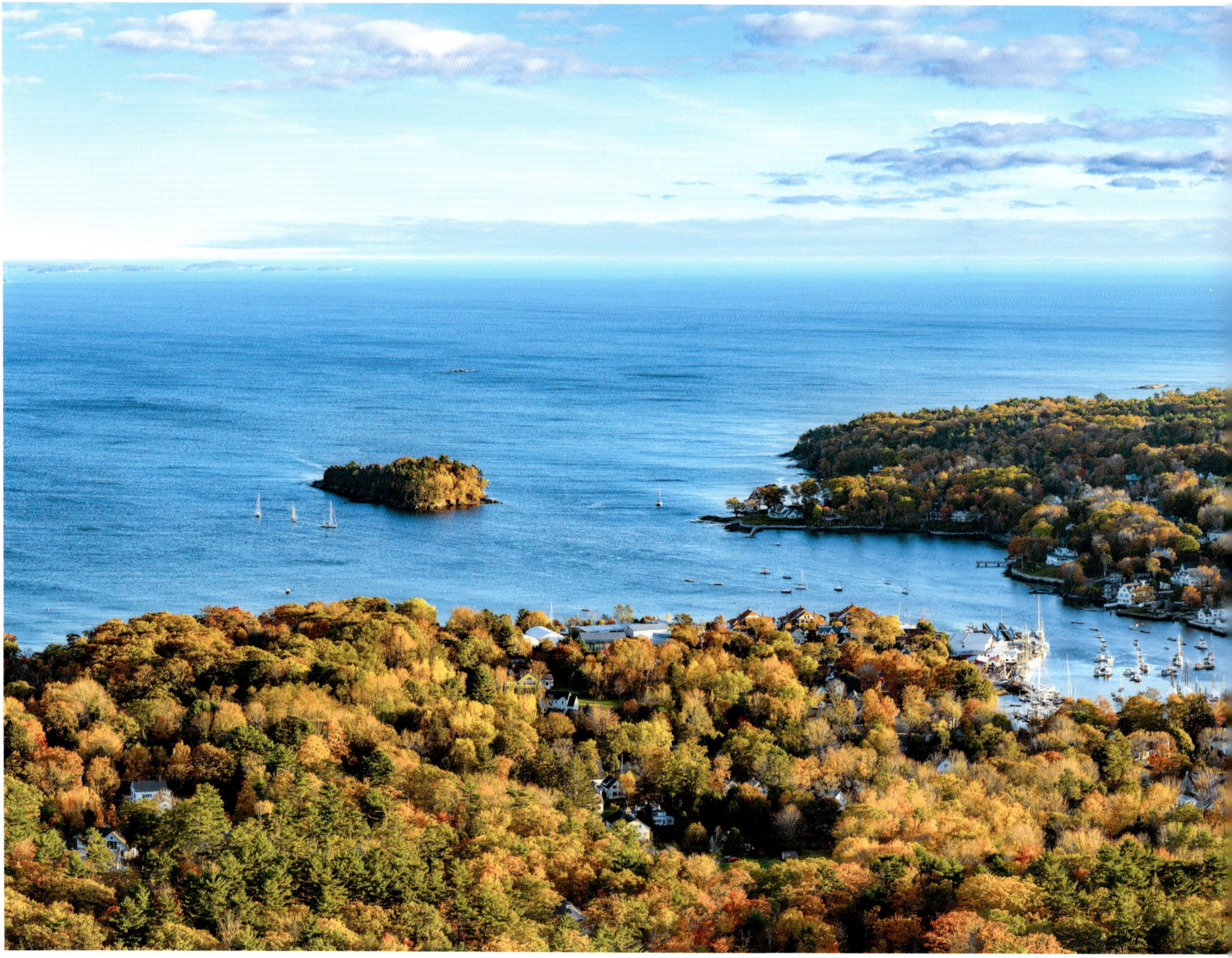

Penobscot Bay and Camden, Maine, from the top of Mount Battie (780 feet)

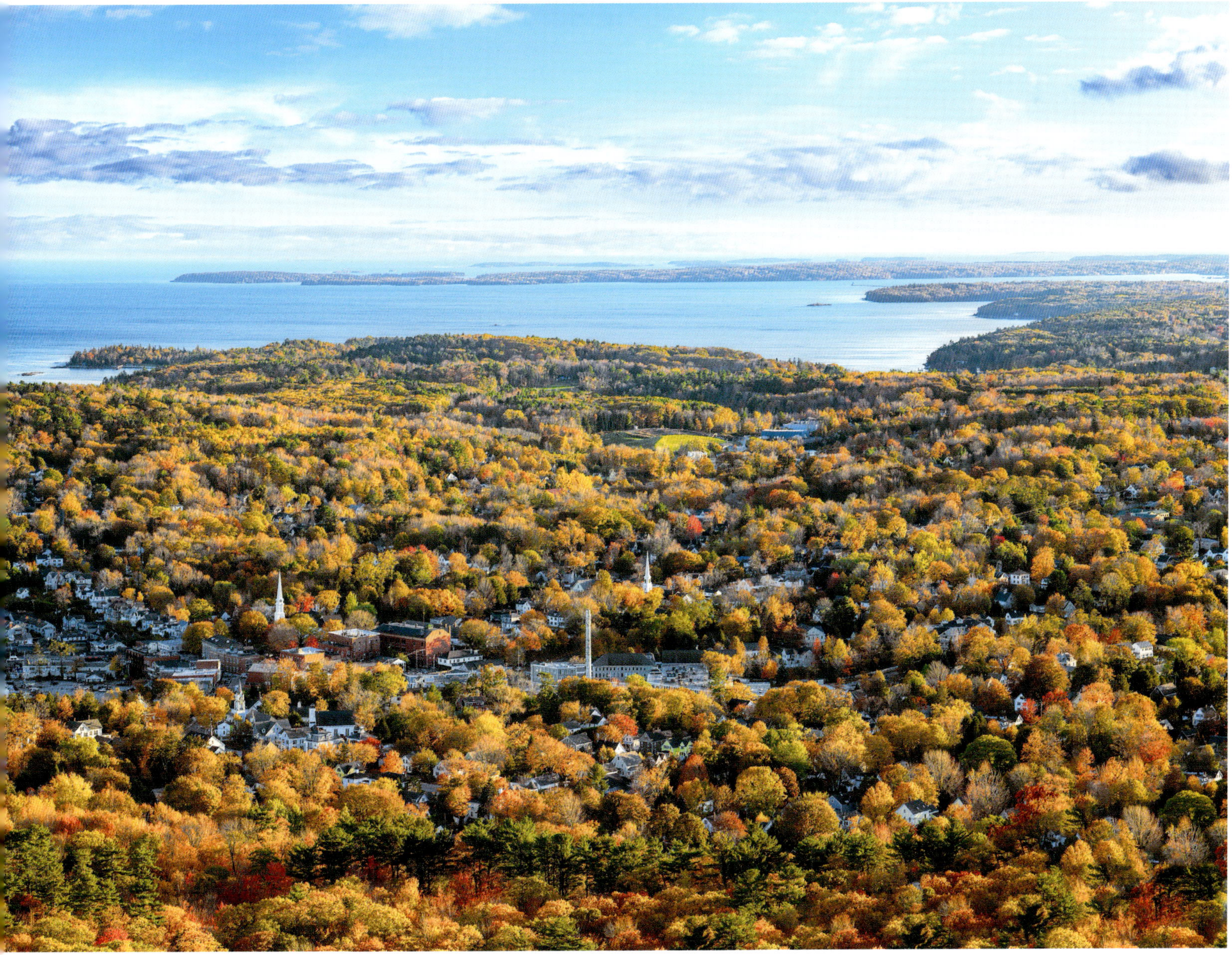

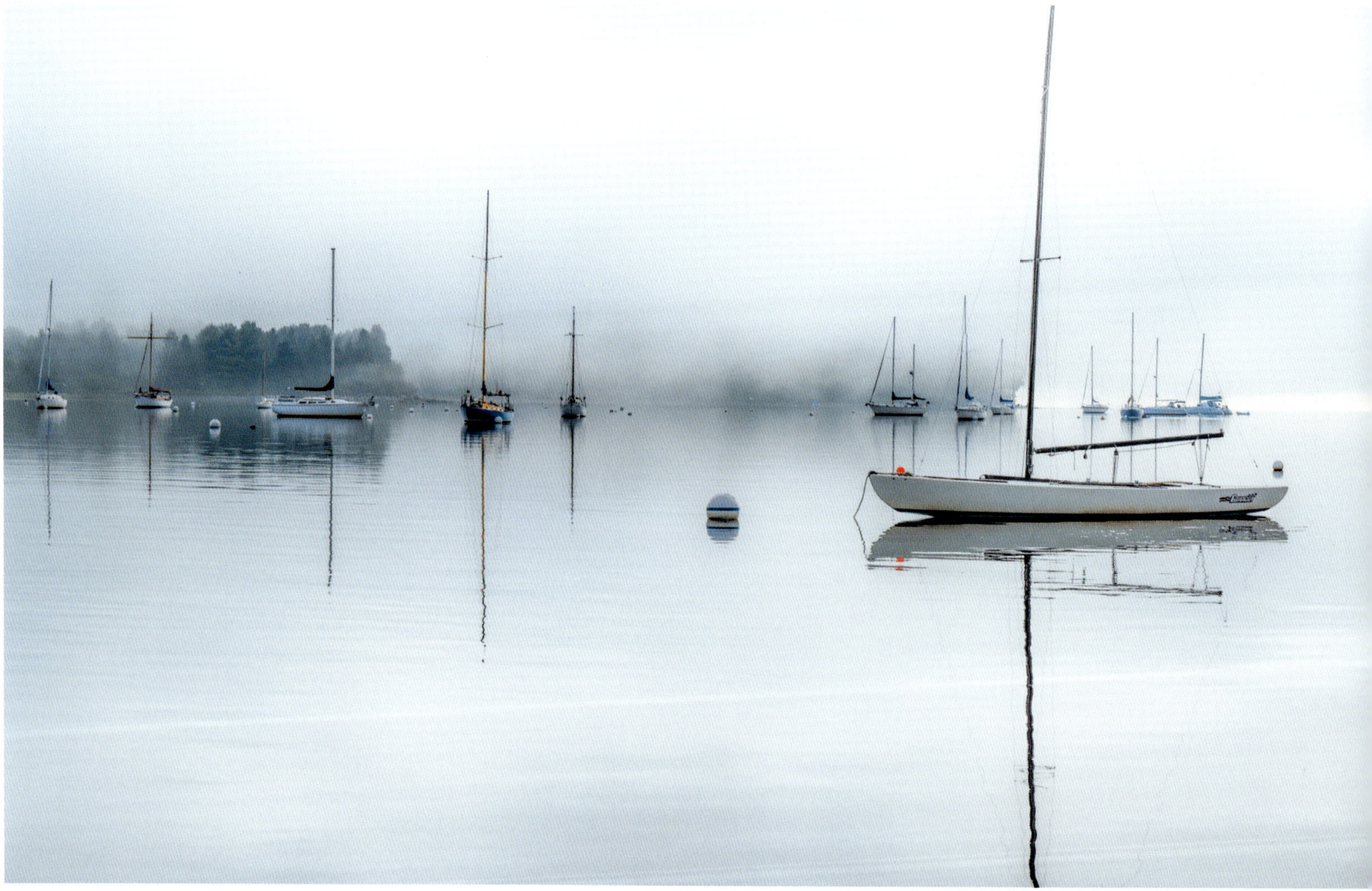

Belfast Harbor, Maine

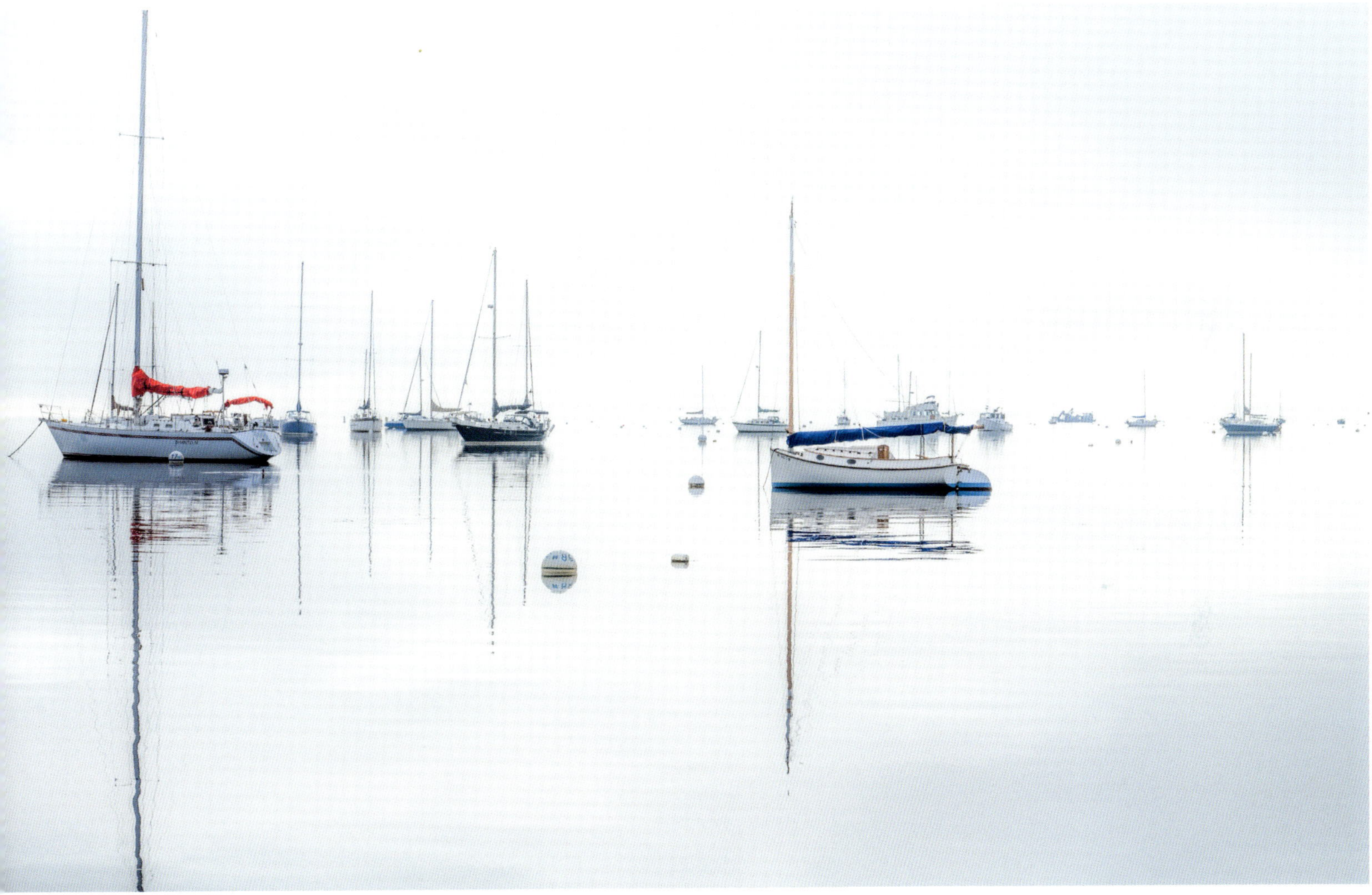

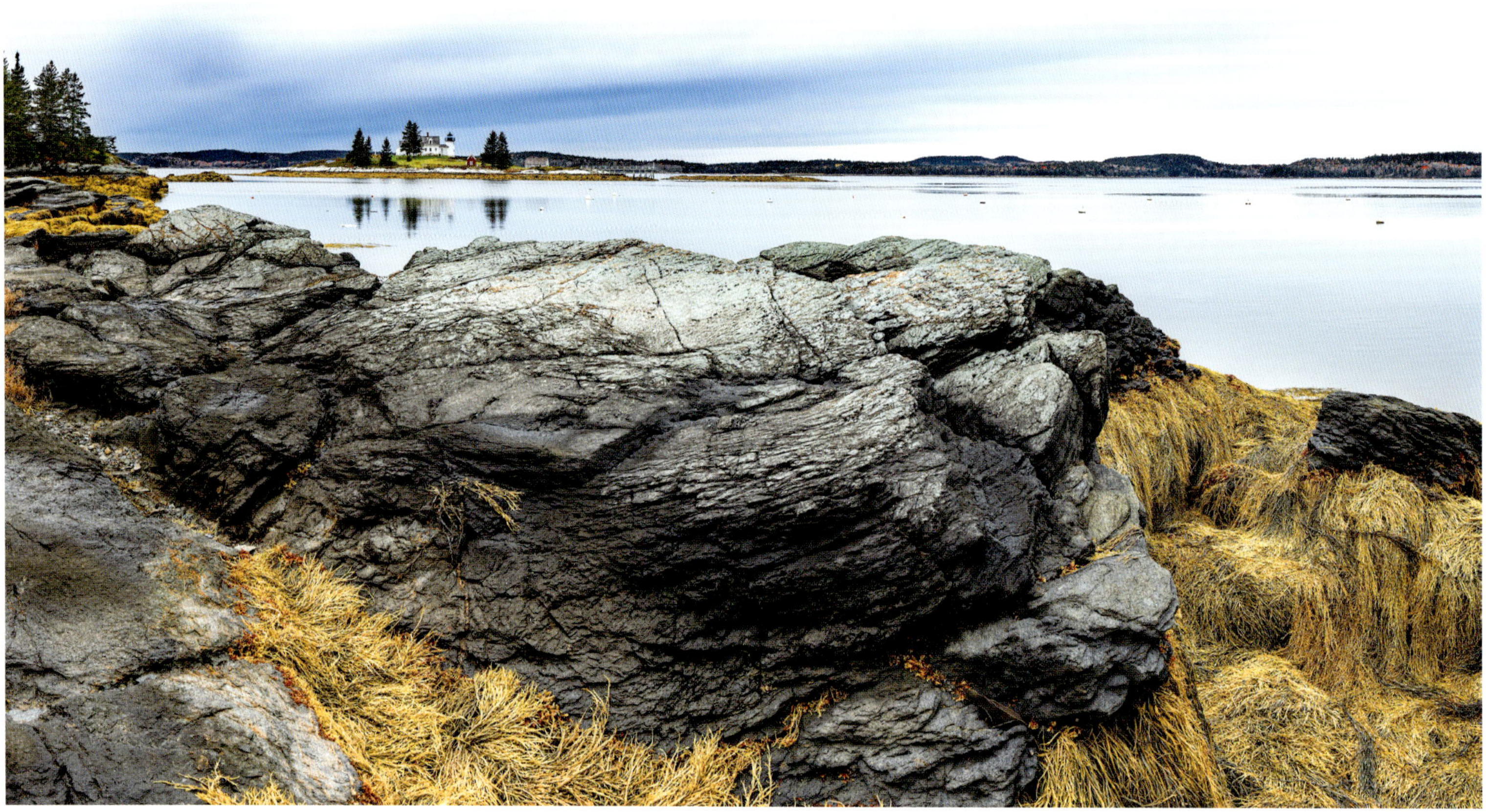

Pumpkin Island Light (1854), Eggemoggin Reach, Maine

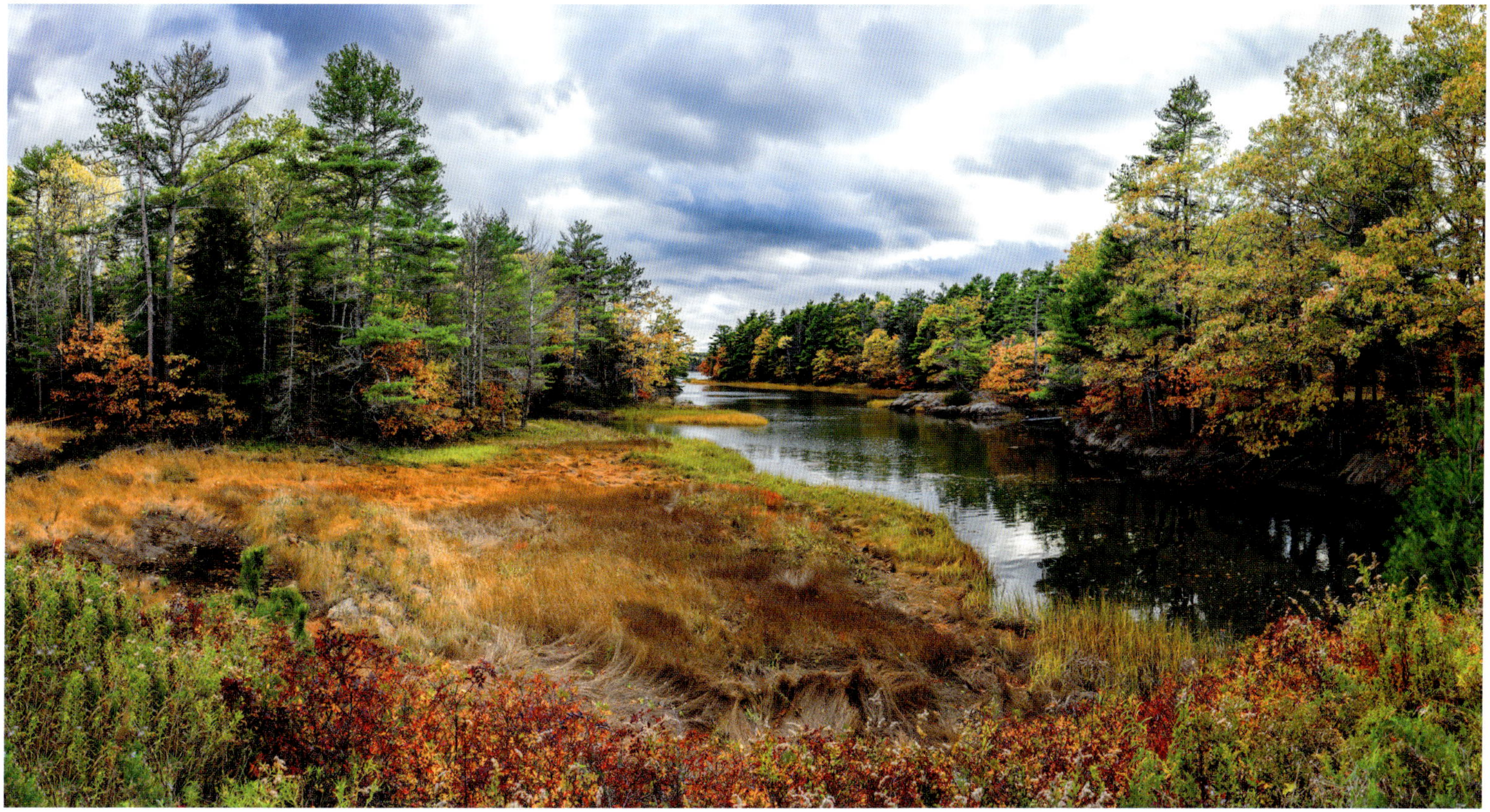

Wildcat Creek, Boothbay, Maine

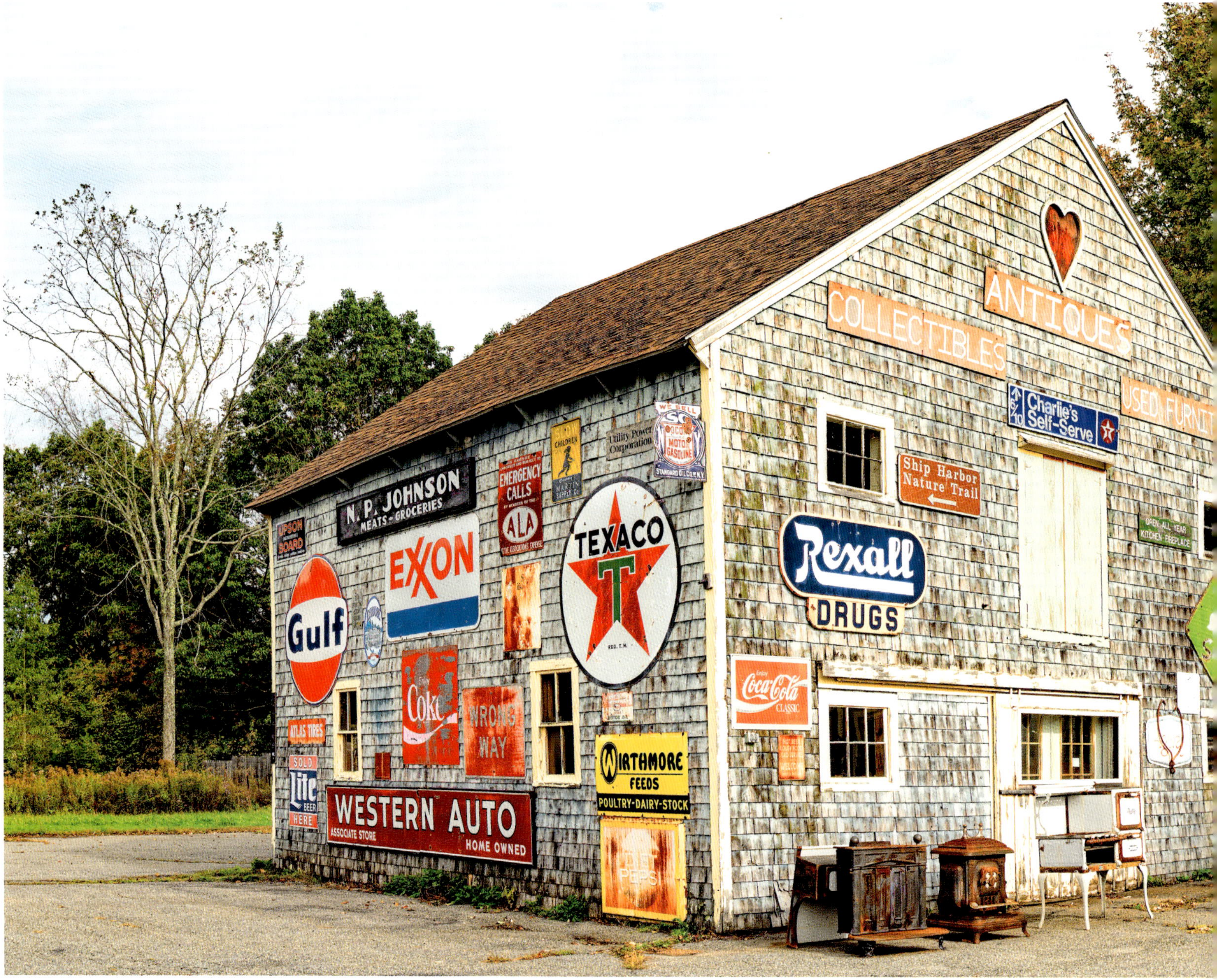

The Love Barn, Orland, Maine

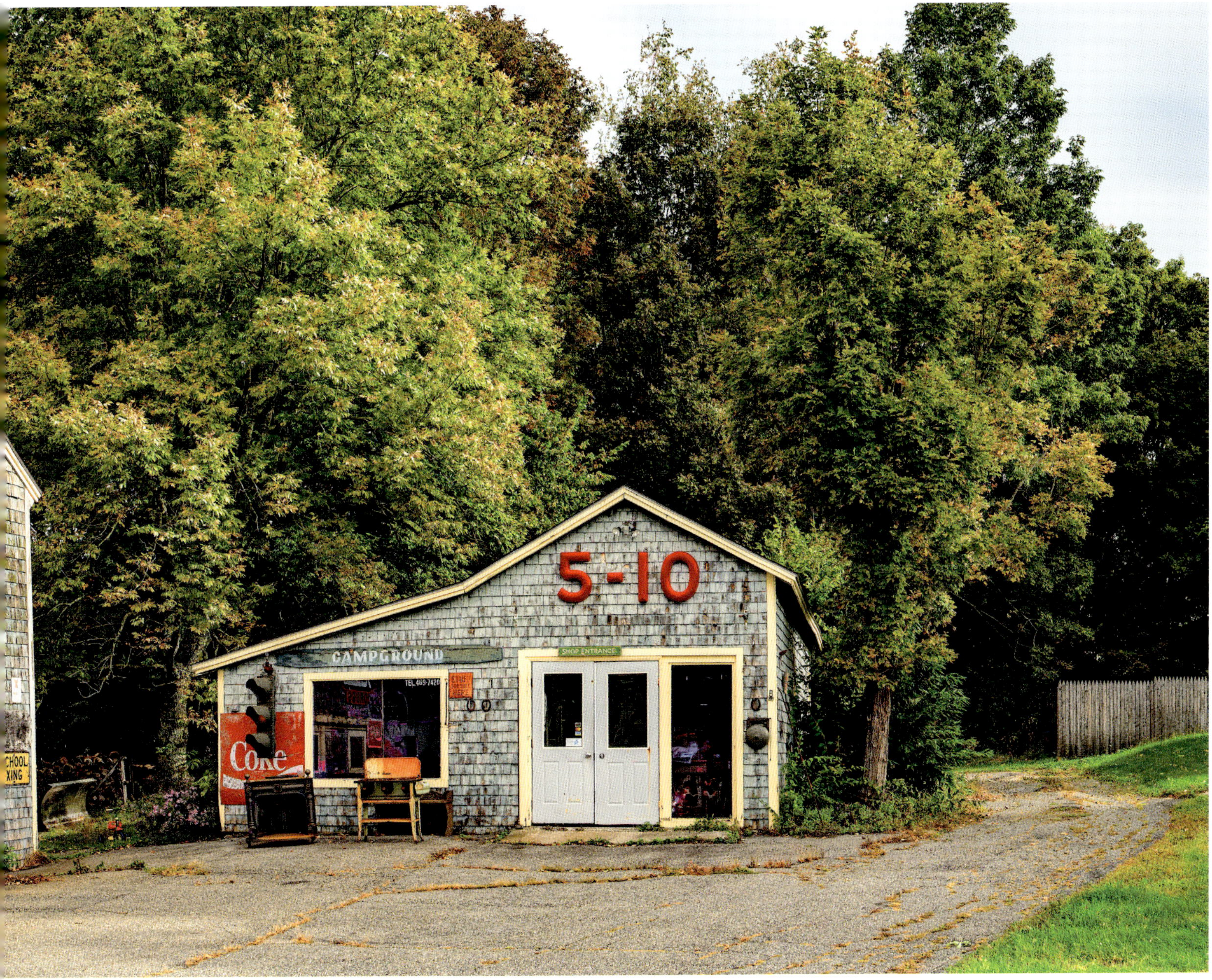
5-10
CAMPGROUND
SHOP ENTRANCE
TEL. 469-7420
Coke

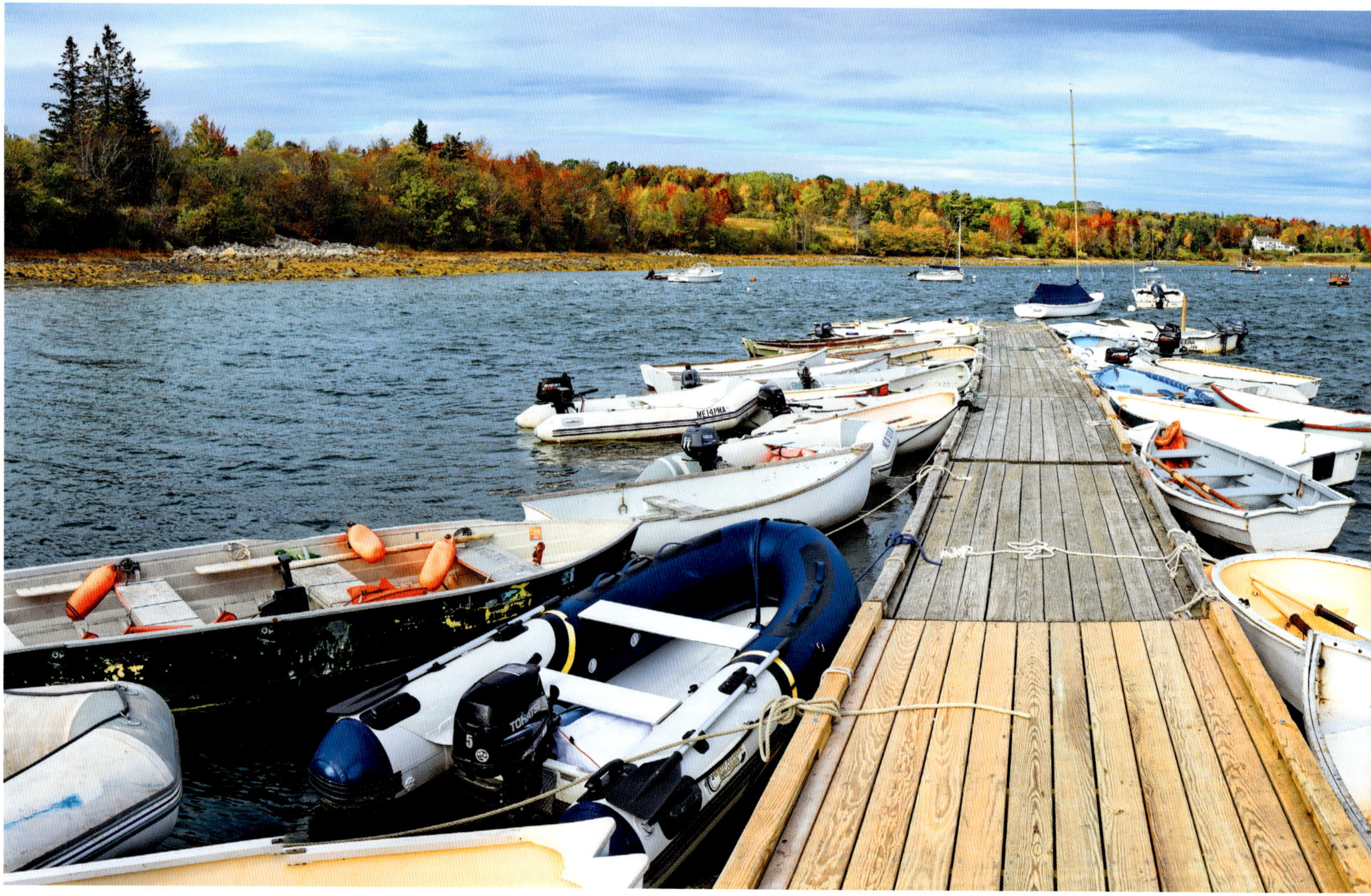

Sedgwick Harbor, Maine

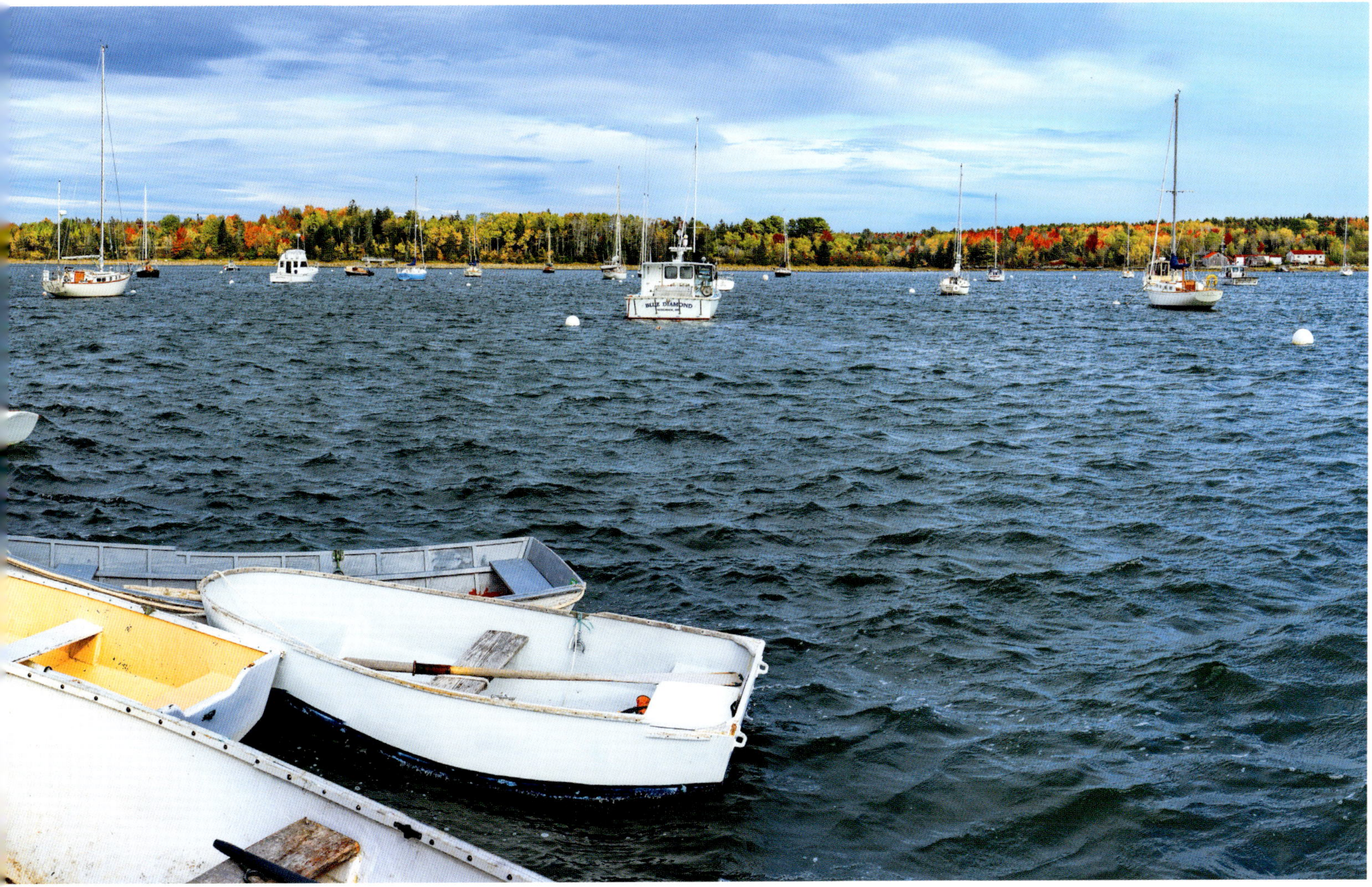

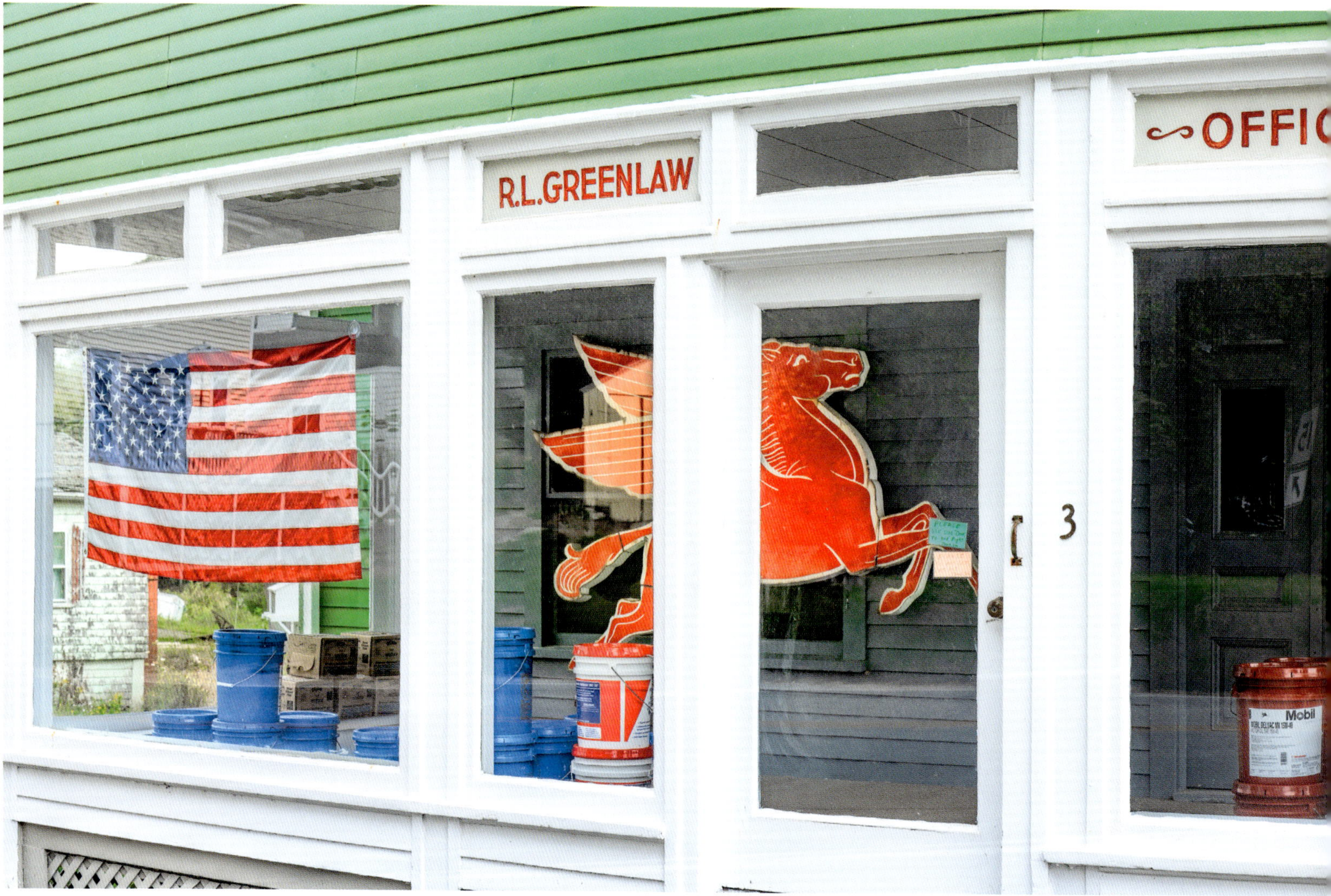

R.L. Greenlaw's office, Deer Isle, Maine

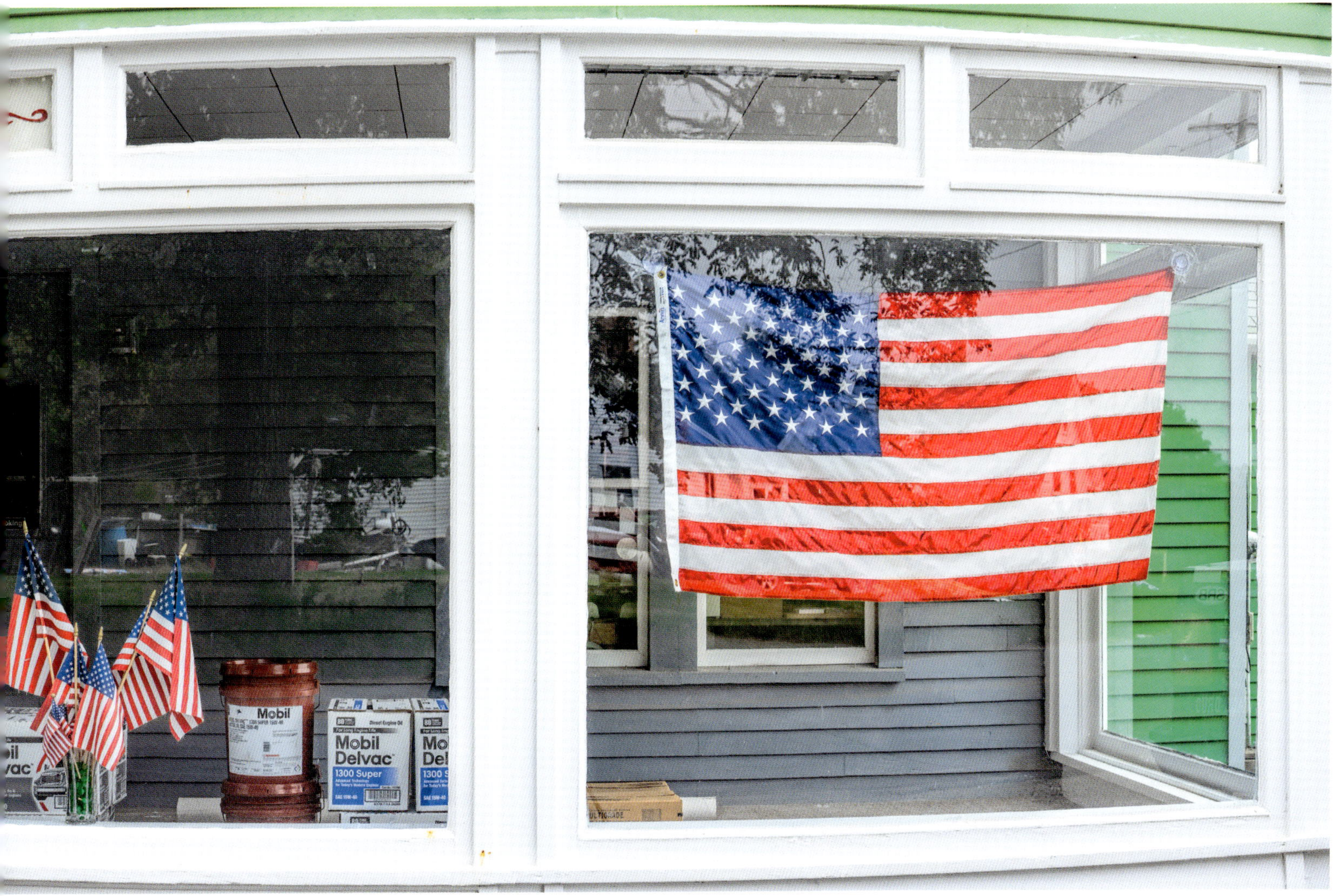

One of the little signs on the door says, “Please do not let cats out. Thank you.” Somehow that made me feel welcome.

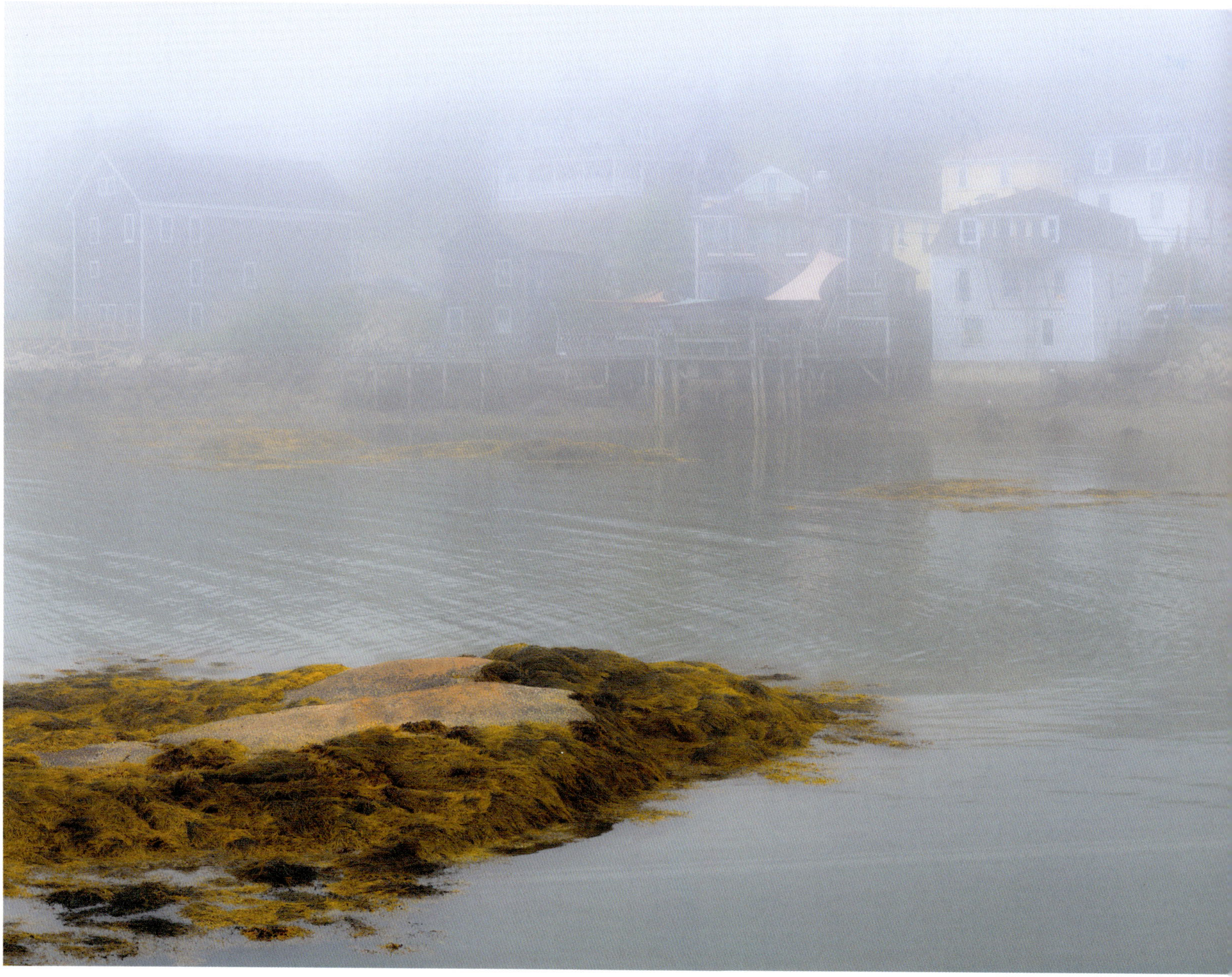

Stonington Harbor, Maine

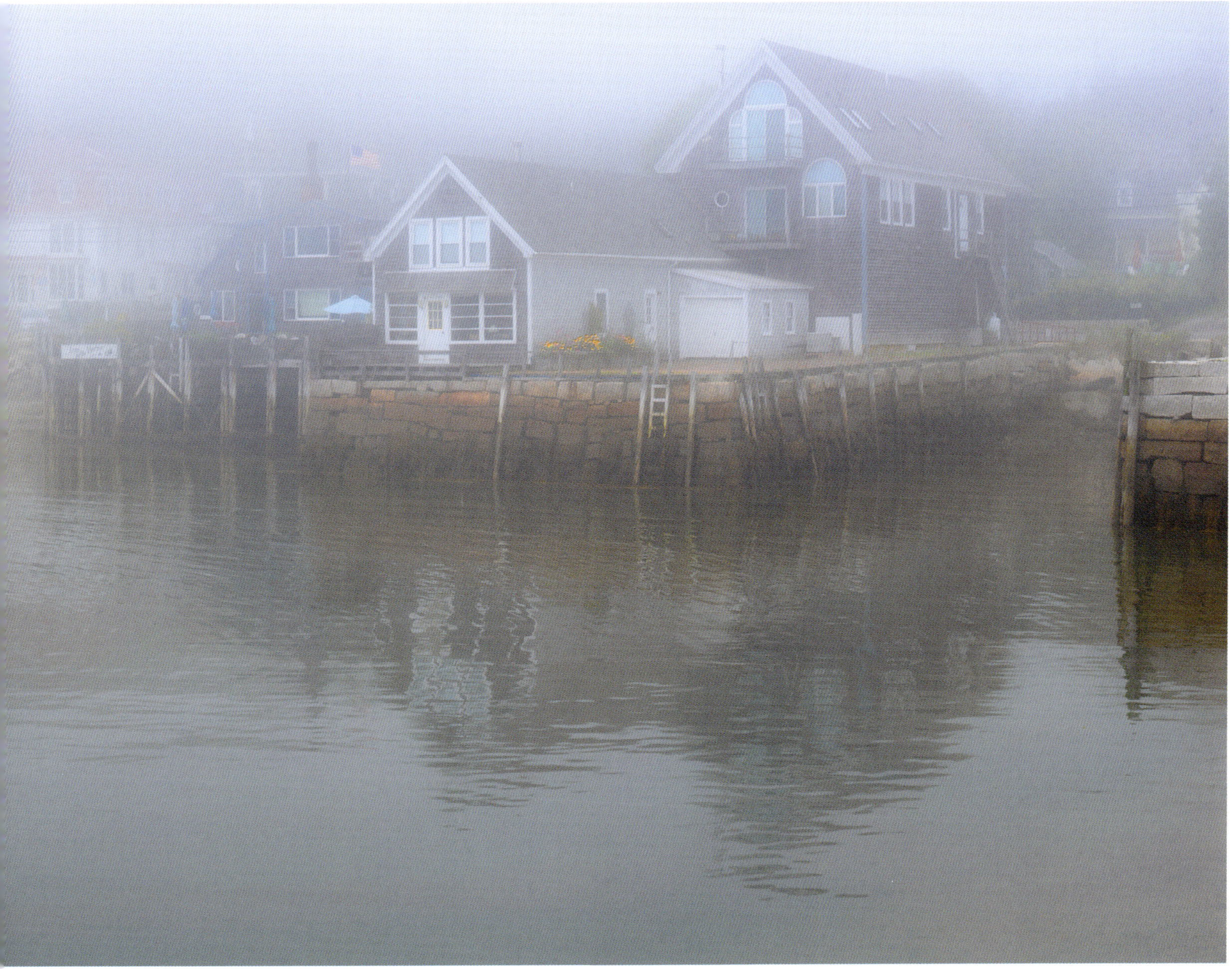

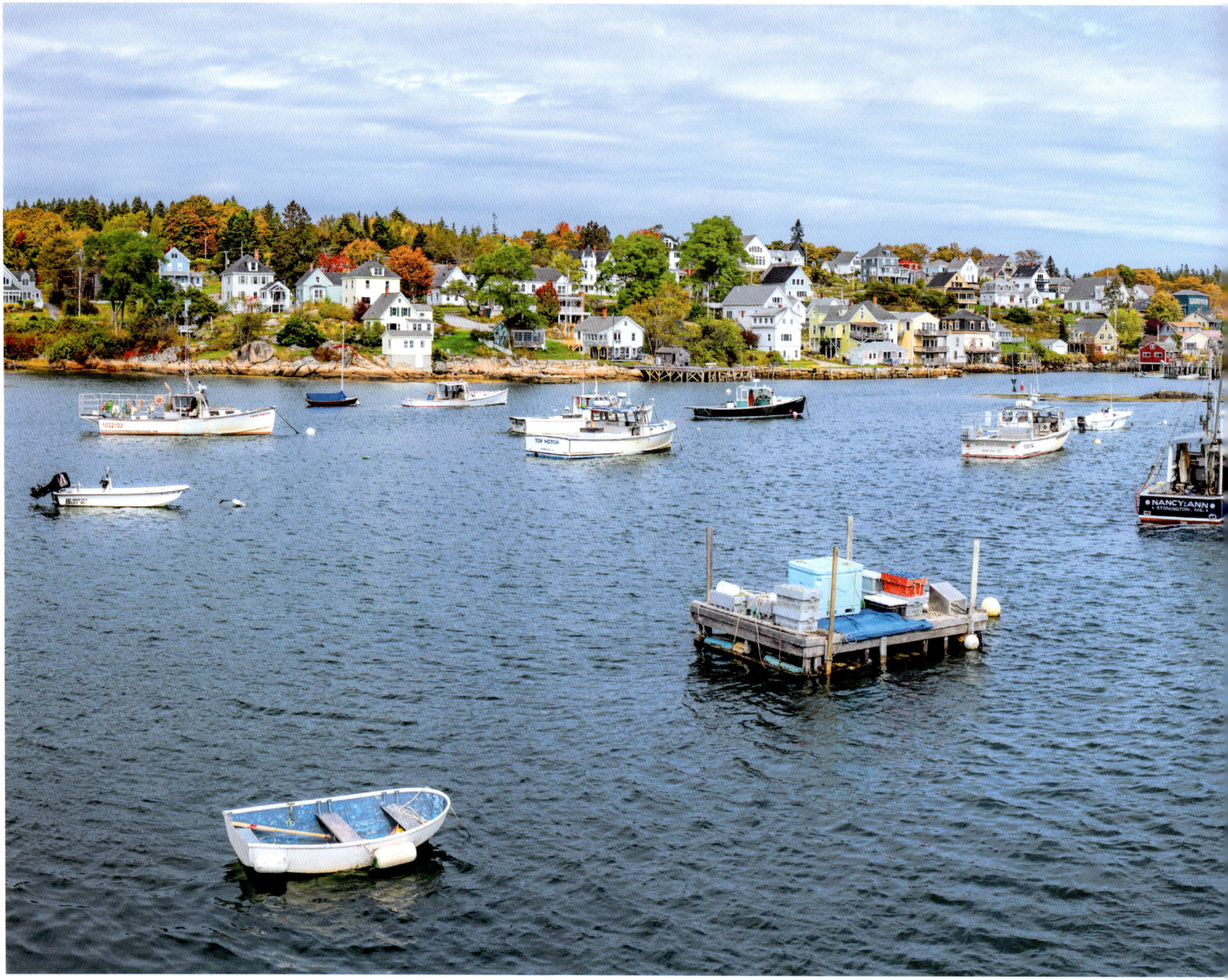

Sunset Harbor, Maine

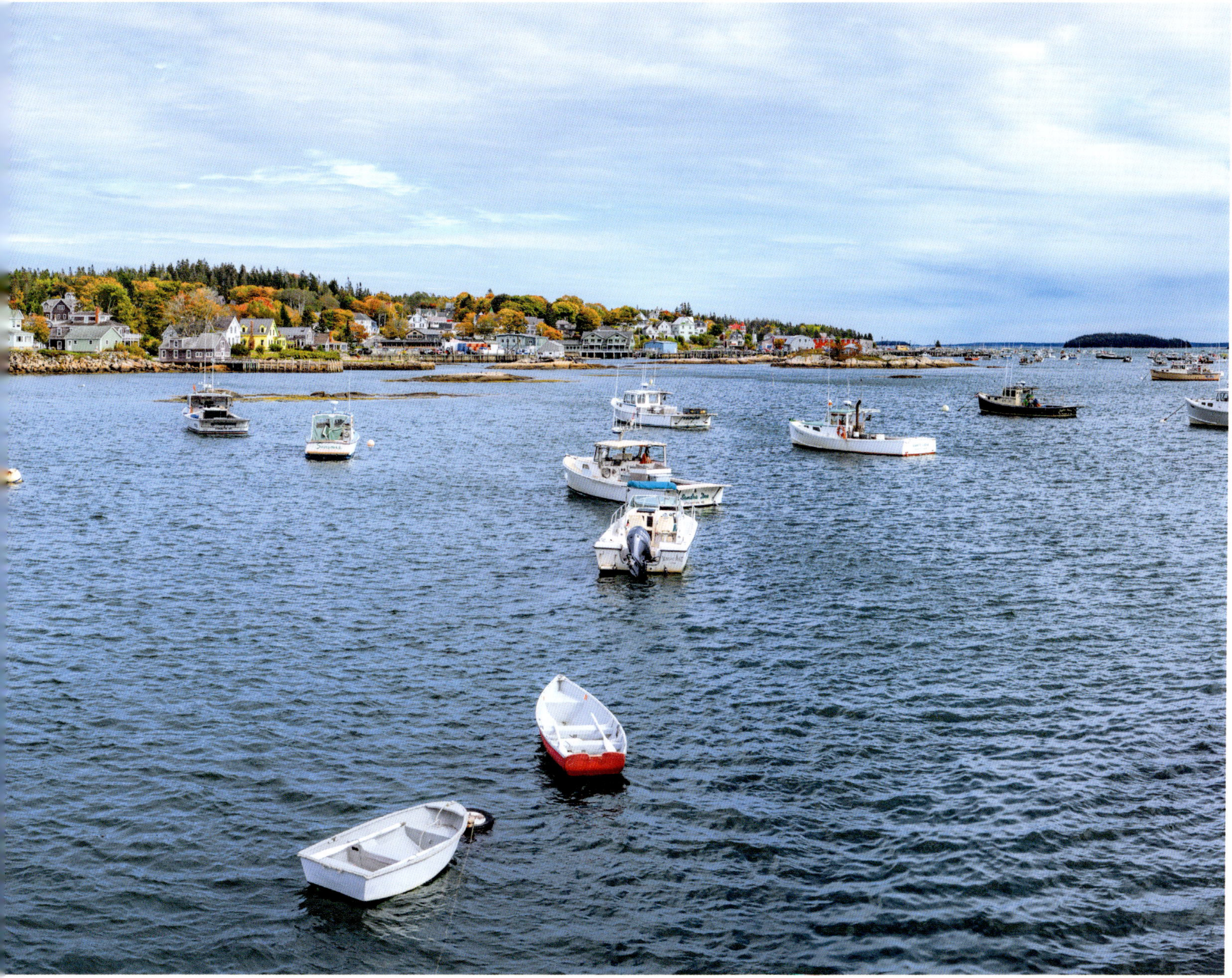

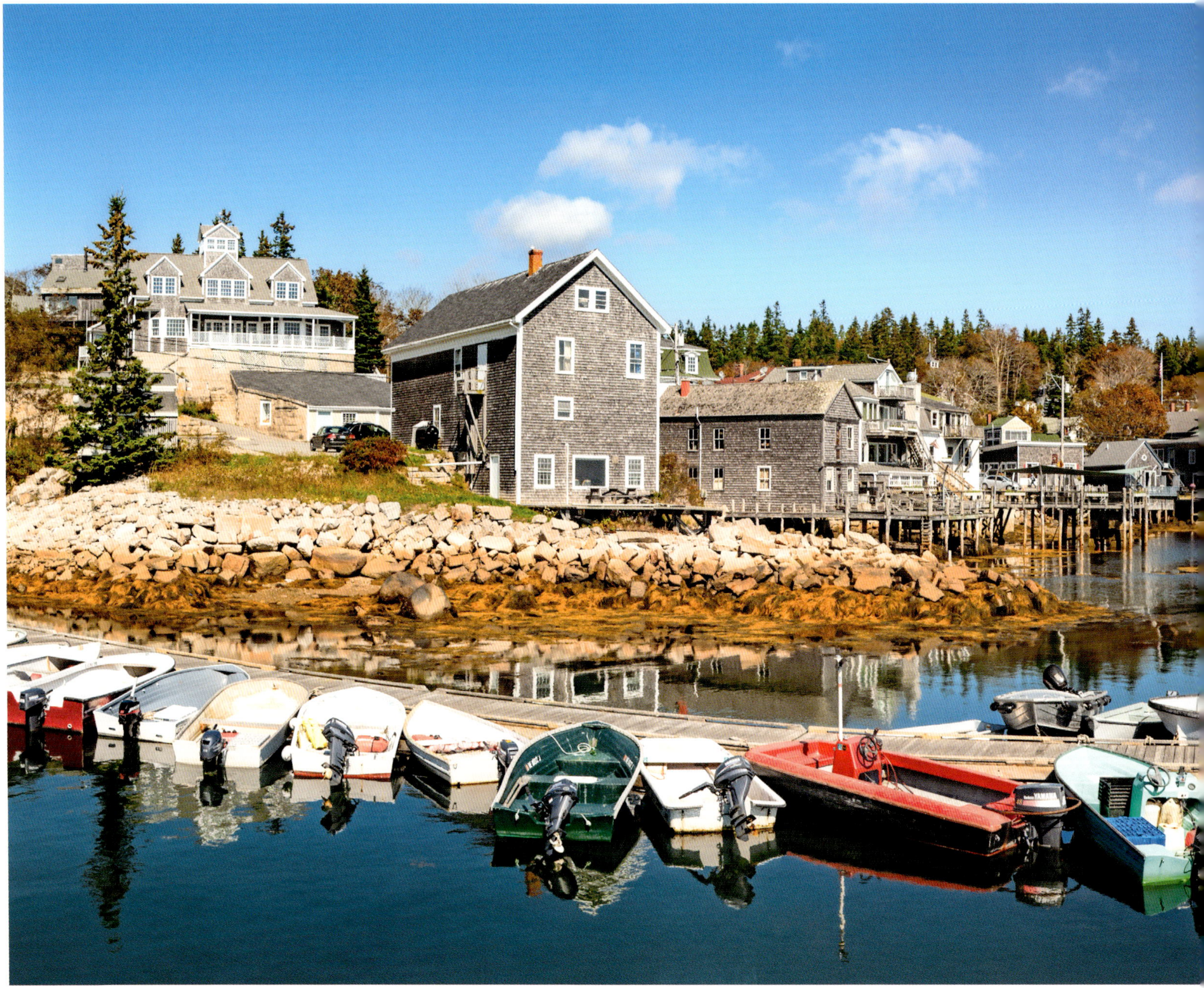

School Street Pier, Stonington, Maine

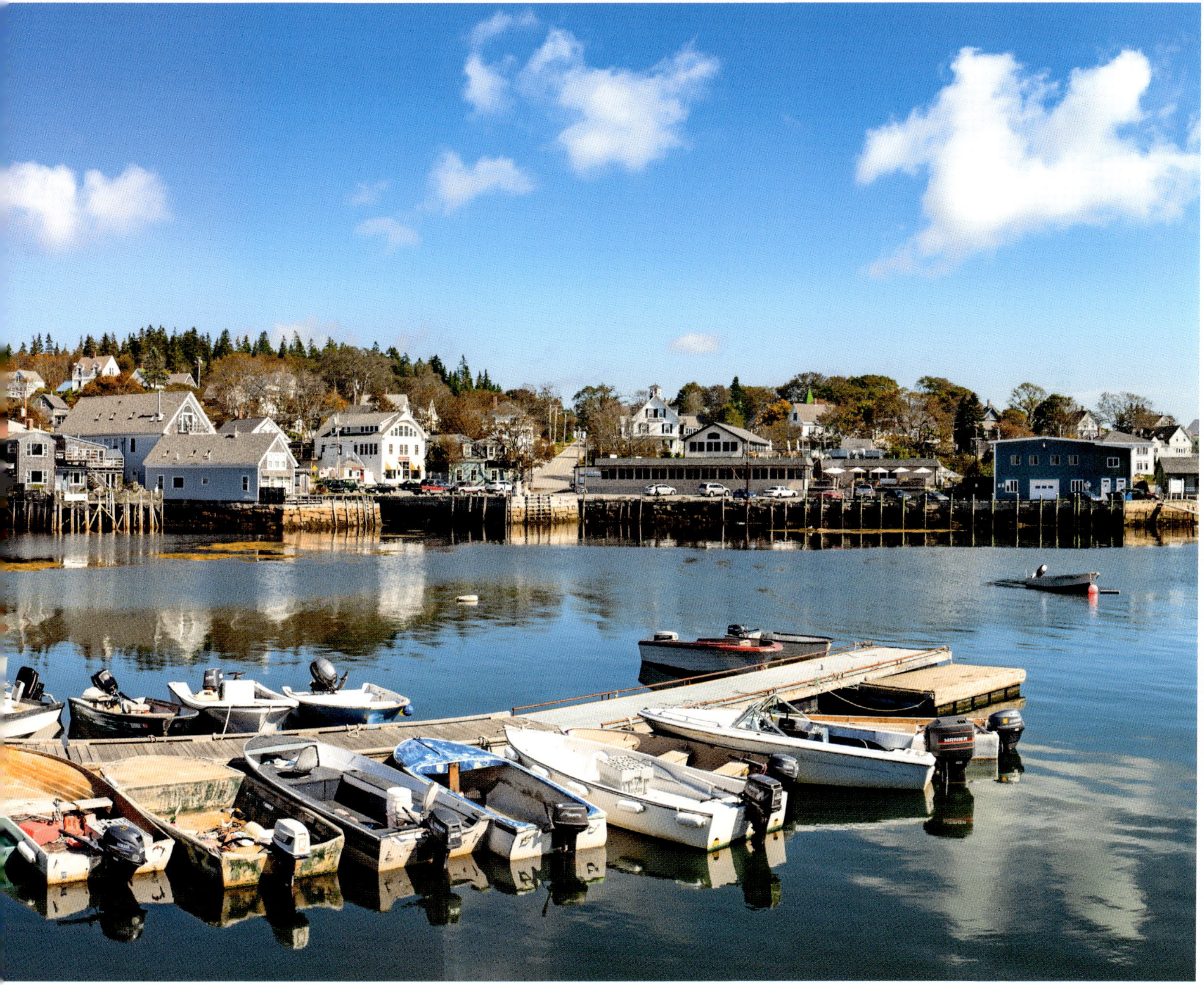

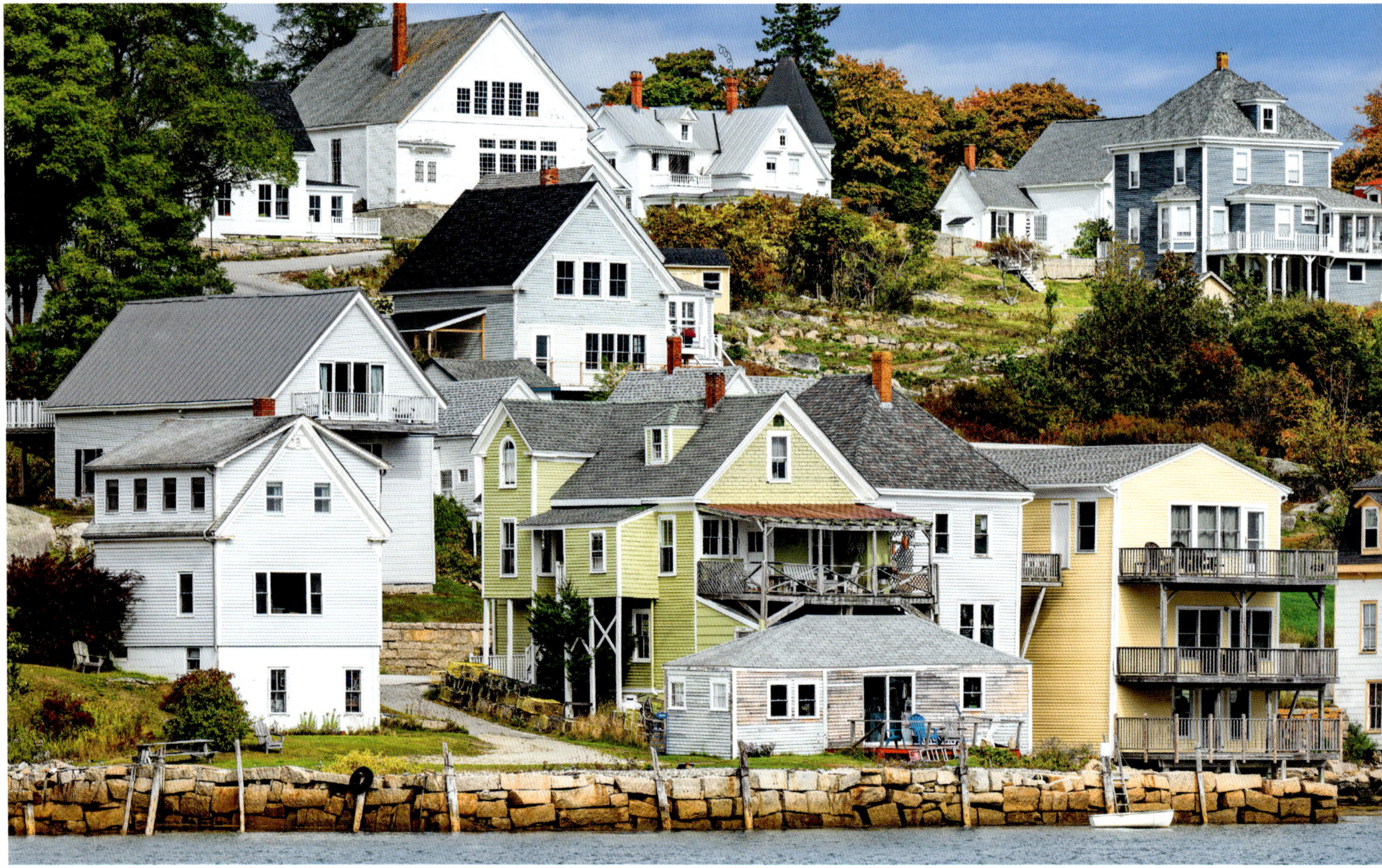

Stonington, Maine

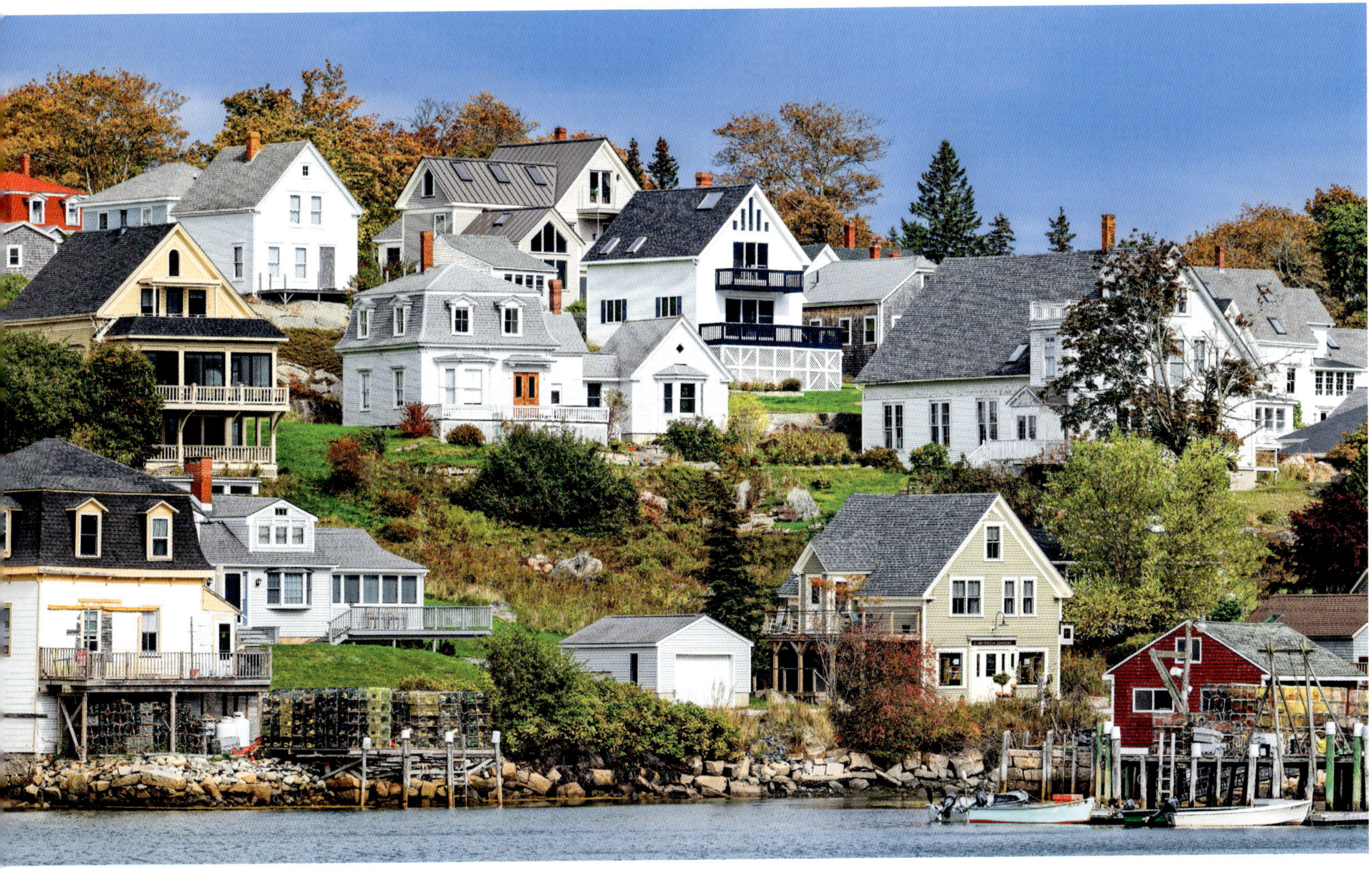

Full disclosure, I Photoshopped out all the poles and wires. It took 18 hours all together. Yeah, crazy!

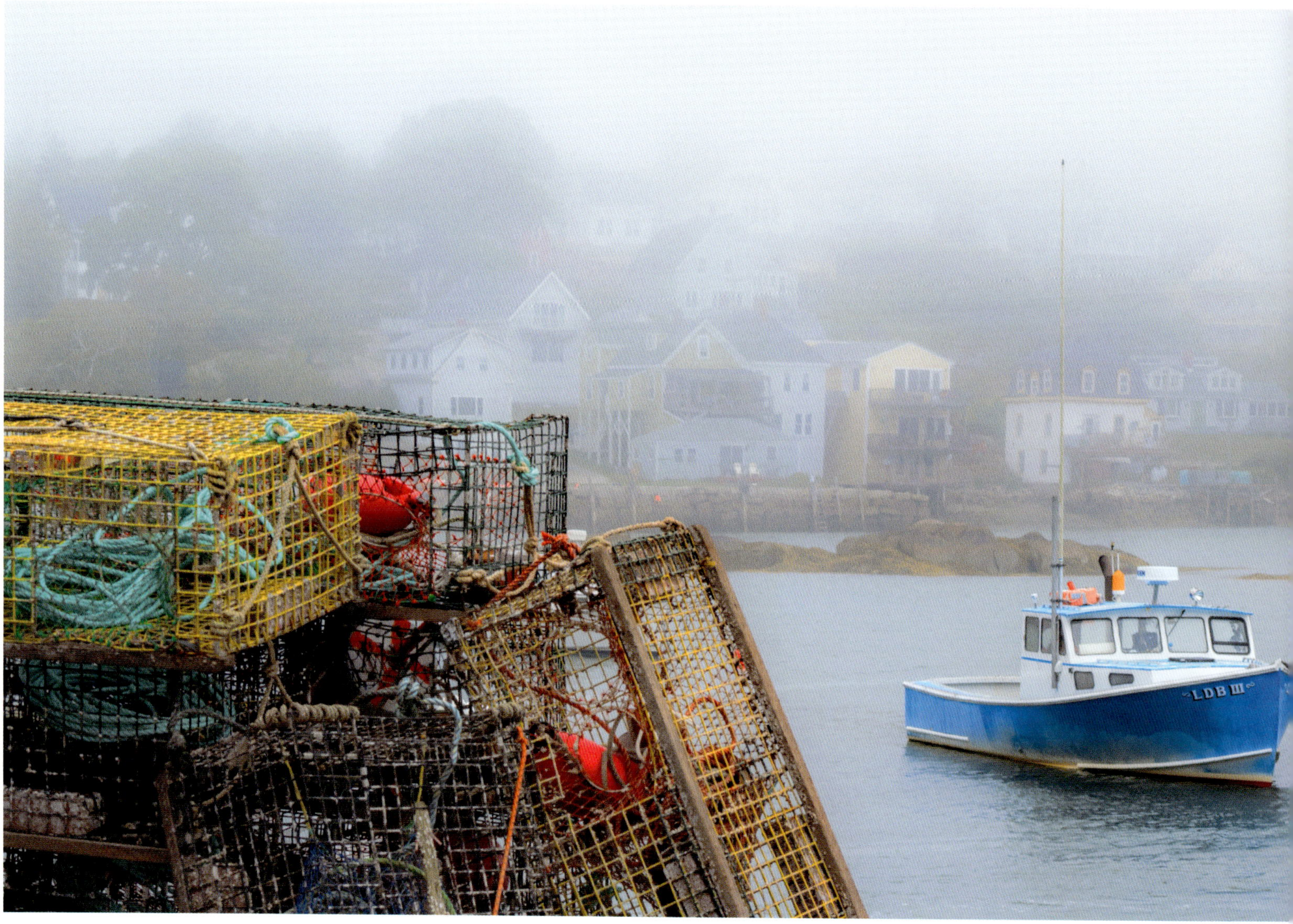

Blue Hill Bay, Maine

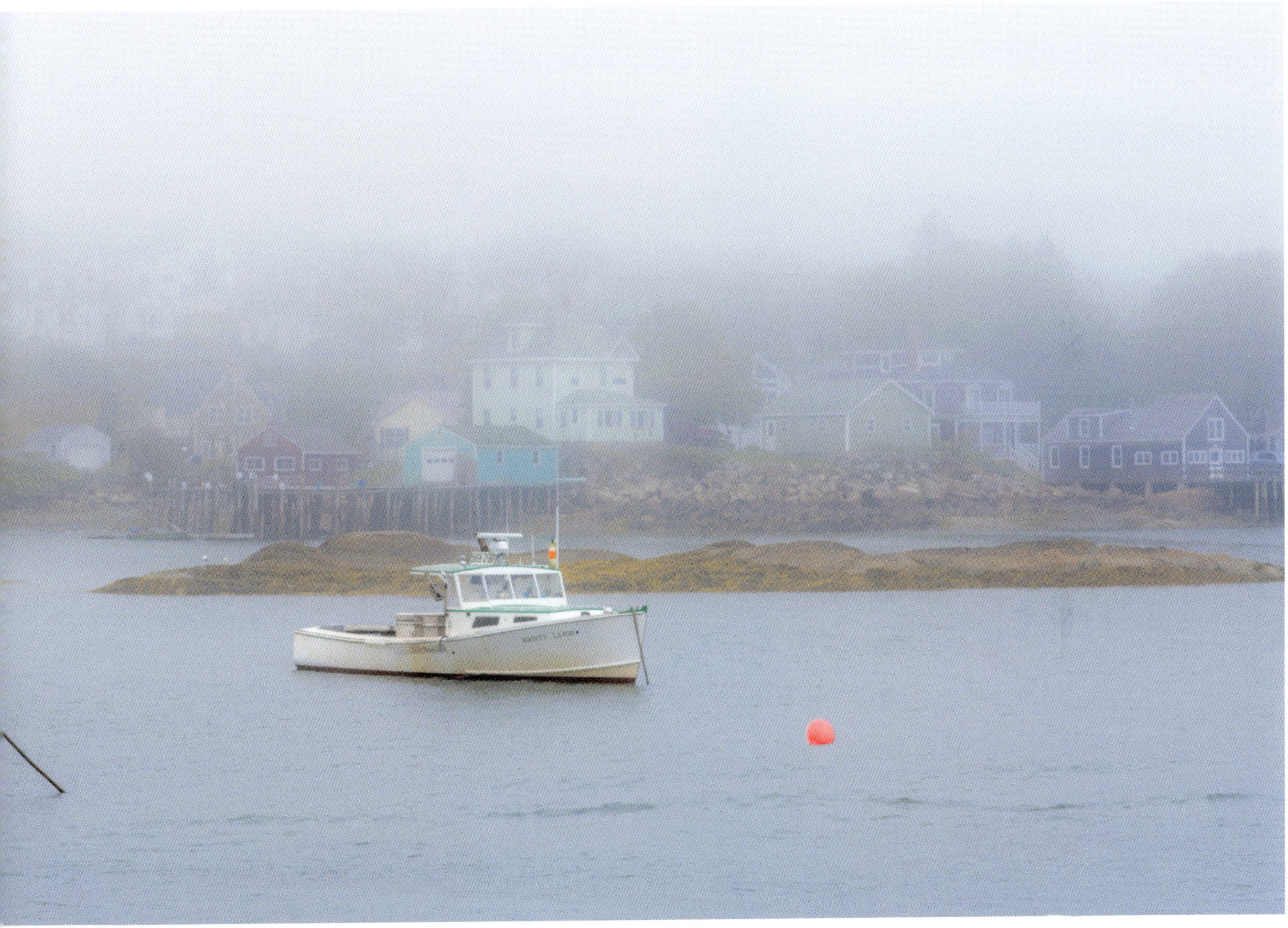

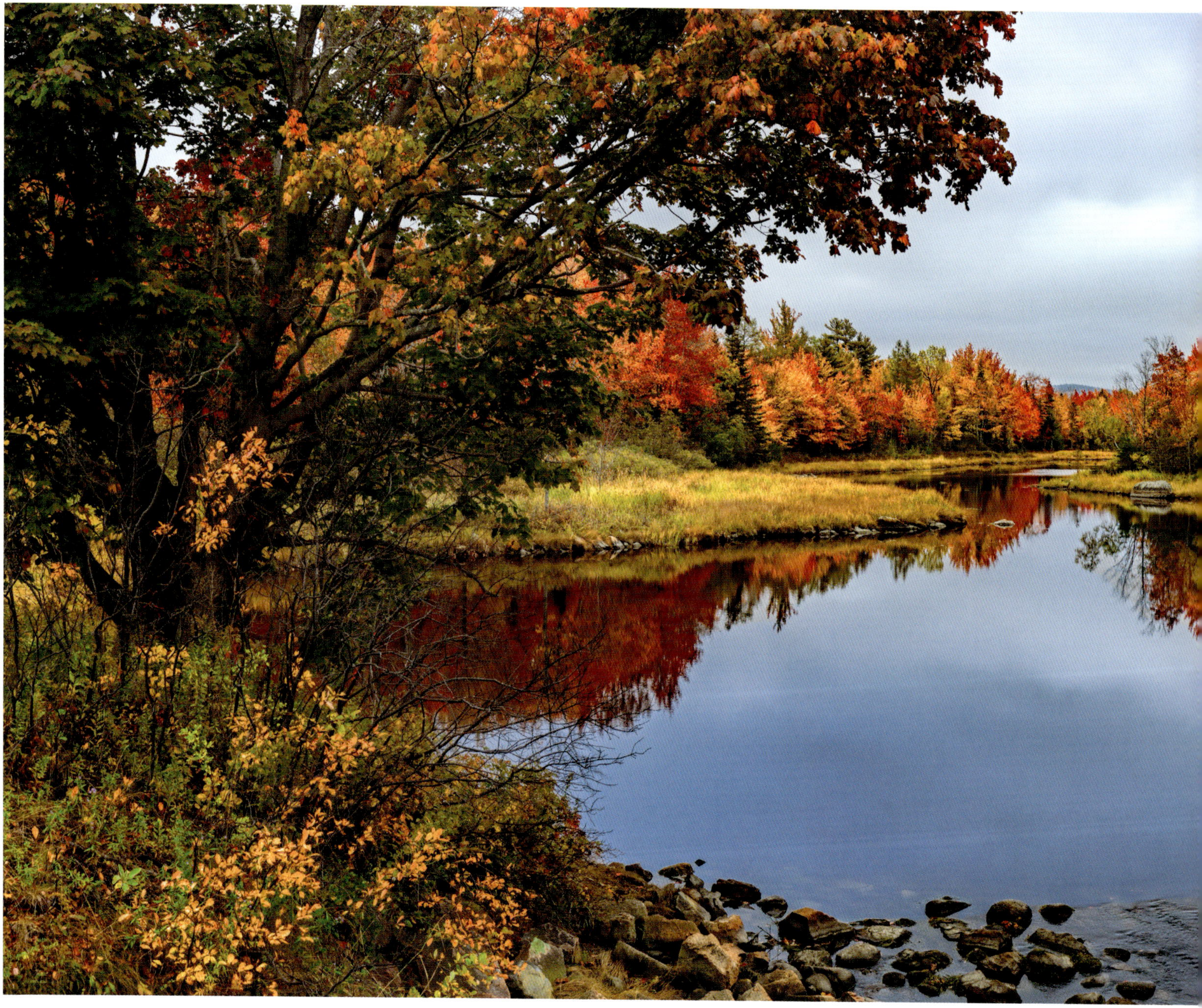

Thomas Bay, Maine

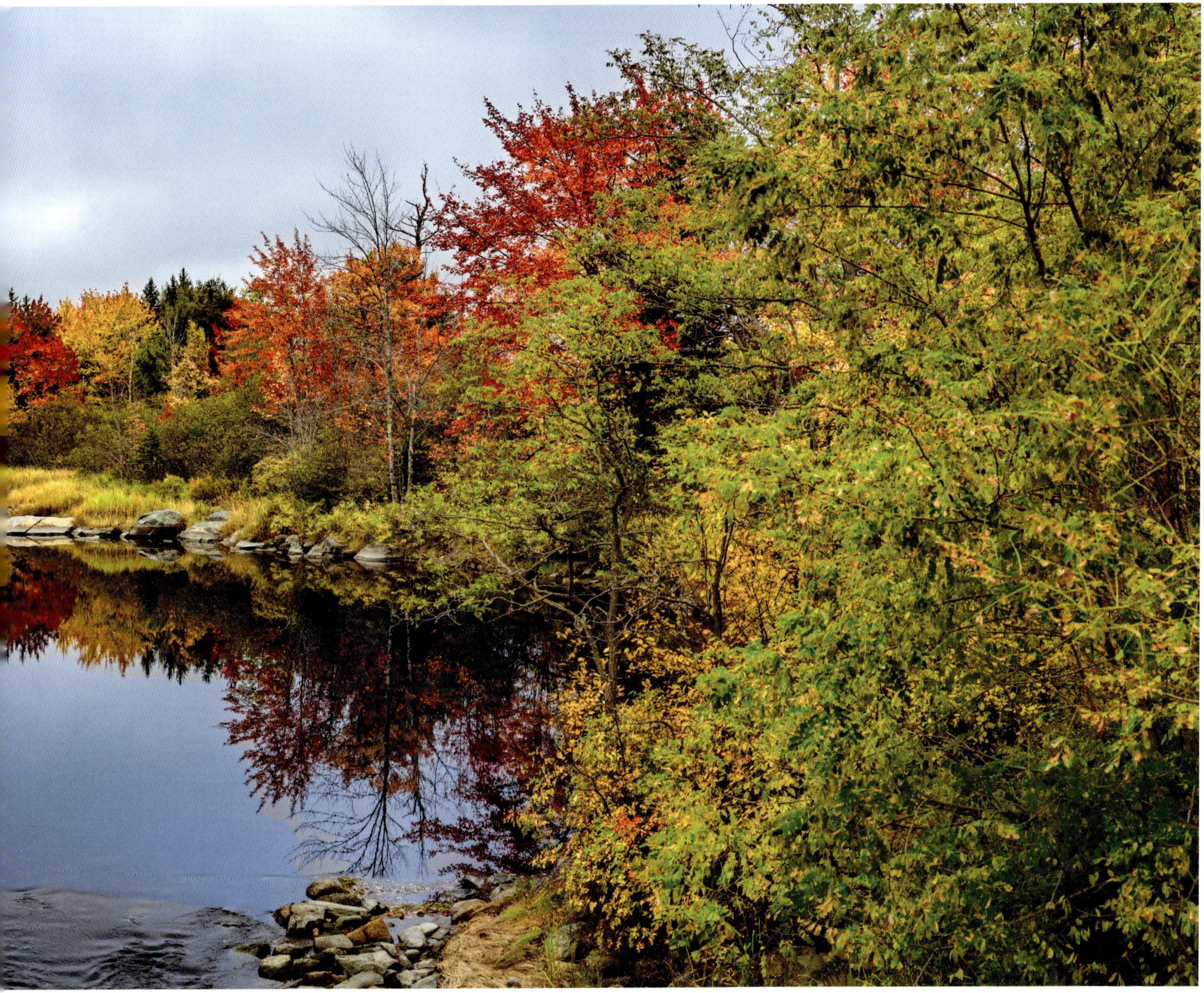

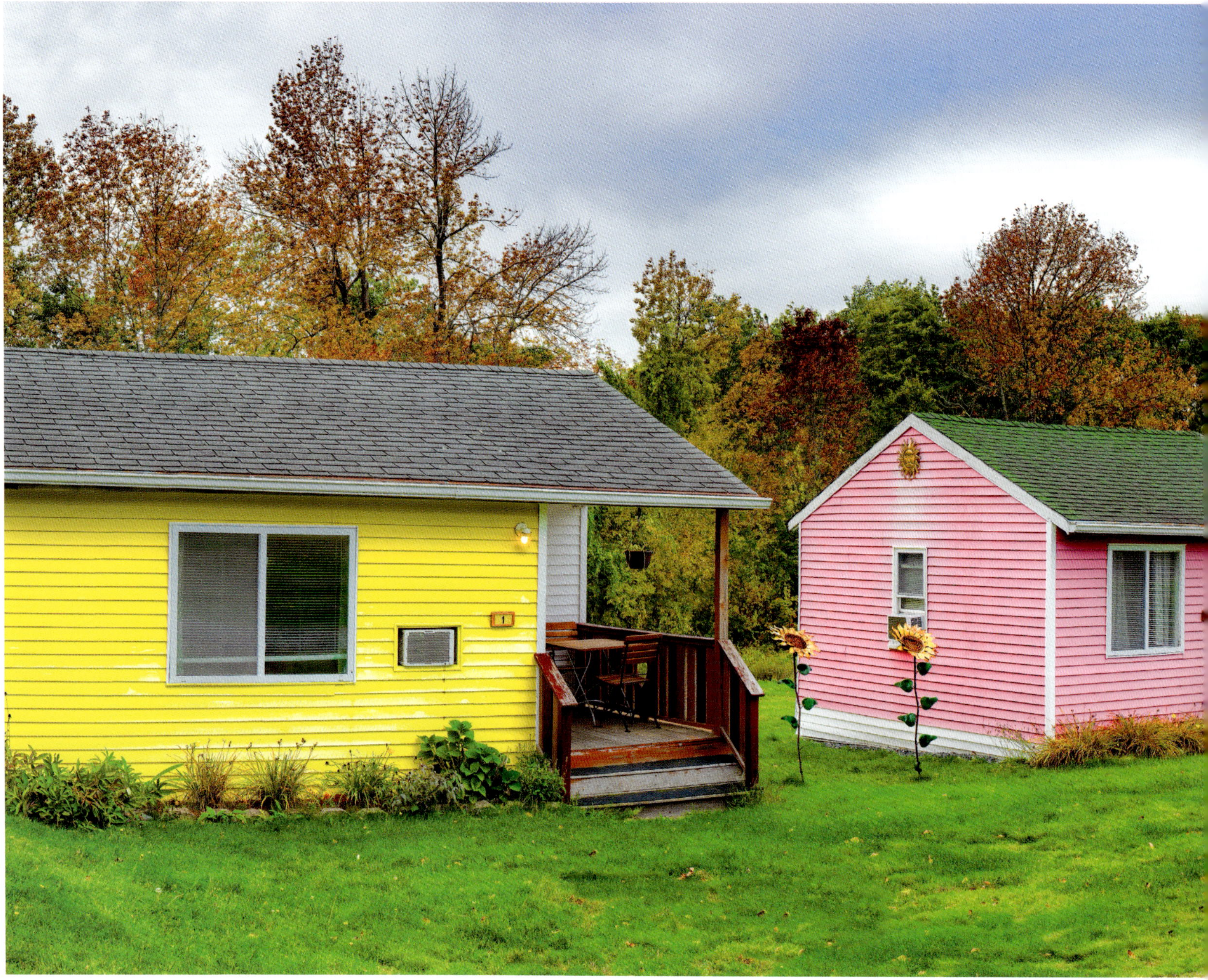

Twin Hills Cottages, Ellsworth, Maine

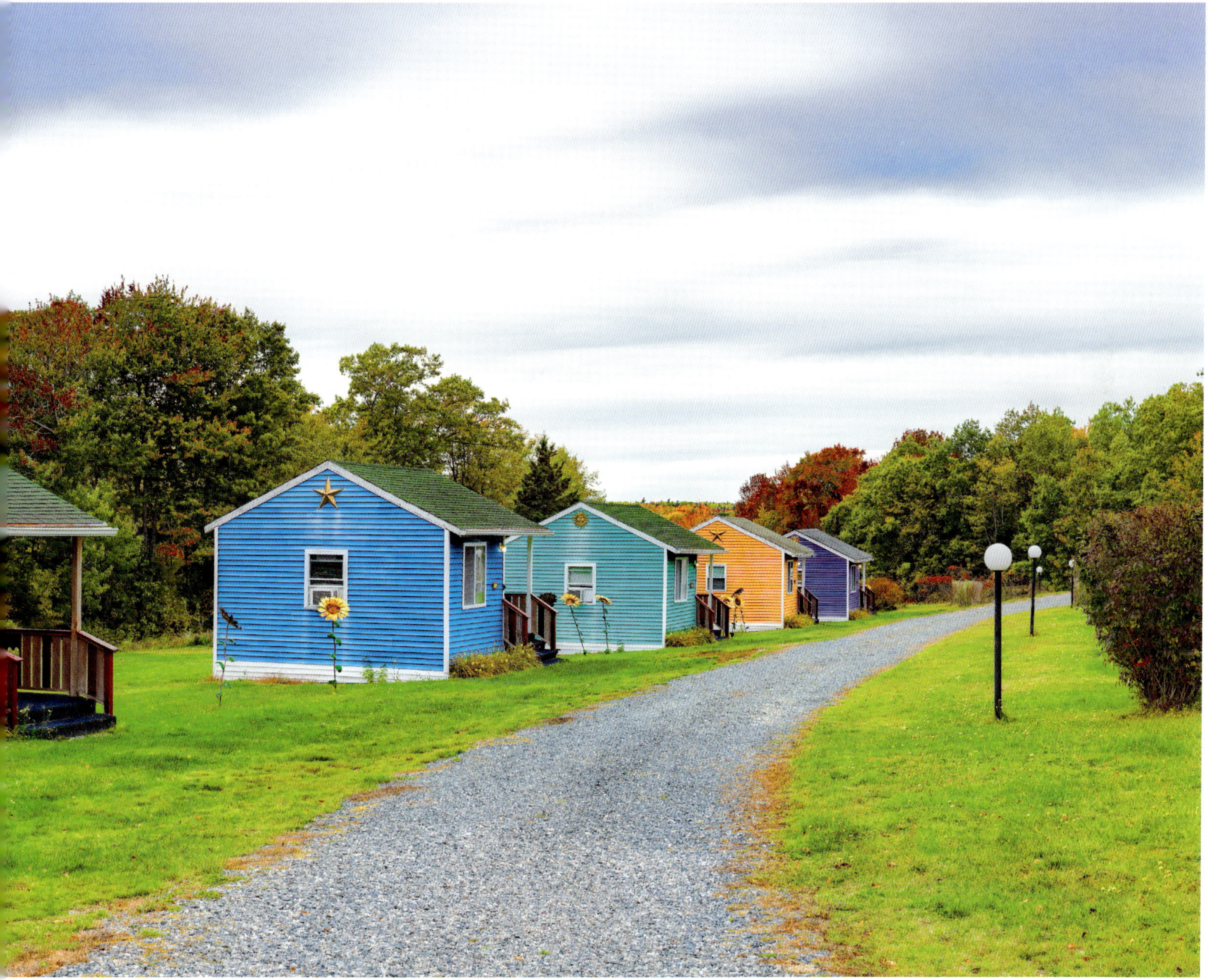

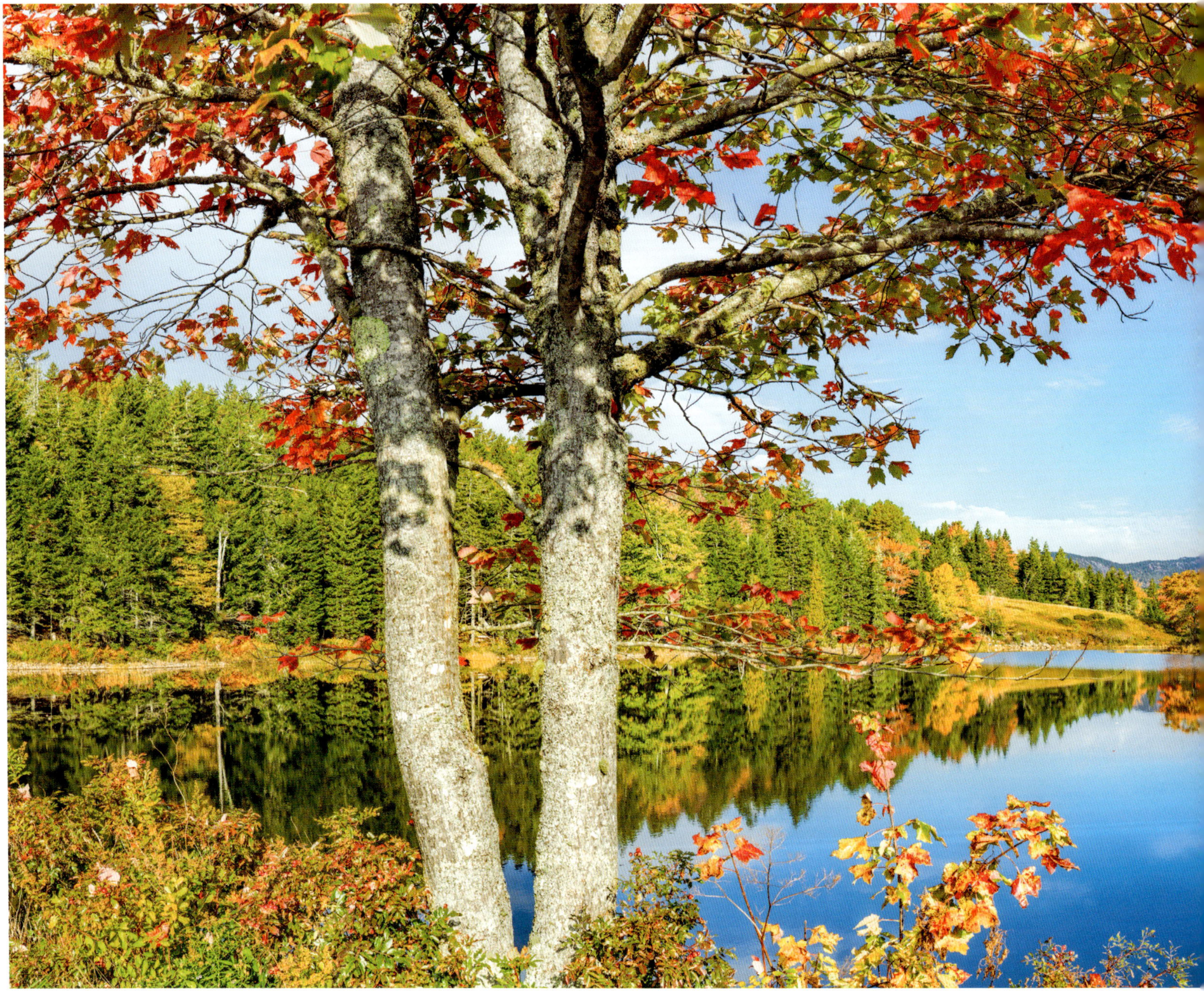

Red maple tree, Little Long Pond, and Penobscot Mountain, Maine

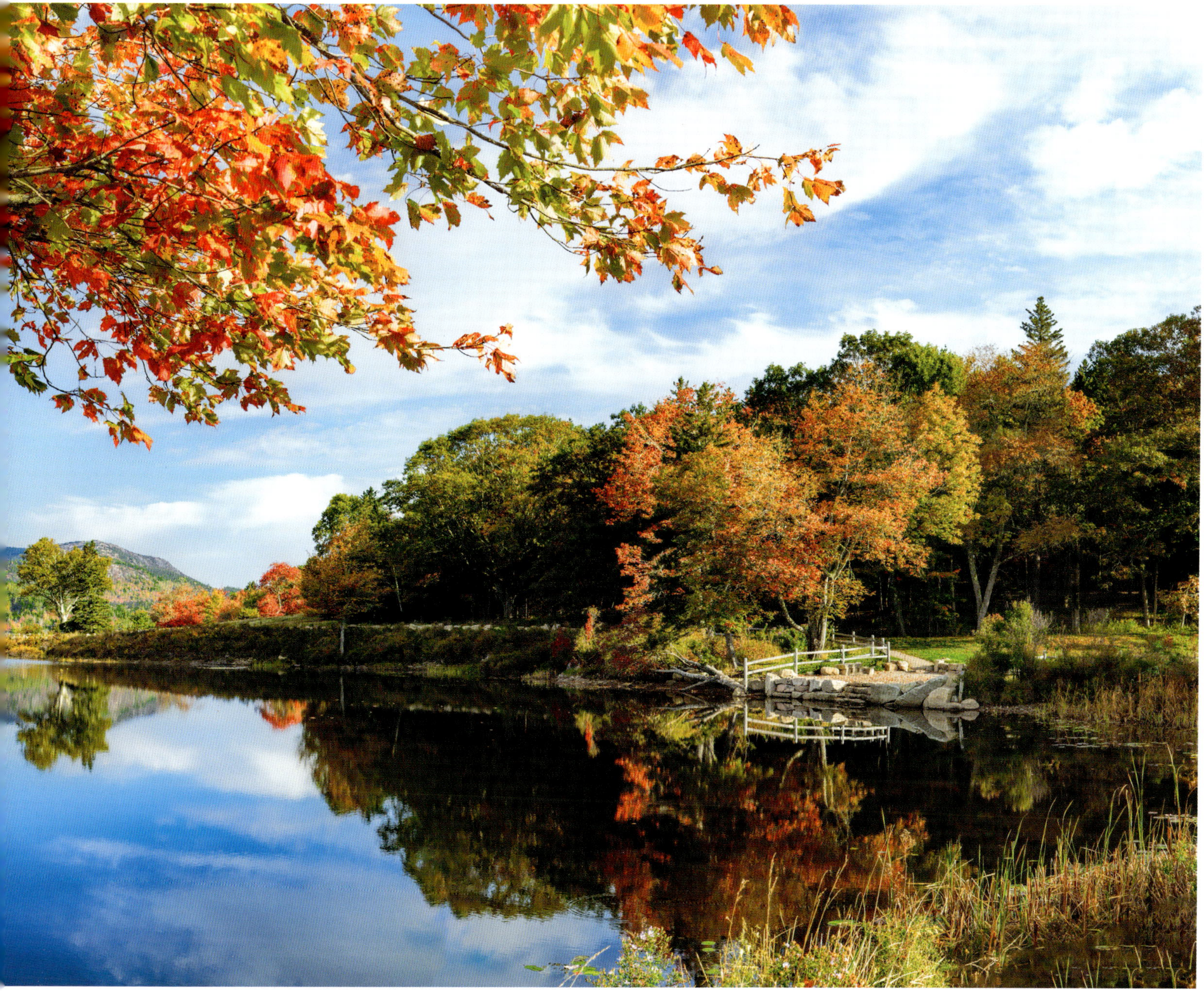

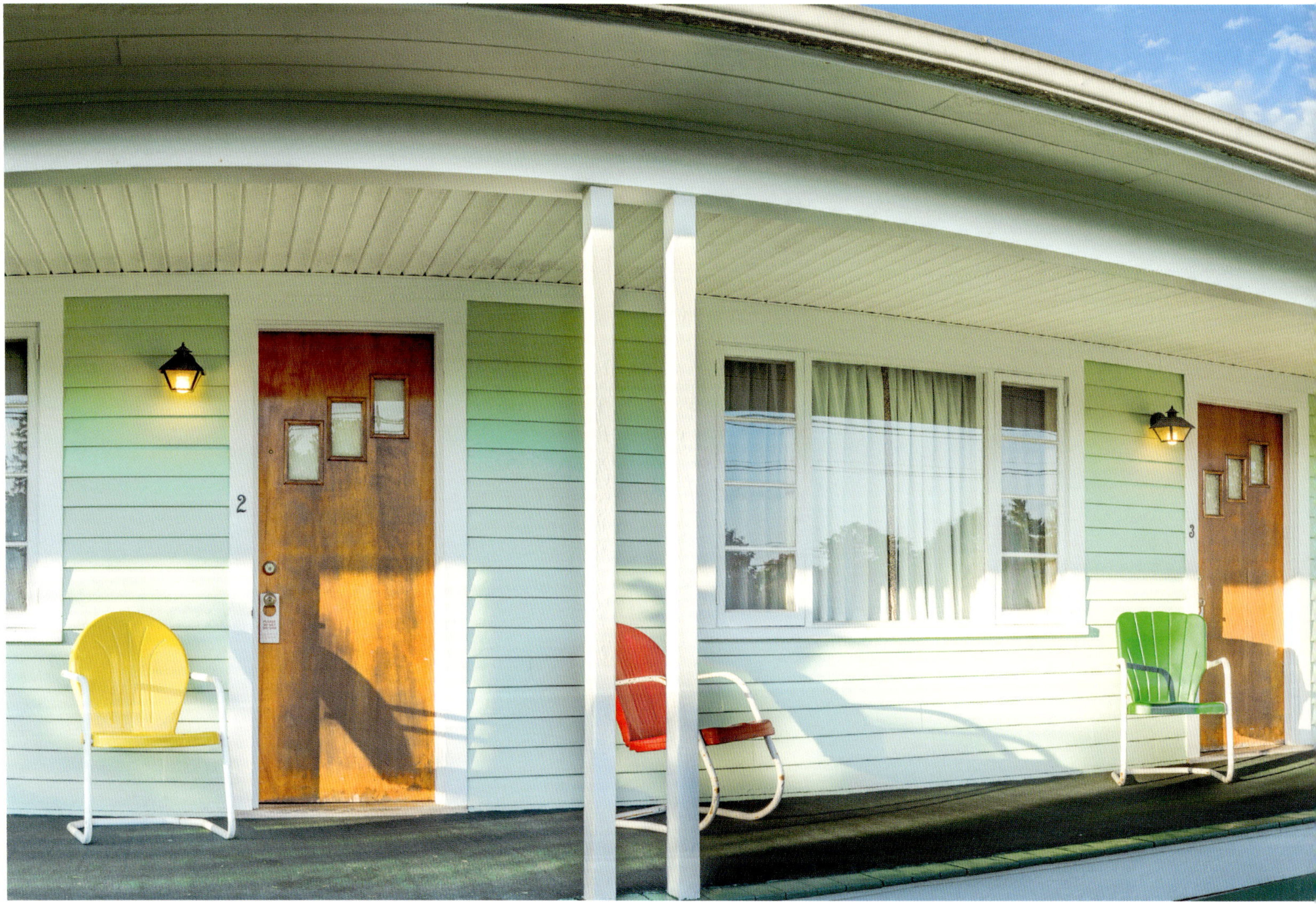

Edenbrook Motel, Bar Harbor, Maine

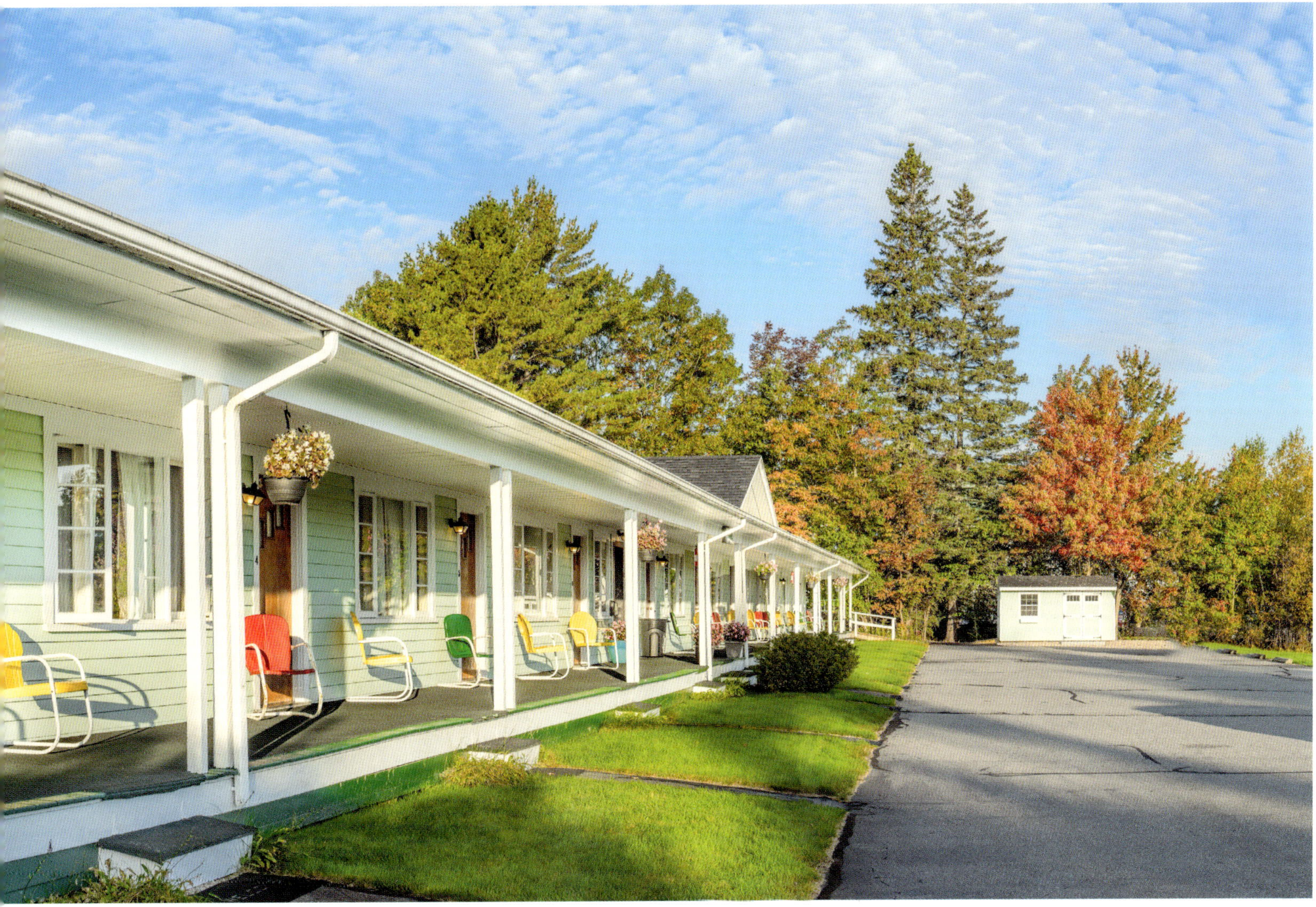

I always stay here when I'm in Bar Harbor. It's kind of like home.

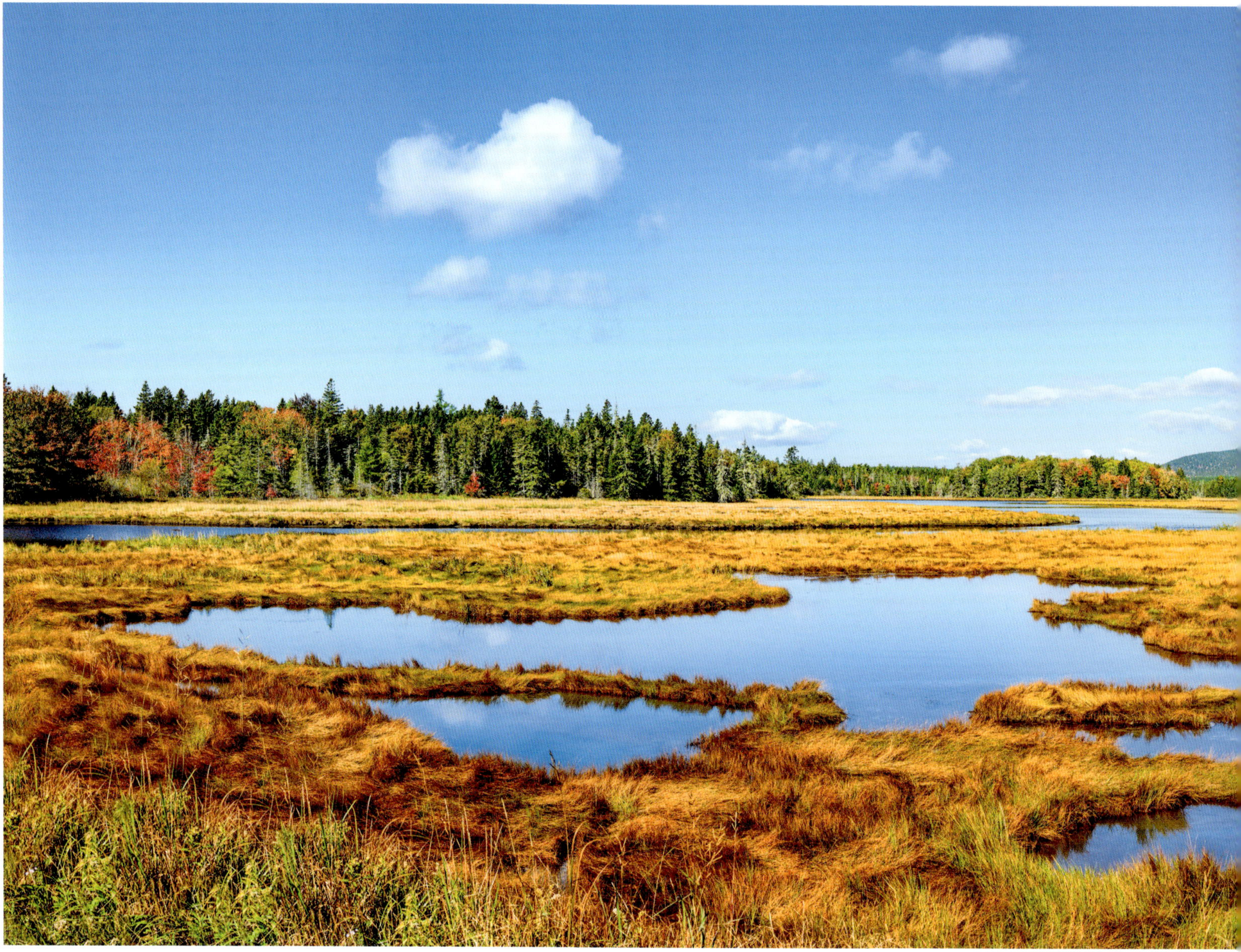

Somes Sound, Mount Desert Island, Maine

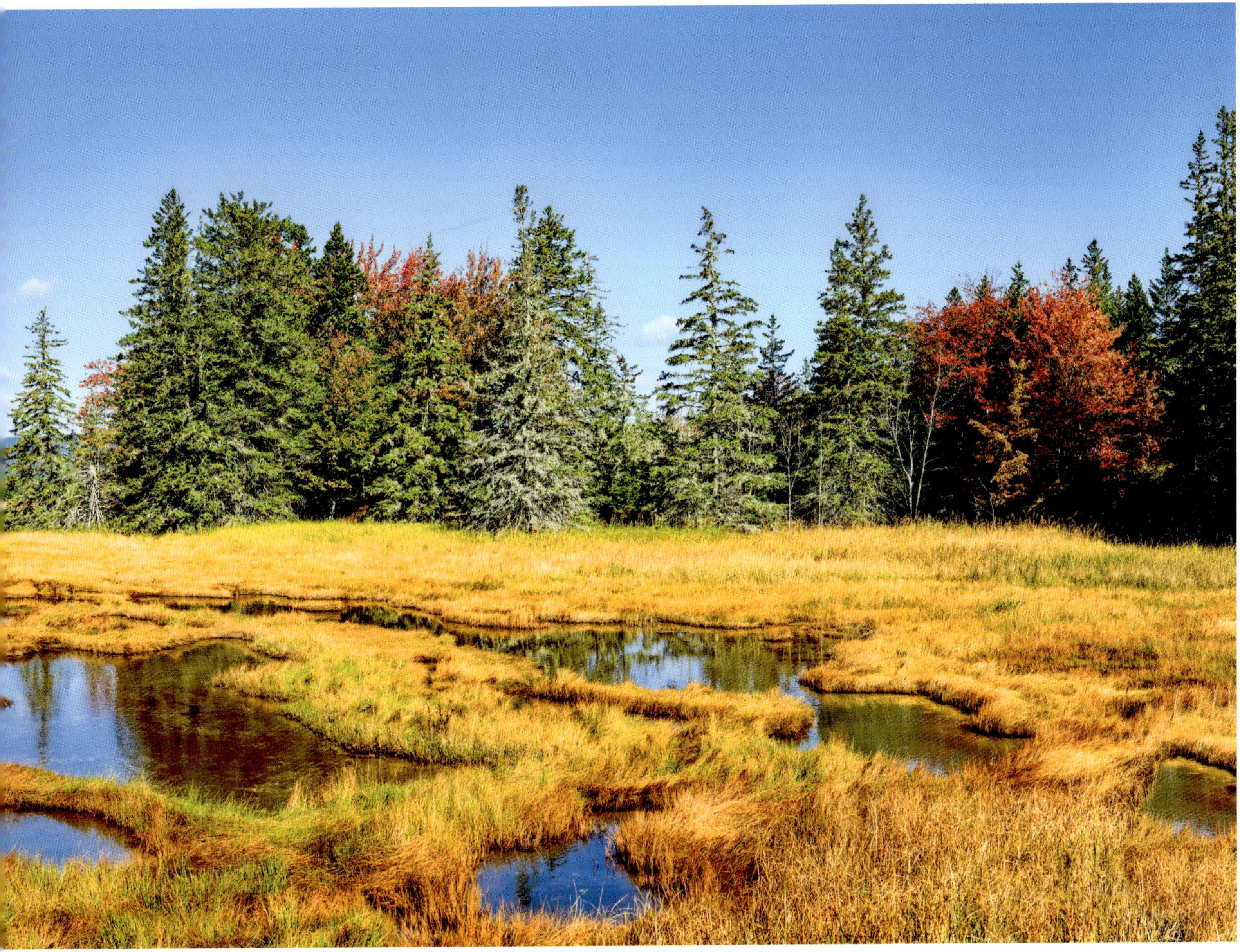

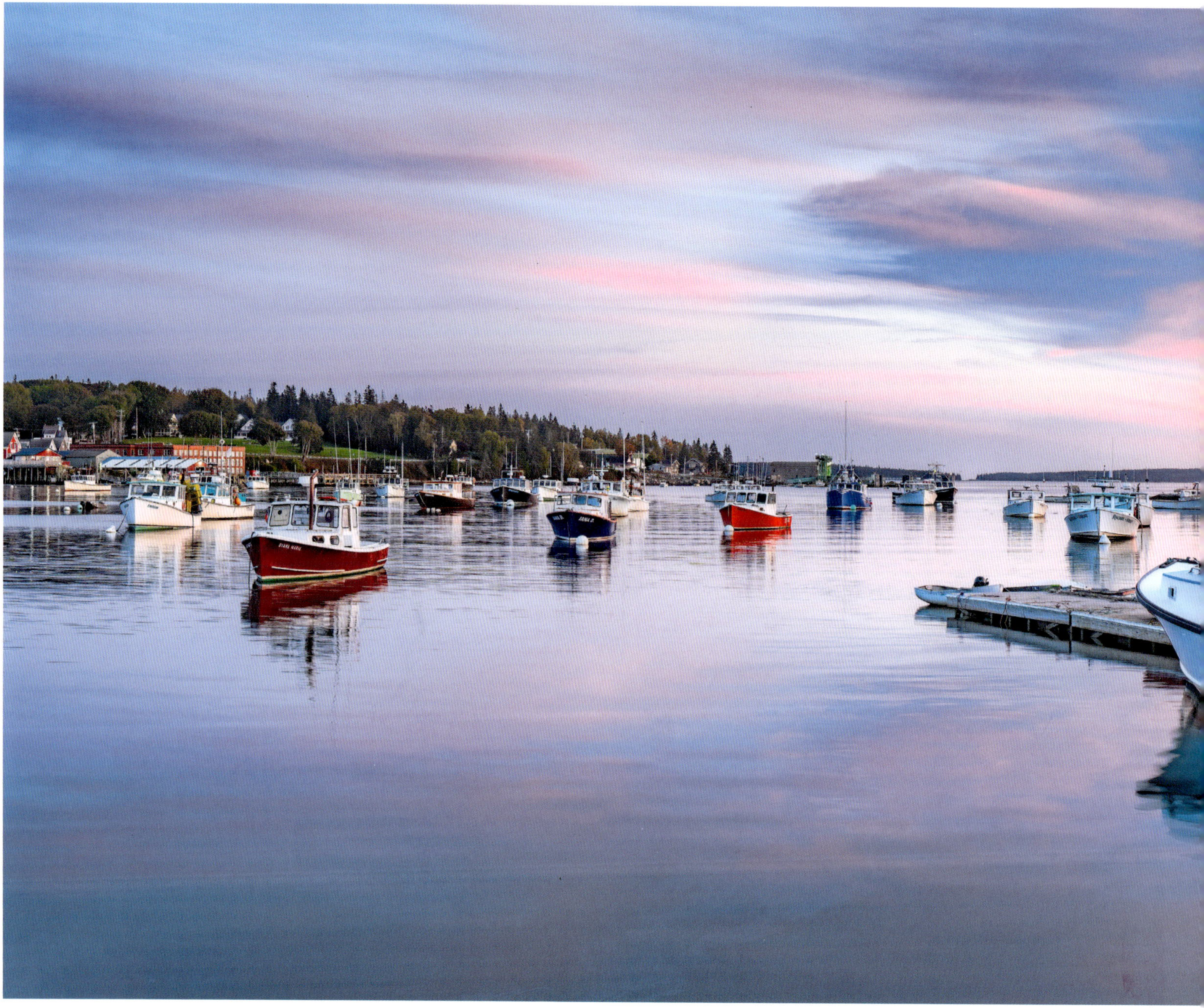

Sunset at Tremont Wharf, Bernard, Maine

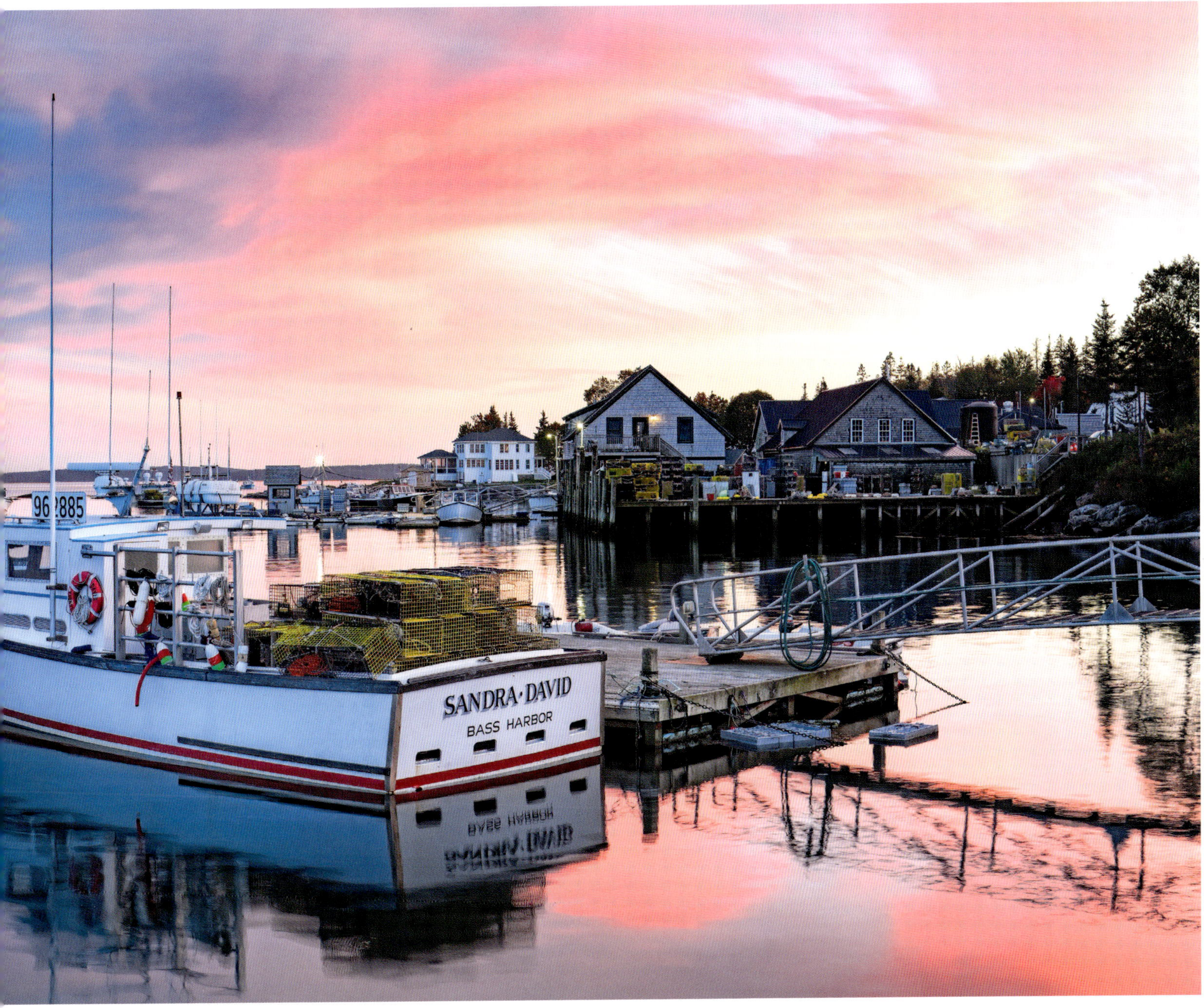
96?885
SANDRA·DAVID
BASS HARBOR

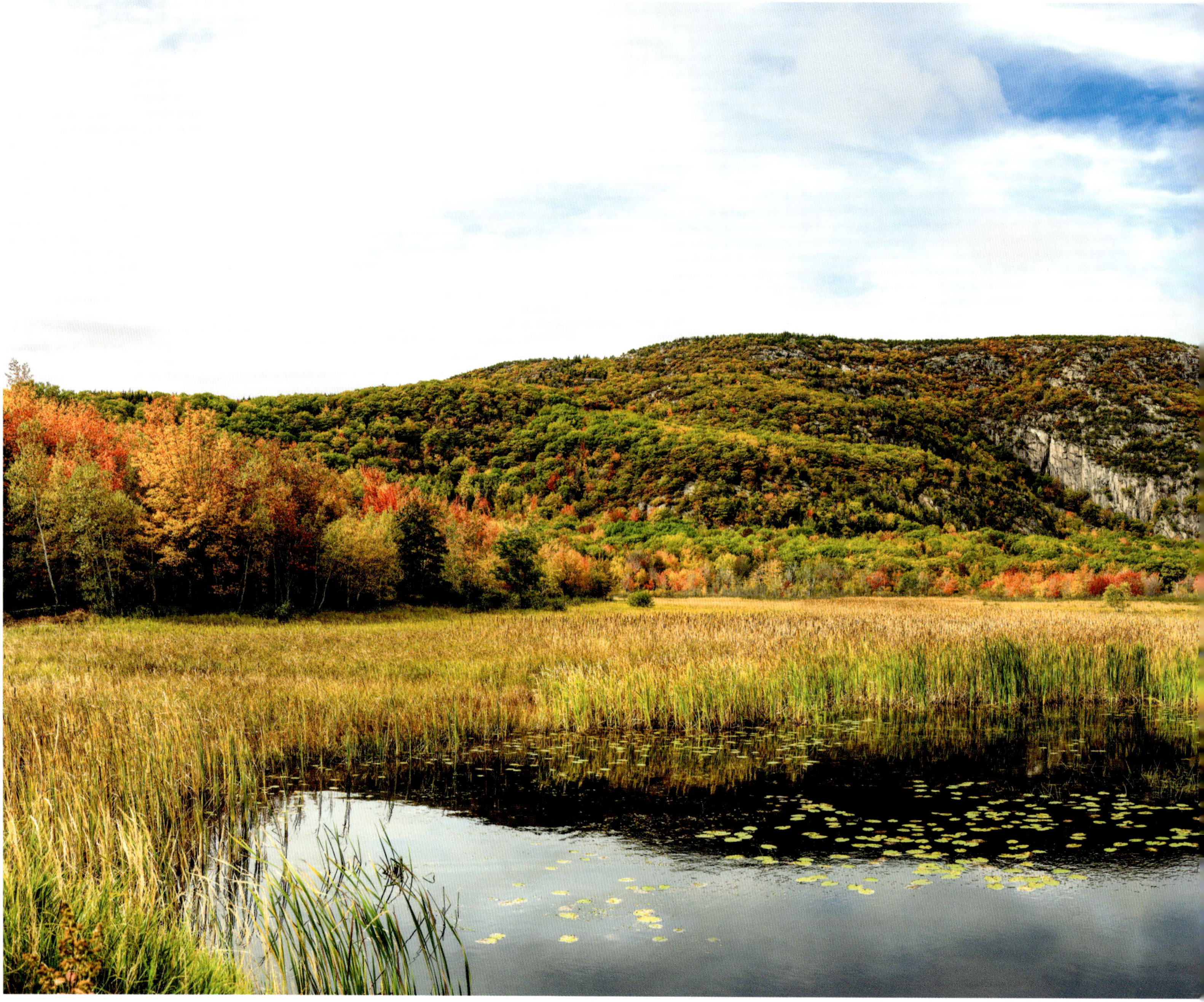

Champlain Mountain, Mount Desert Island, Maine

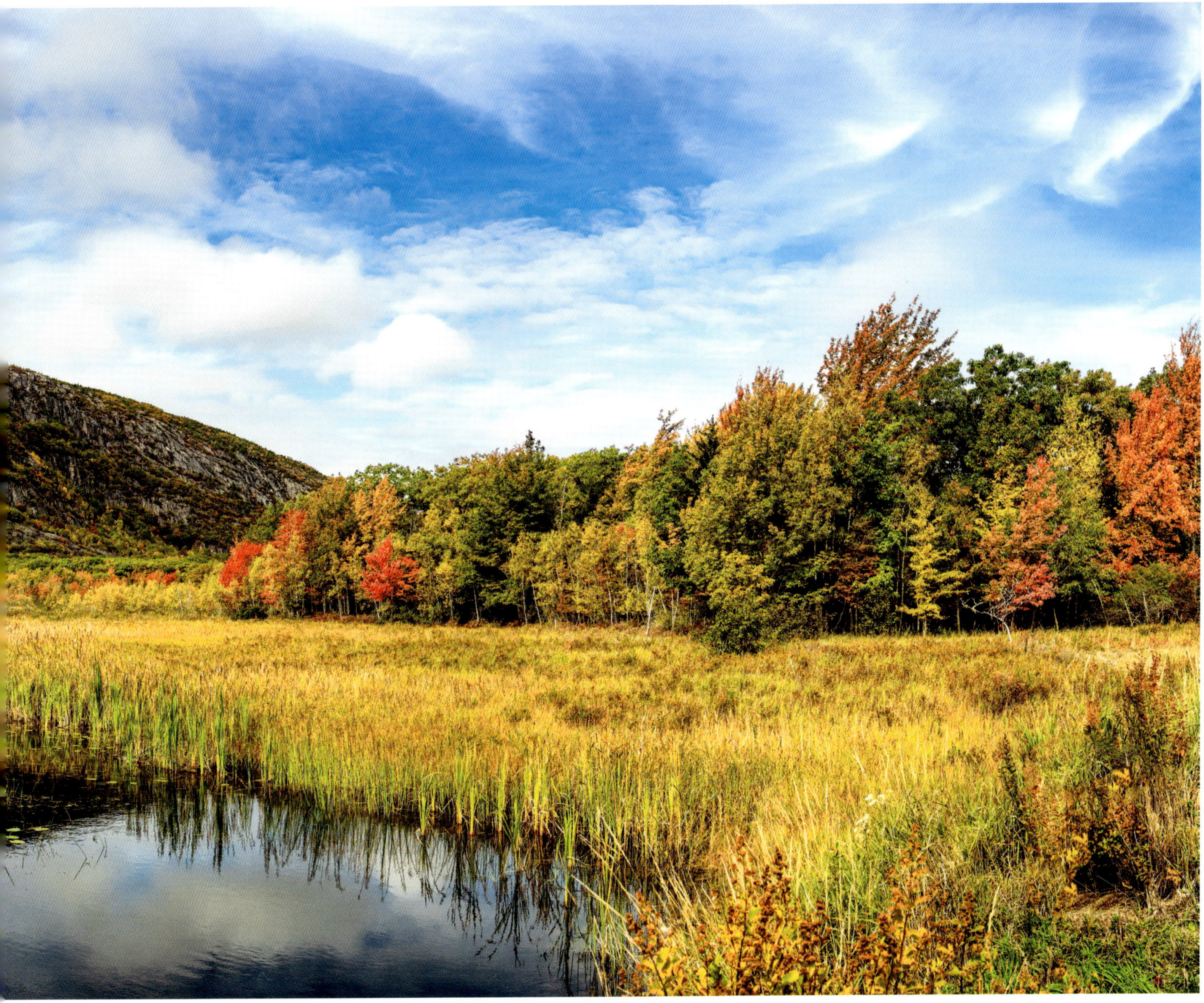

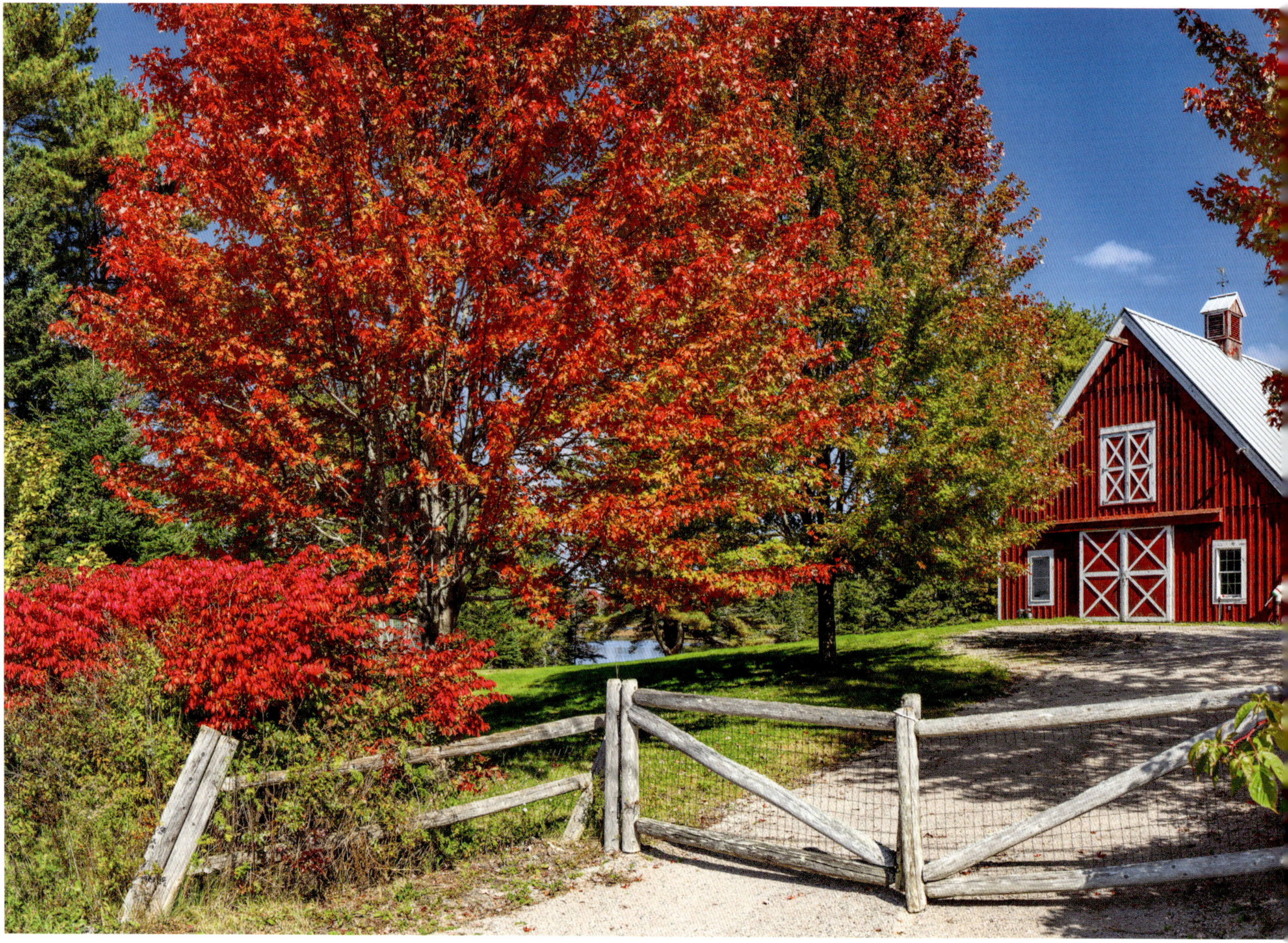

Red barn and spindle trees, Bartletts Landing, Maine

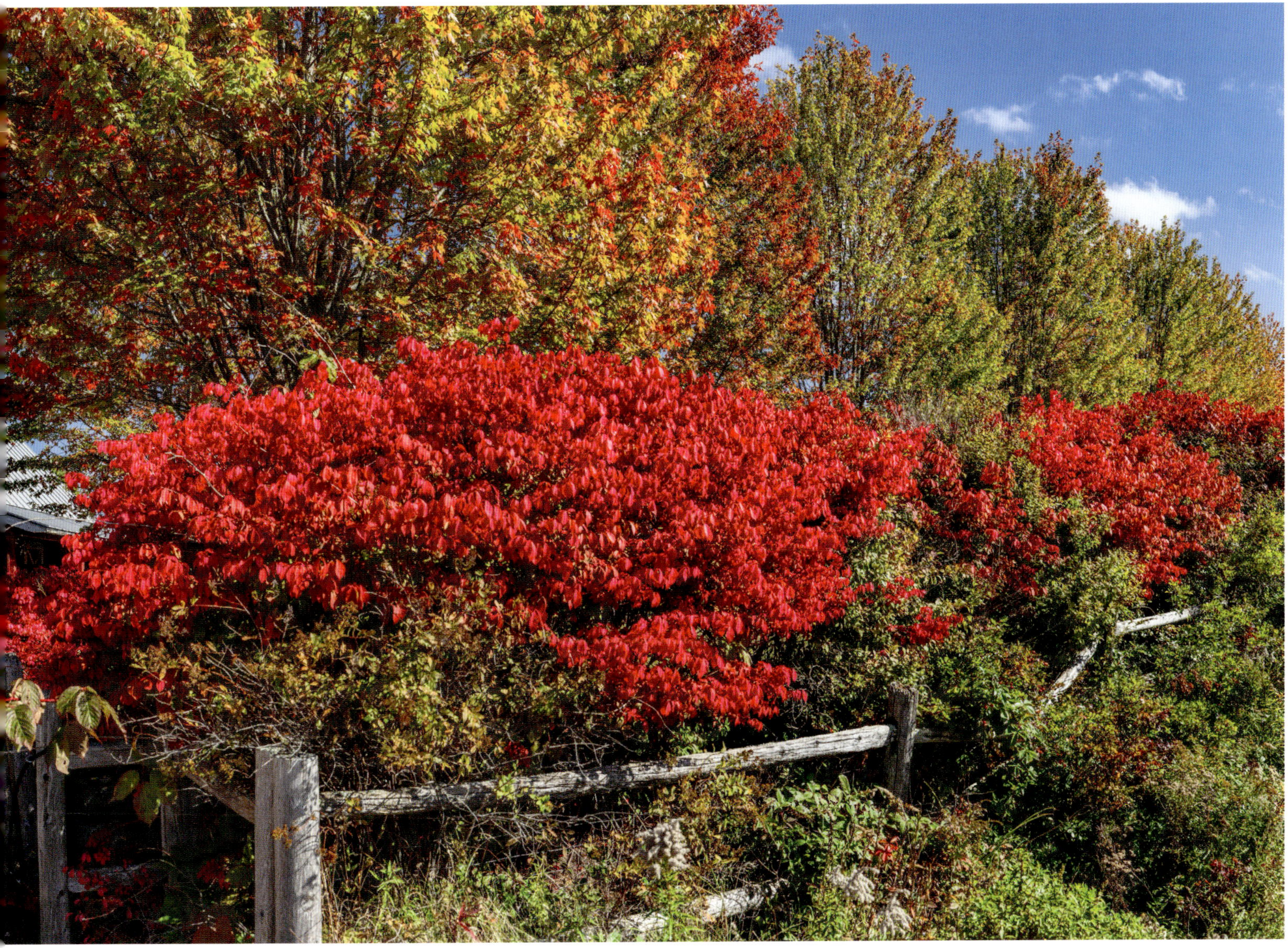

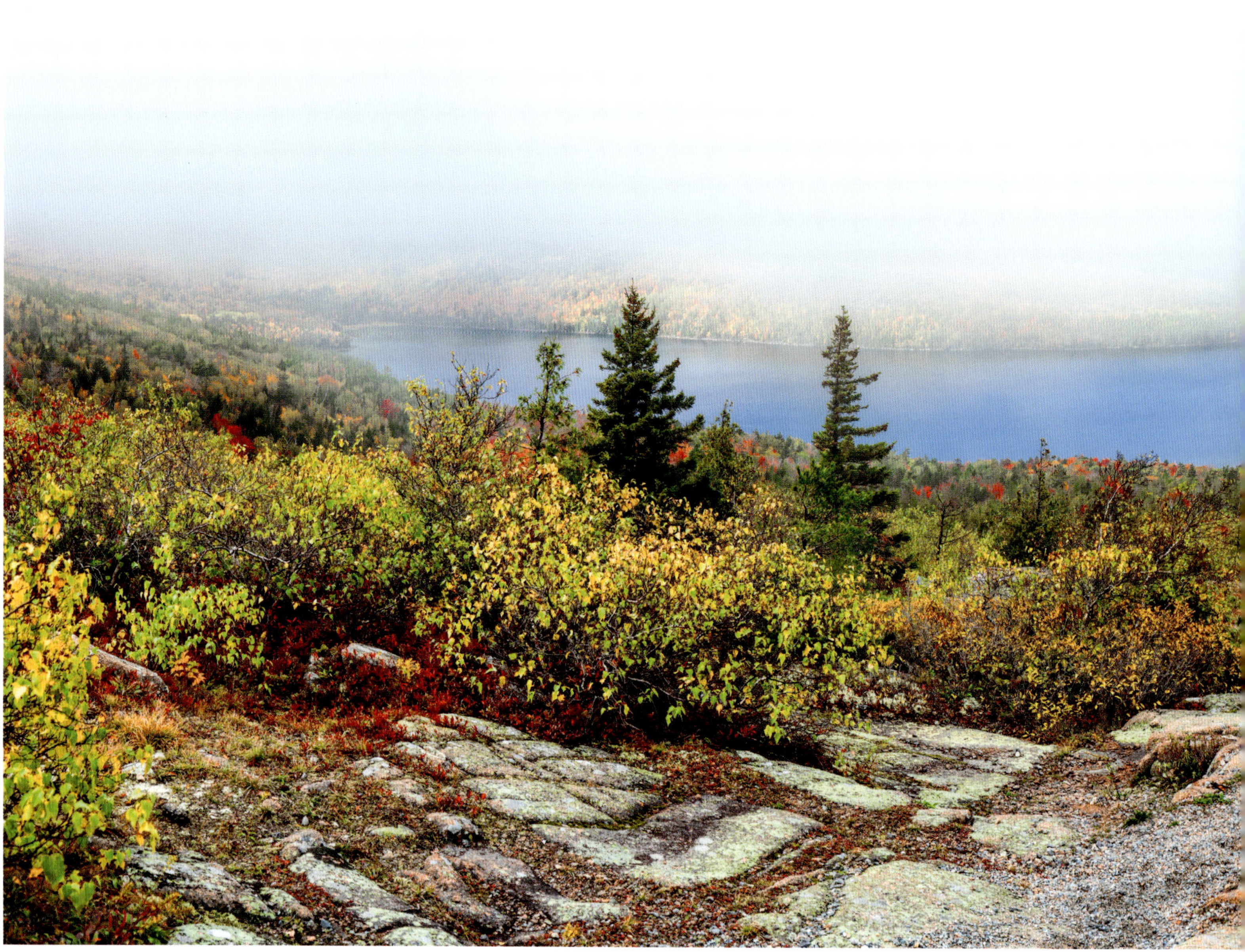

Eagle Lake from Cadillac Mountain, Acadia National Park, Maine

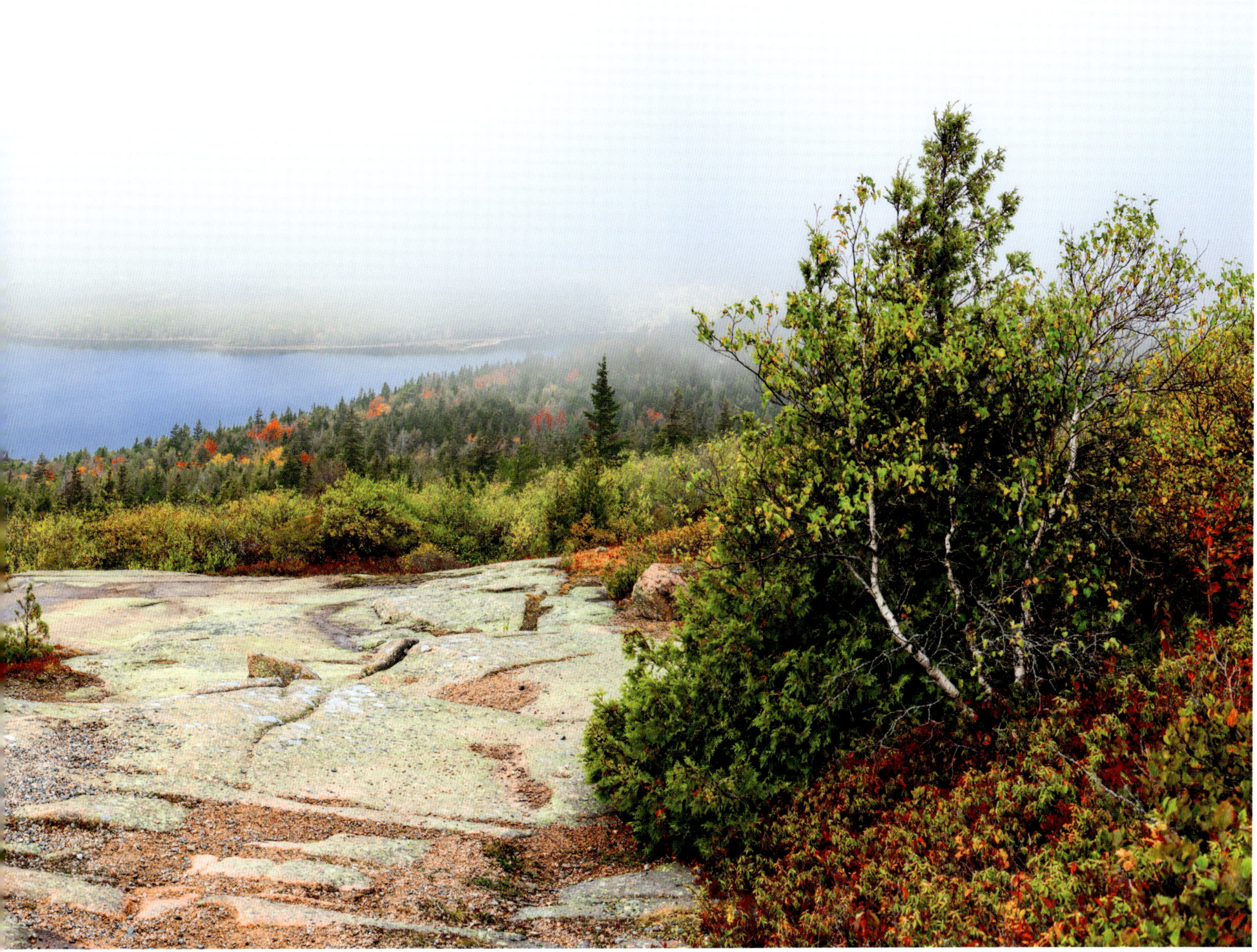

As the fog lifted, the lake seemed to magically appear.

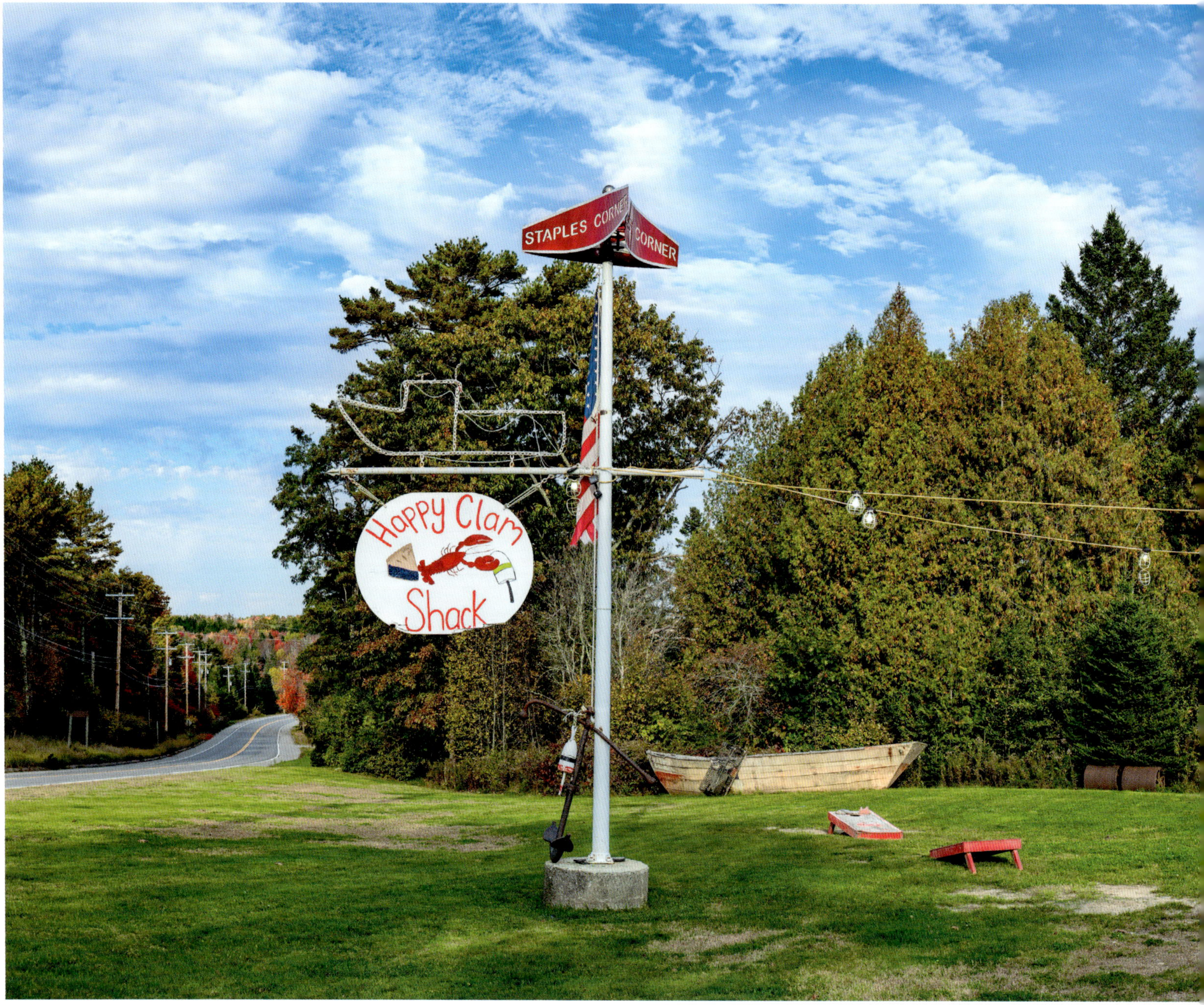

The Happy Clam Shack on Maine State Route 3

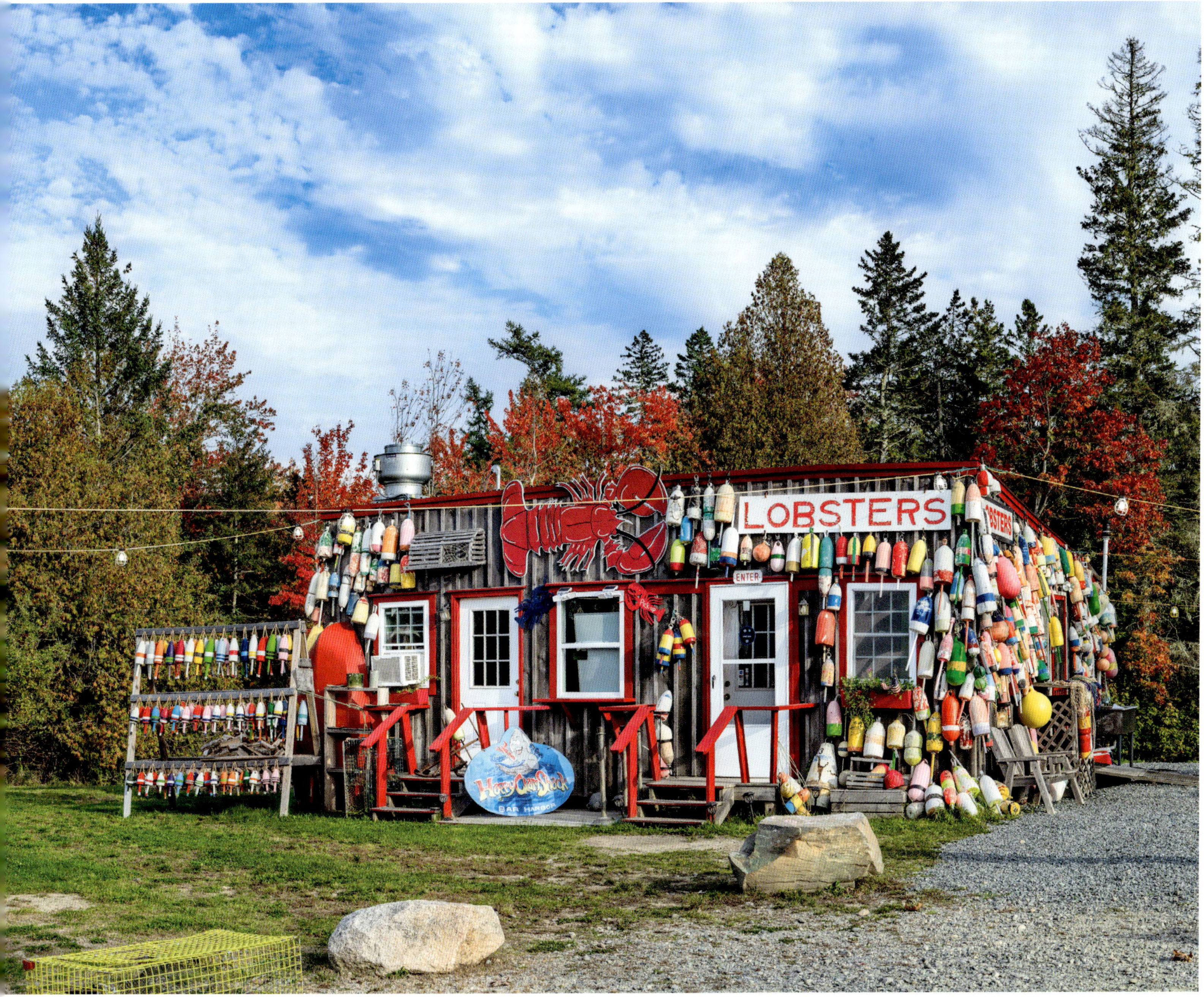
LOBSTERS
ENTER
BAR HARBOR

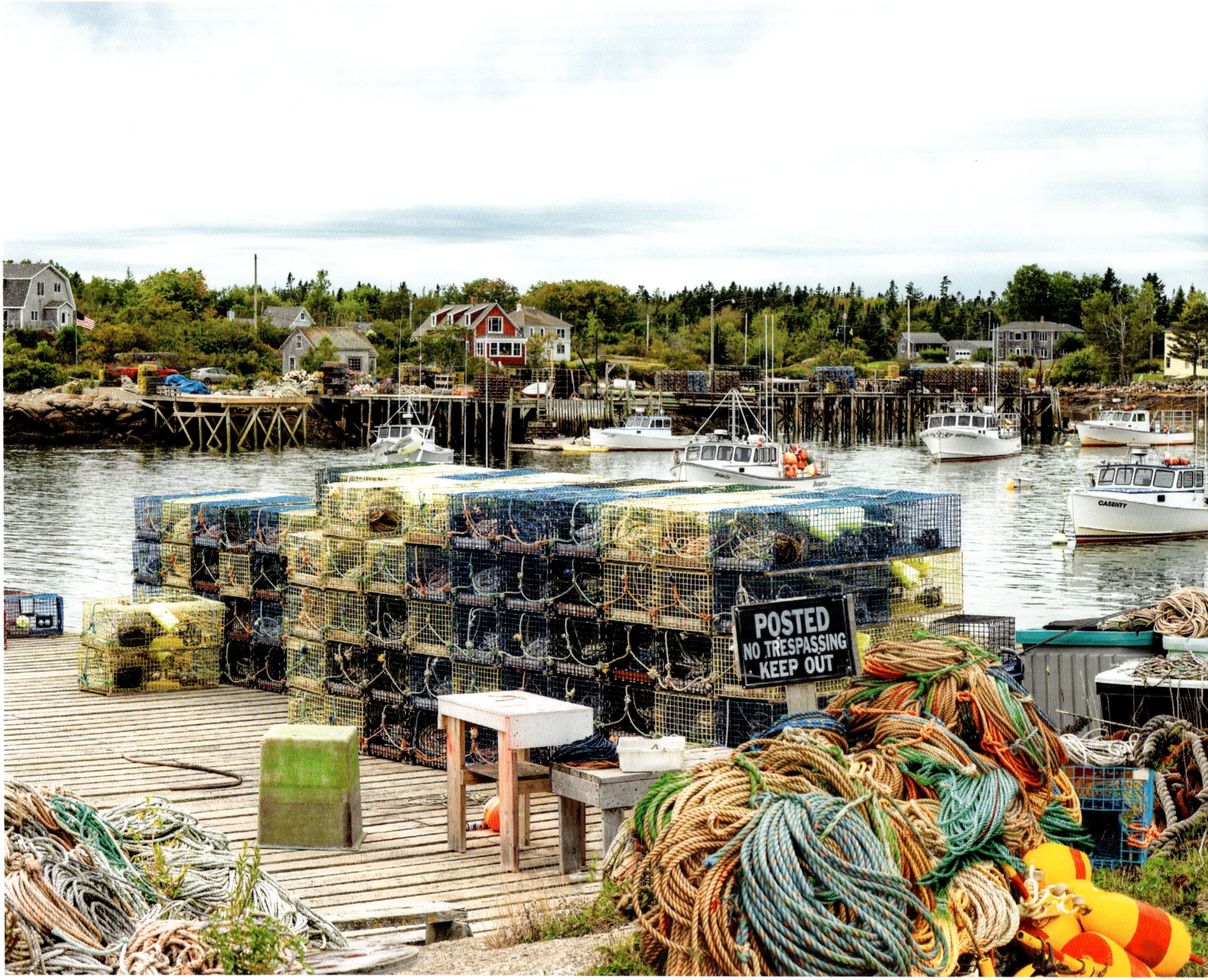

Lobster Co-Op, Corea Harbor, Maine

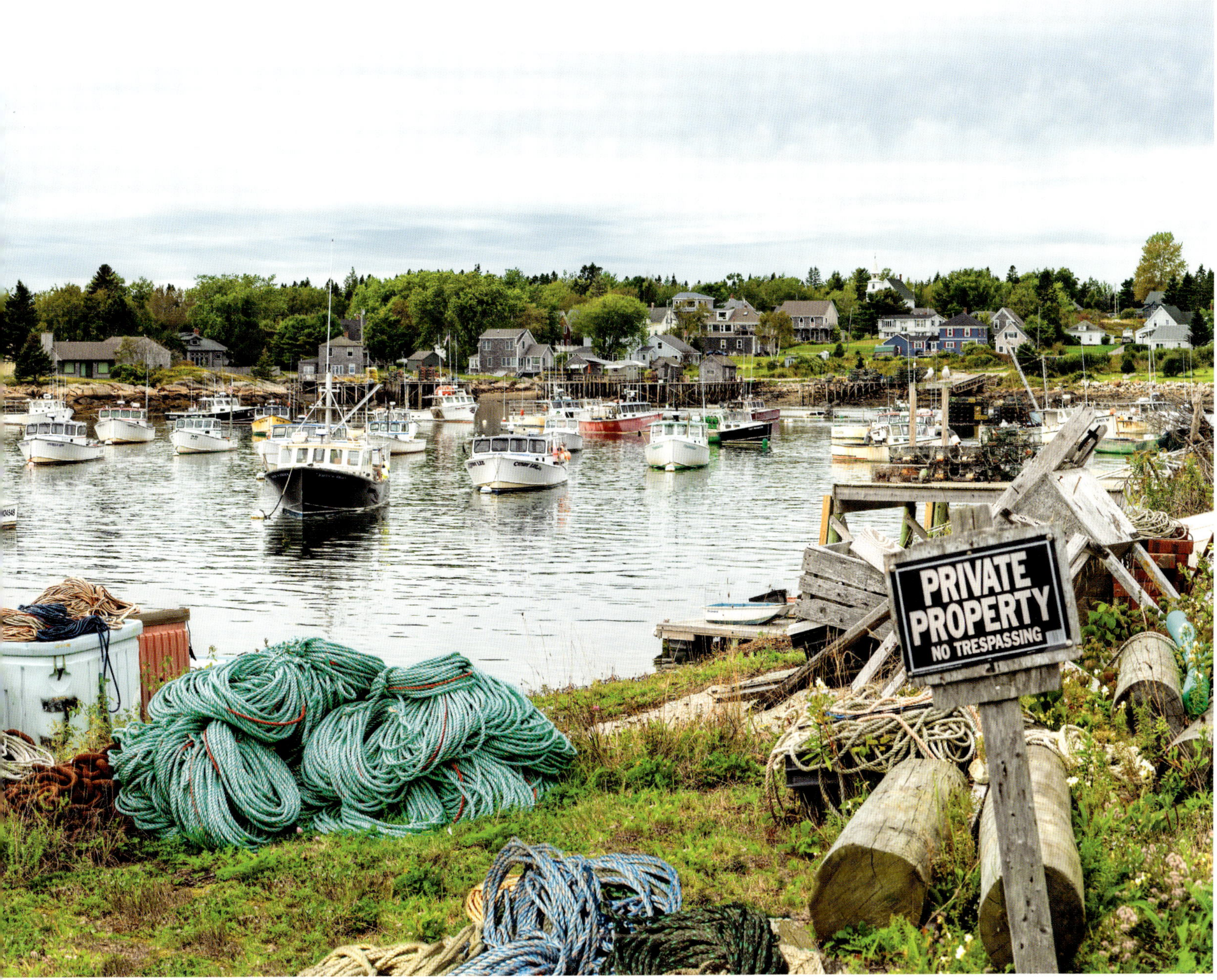

I could spend years photographing this stuff. It was nice of them to let me wander around.

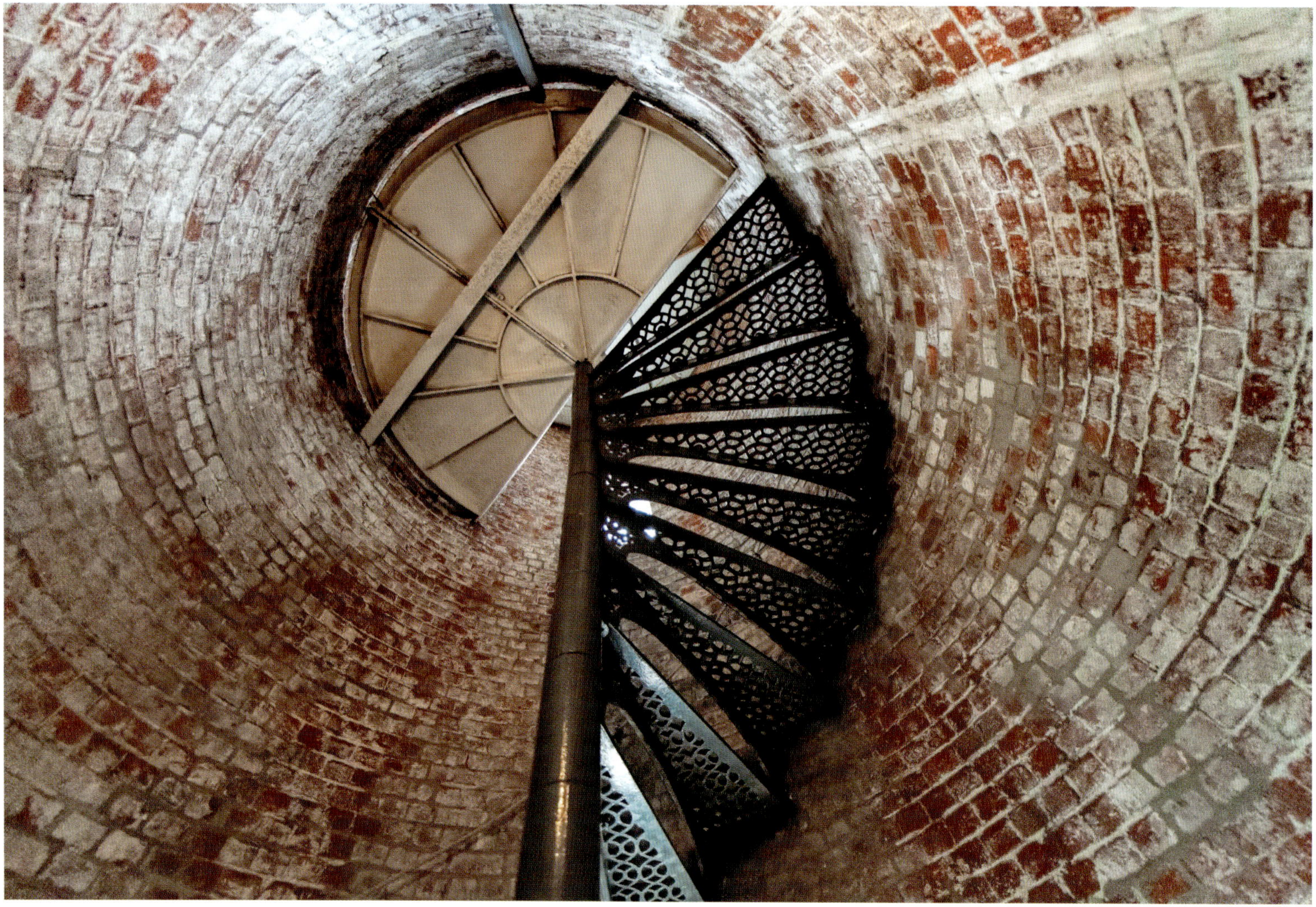

Fort Point Light (1857), Stockton Springs, Maine

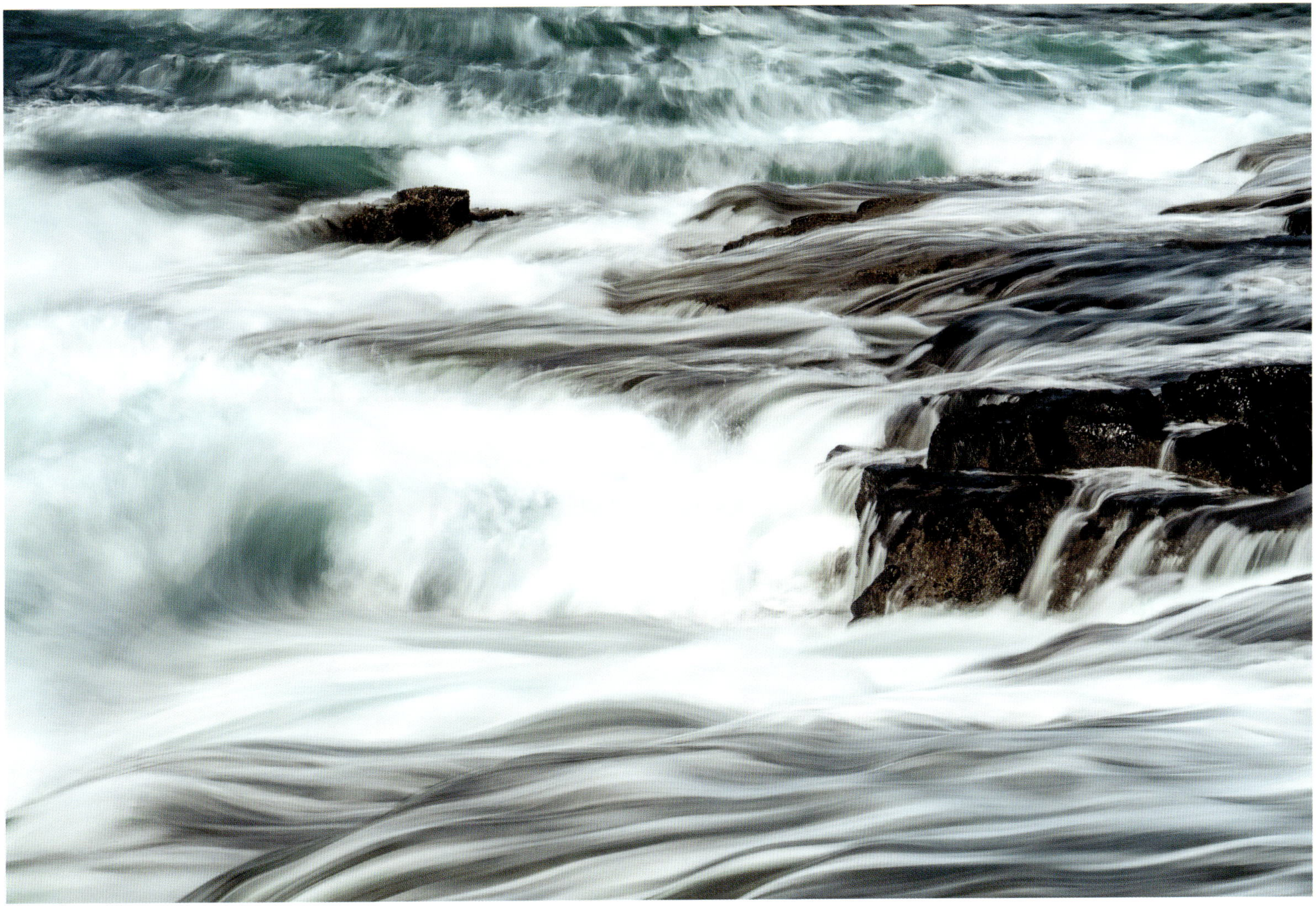

Schoodic Point, Acadia National Park, Maine

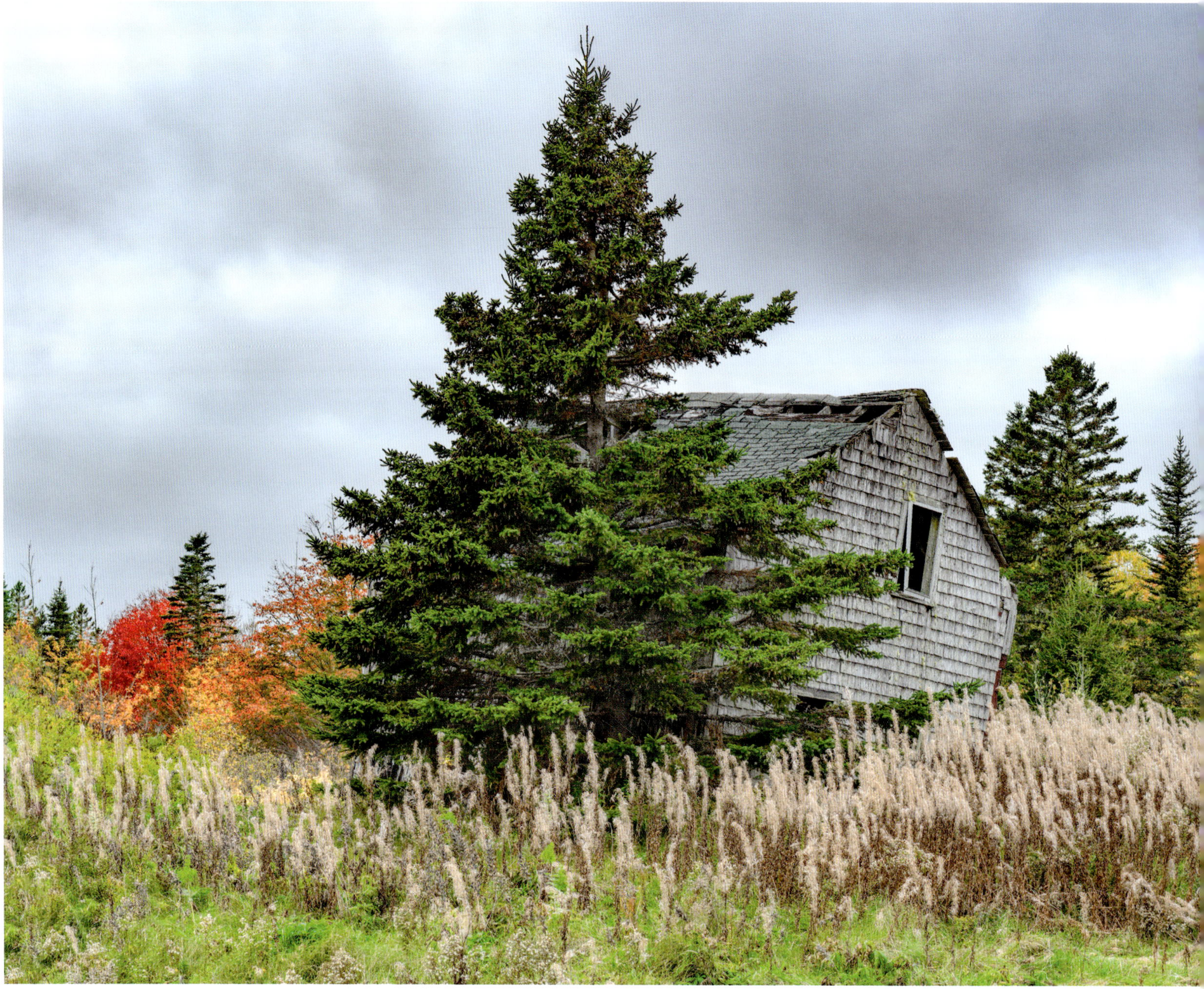

Abandoned house, Cutler, Maine

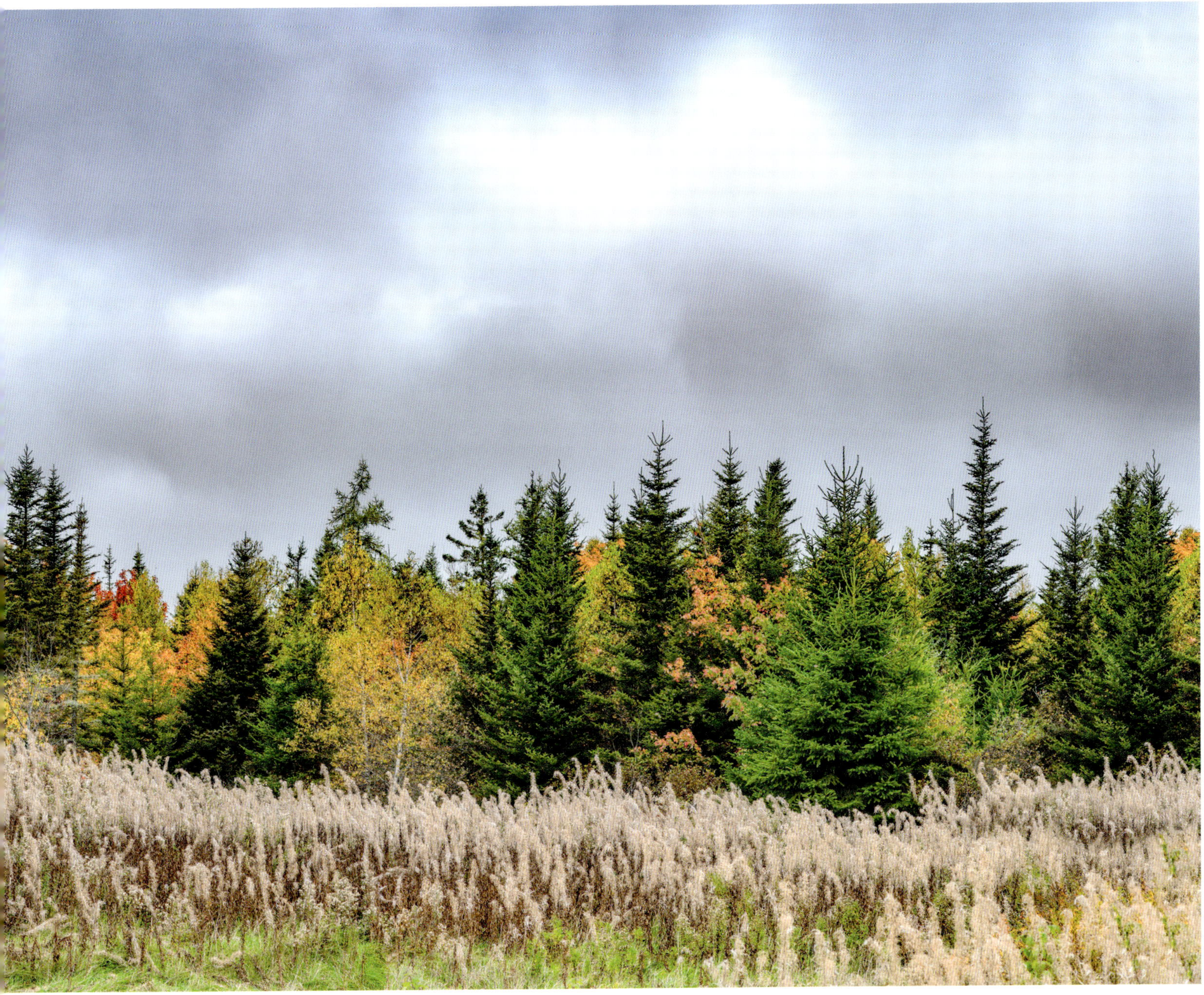

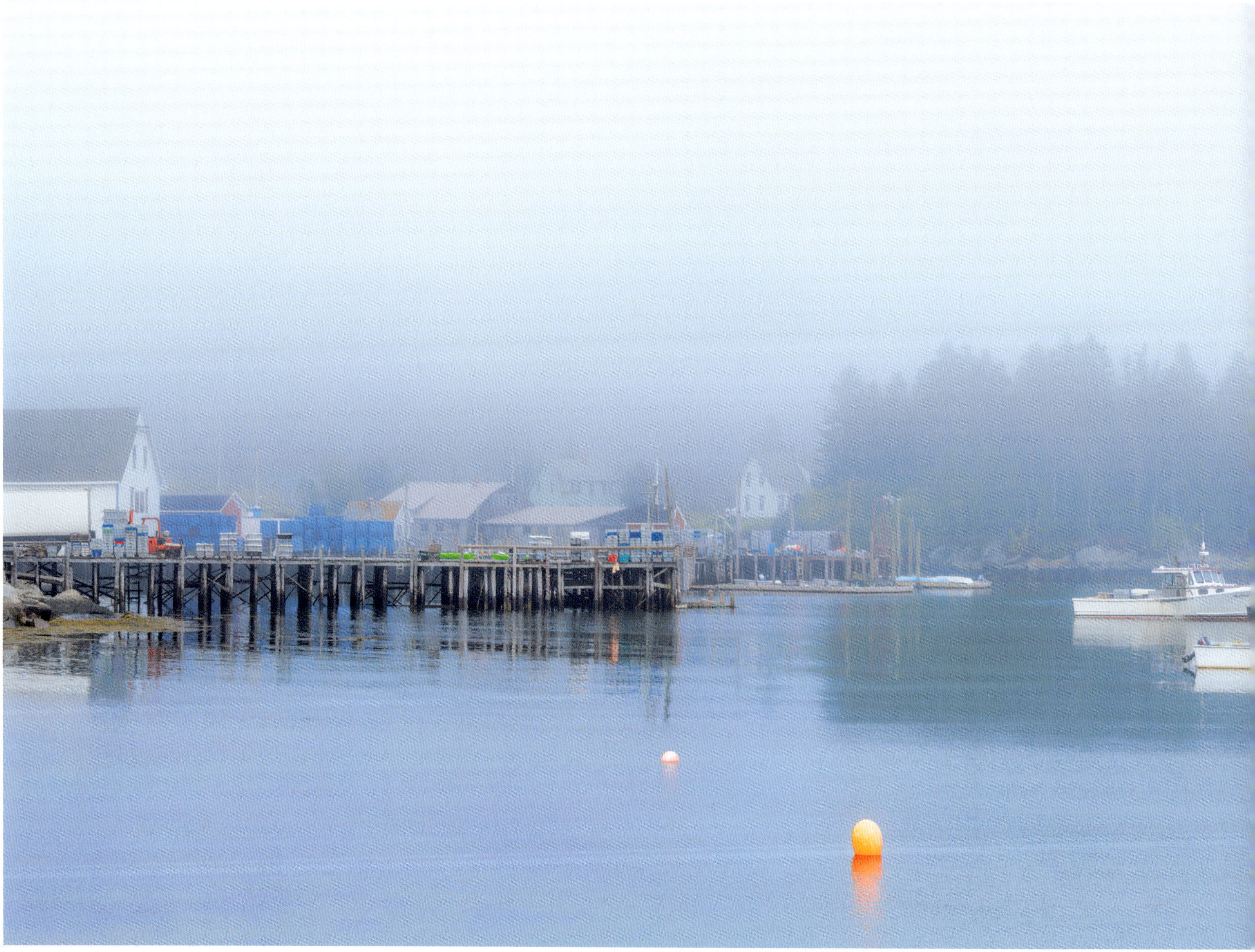

Destiny Cove, Culver, Maine

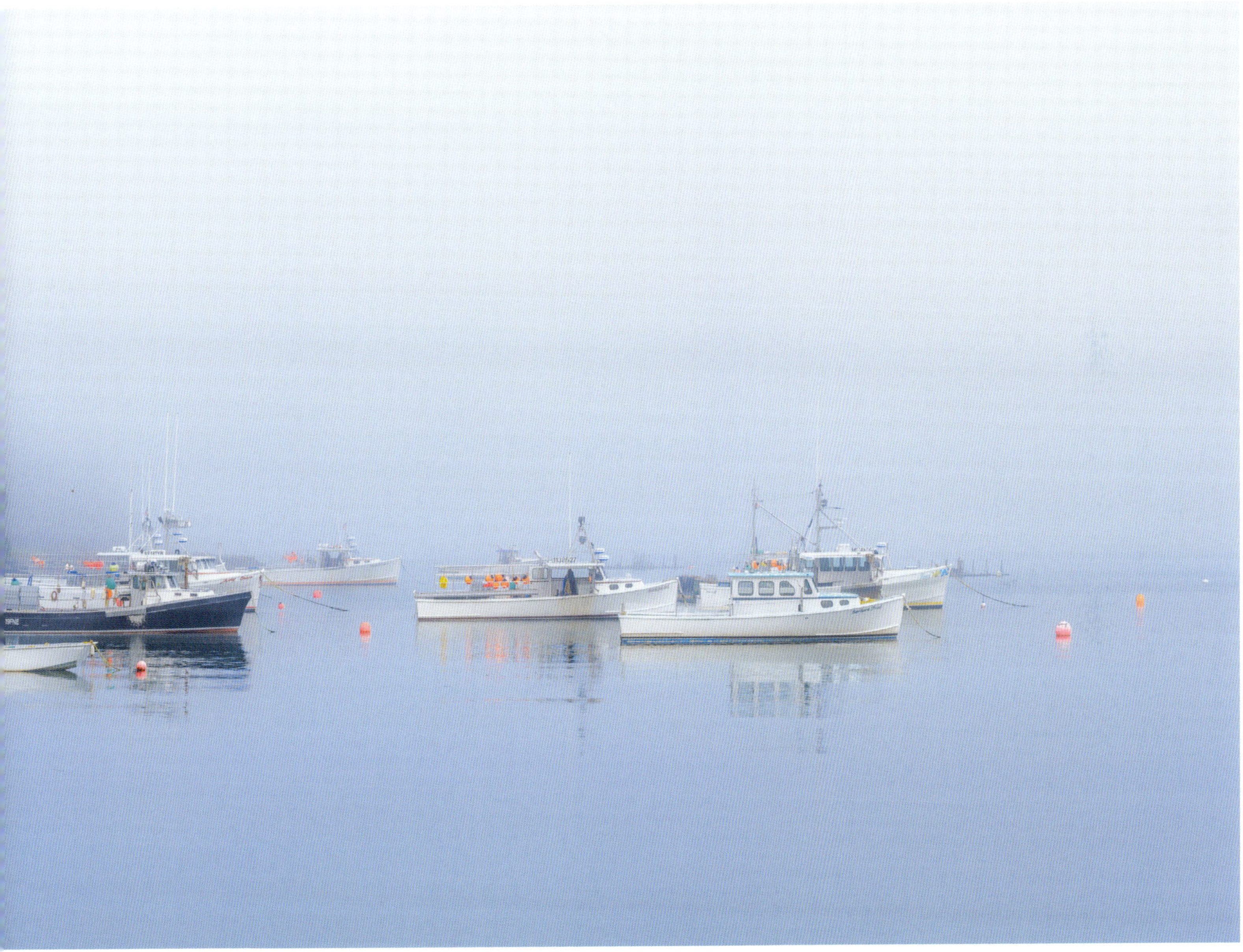

There were some local teens hanging out here. After they told me the name of the cove, we talked awhile about their hopes and dreams. I hope they're following them.

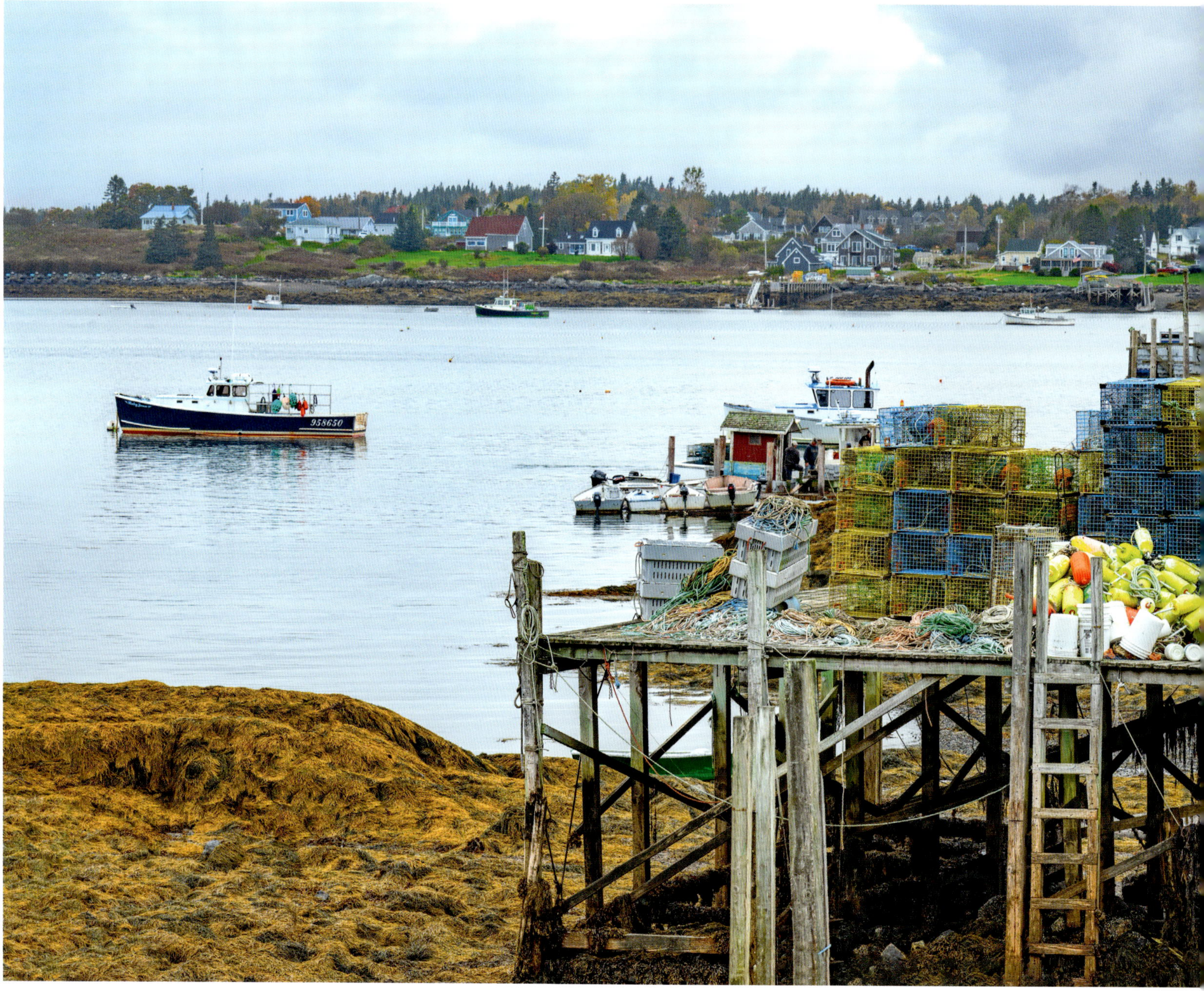

Donovan Cove, Beals Island, Maine

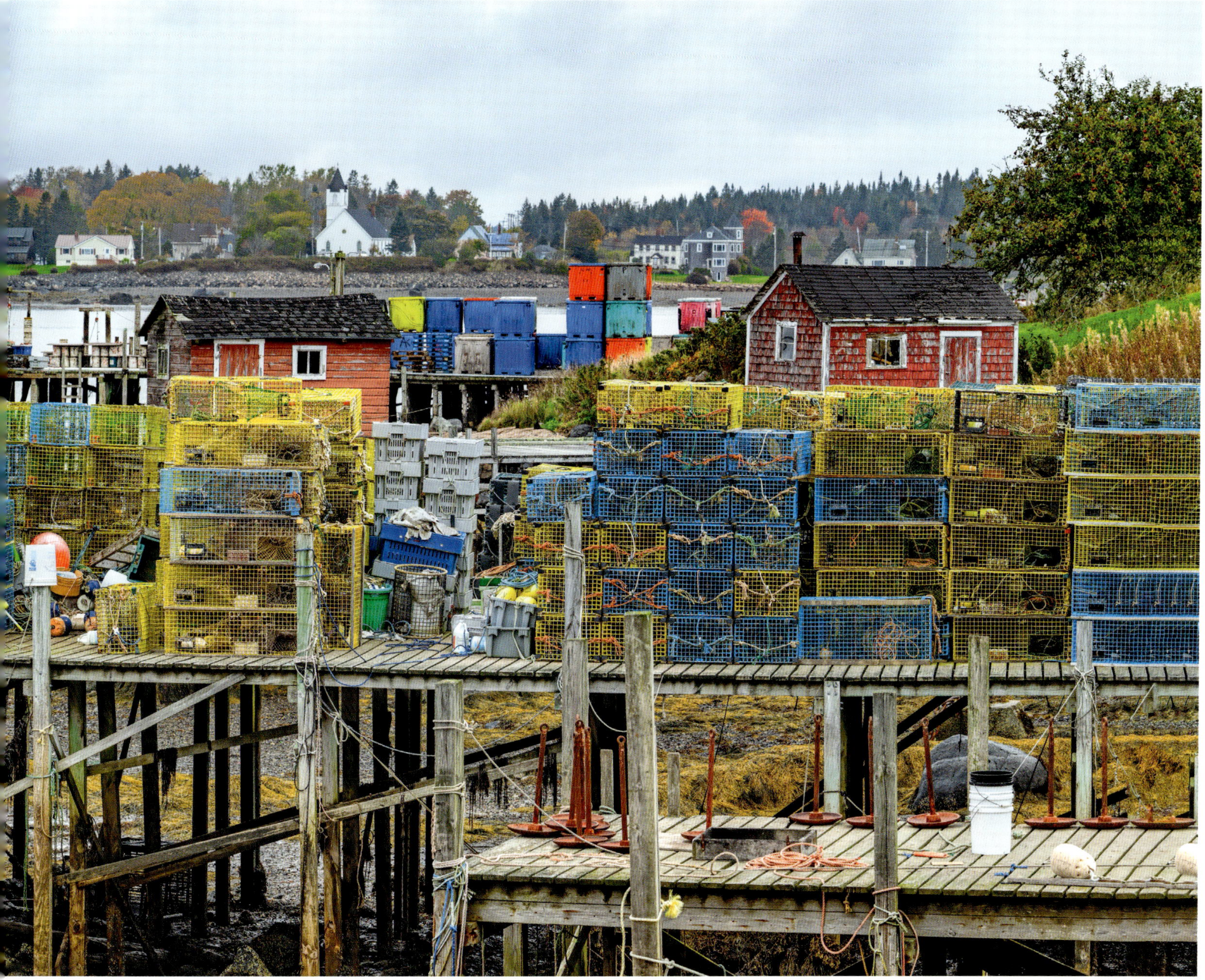

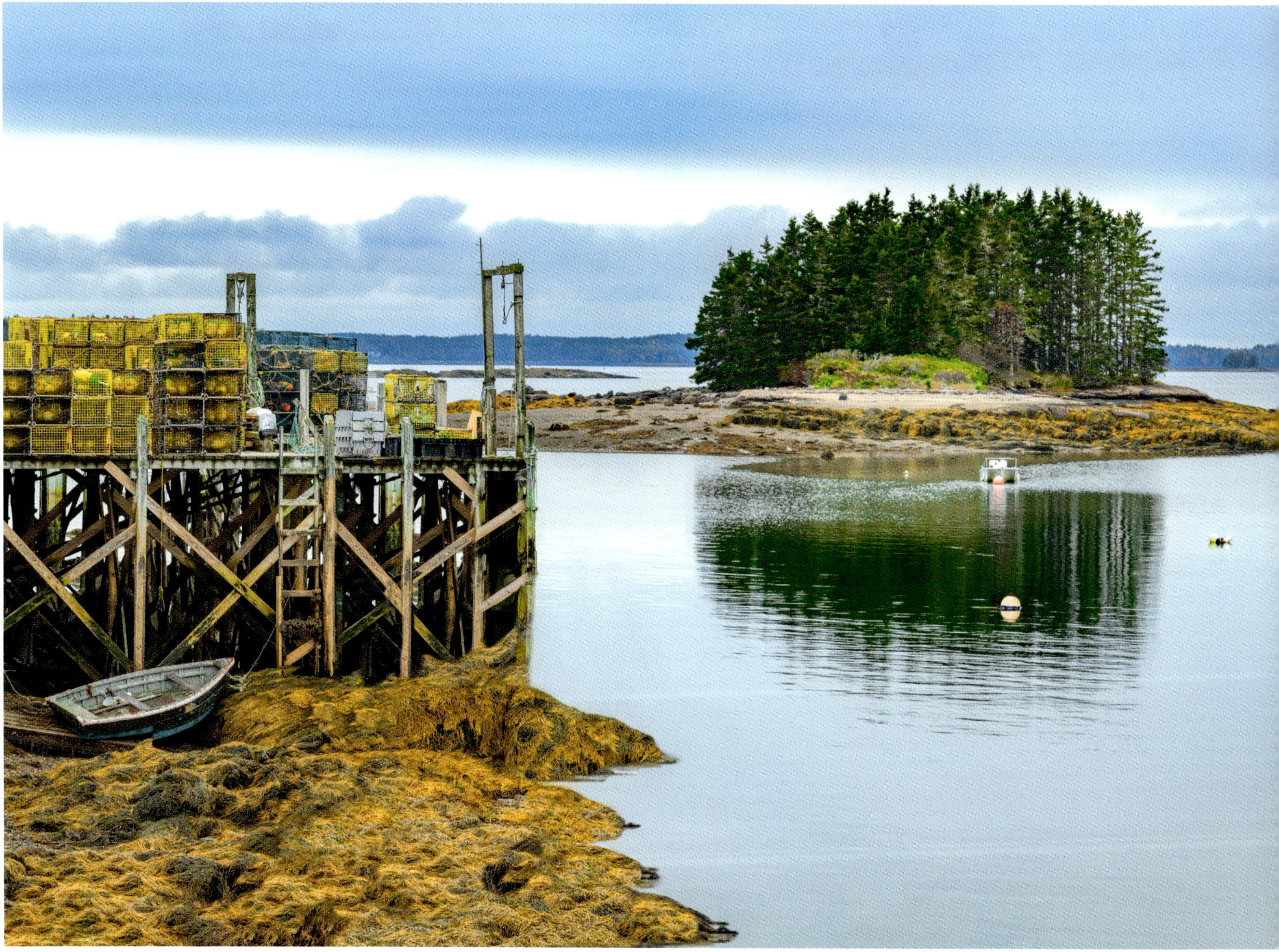

Mill Pond, Beals Island, Maine

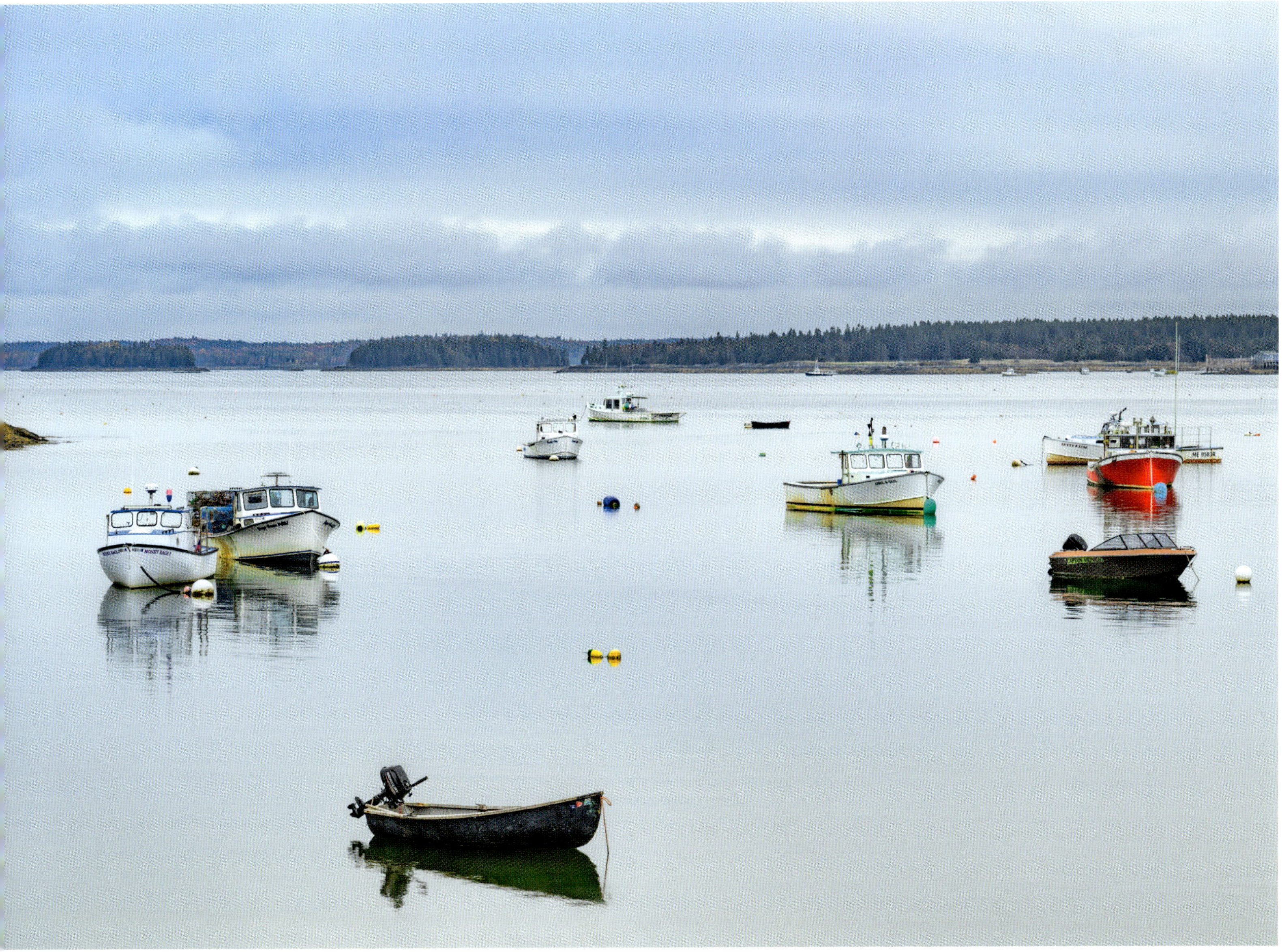

I had to hang over a railing for this one. I almost fell in.

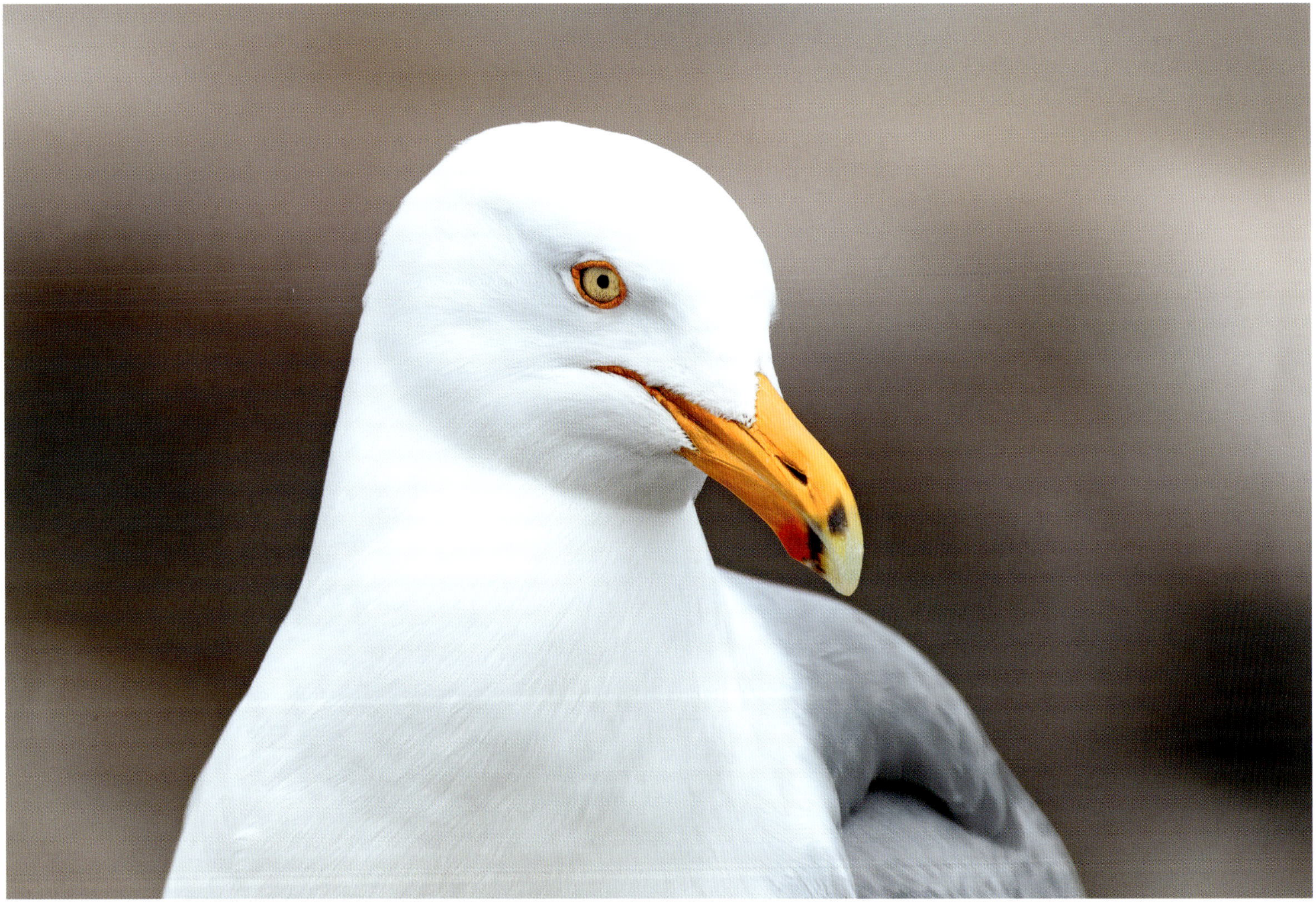

Posing gull, Schoodic Point, Acadia National Park, Maine

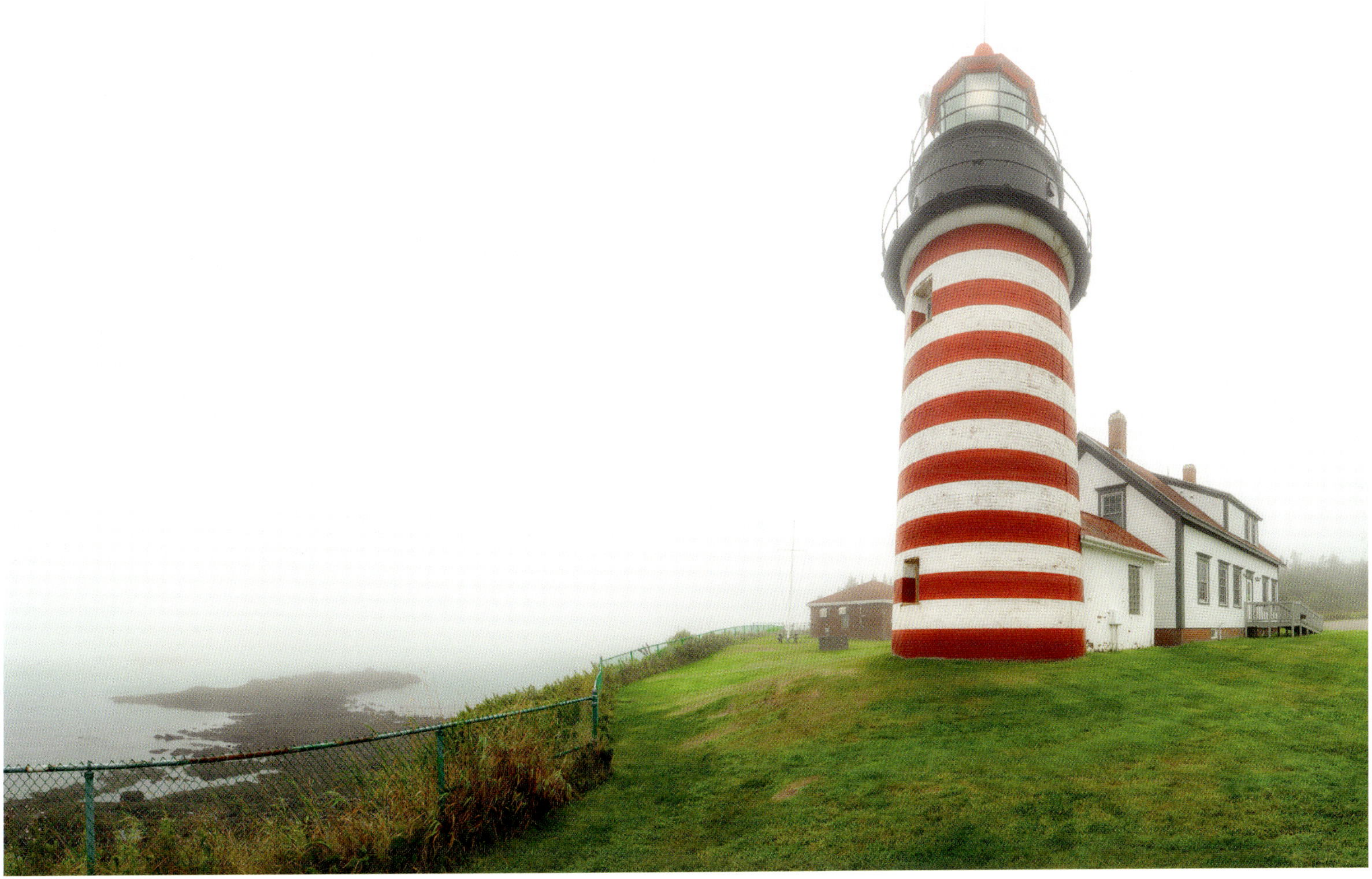

West Quoddy Head Lighthouse (1808), Lubec, Maine

This is the easternmost point in the United States.

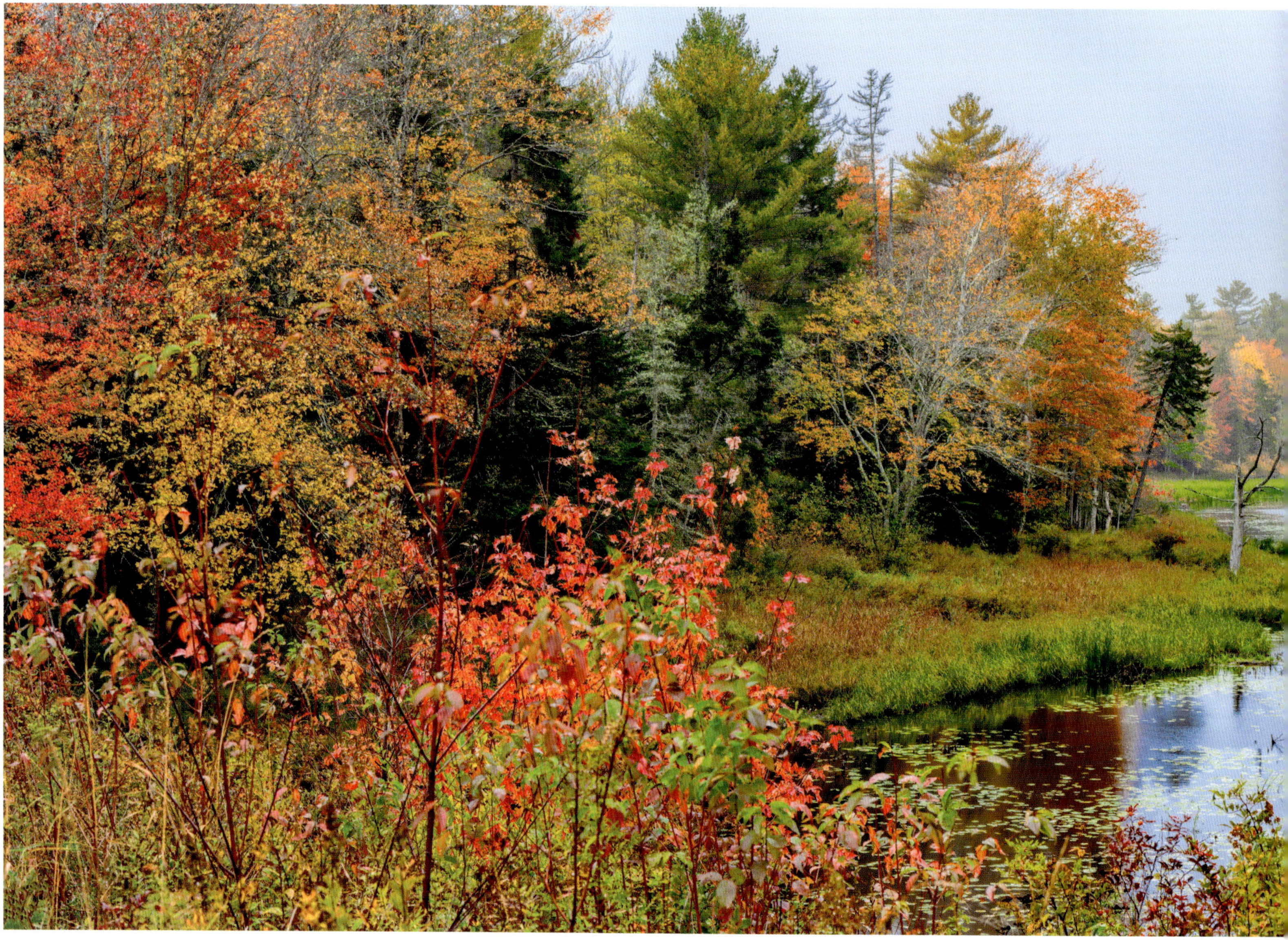

Long Cove, Maine

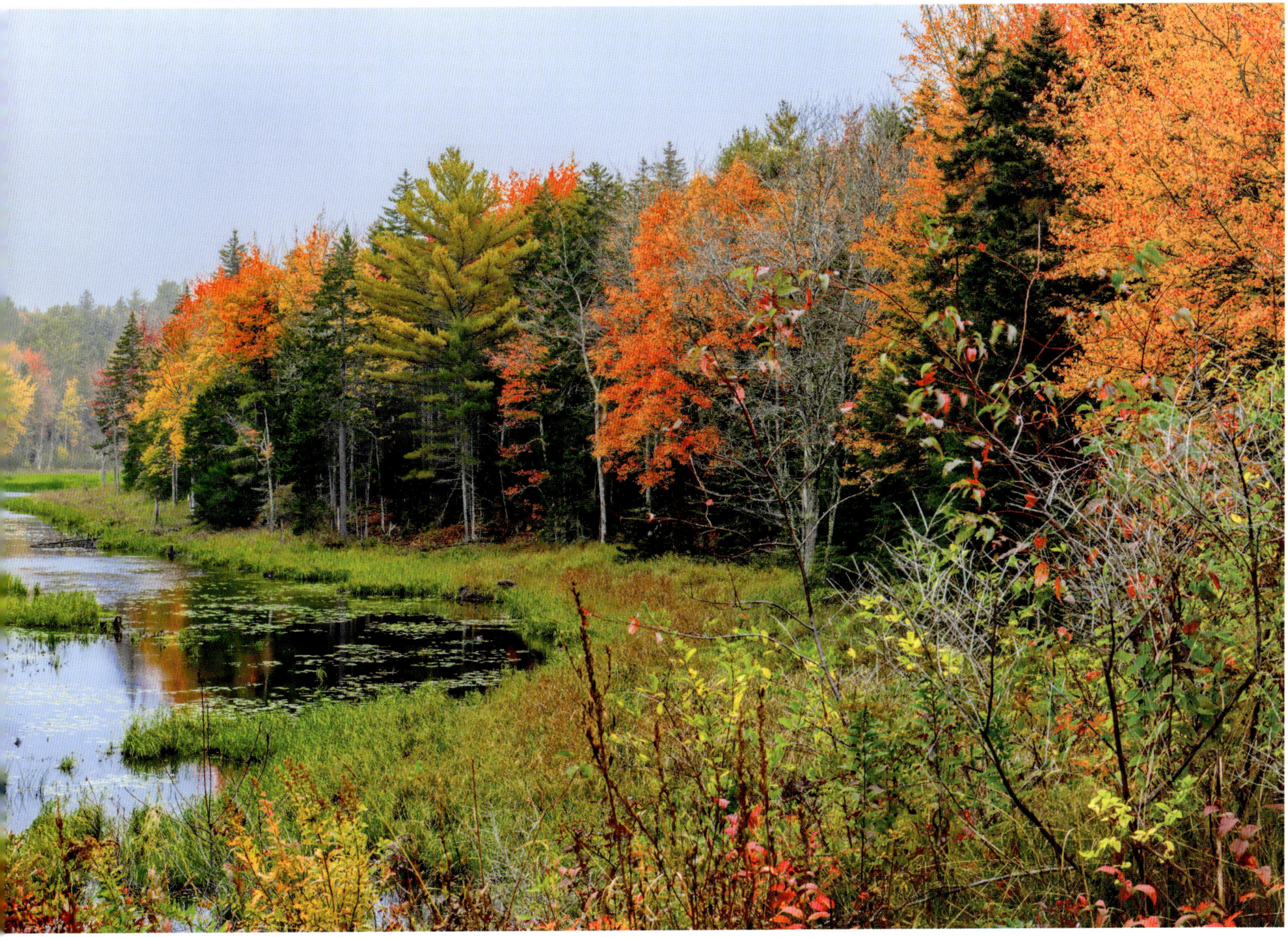

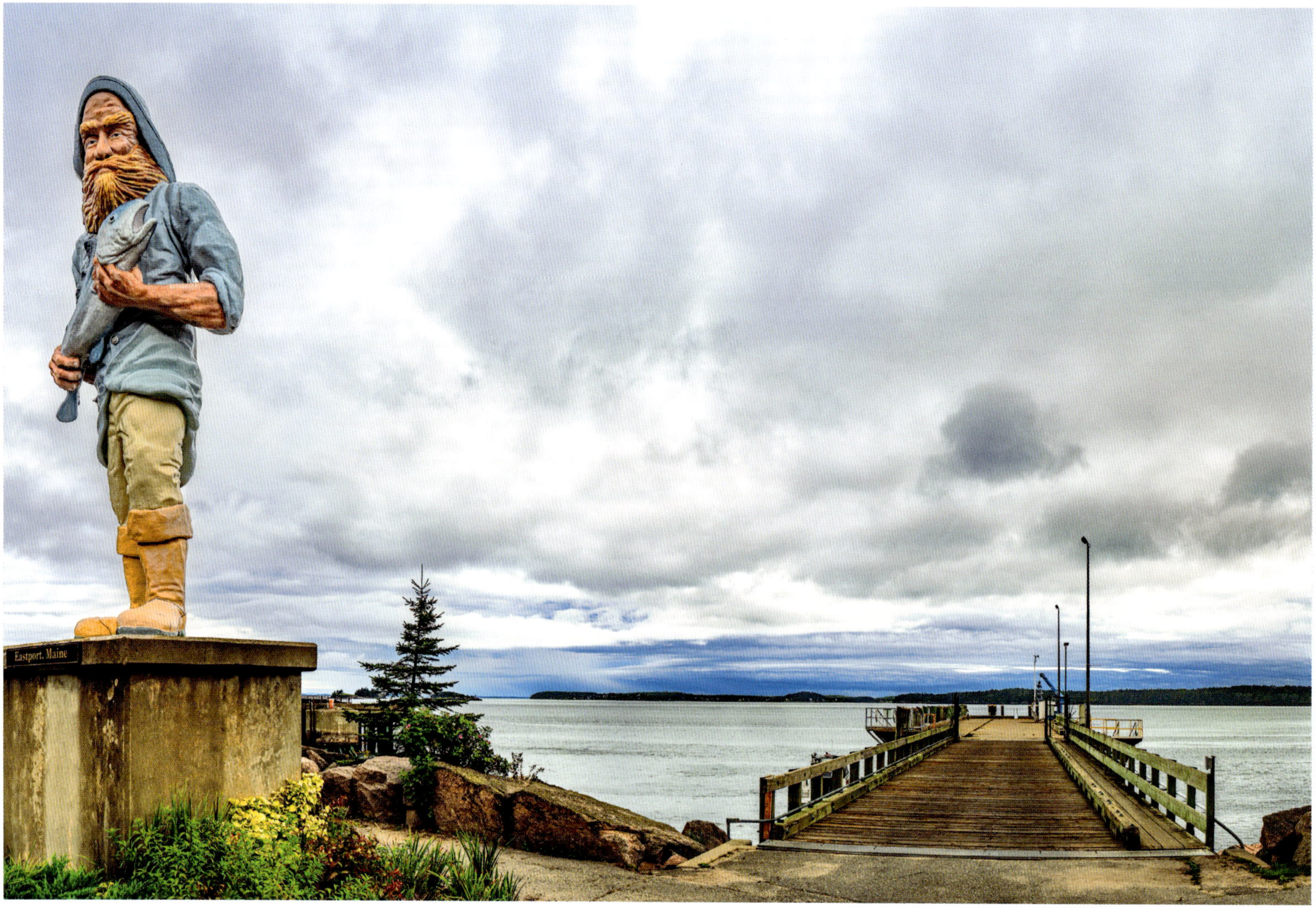

Pier at Eastport, Maine, and a statue honoring fishermen

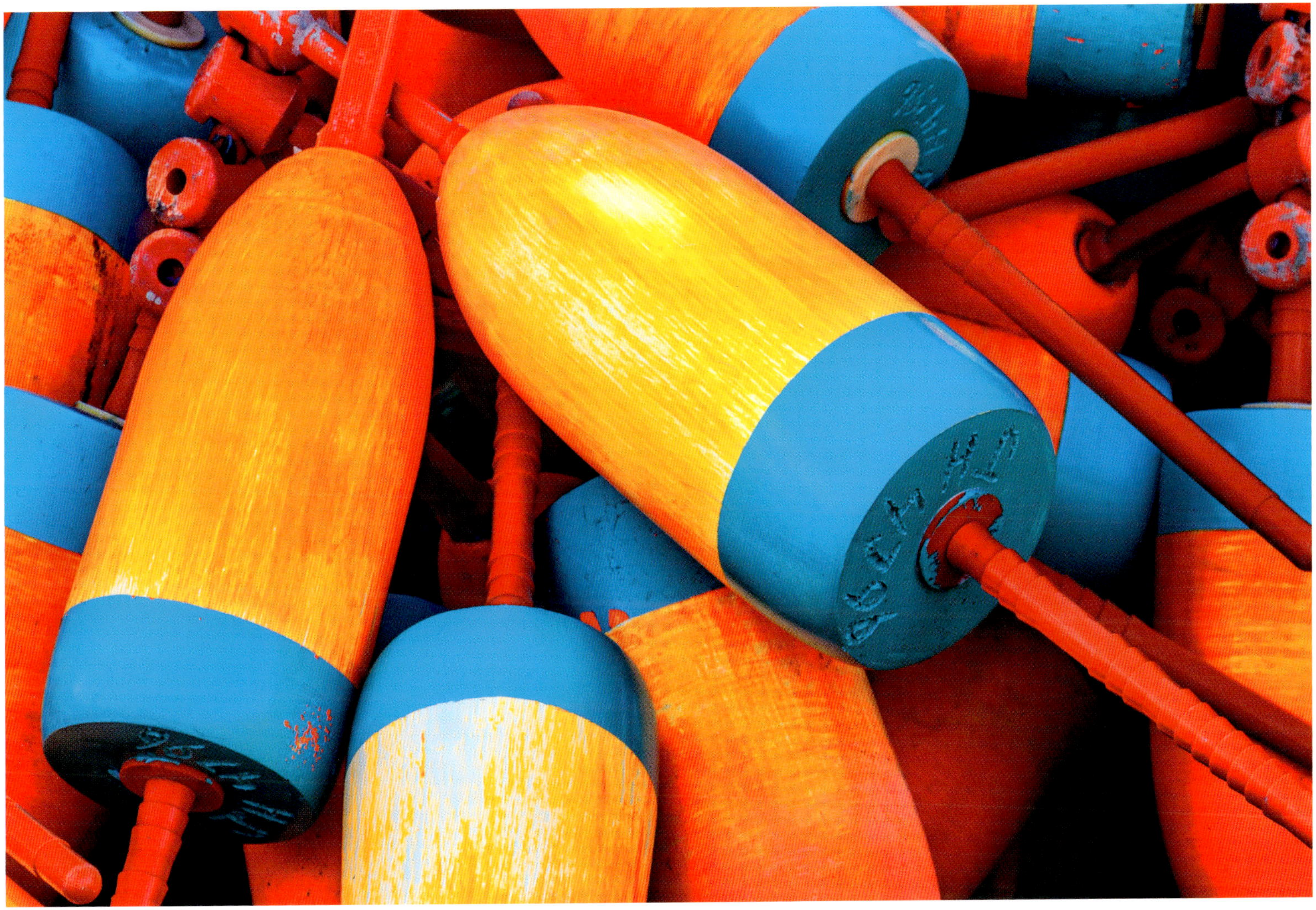

Lobster trap floats, Calais, Maine

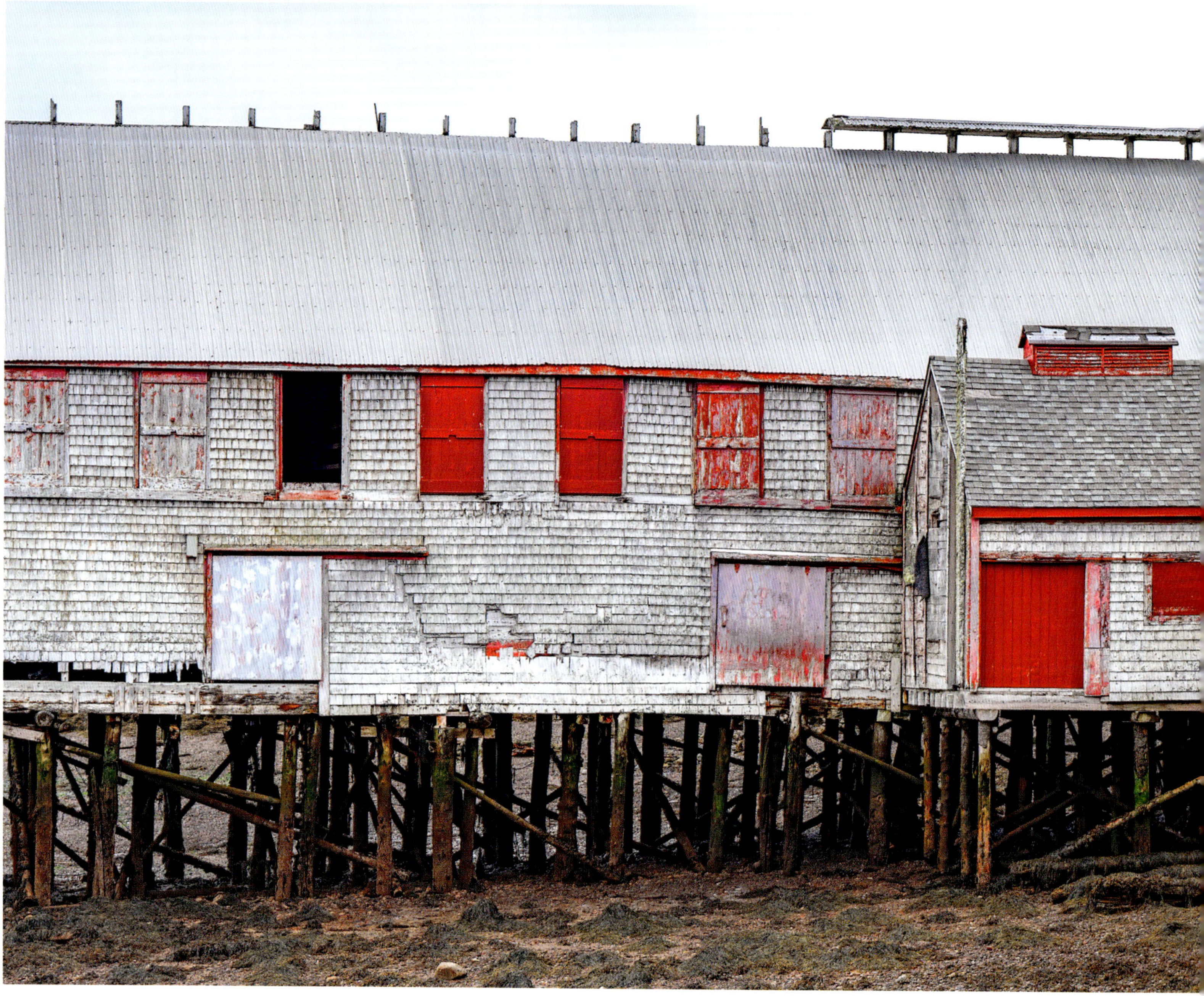

Lubec, Maine

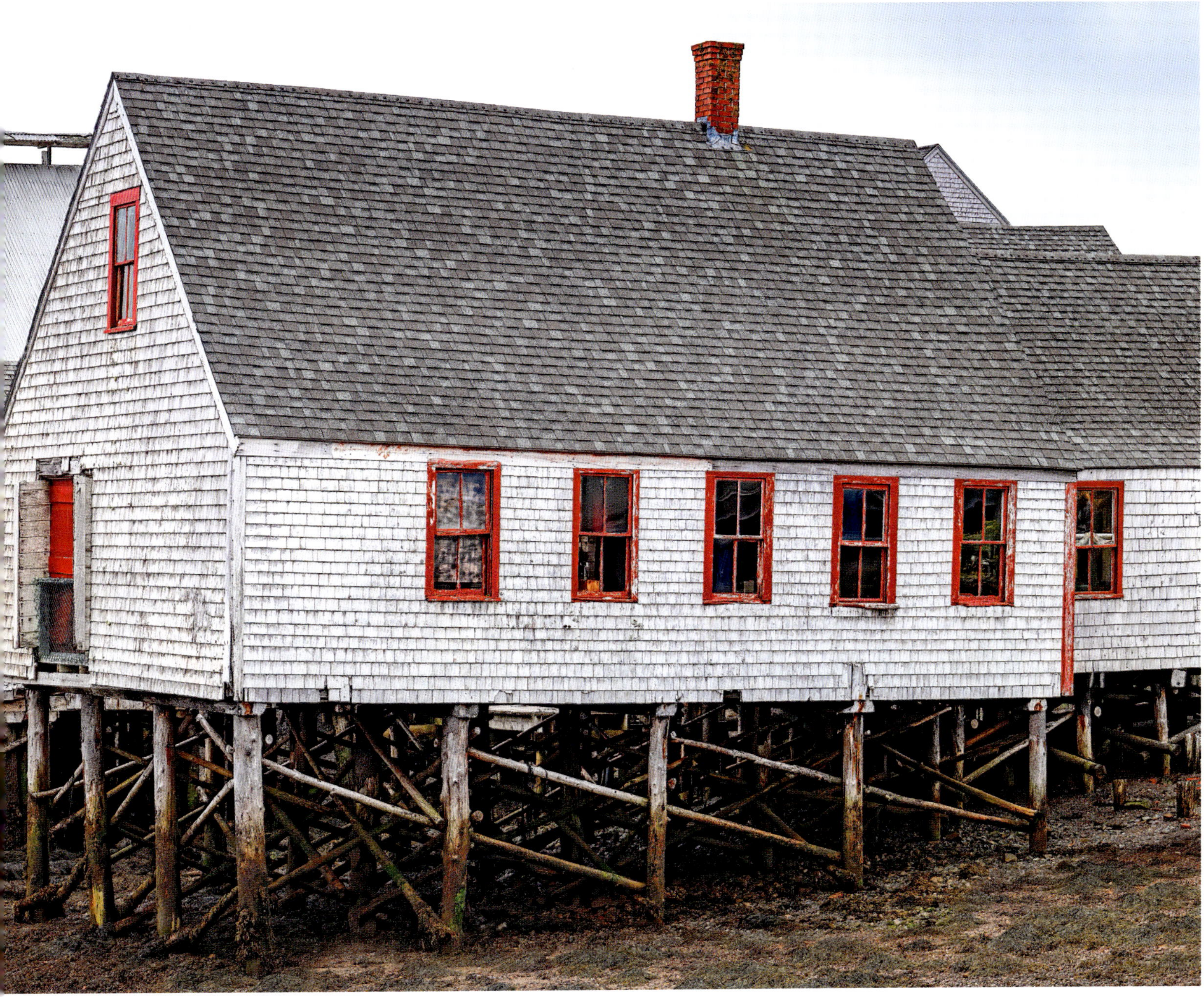

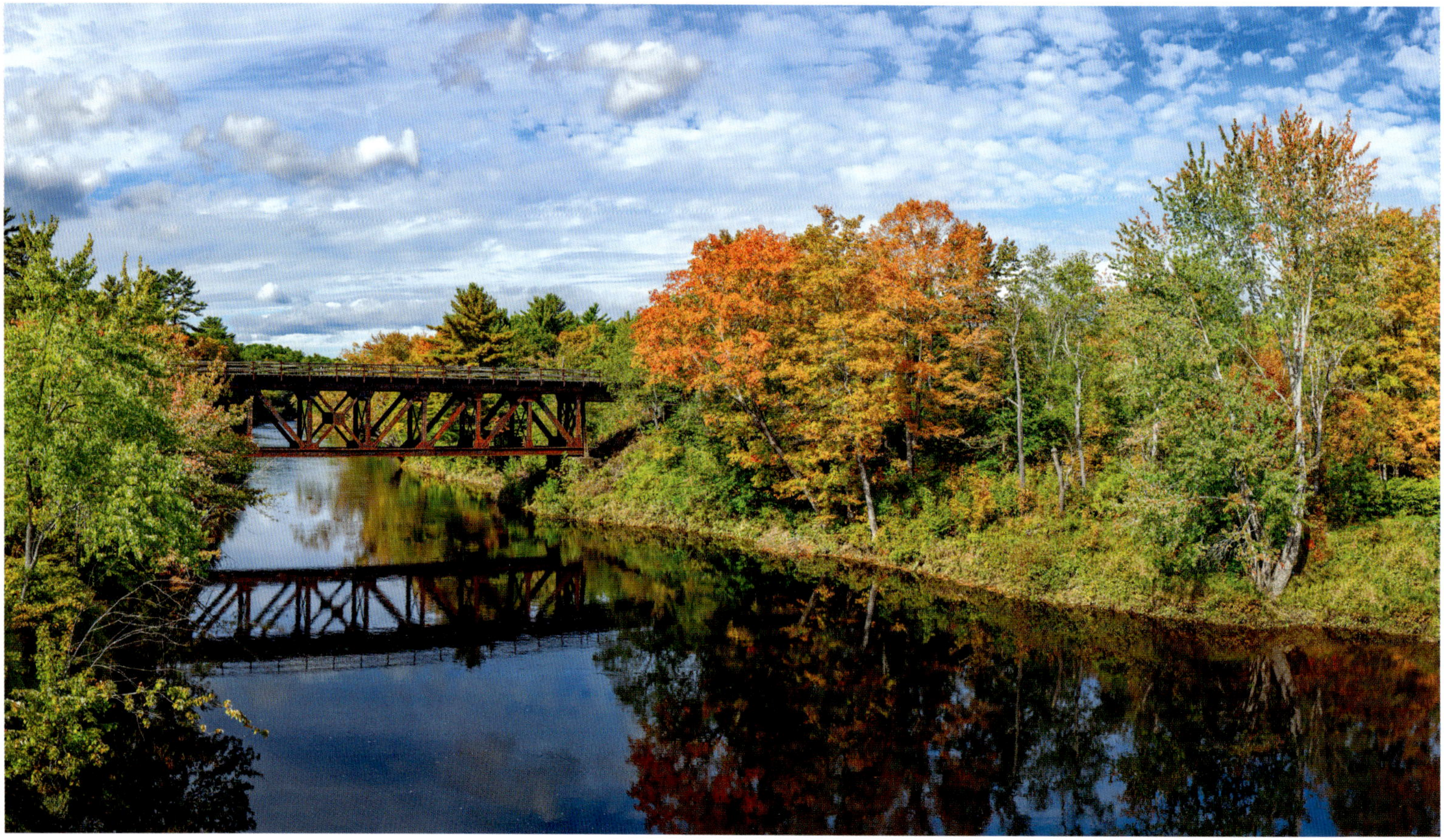

Railroad bridge over the Pleasant River, Brownsville, Maine

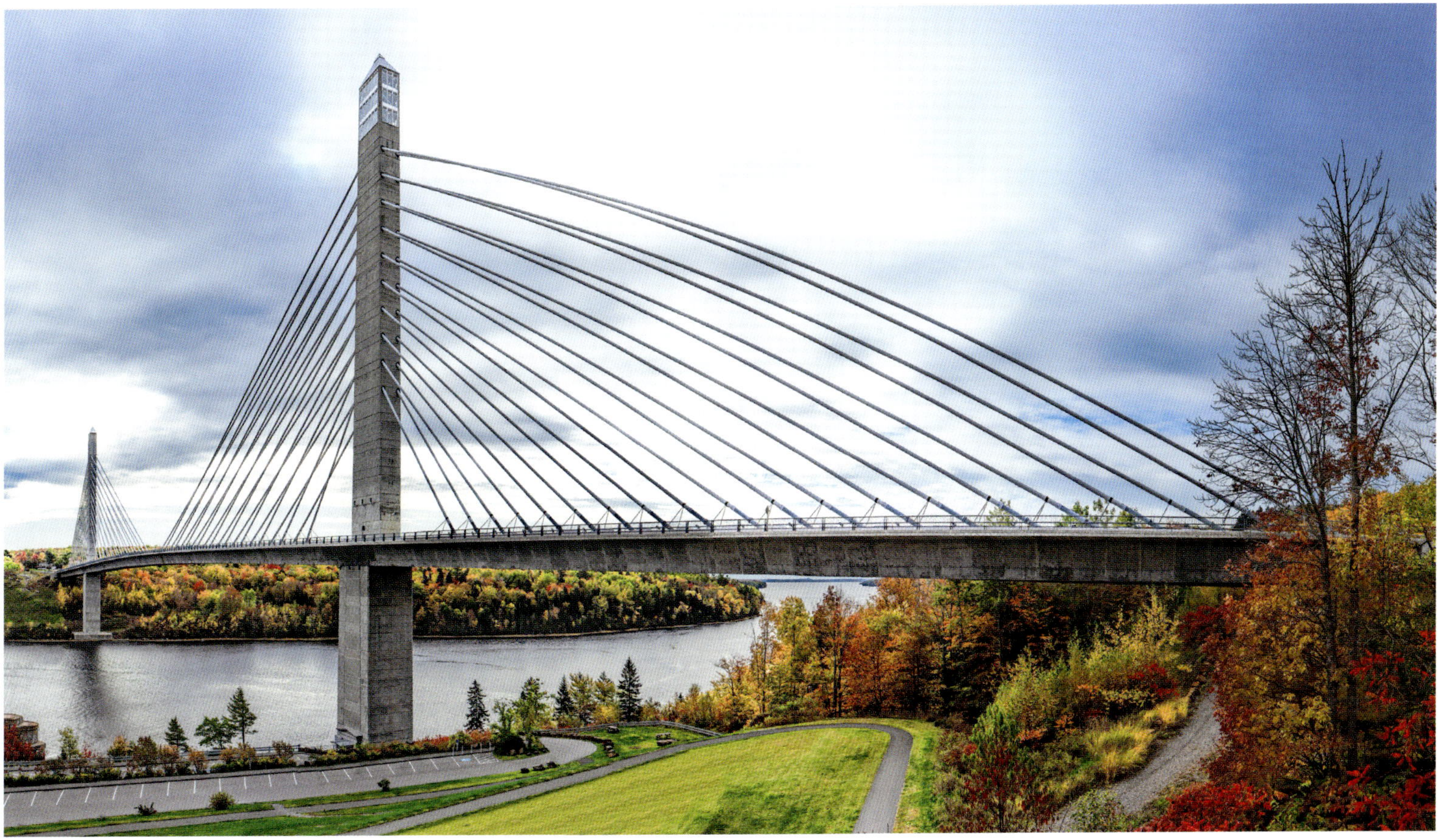

Penobscot Narrows Bridge

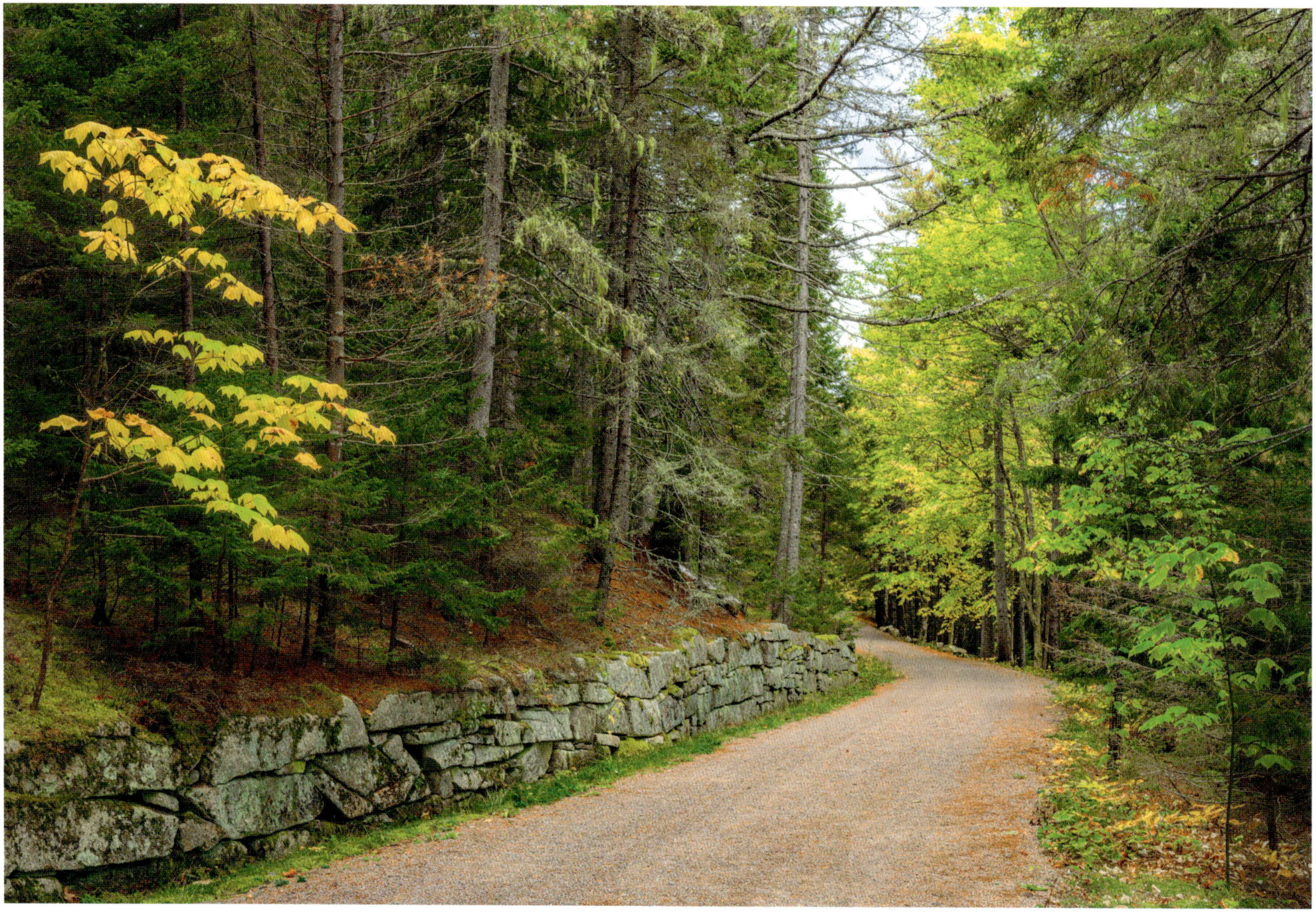

Striped maple tree and Little Long Pond Road, Maine

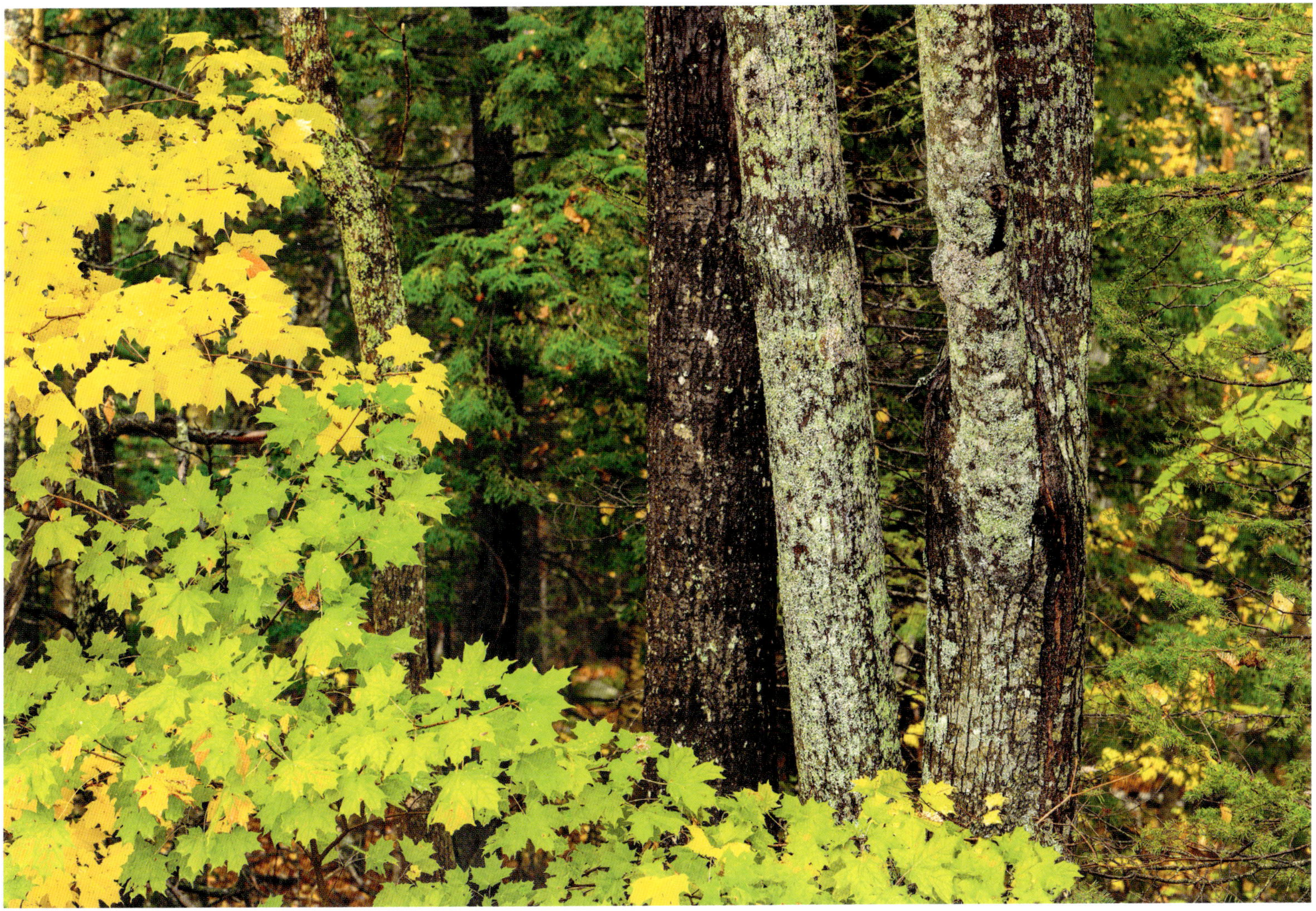

Sugar maples along Maine State Highway 191

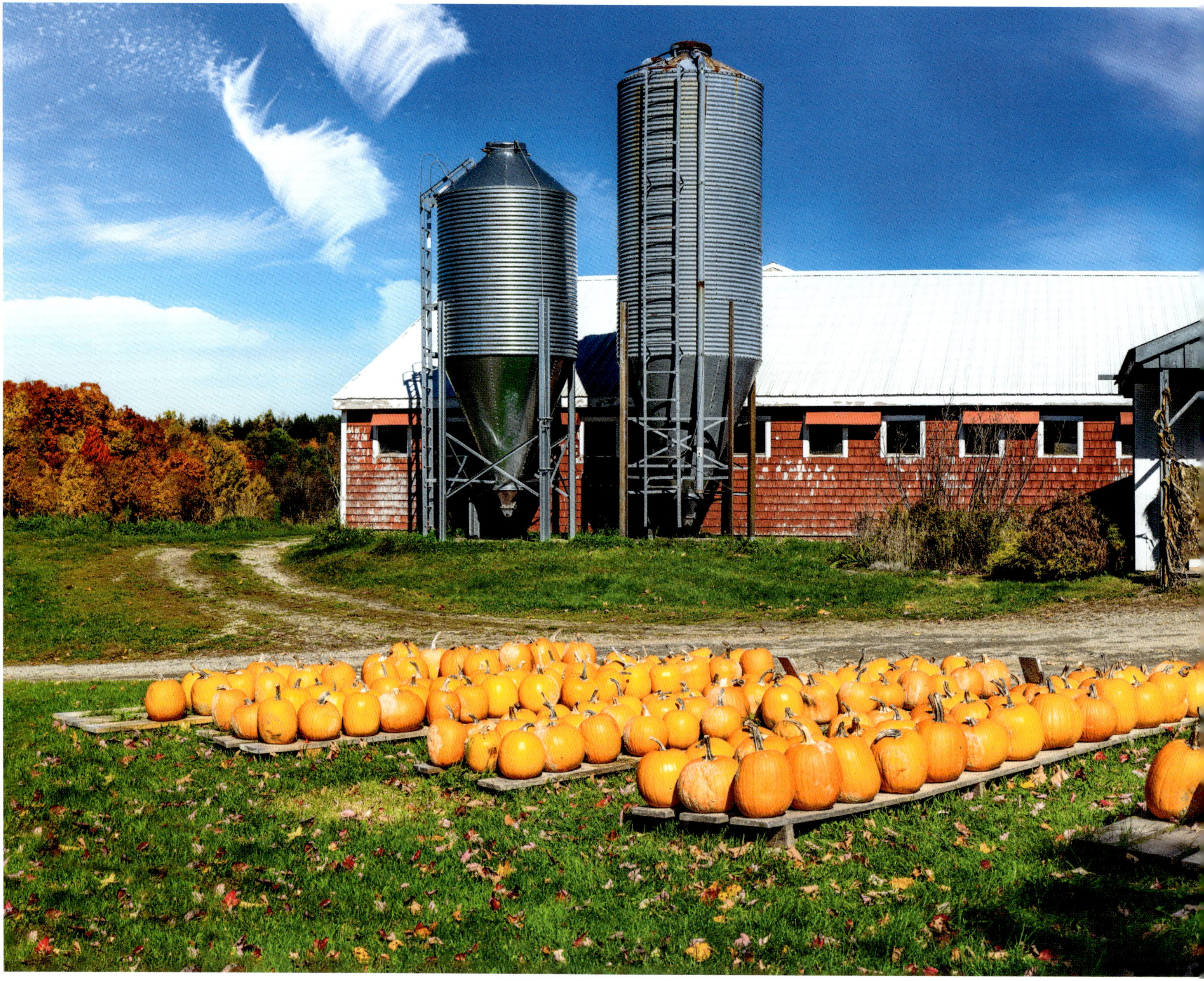

Barn and pumpkins, Monroe, Maine

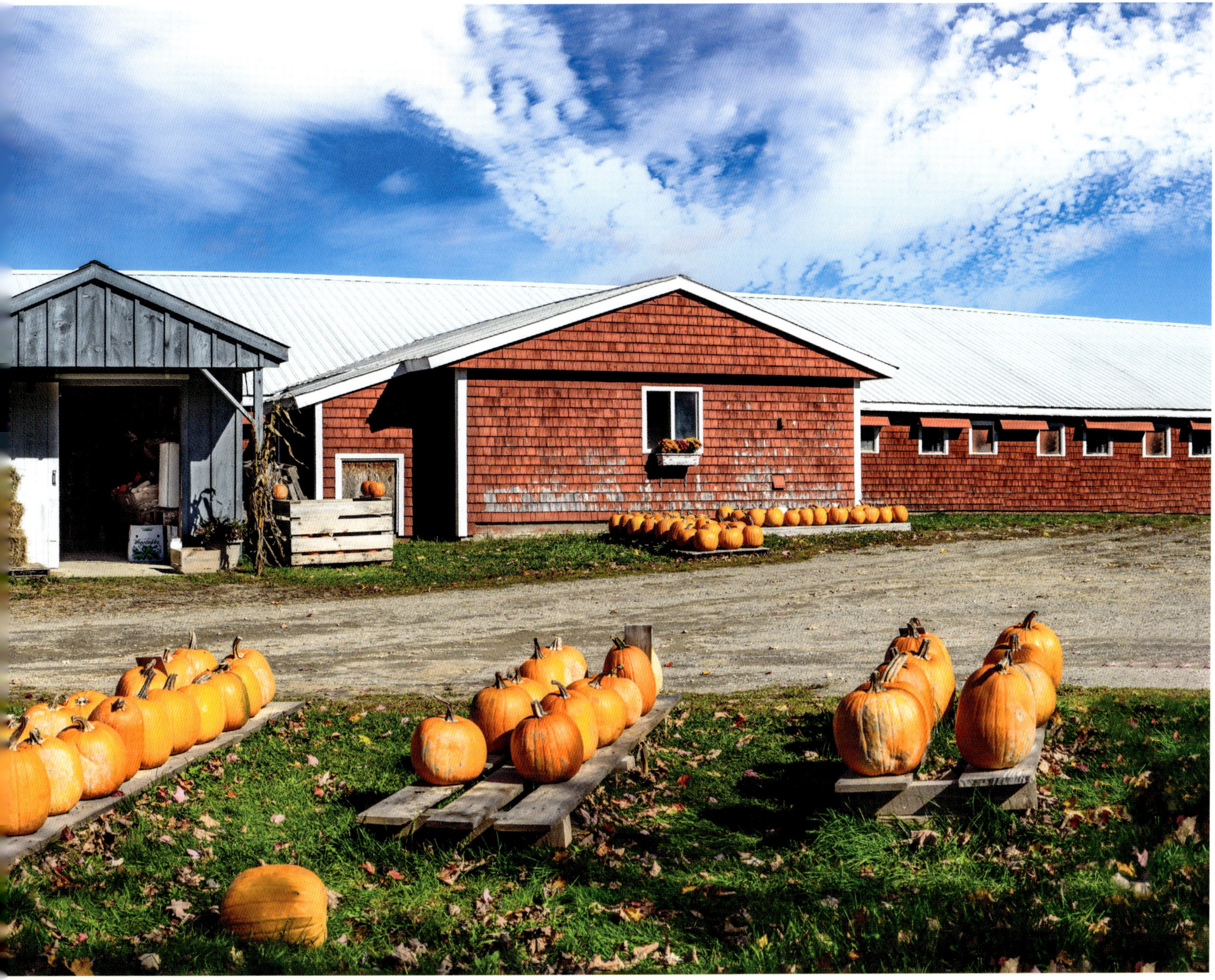

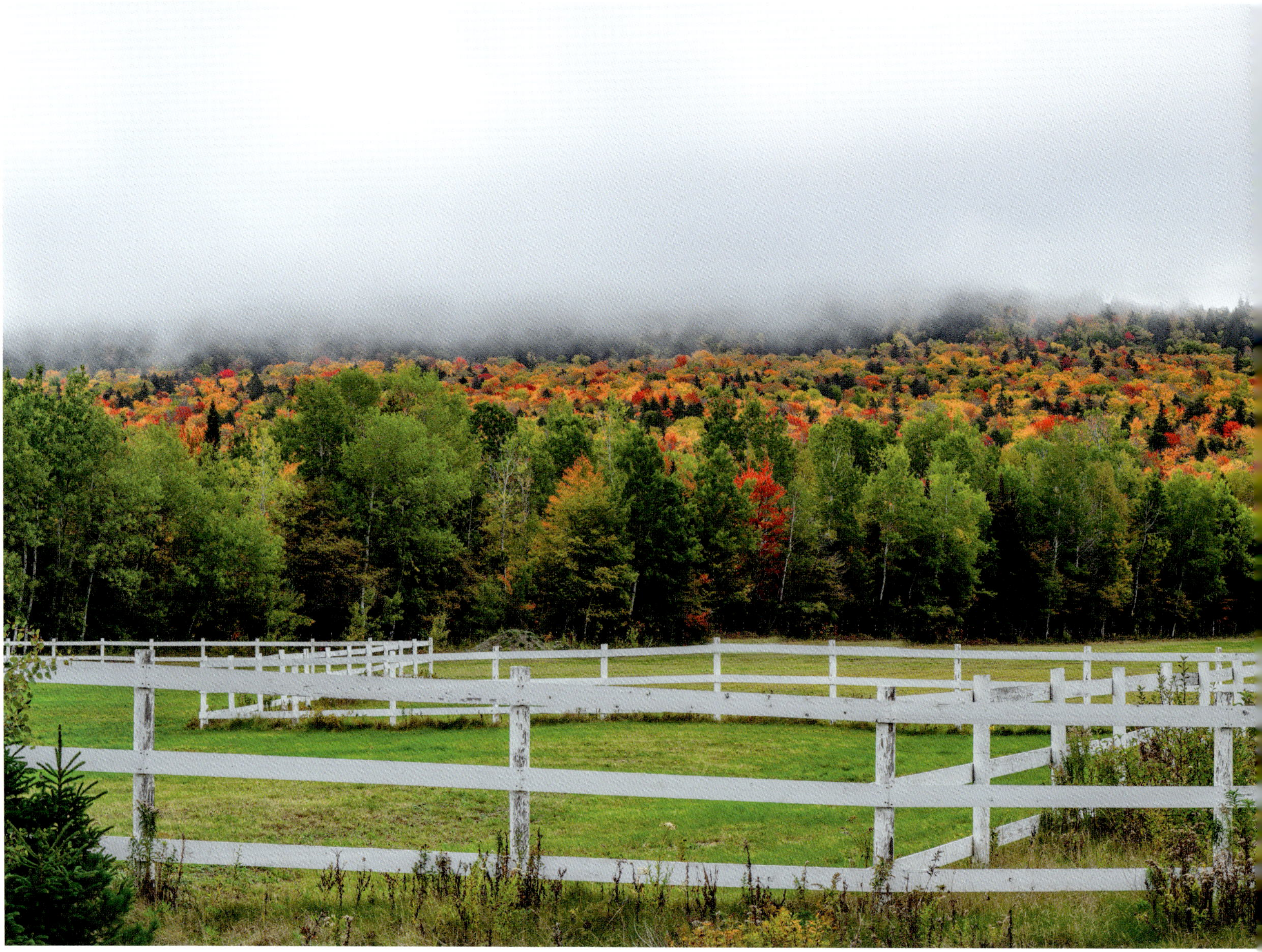

Fences, fog, and fall, Rockwood, Maine

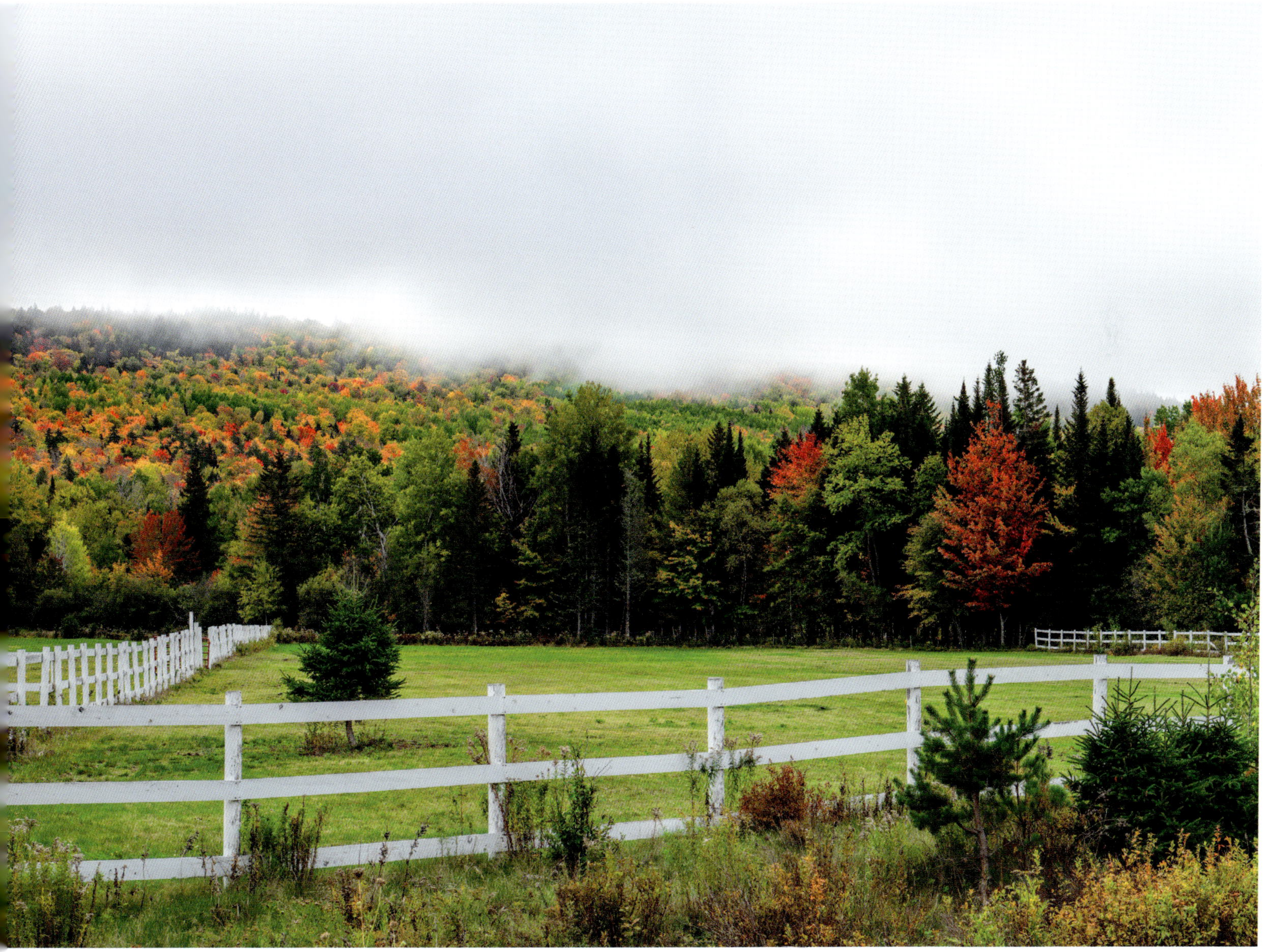

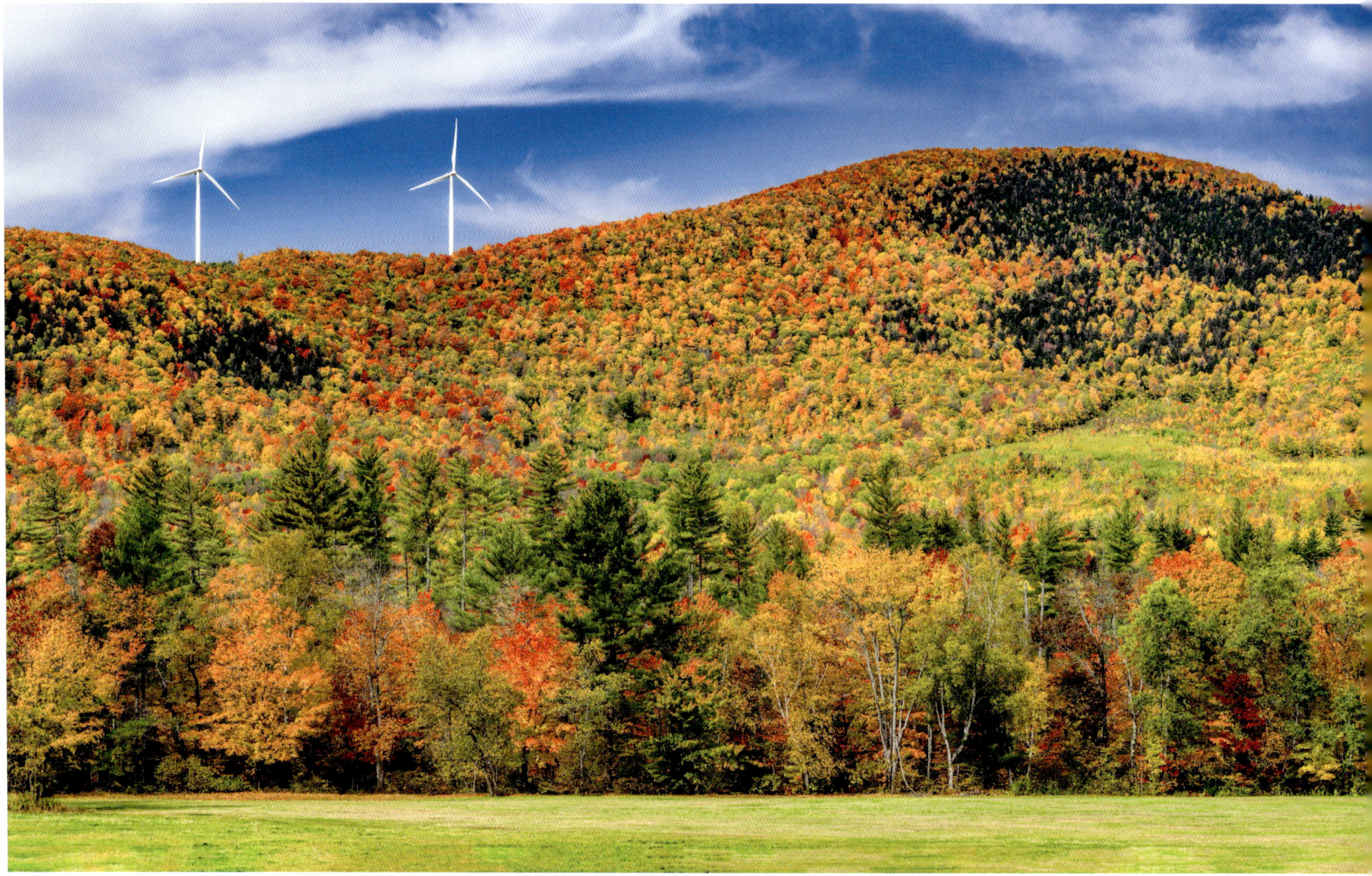

Giant windmills, Roxbury, Maine

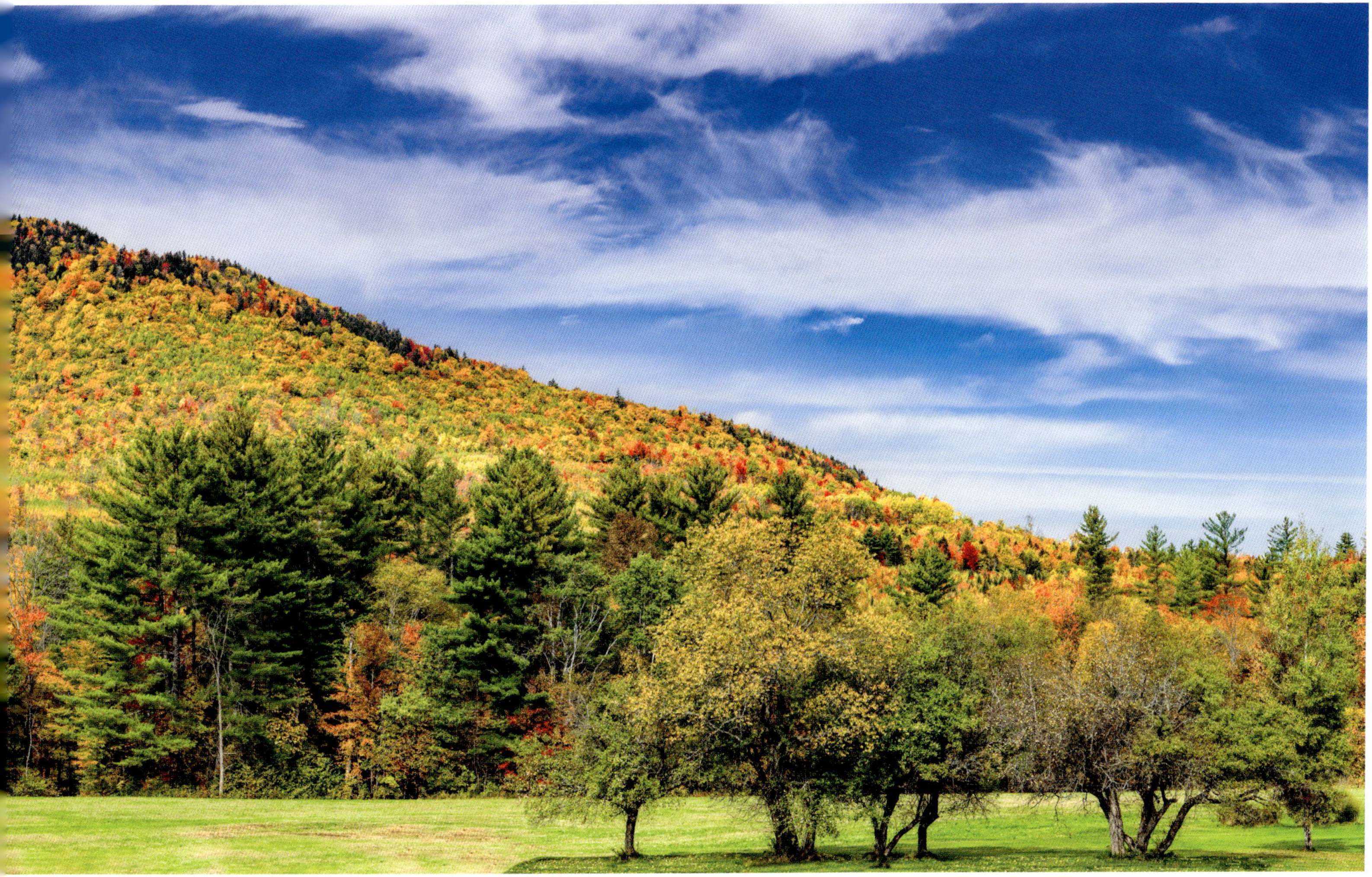

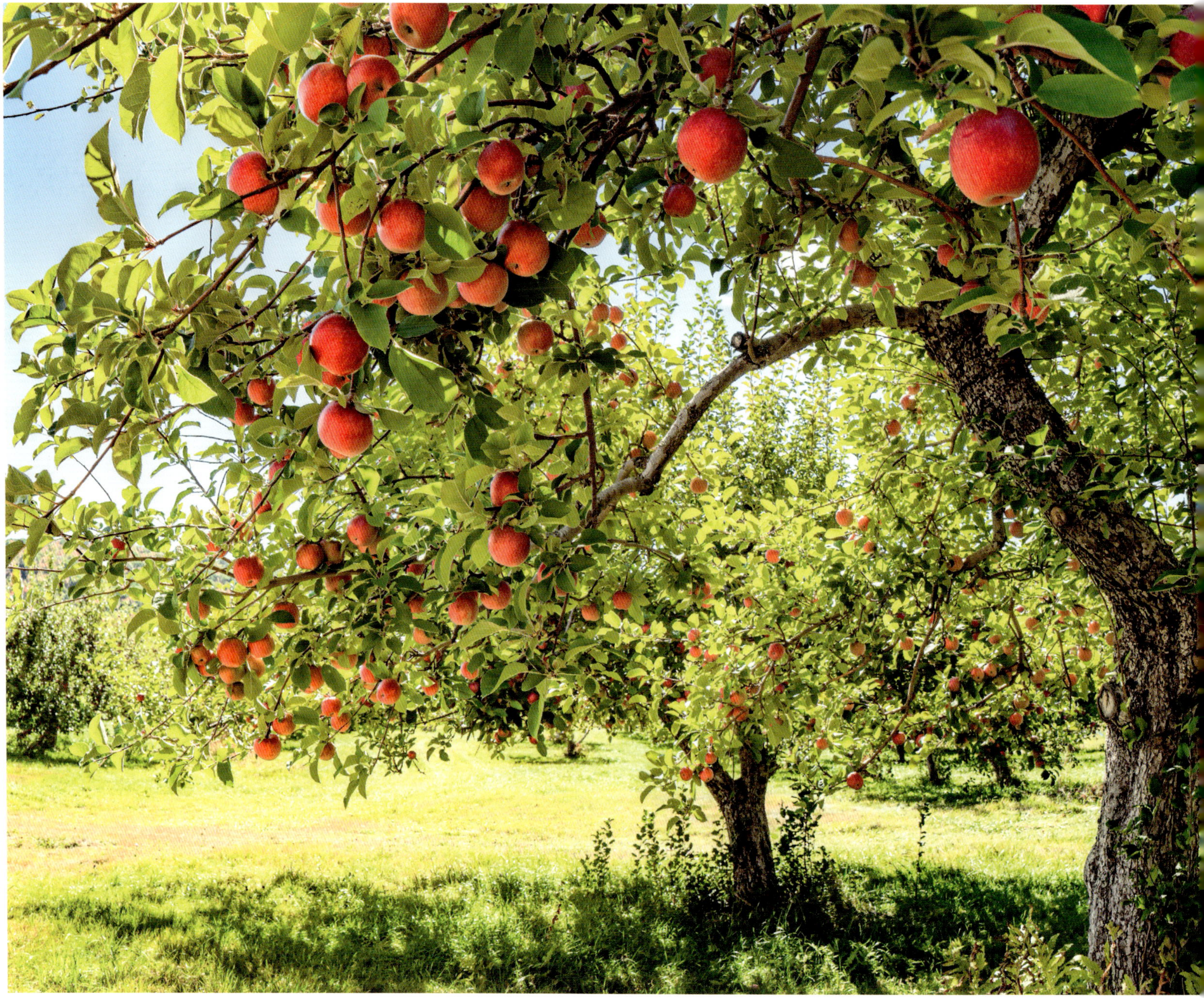

Paradise apples, Lyon's Apple Orchard, Bethel, Maine

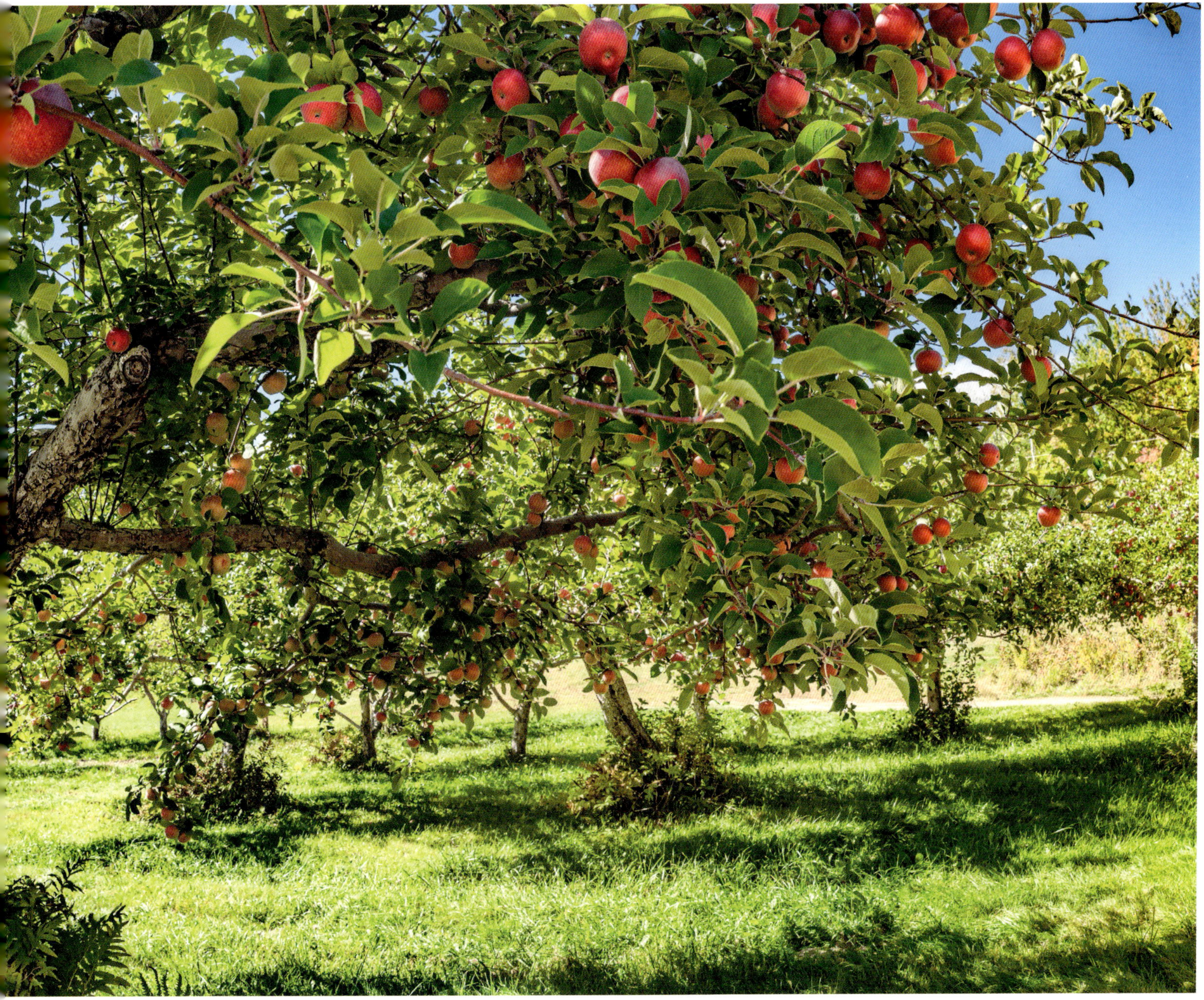

These were every bit as tasty as they look!

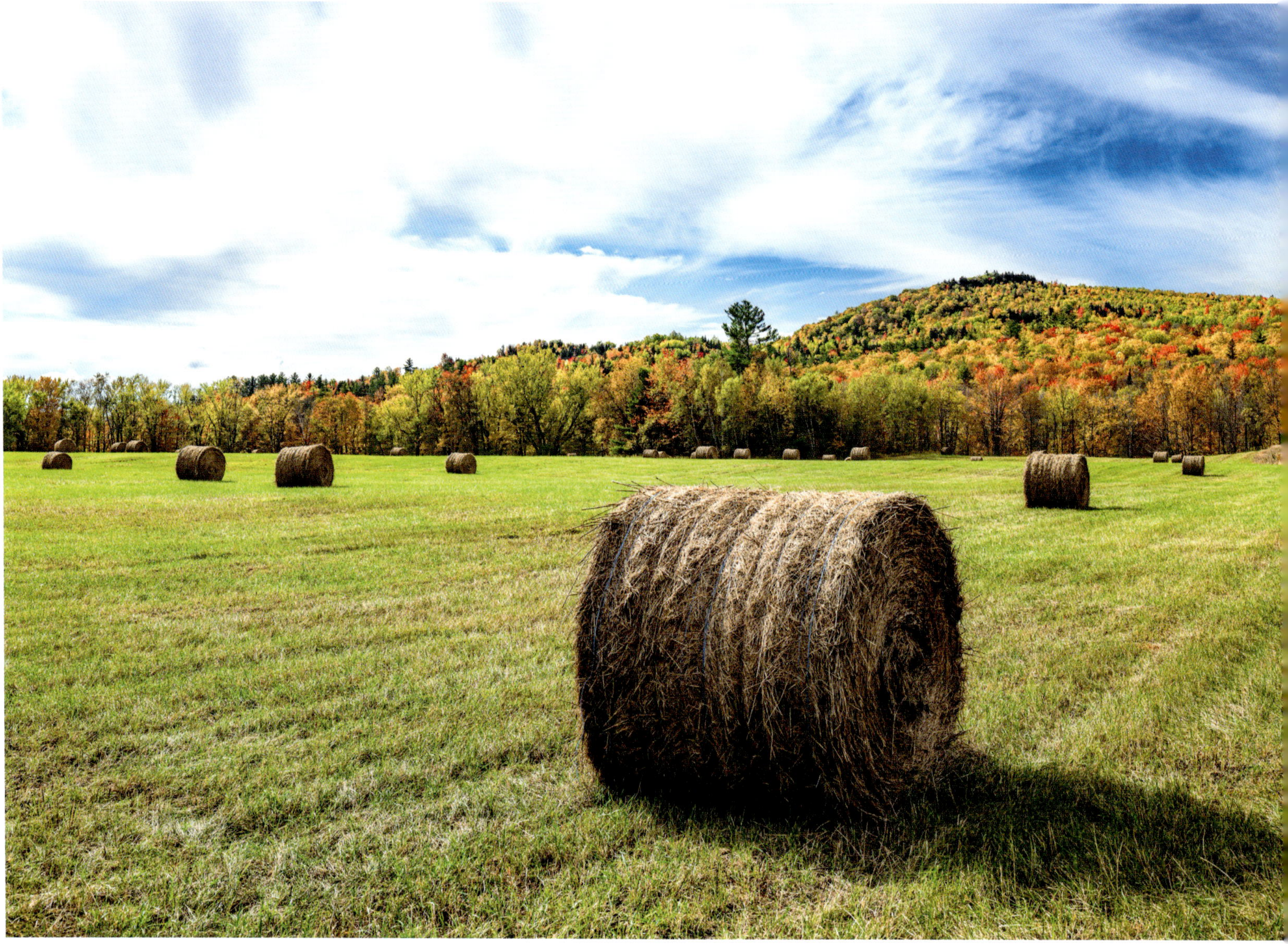

Hayfield, in Mexico, Maine

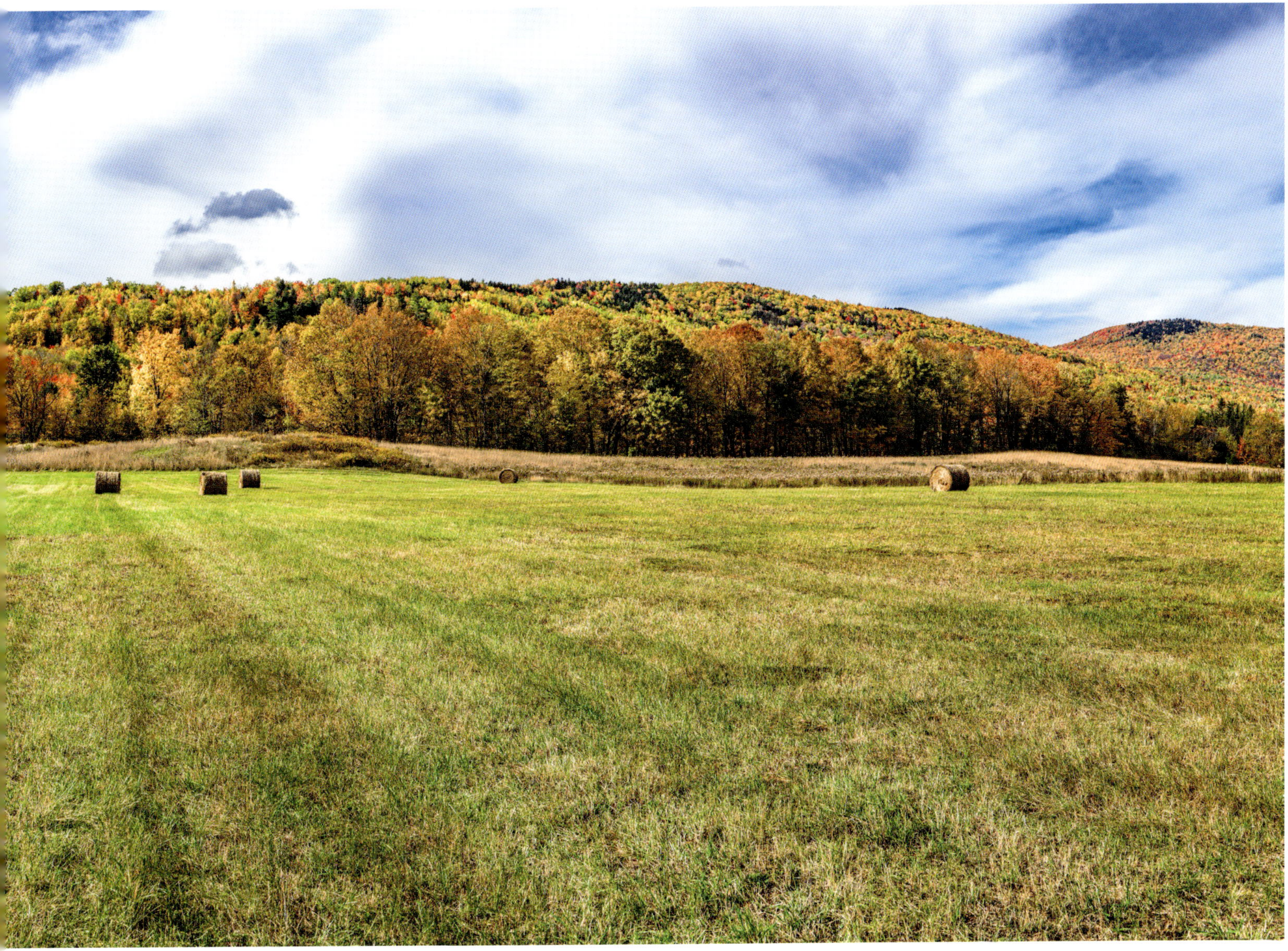

Incorporated in 1818, the town's name was inspired by local sympathy for Mexico's fight for independence from Spain.

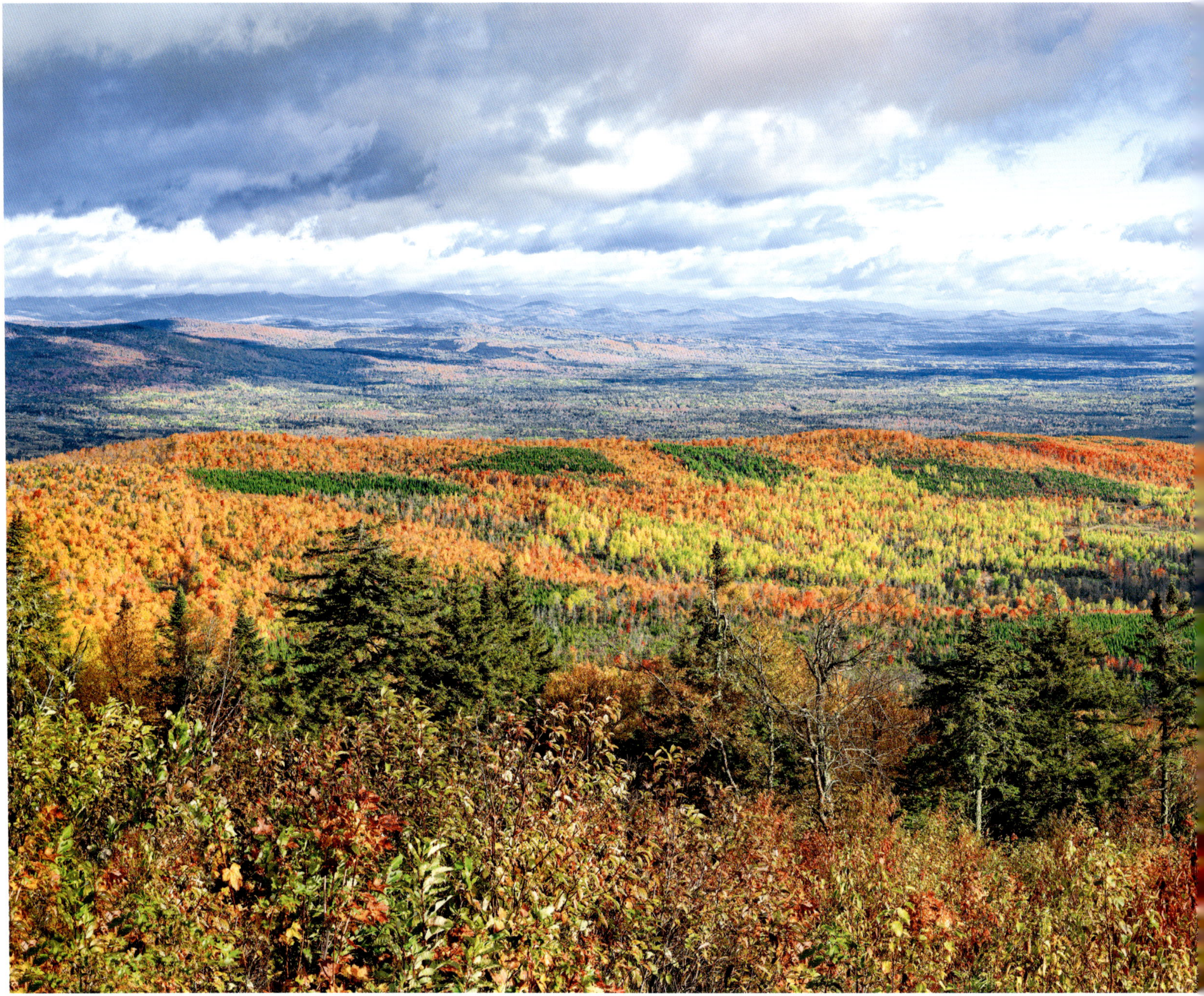

View from Quill Hill (2,848 feet), Dallas Plantation, Maine

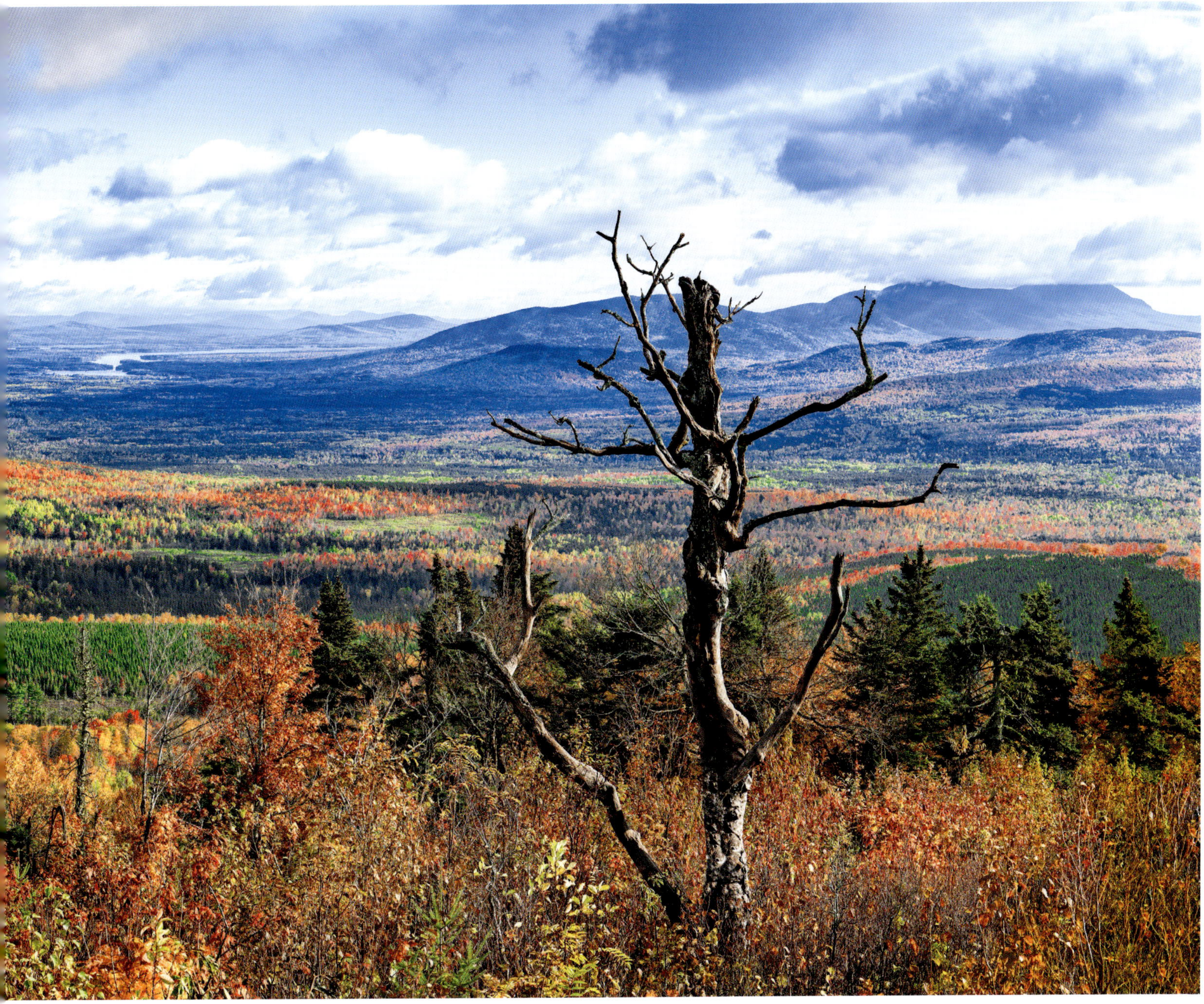

The sign simply said "View." They weren't kidding!

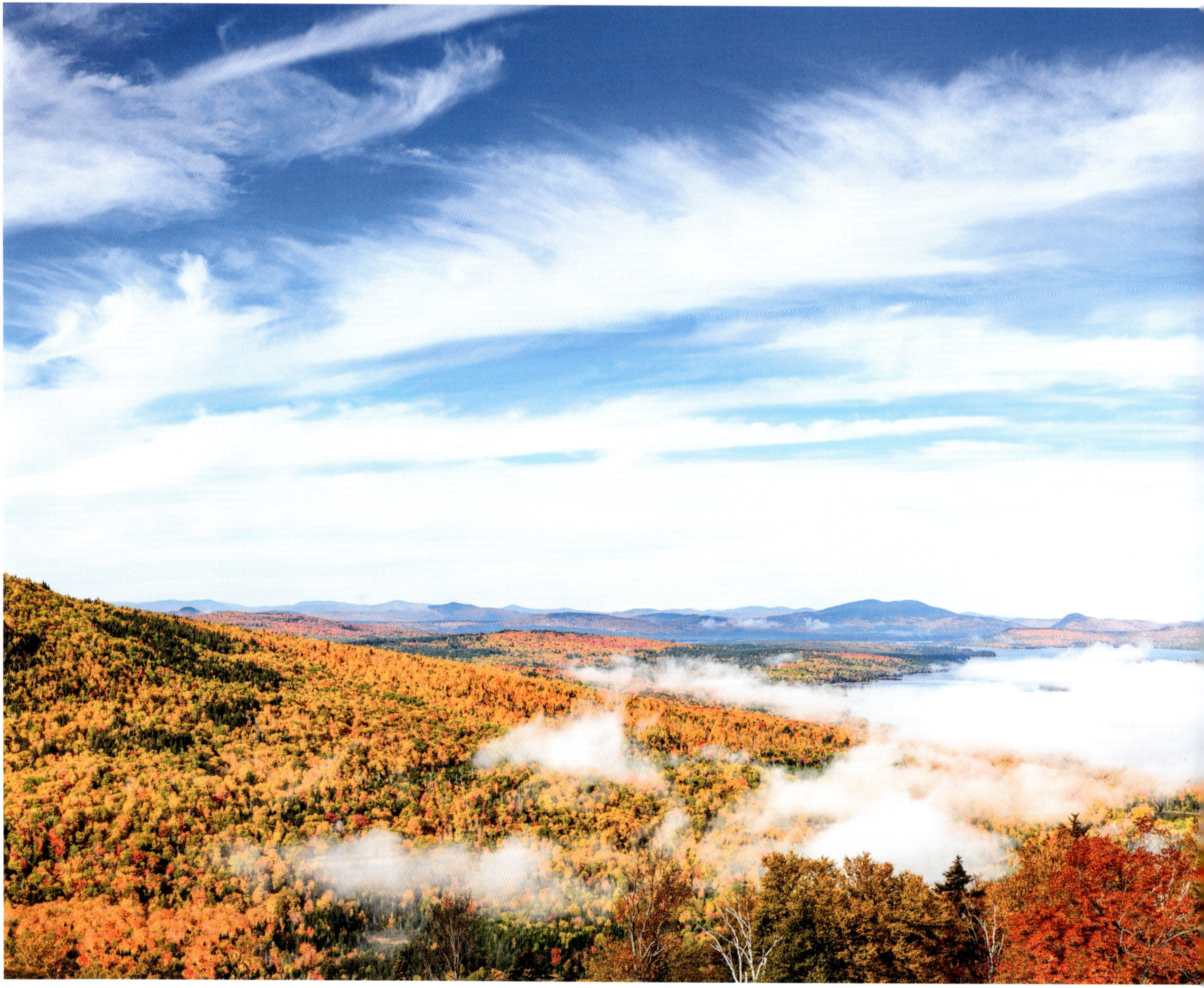

Fog over Mooselookmeguntic Lake, Maine

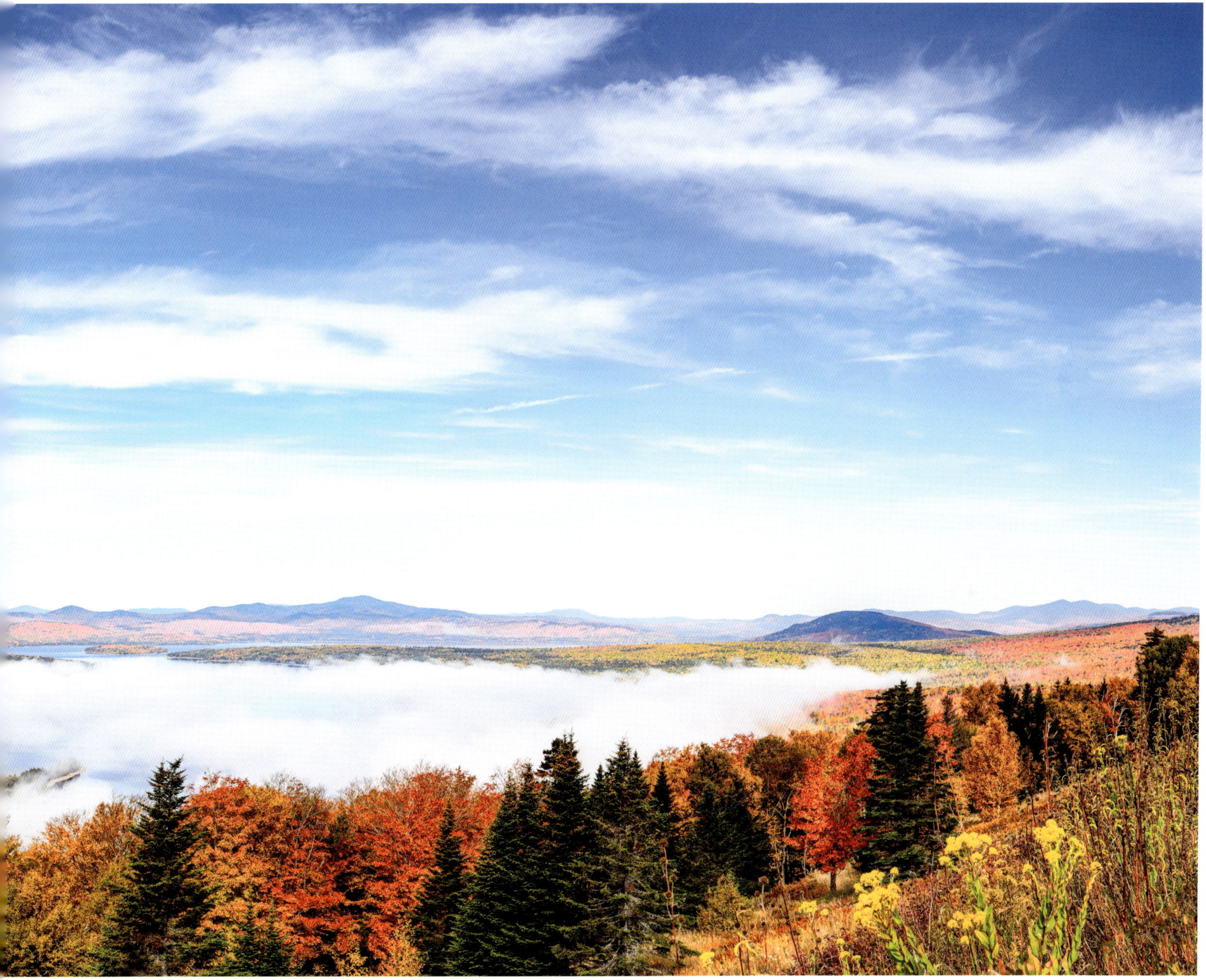

I checked the spelling three times. “Mooselookmeguntic” means “moose feeding place” in the endangered language of Abnaki.

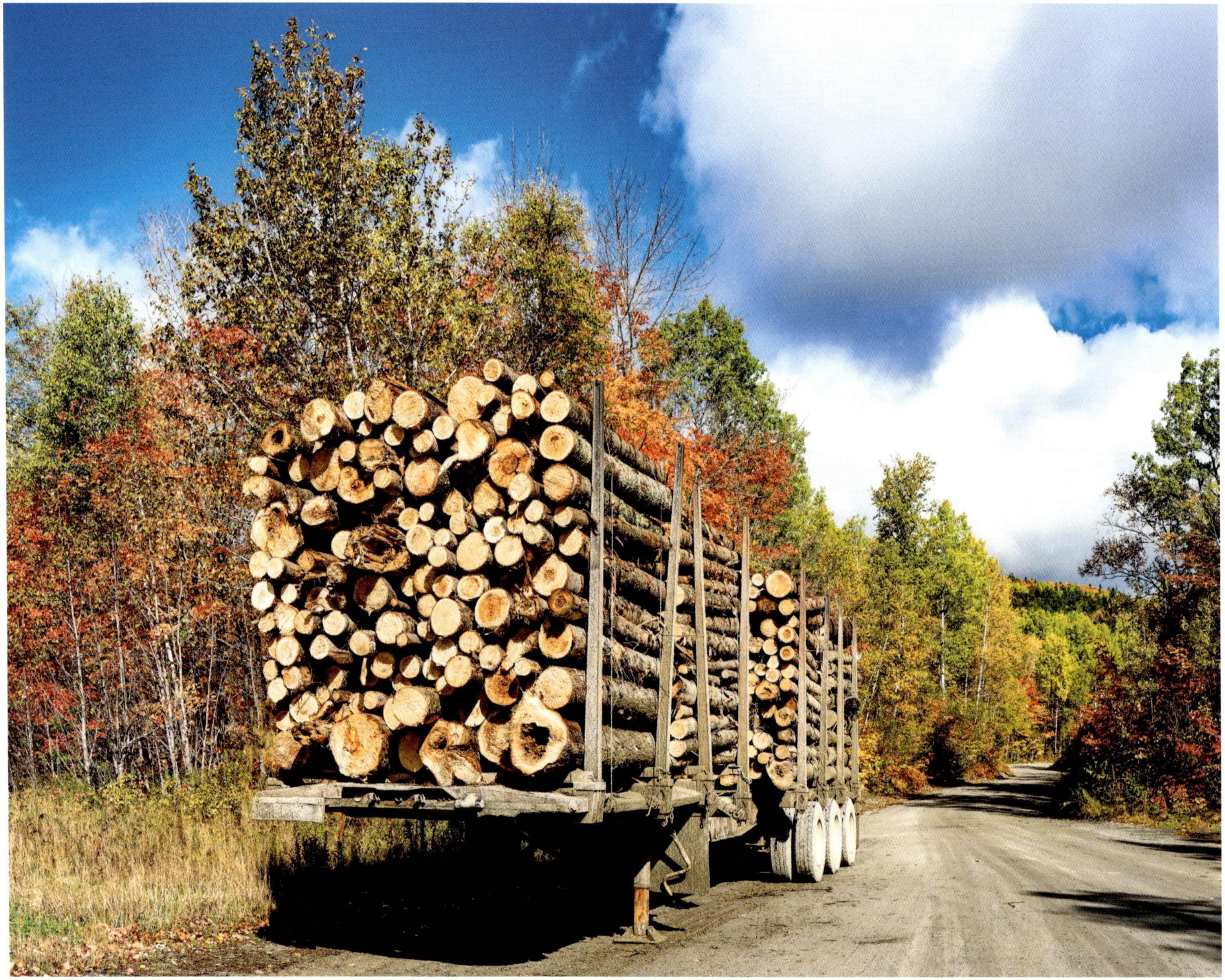

Gold Brook Road, western Maine

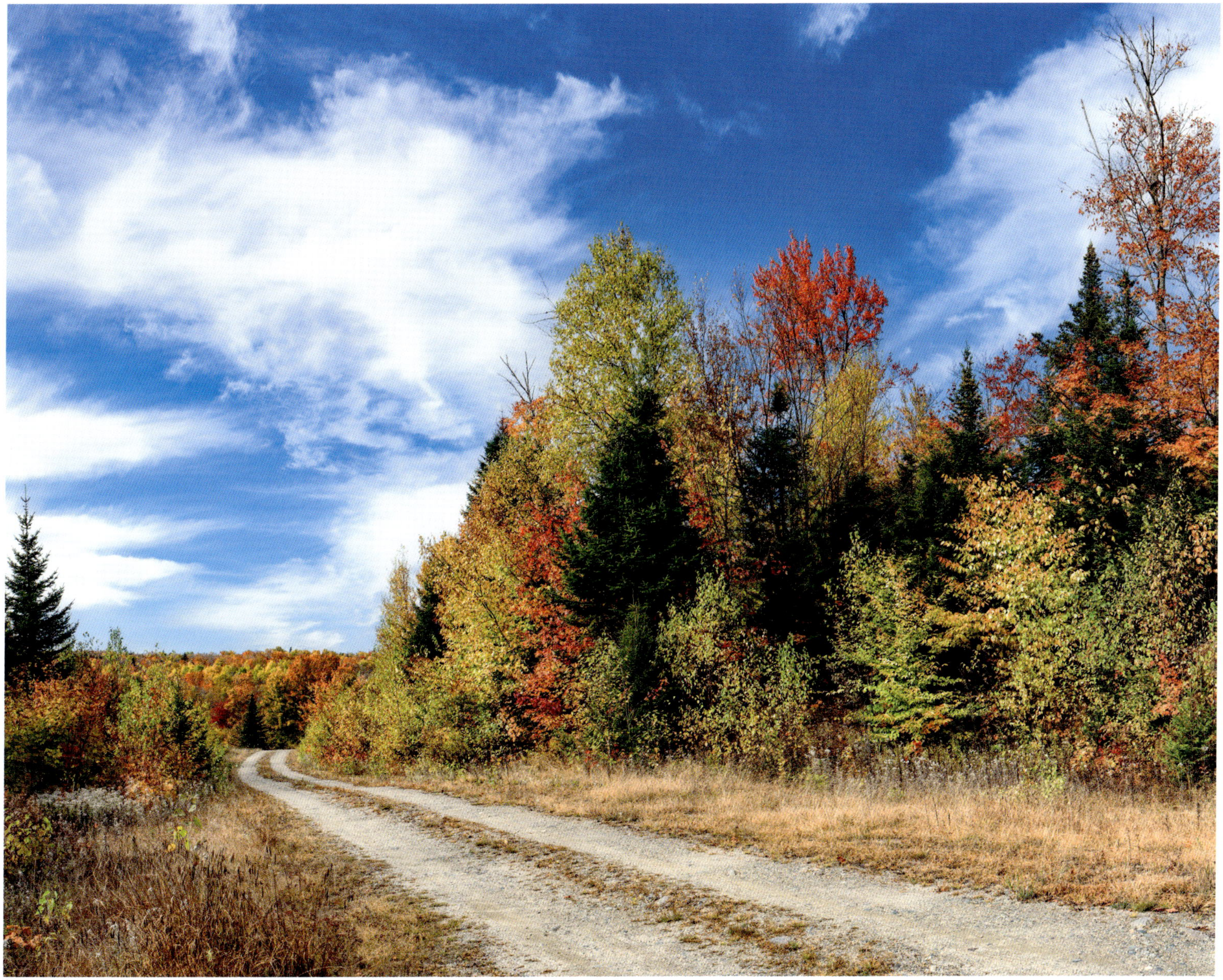

Logging road, Franklin County, Maine

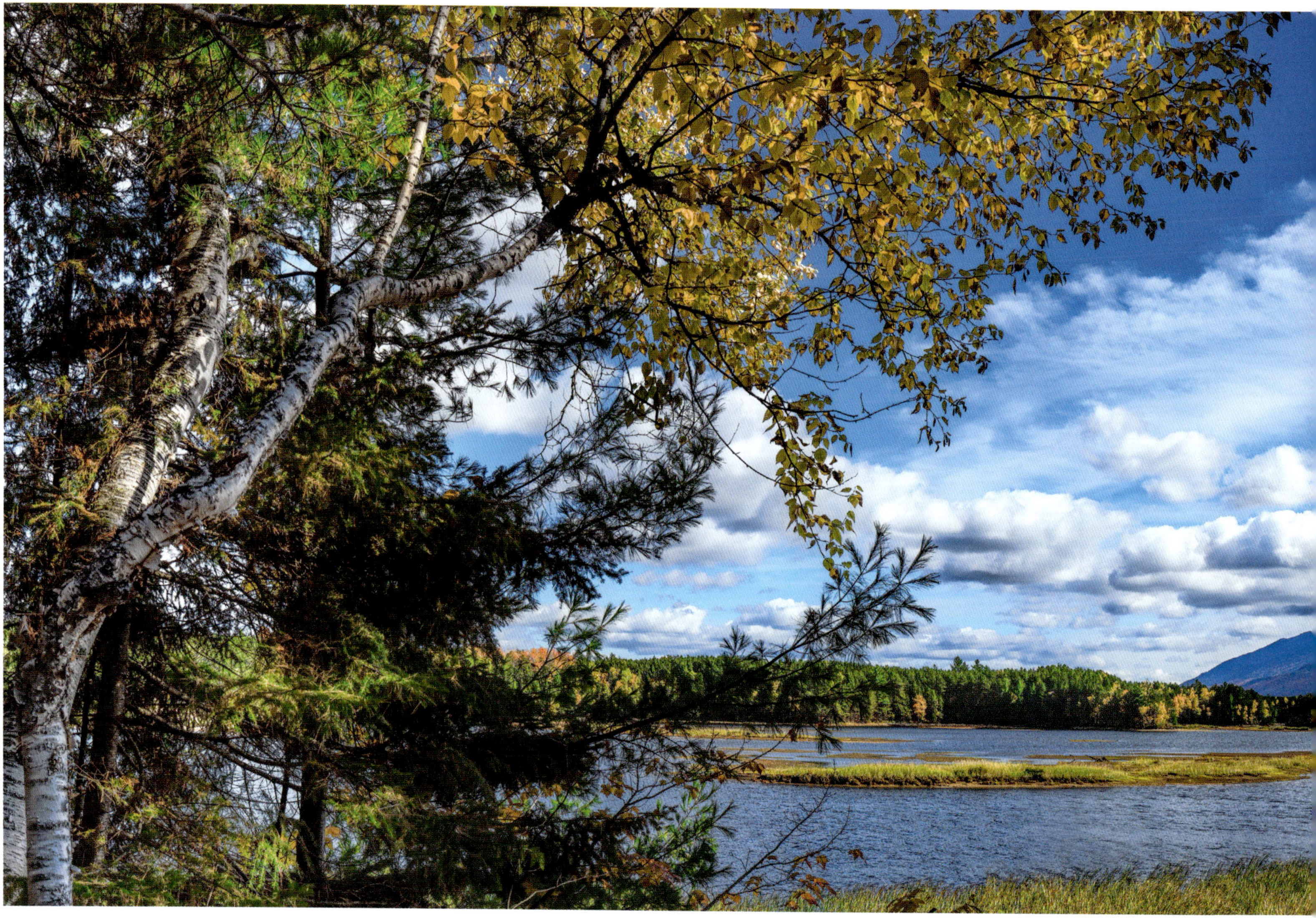

Flagstaff Lake and the Bigelow Mountains, Maine

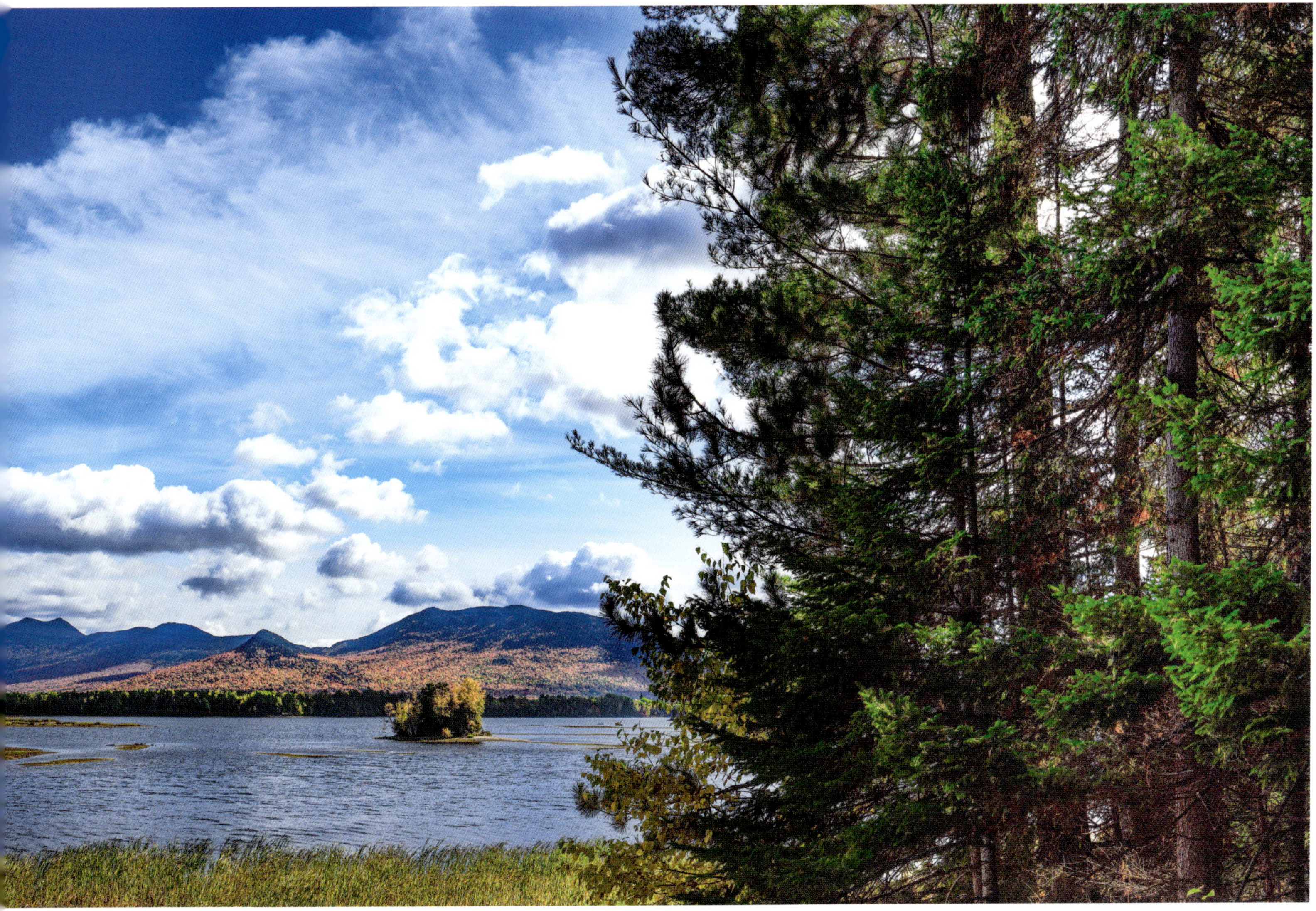

I pulled into Trout Brook Campground to check for wildlife and found this view instead.

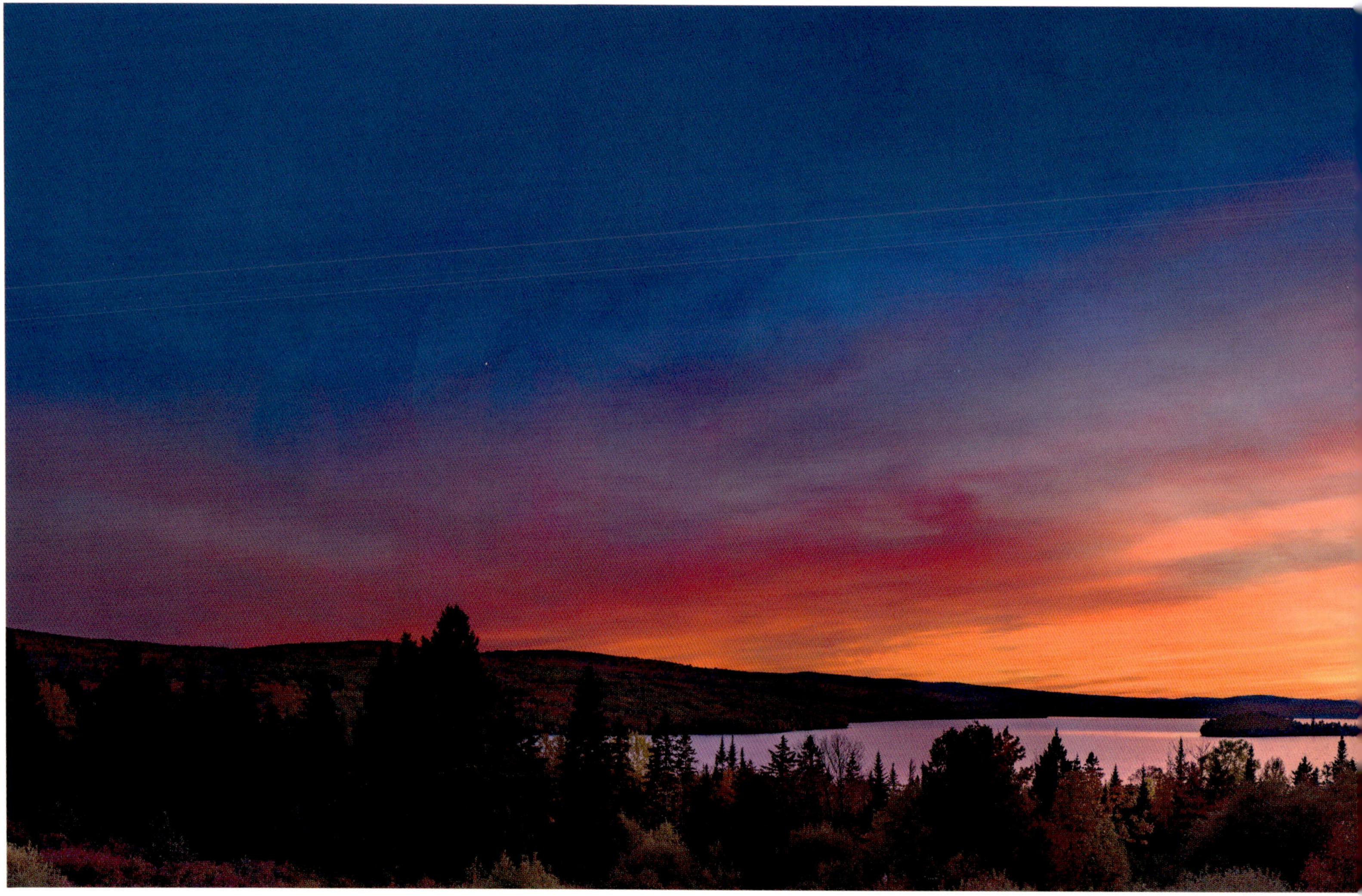

Sunset over Rangeley Lake, Franklin County, Maine

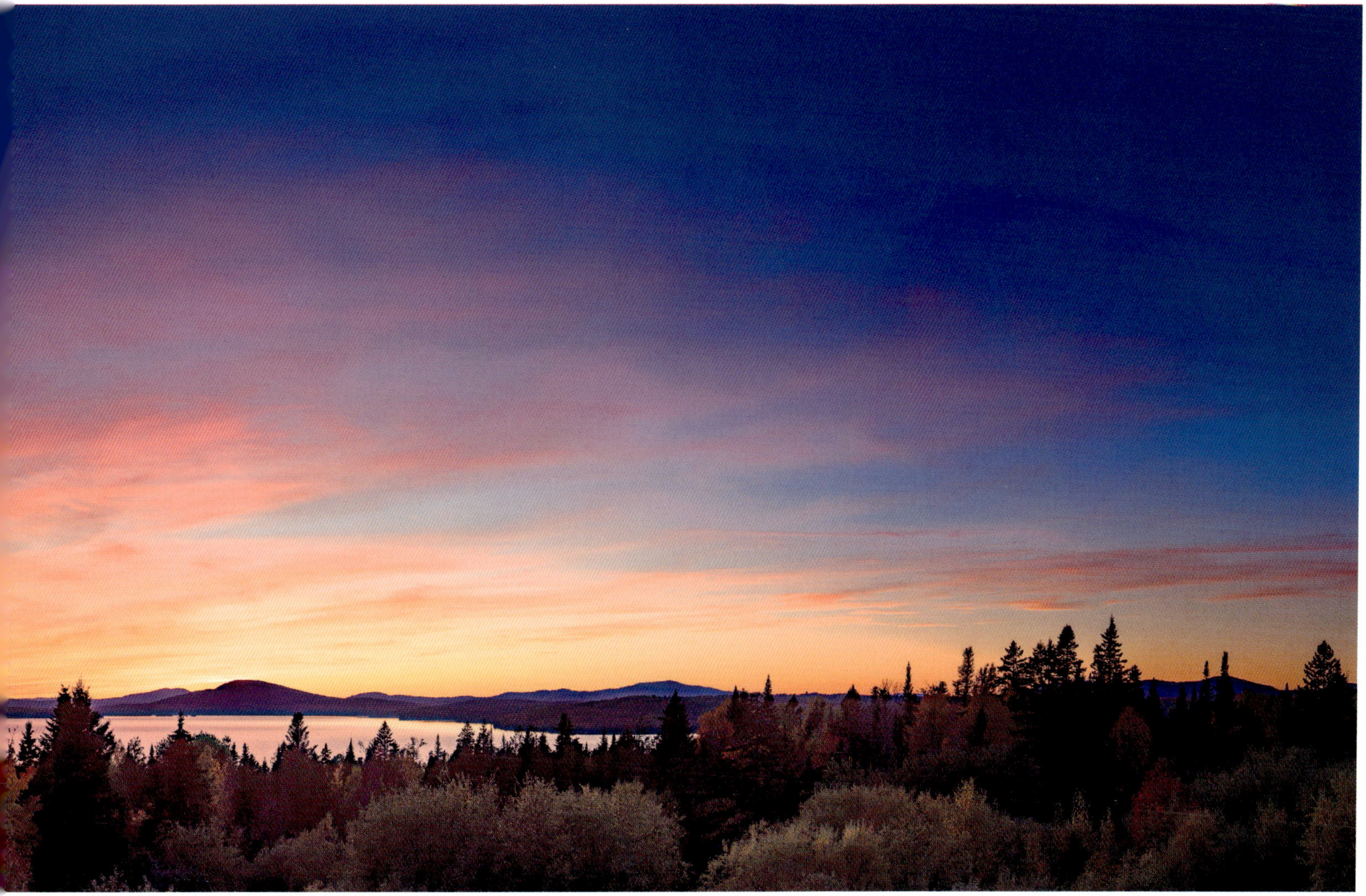

This sunset seemed to go on forever. It kept getting better and better. There were some other people standing around watching. We were all clapping and cheering.

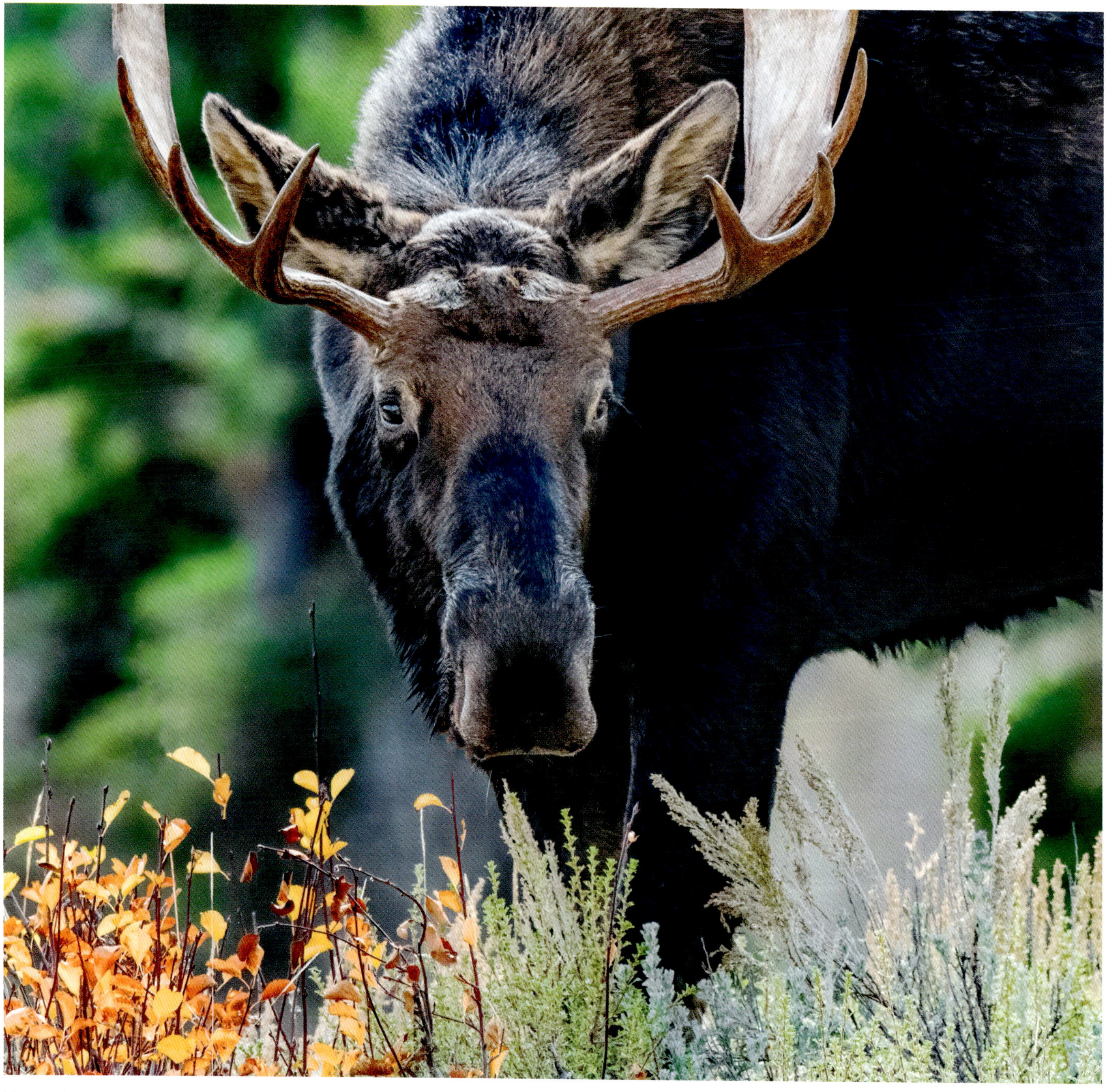

Moose, logging road, Maine

I searched for days to find a moose, then I rounded a curve and he was just there.

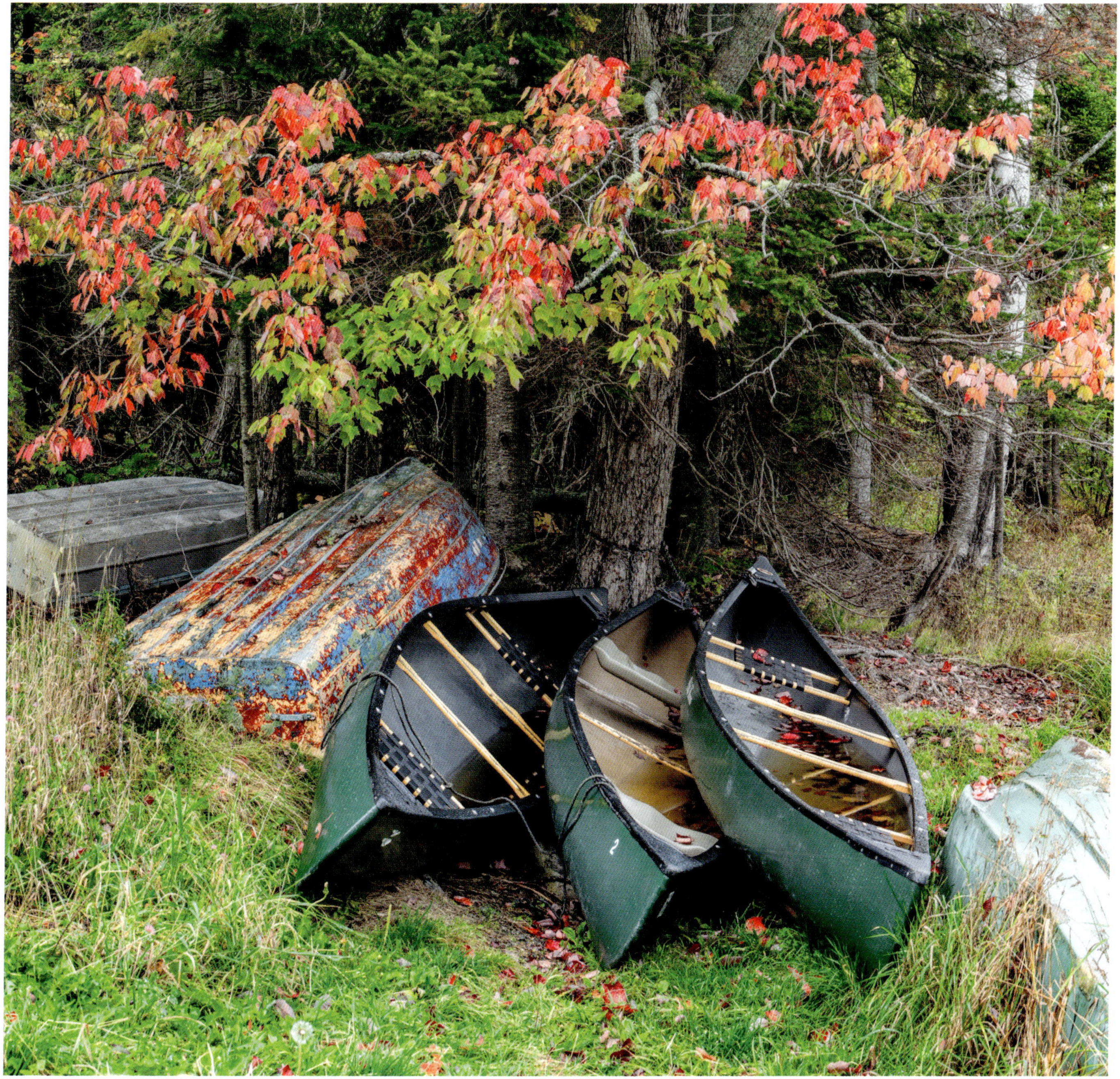

Red maple tree and boats at Prong Pond, Maine

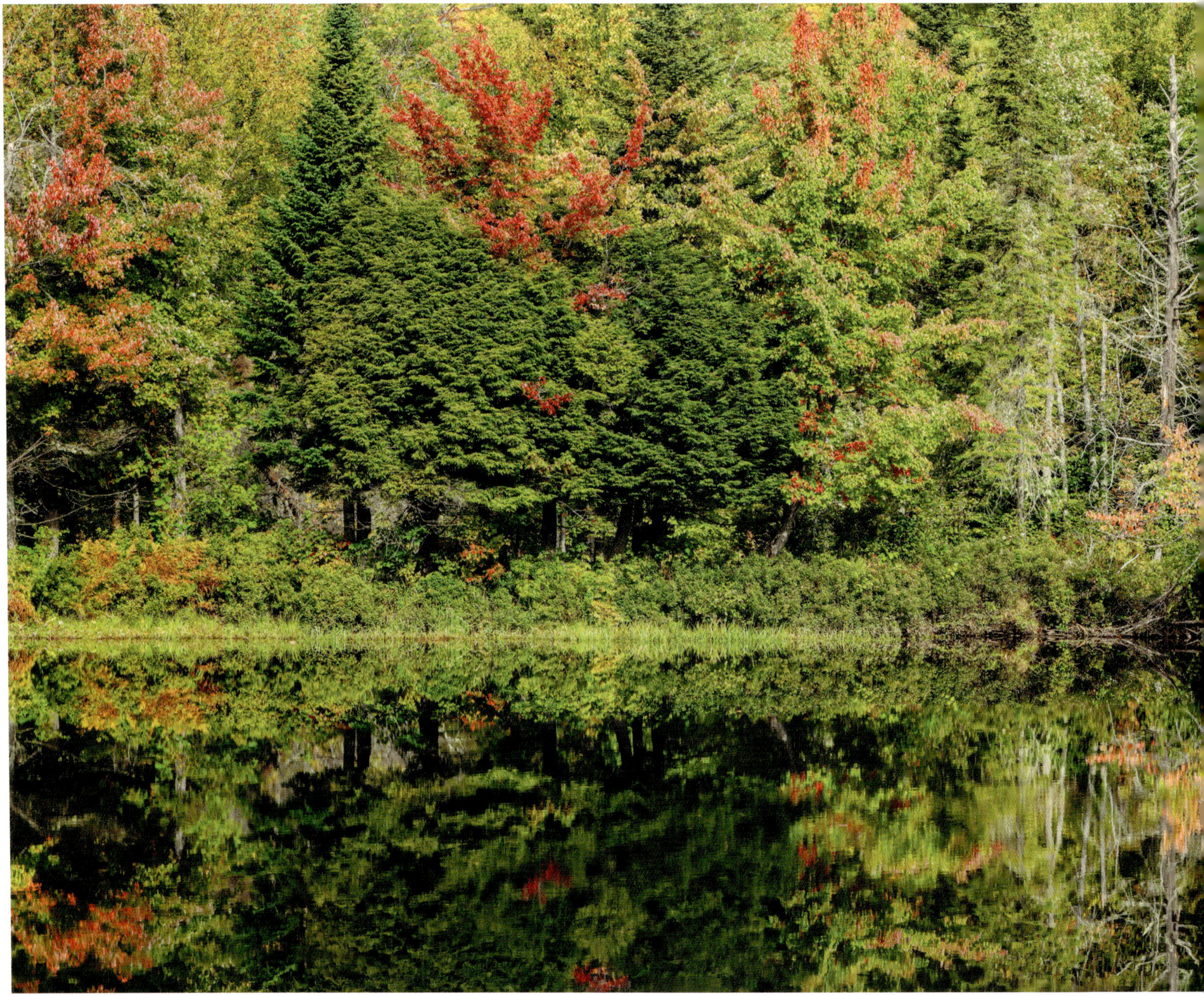

Fall reflection, Kingsbury Stream, Maine

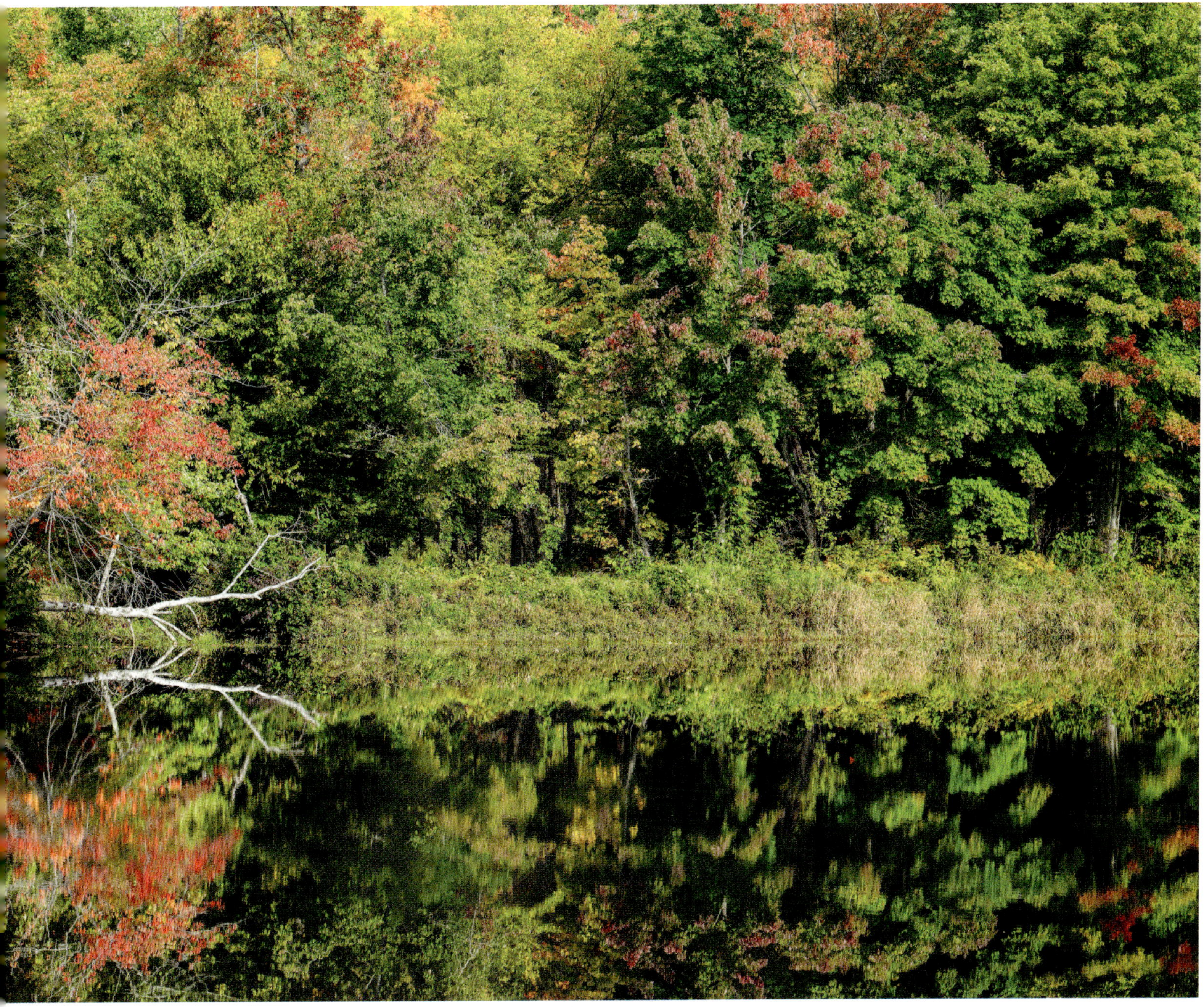

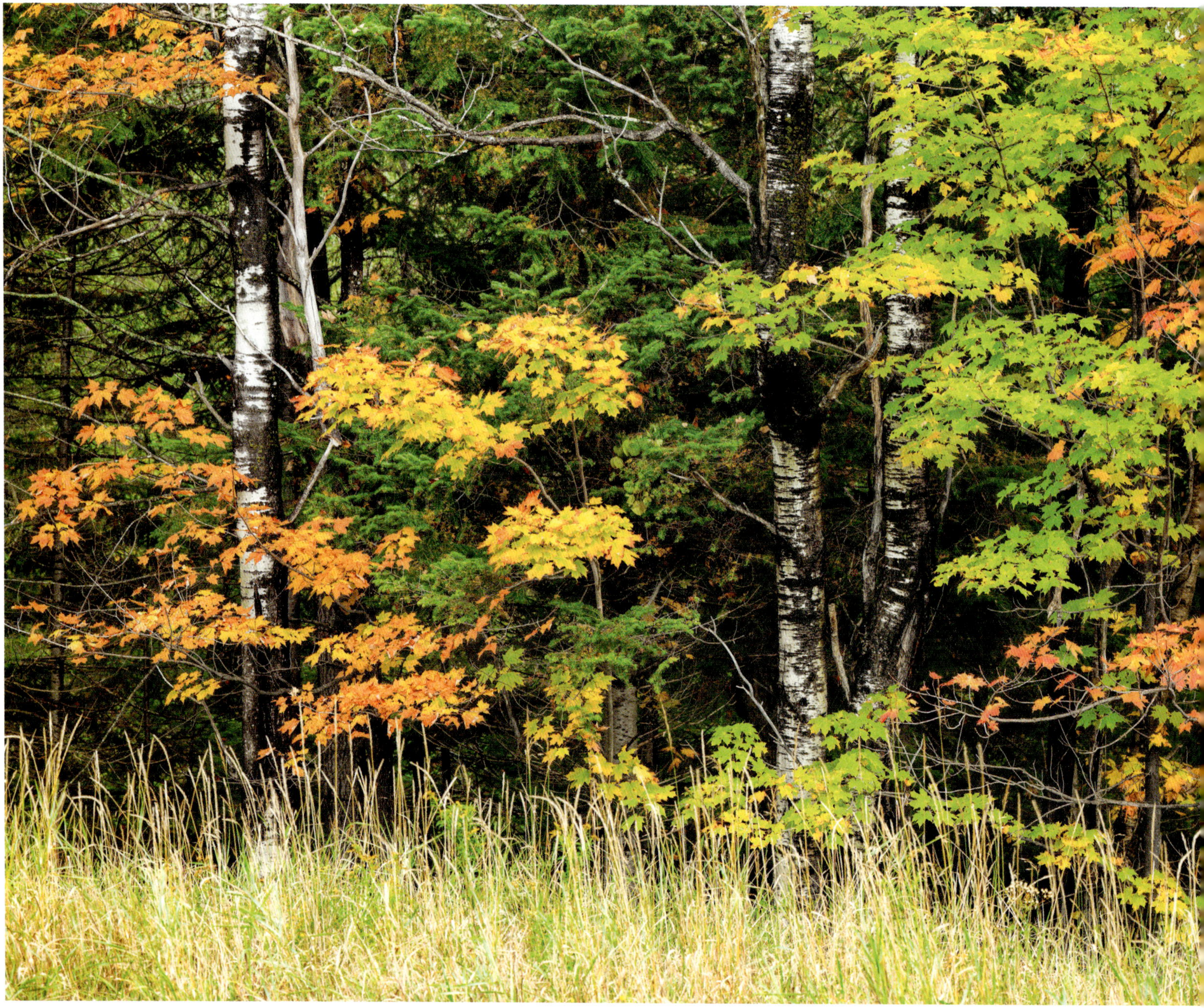

Birch and sugar maple trees along Maine State Highway 201

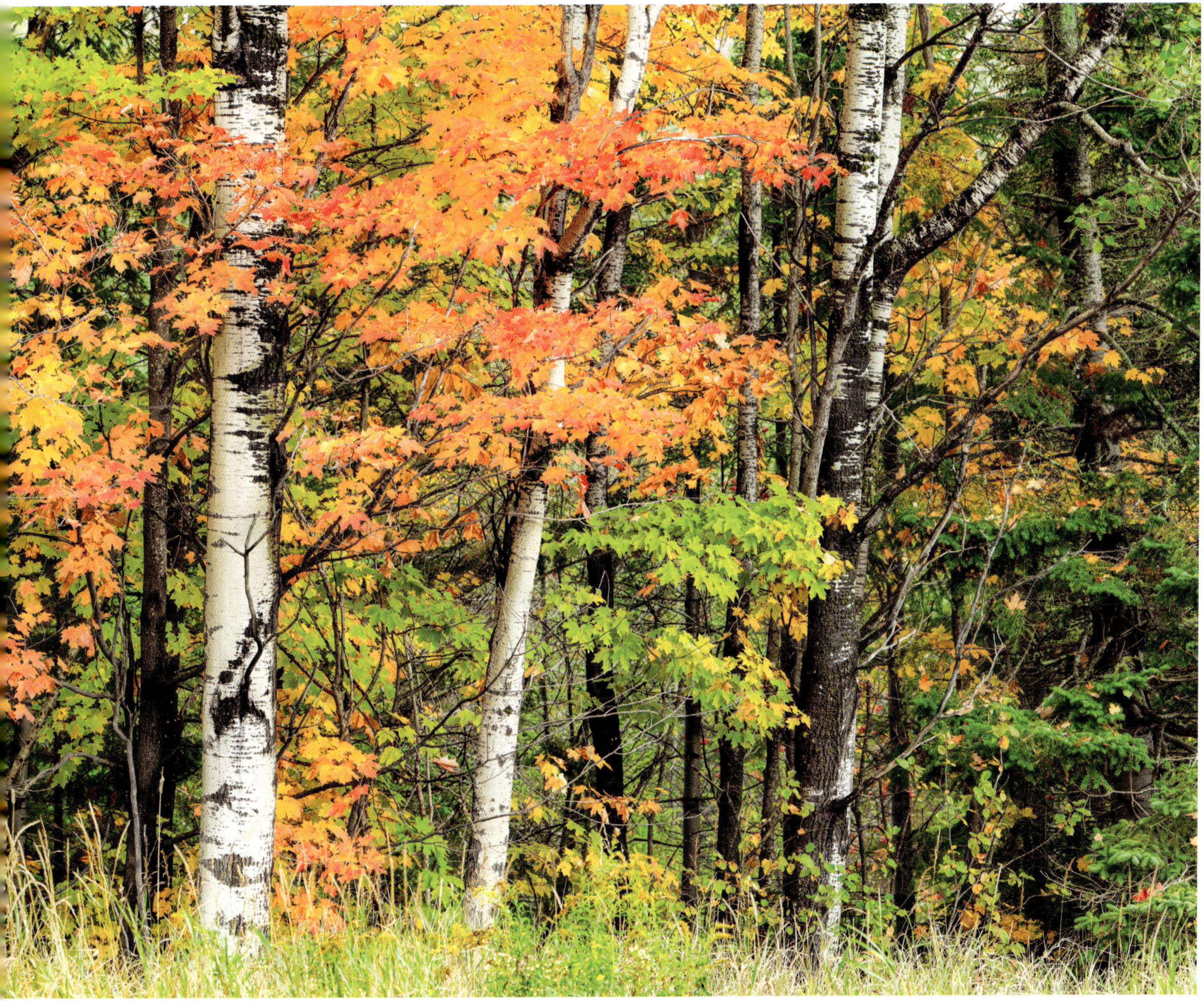

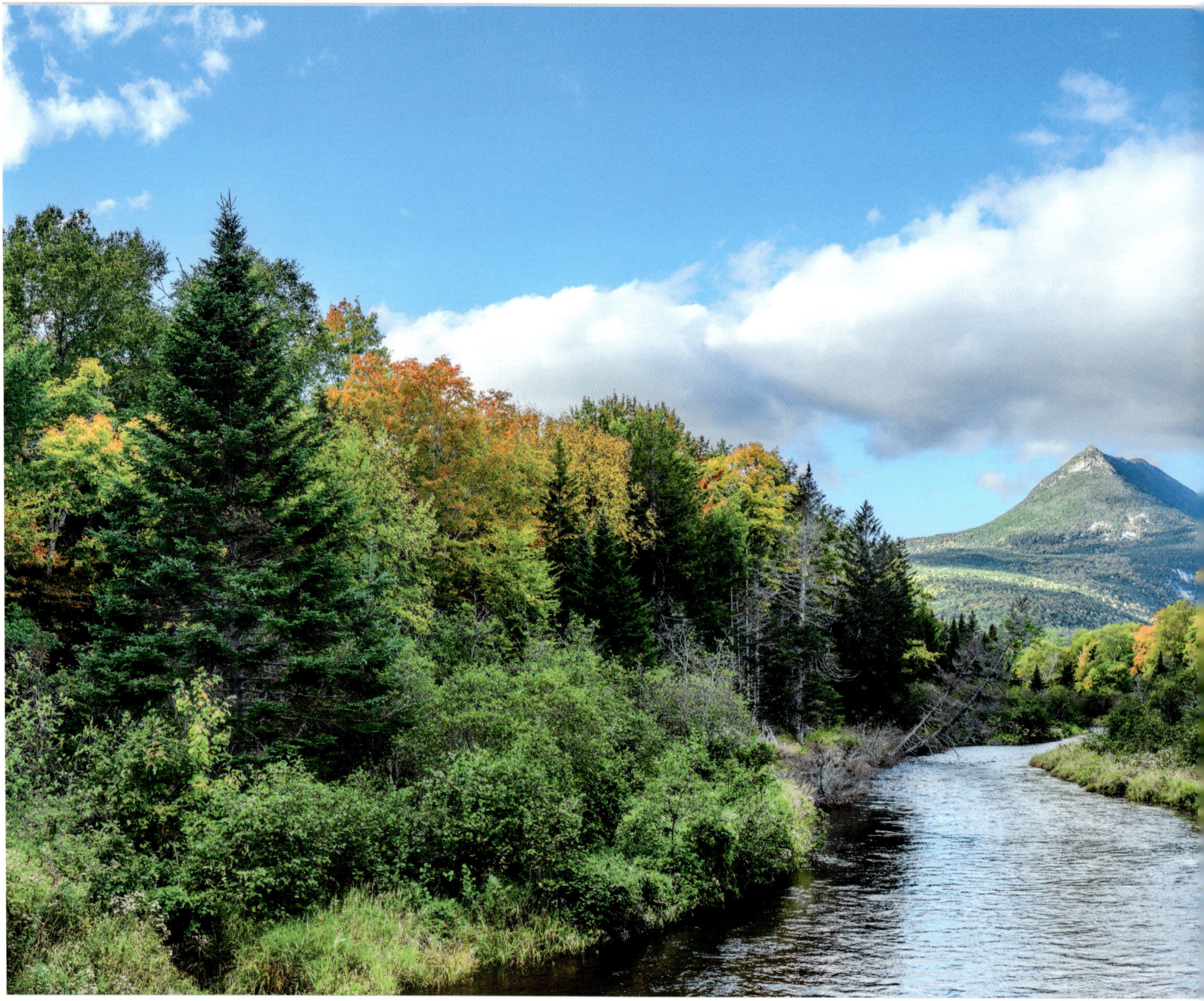

Double Top Mountain, Baxter State Park, Maine

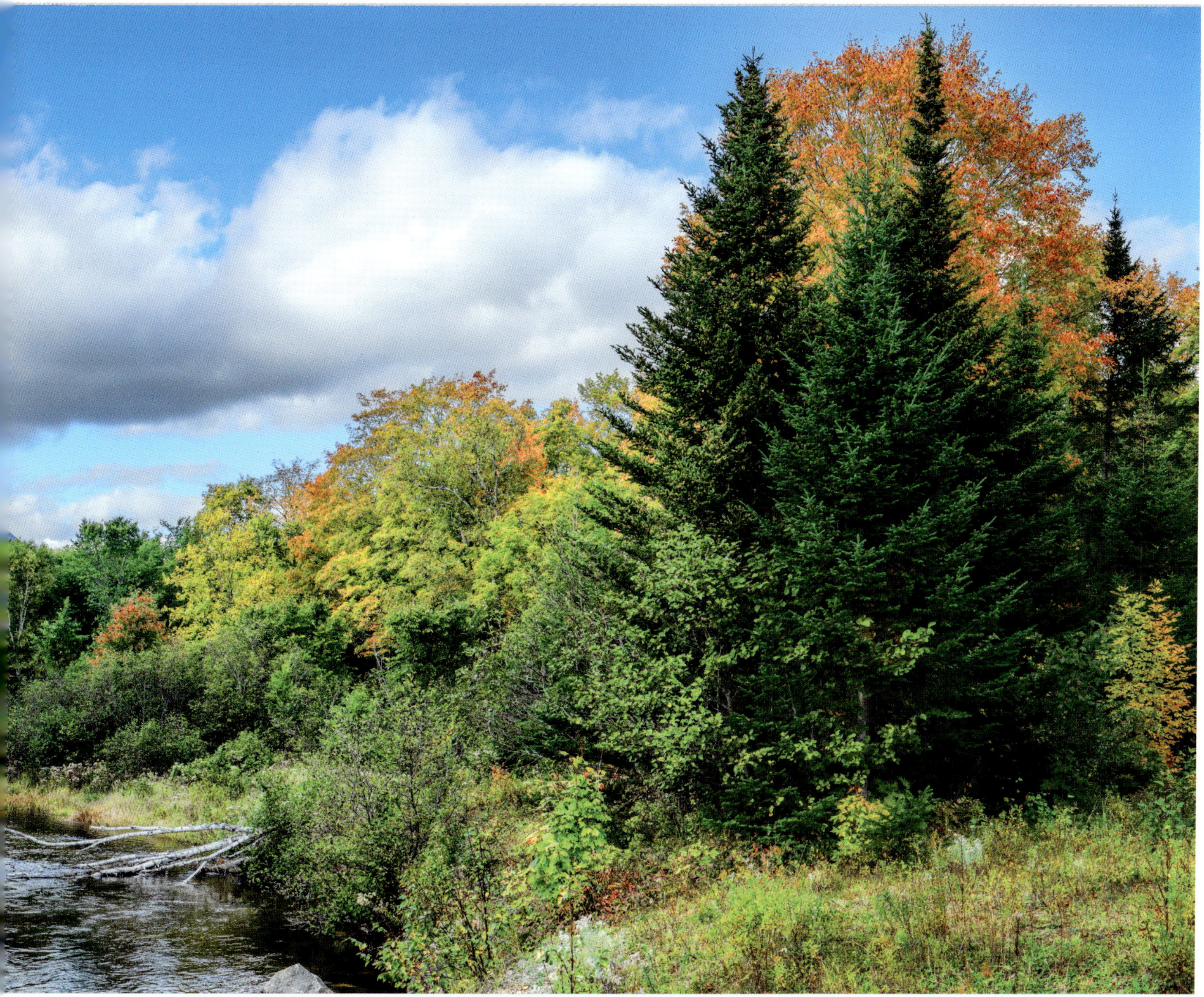

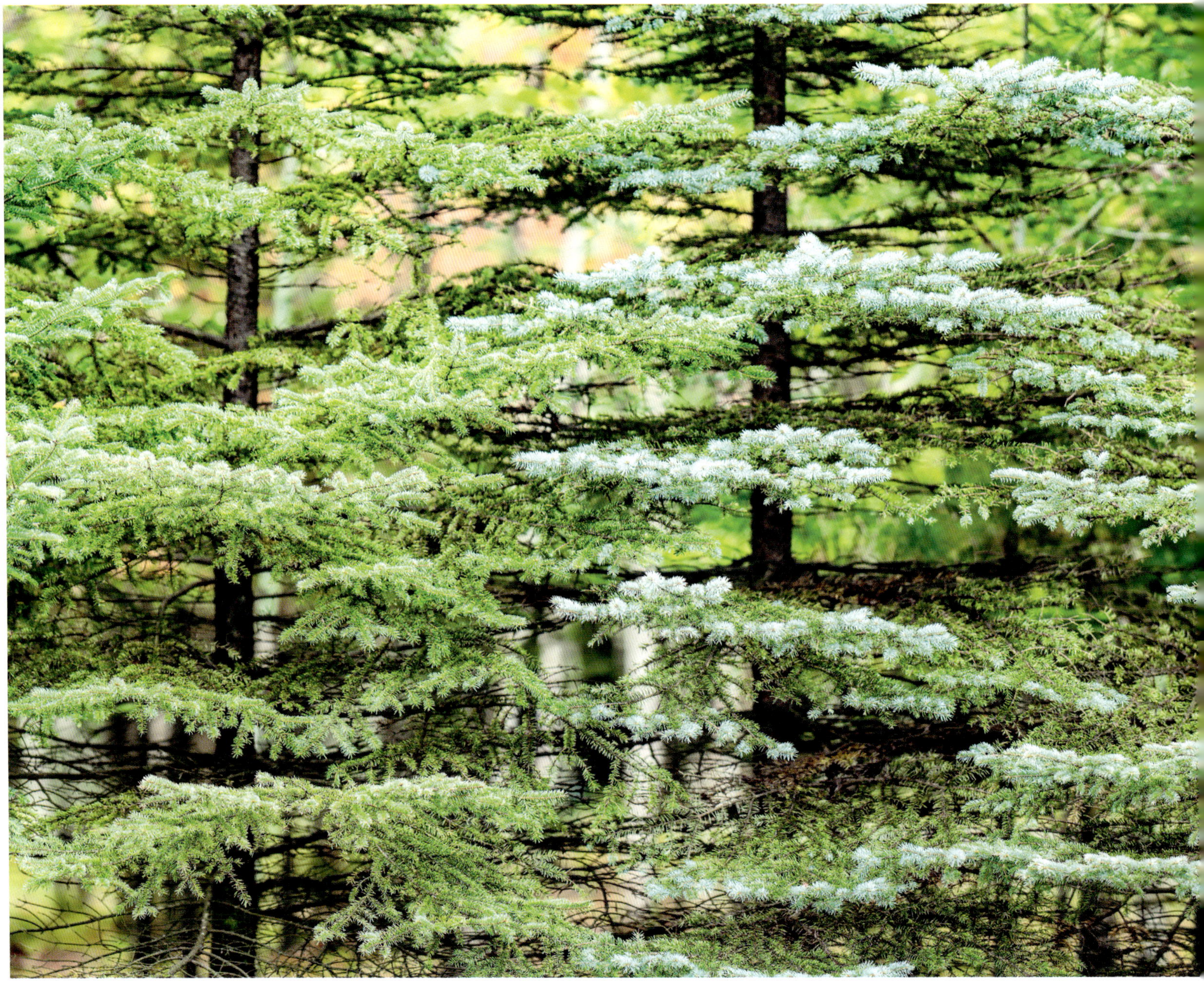

Blue spruce trees on Kineo Drive, Maine

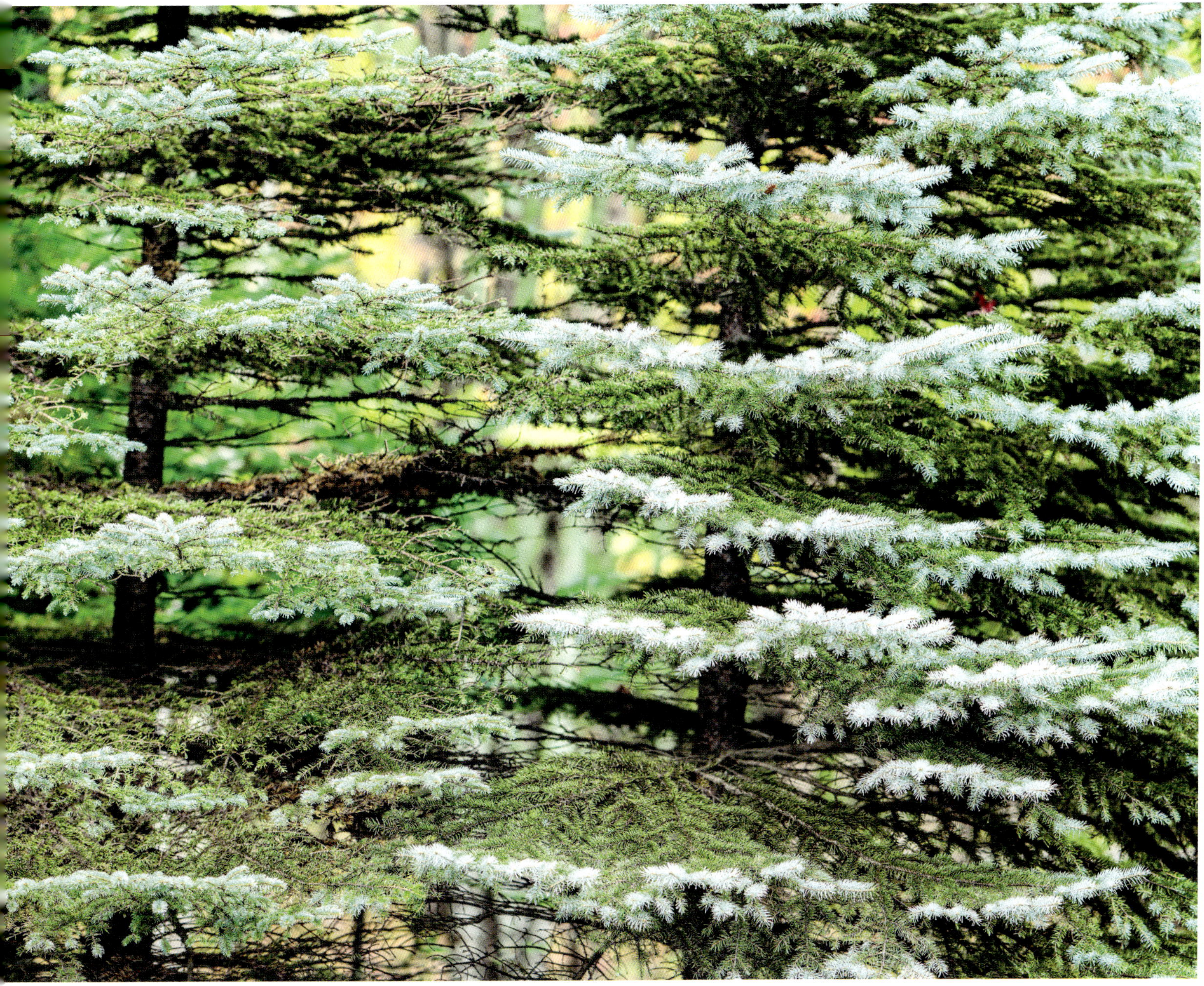

I call this an "underwater" shot because it sort of looks like you're underwater. I've taken many photos like this one, all over the country, of different types of trees.

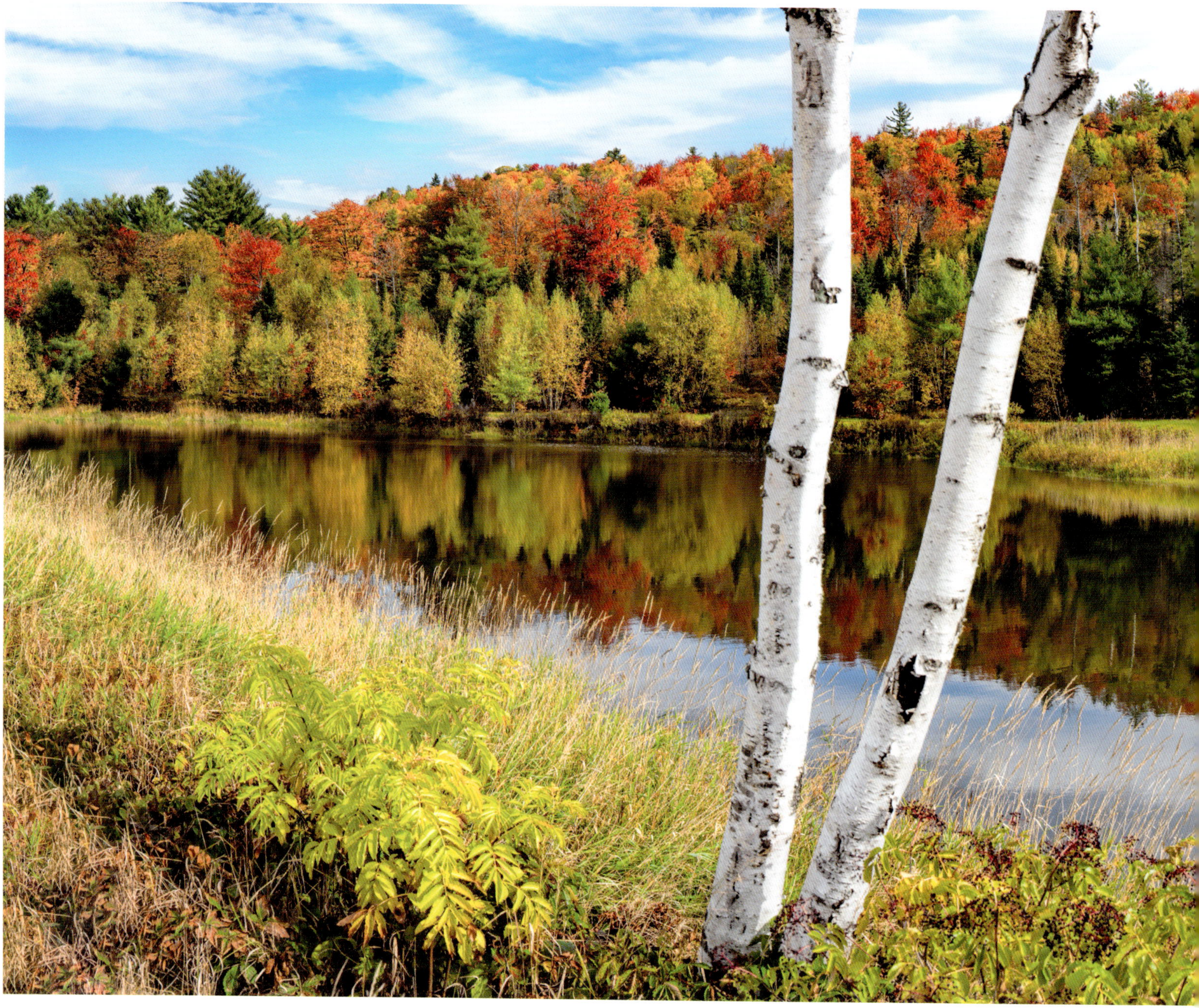

Pond and birch trunks, Roxbury, Maine

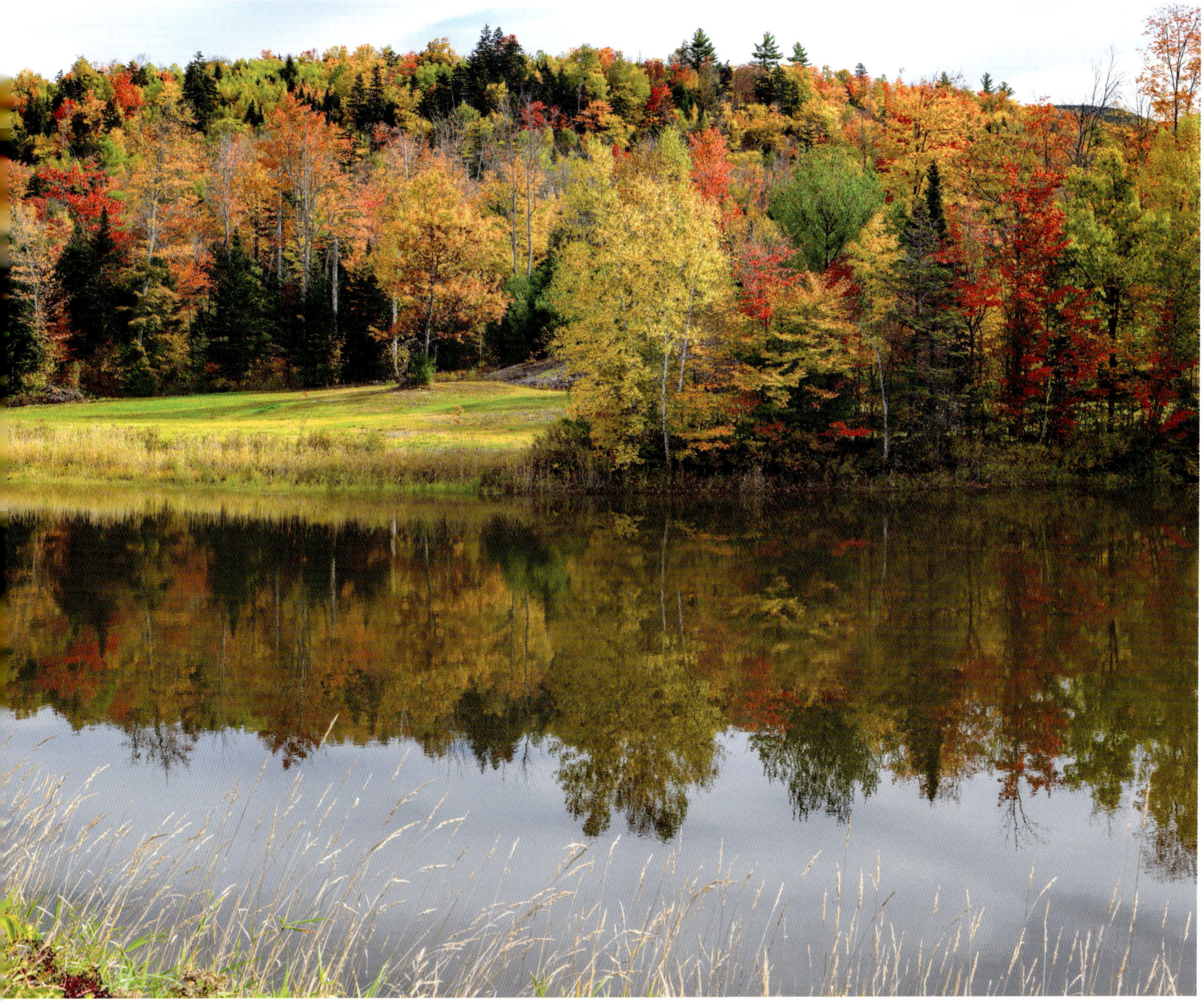

Morning mist on First Roach Pond, Kokadjo, Maine

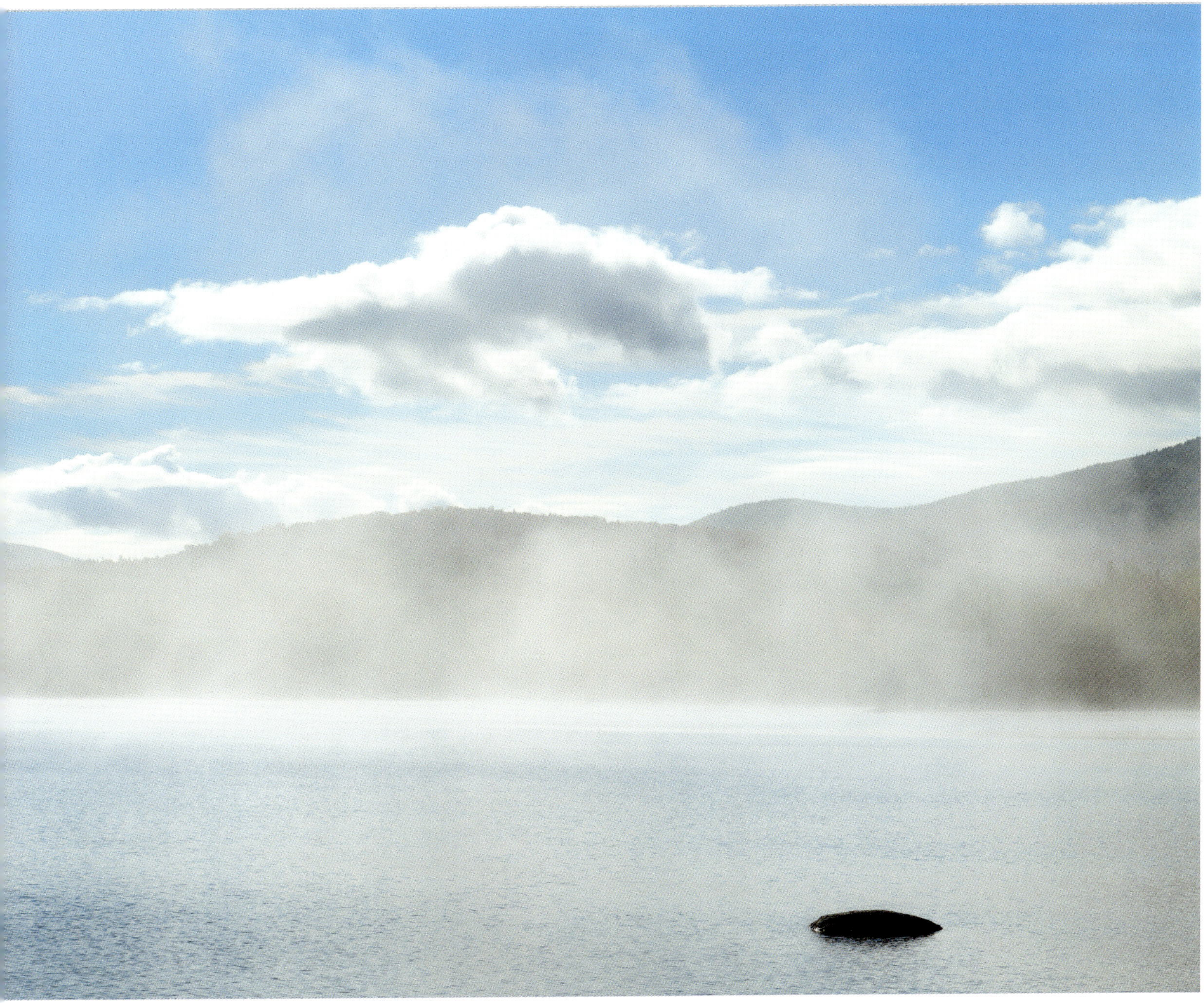

If you're wondering, that's just a rock. I was lucky it was in the right spot.

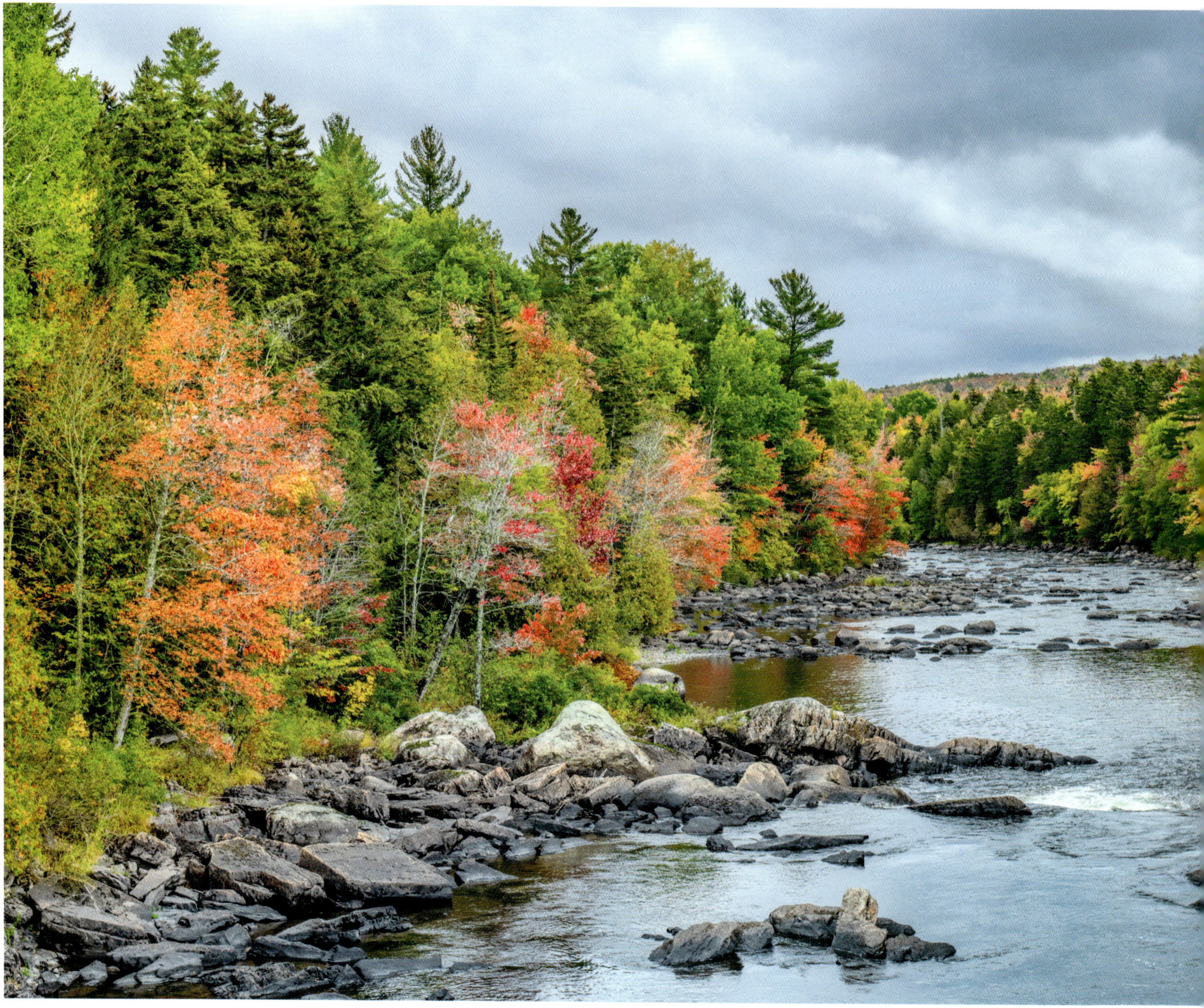

Otter Pond, Maine

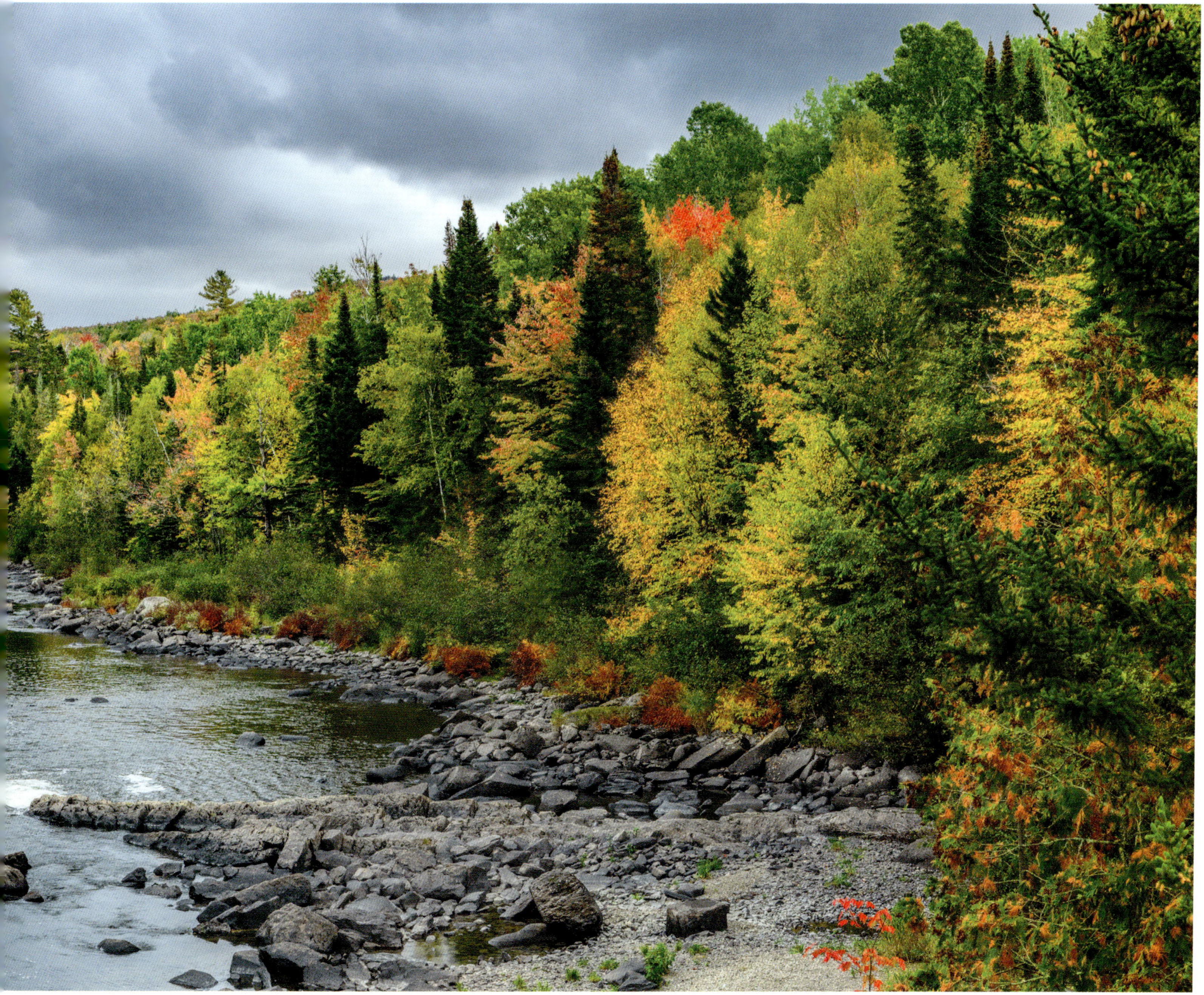

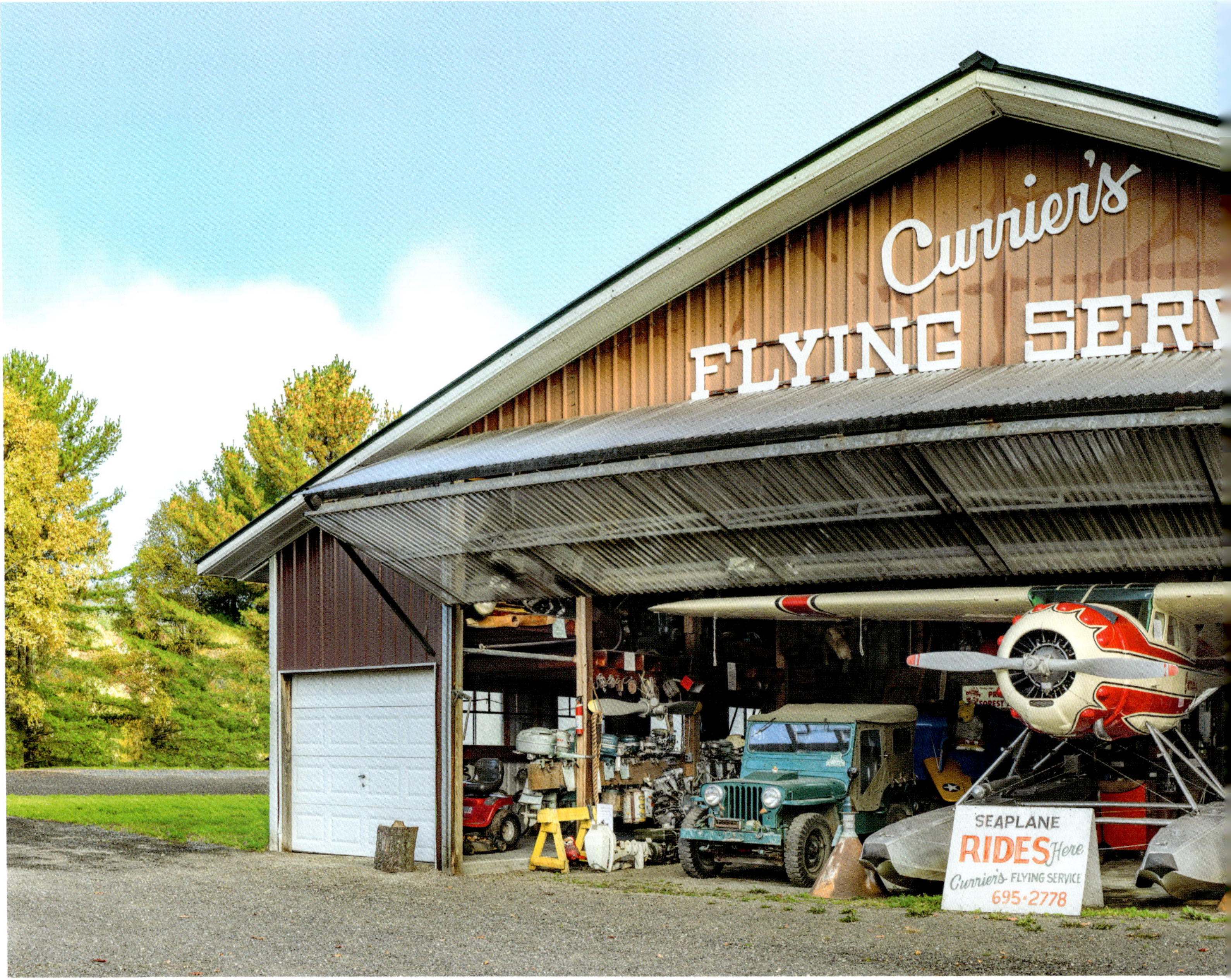

Currier's Flying Service, Greenville, Maine

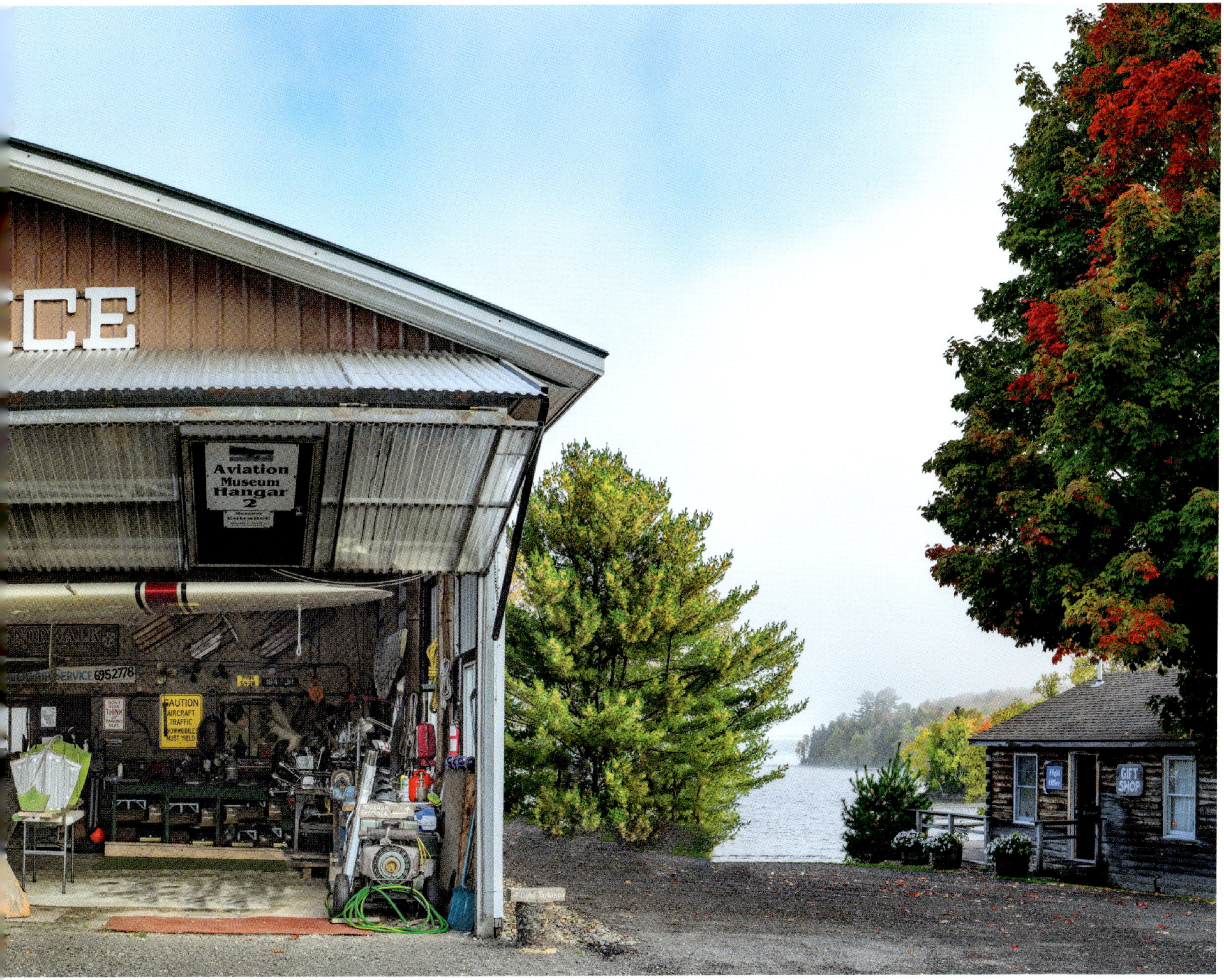

There was too much fog and I had to move on. Next time I'm going to take a ride!

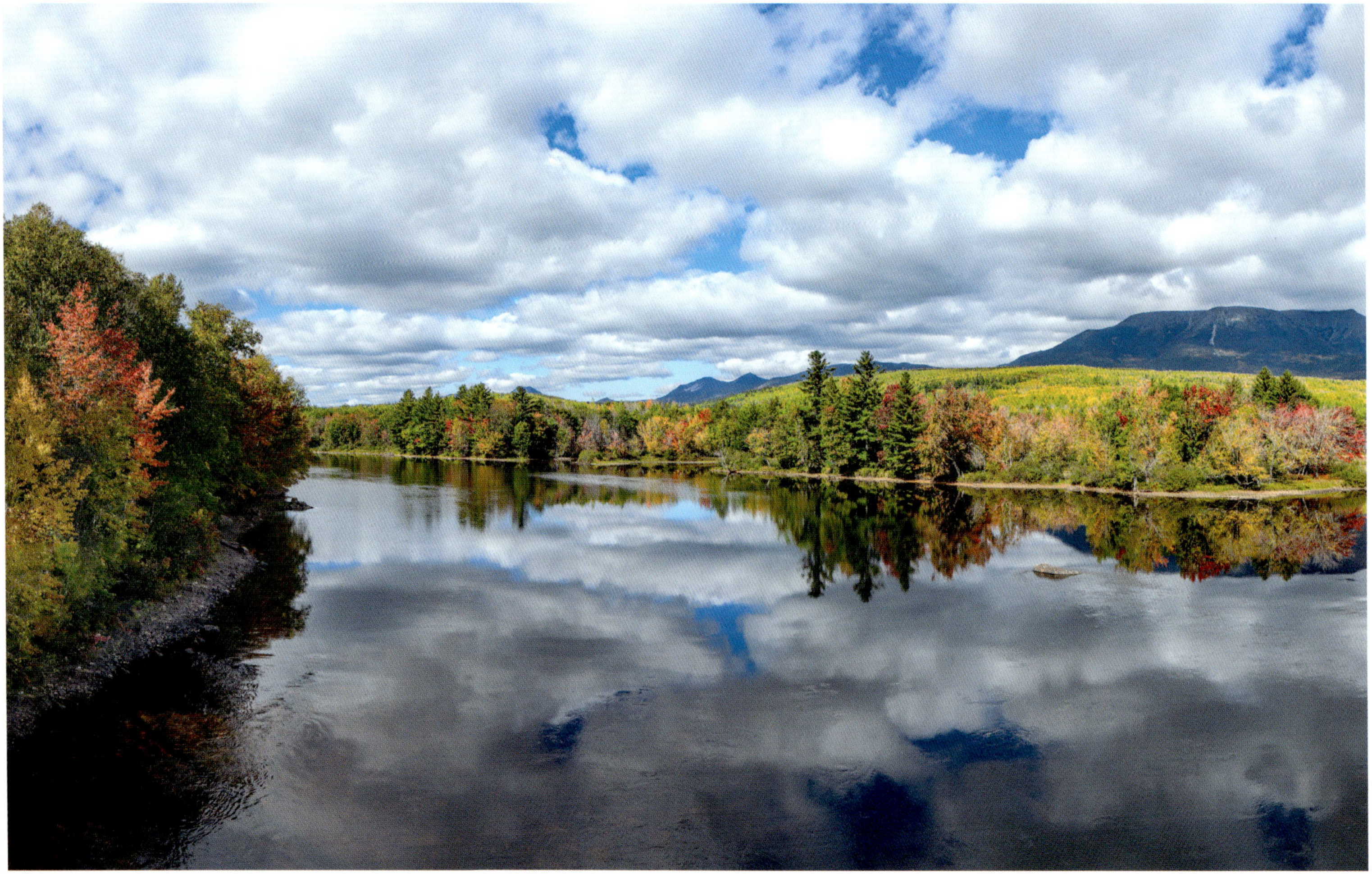

Mount Katahdin and Abol Stream, Maine

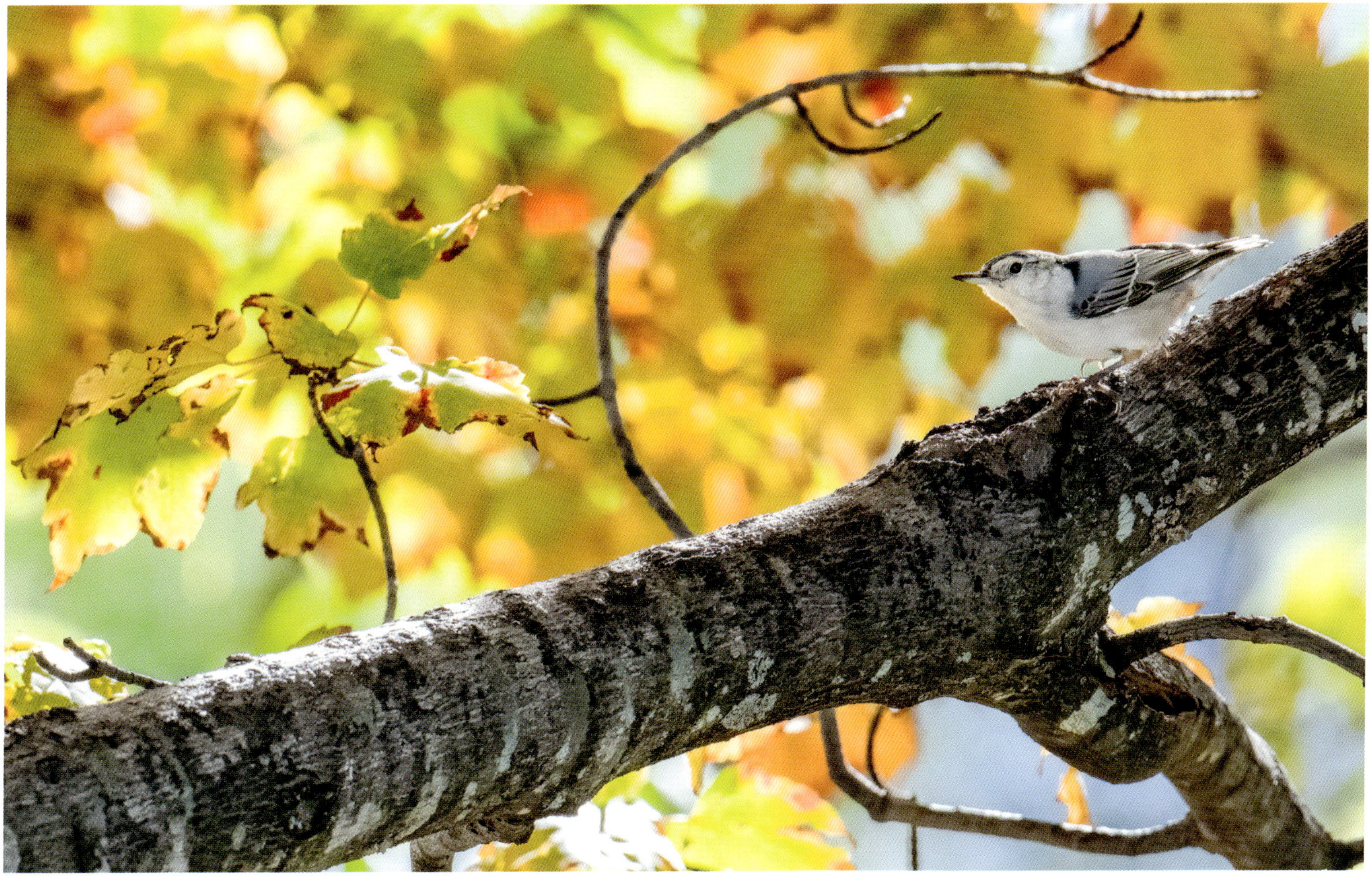

White-breasted nuthatch in red maple tree, Maine

Thanks to a nice guy named Frances, who let me trespass on his property to get this photo. He even brought out a book to identify the bird.

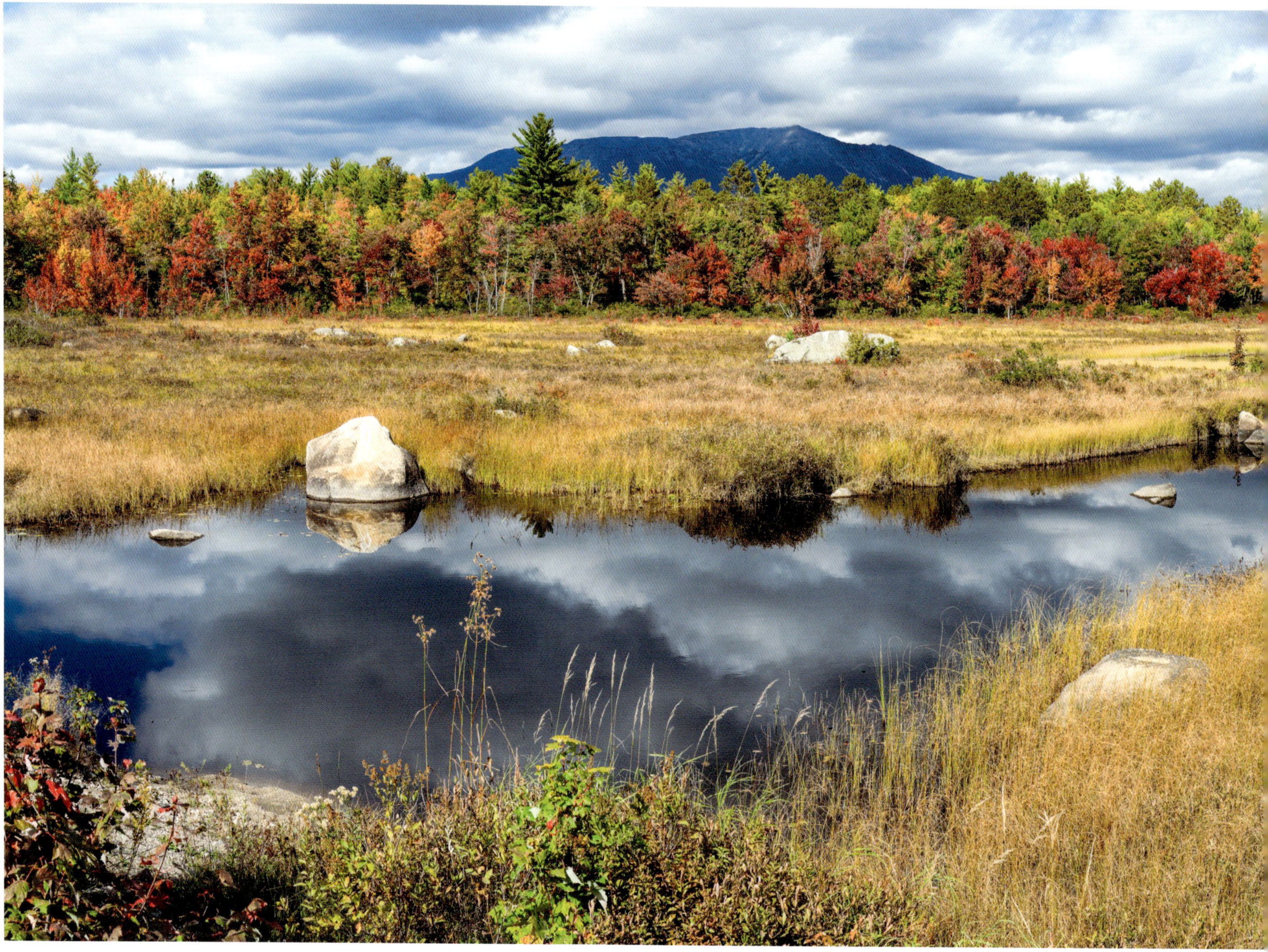

Mount Katahdin and Rainbow Lake, Maine

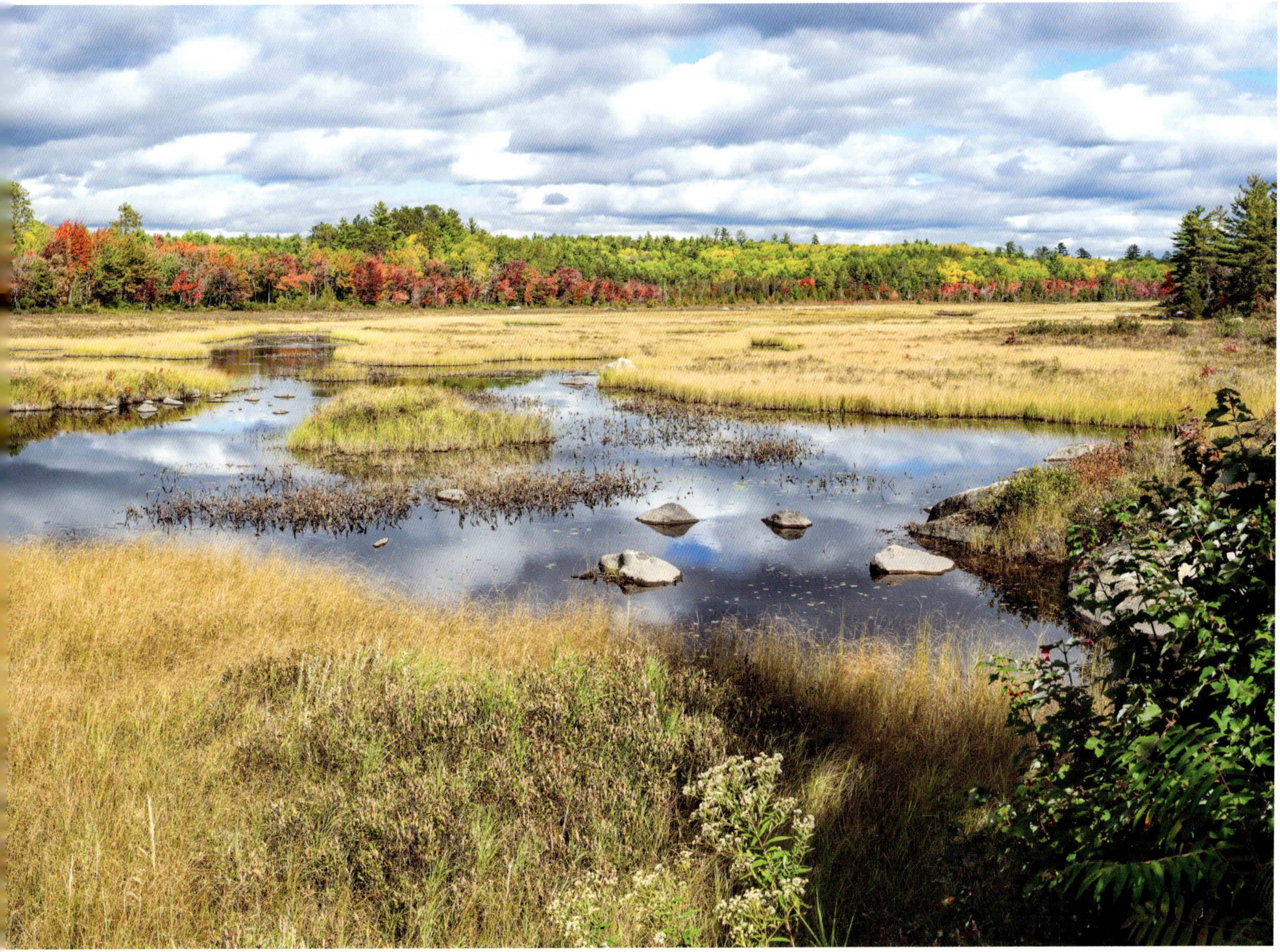

Katahdin means "the Greatest Mountain" in the language of the native Penobscot people. At an elevation of 5269 feet, it is the highest mountain in Maine.

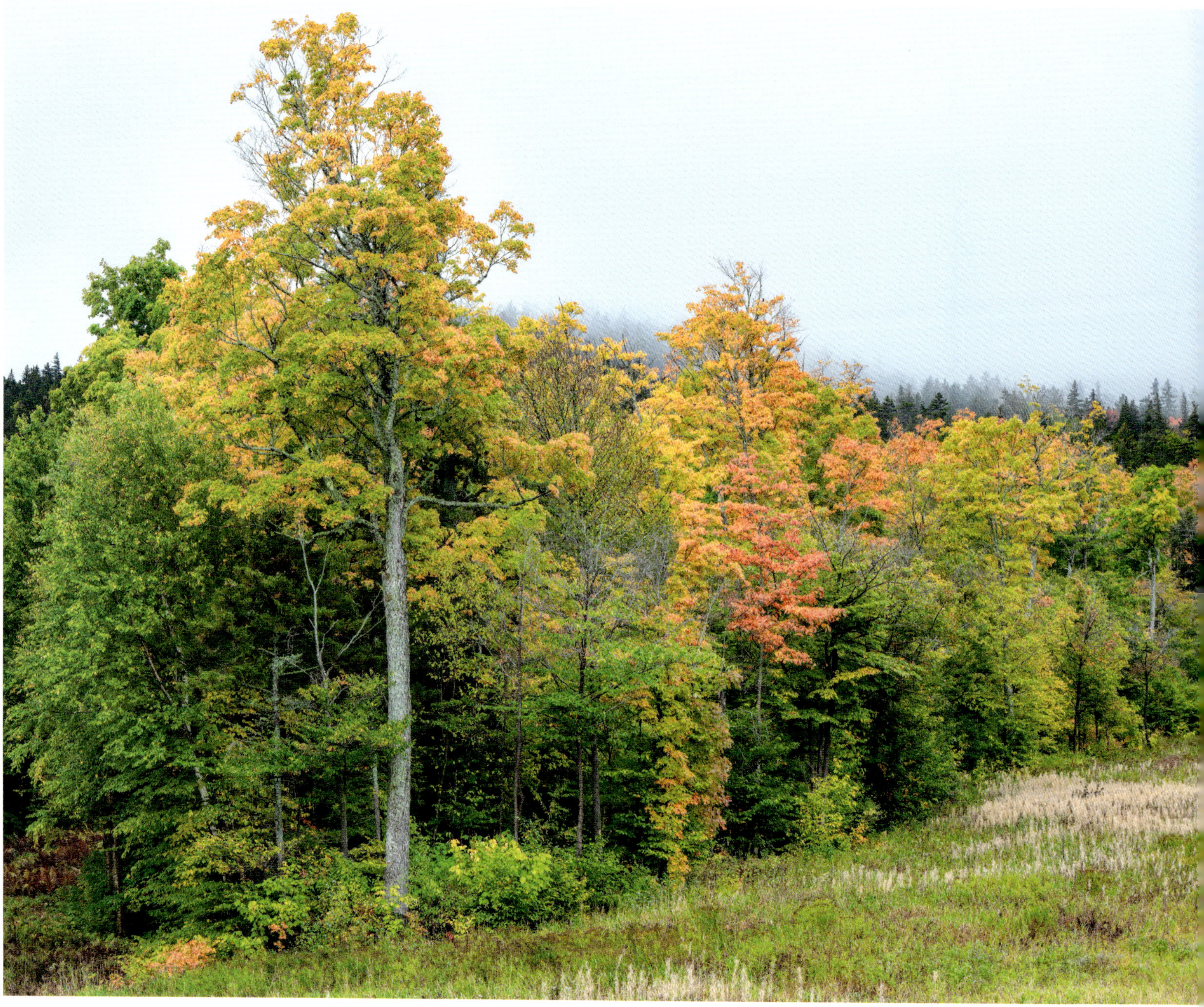

Big Squaw Mountain, Piscataquis County, Maine

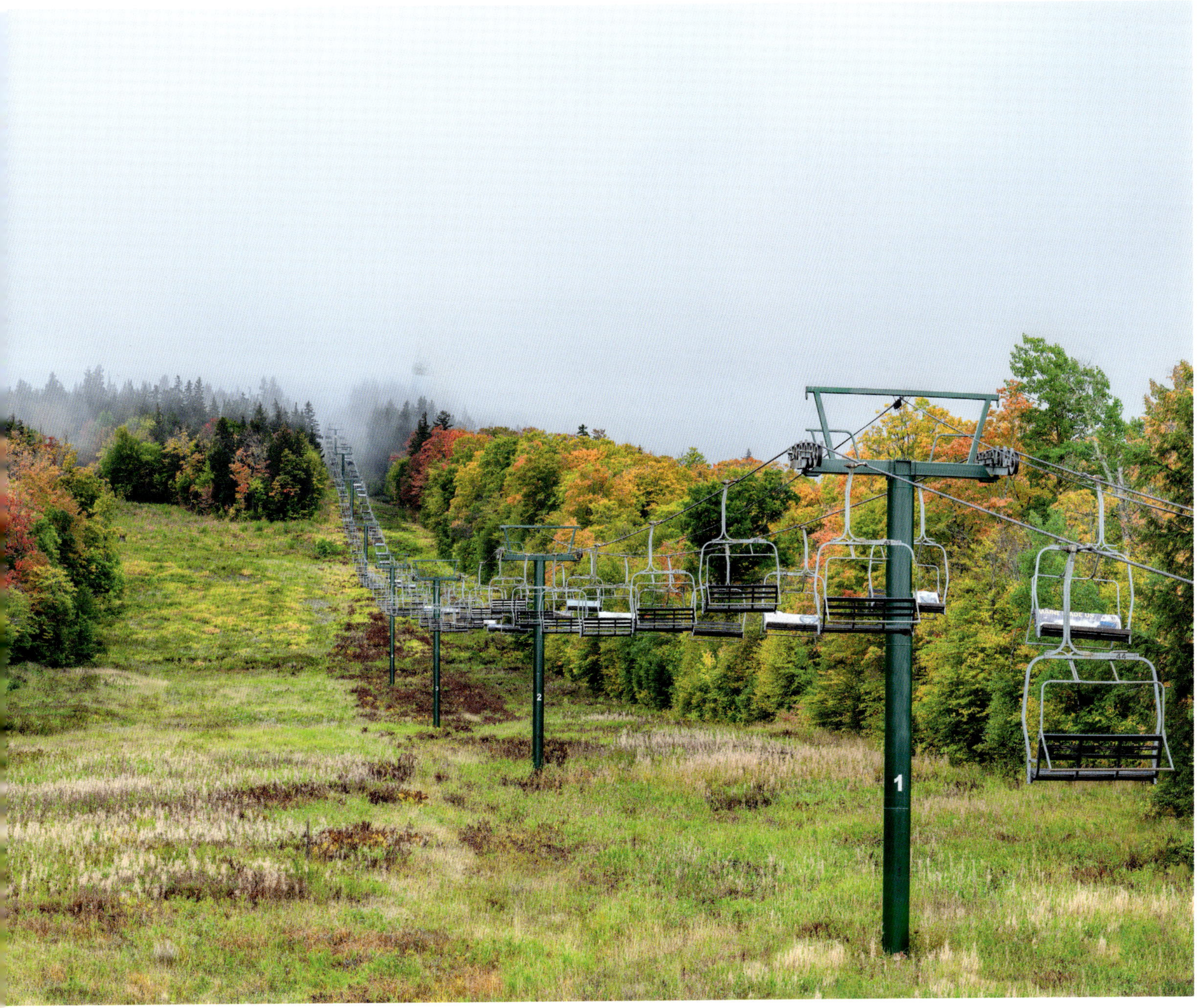

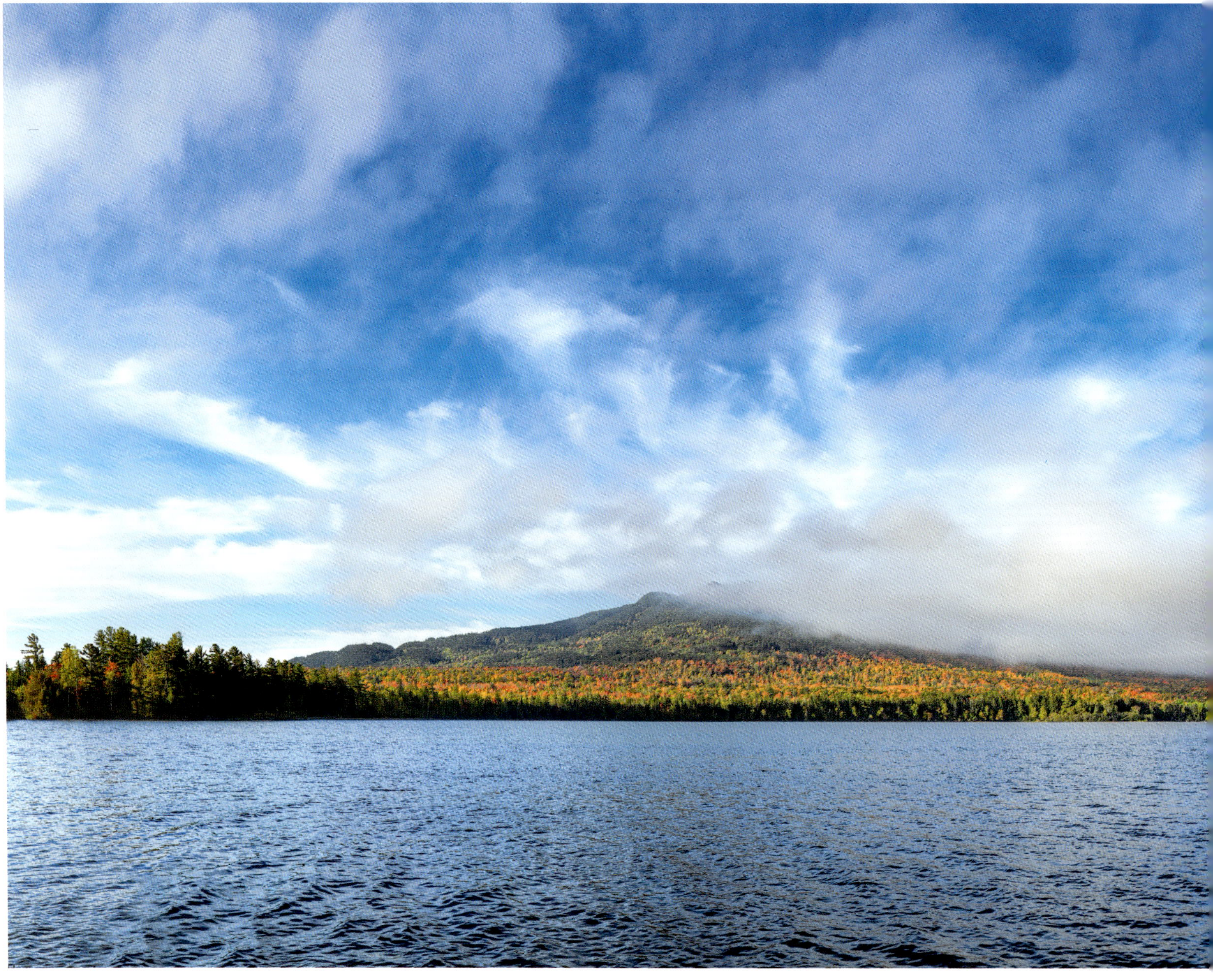

Mountain View Pond and Squaw Mountain, Maine

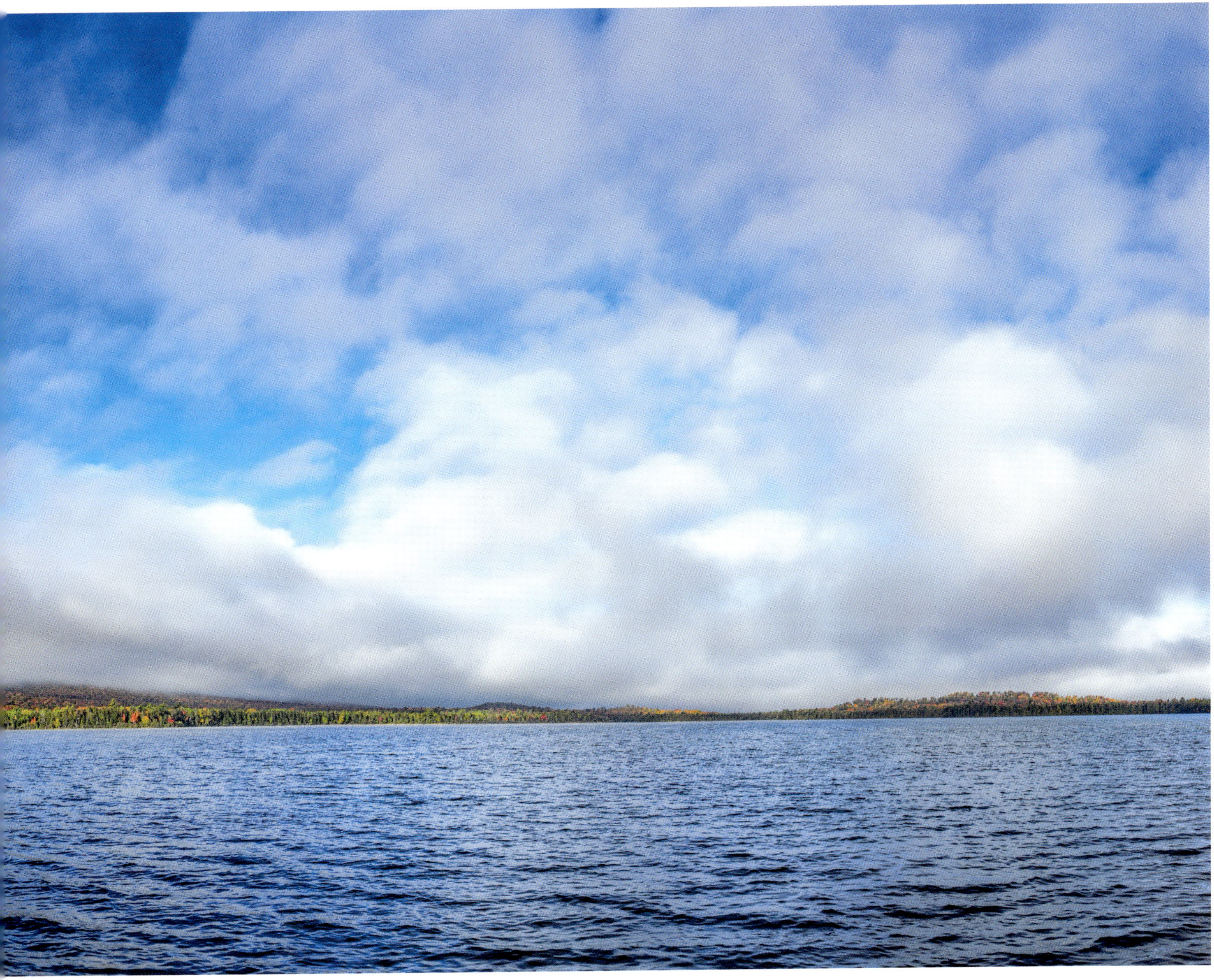

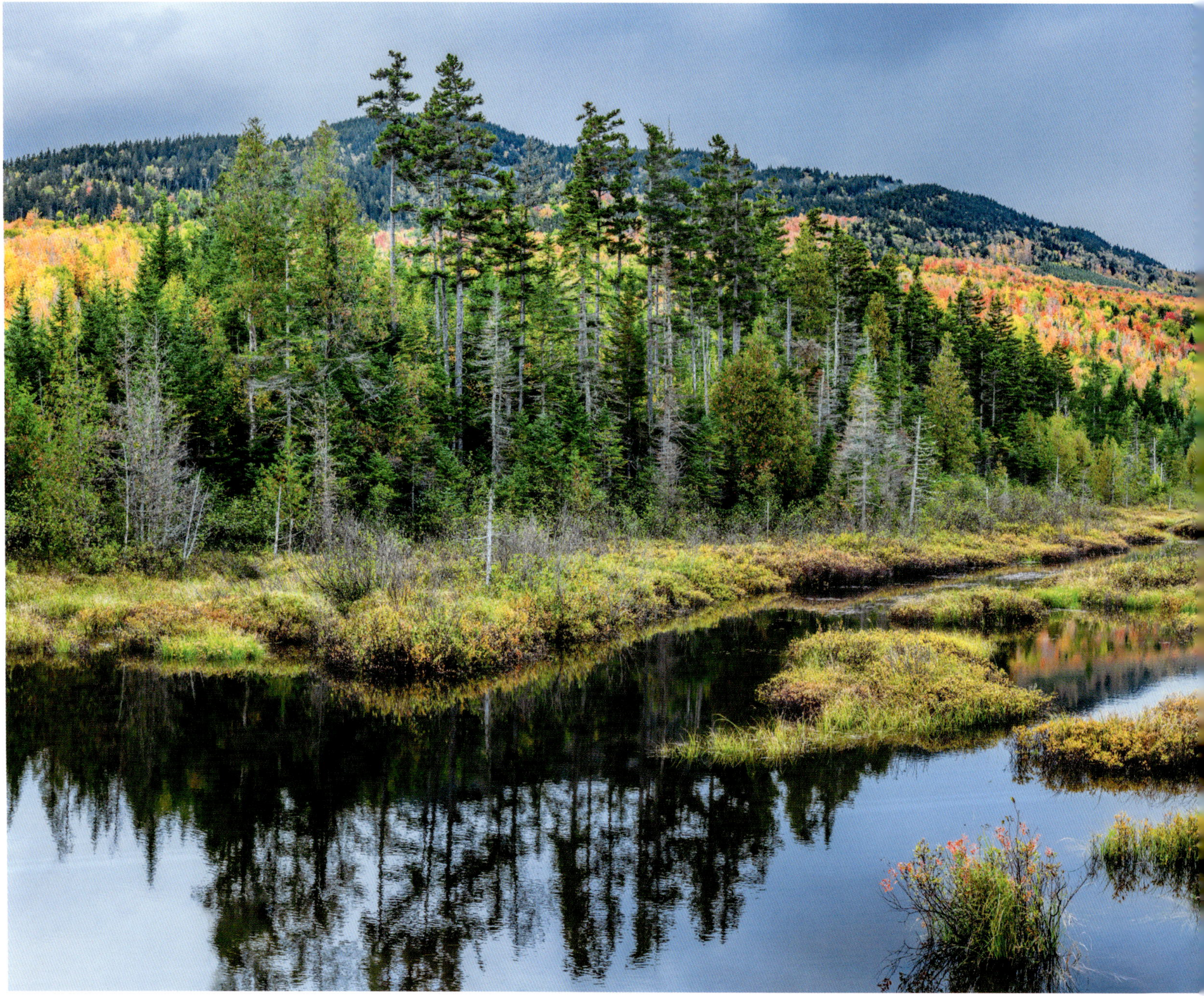

Parlin Stream, West Forks, Maine

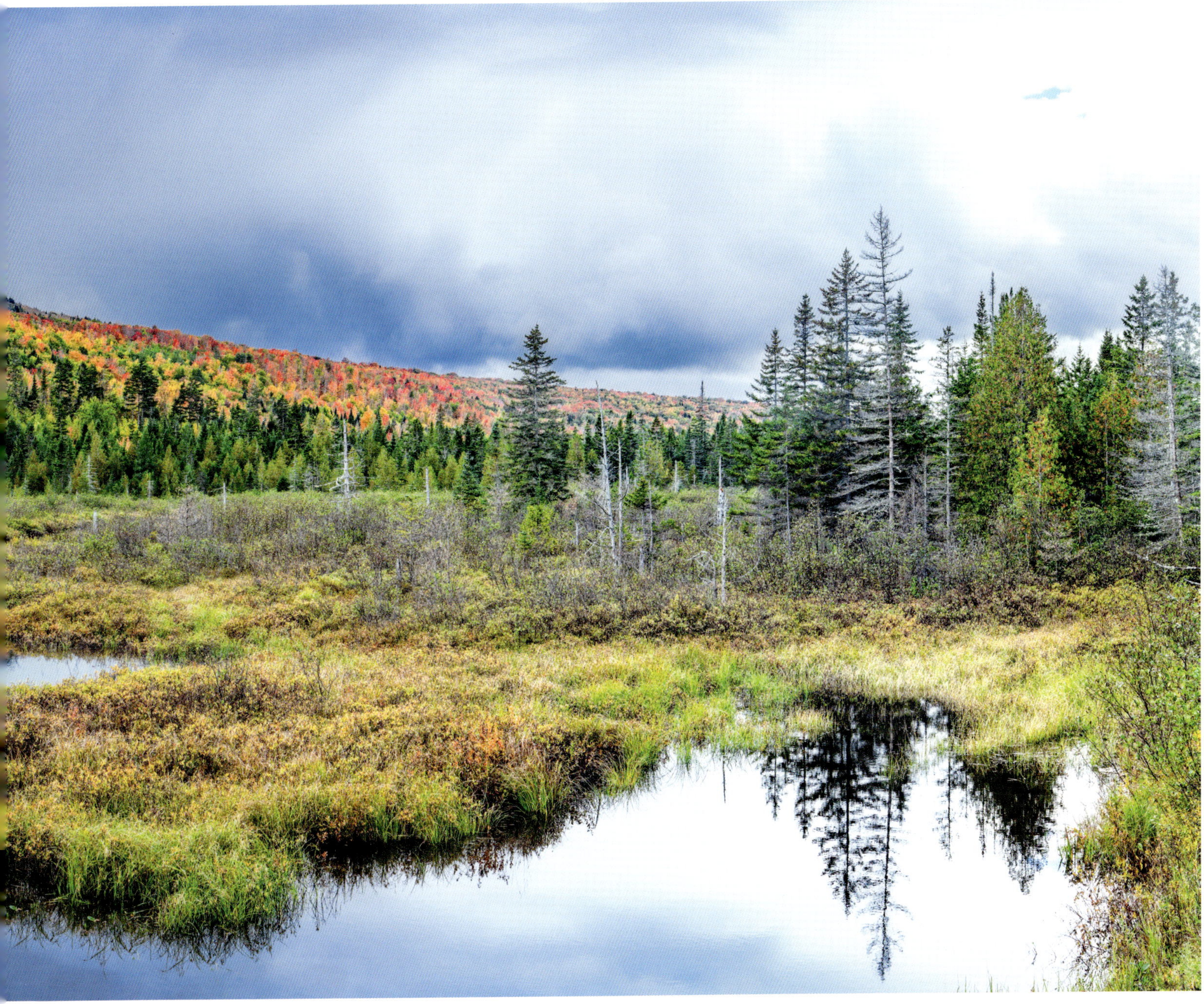

The sun and the rain were playing tag with each other.

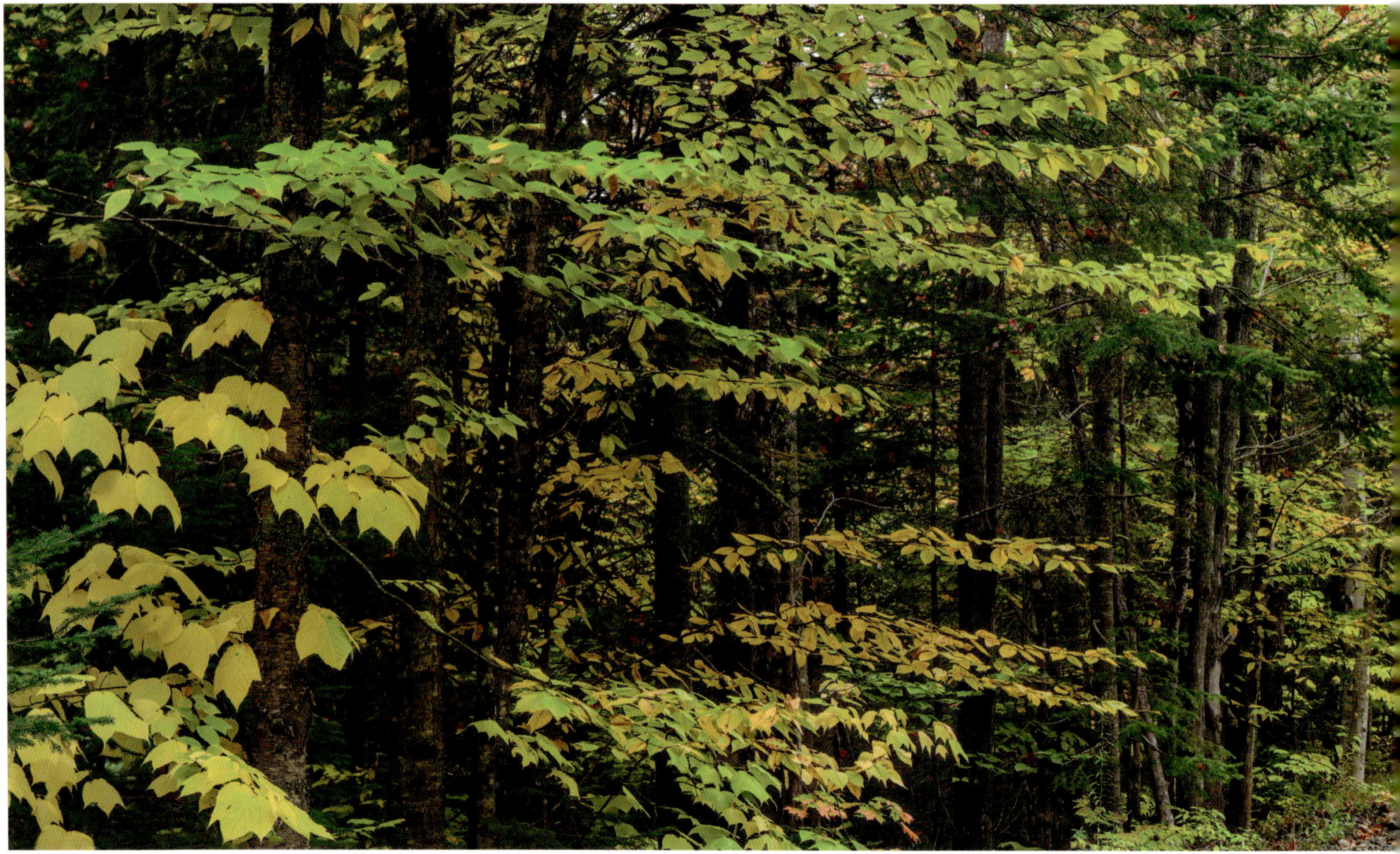

Sumerset Junction Road, Rockwood, Maine

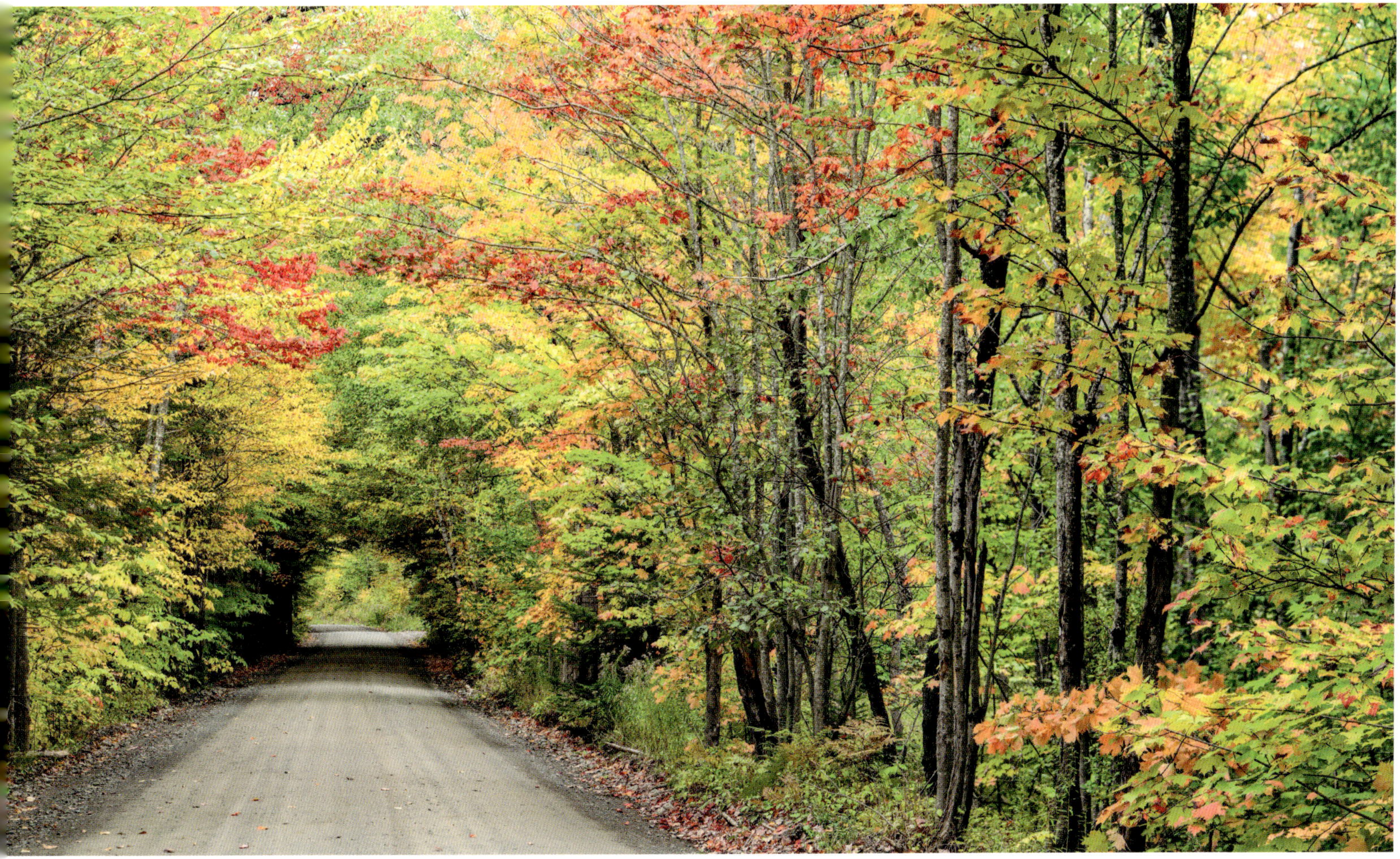

Driving through that tunnel felt a little like going down the rabbit hole.

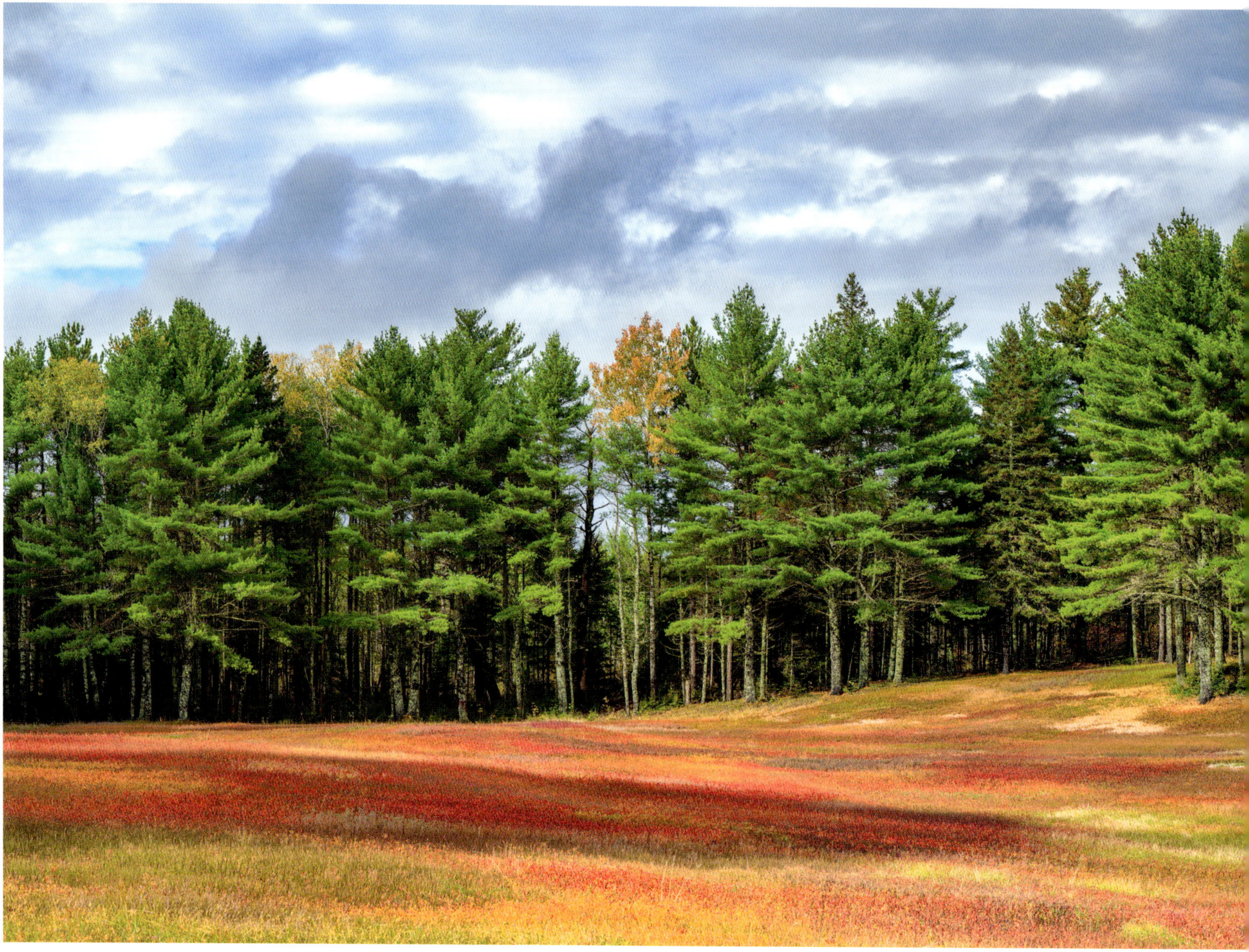

Wild blueberries, Down East, Maine

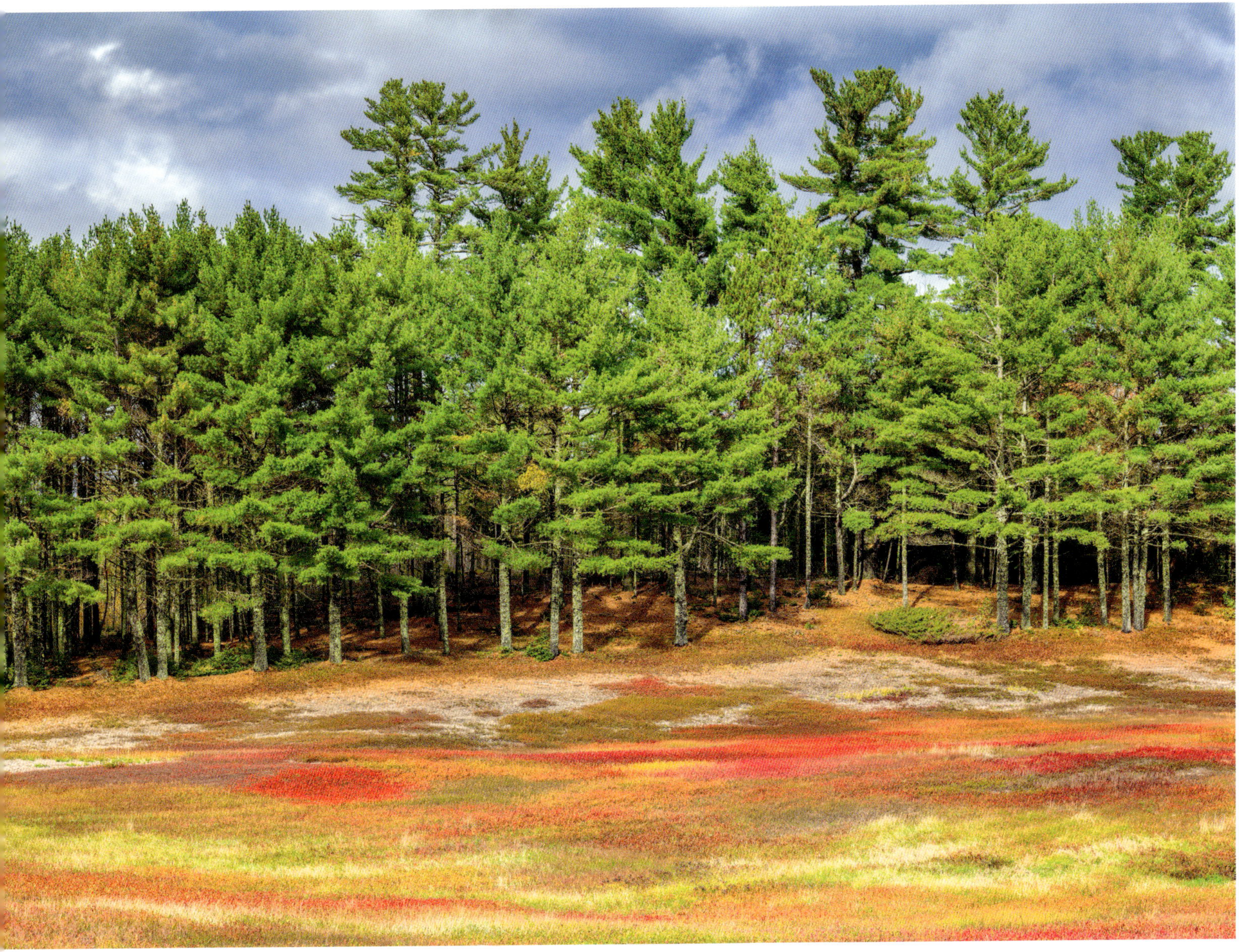

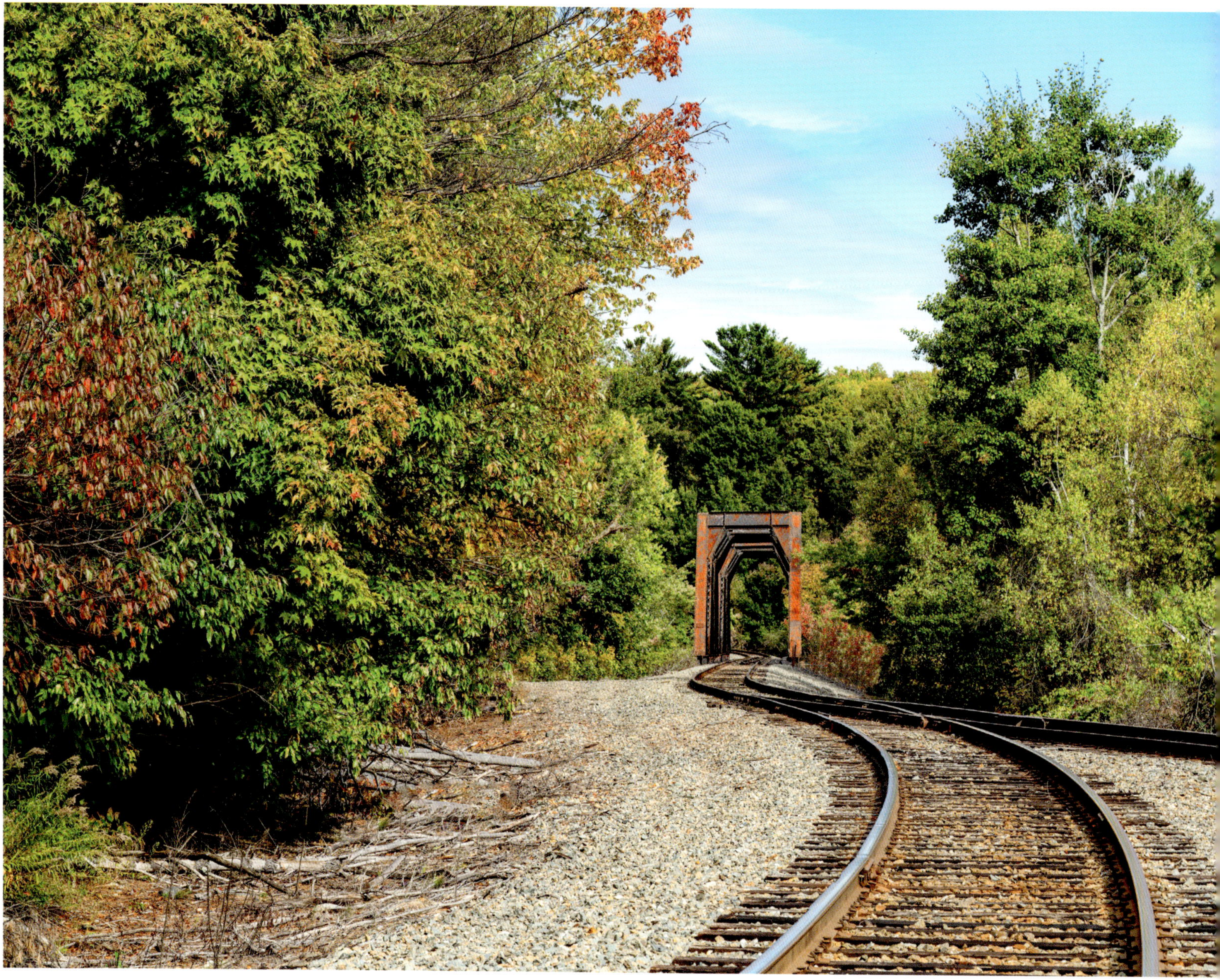

Railroad bridge, Brownville Junction, Maine

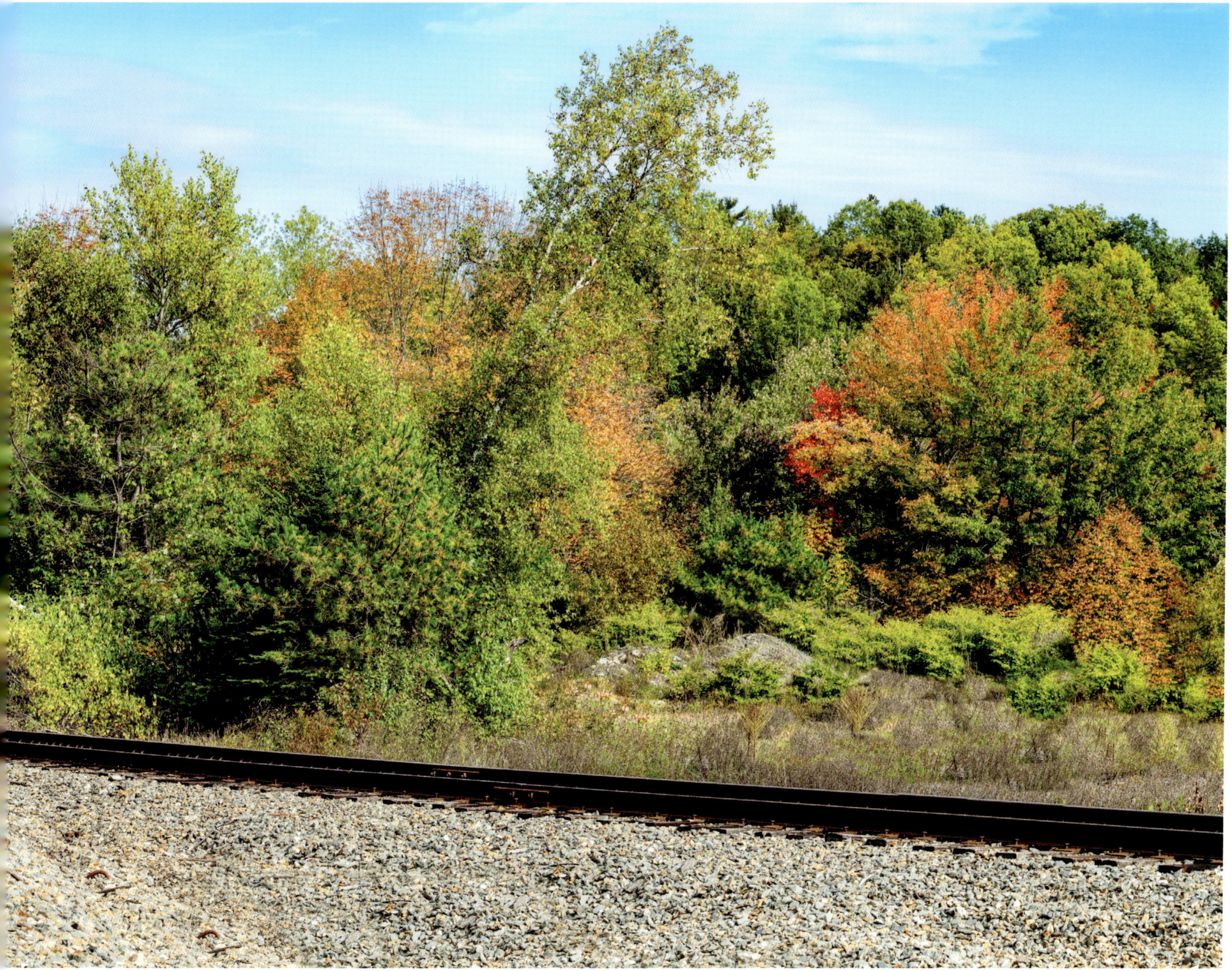

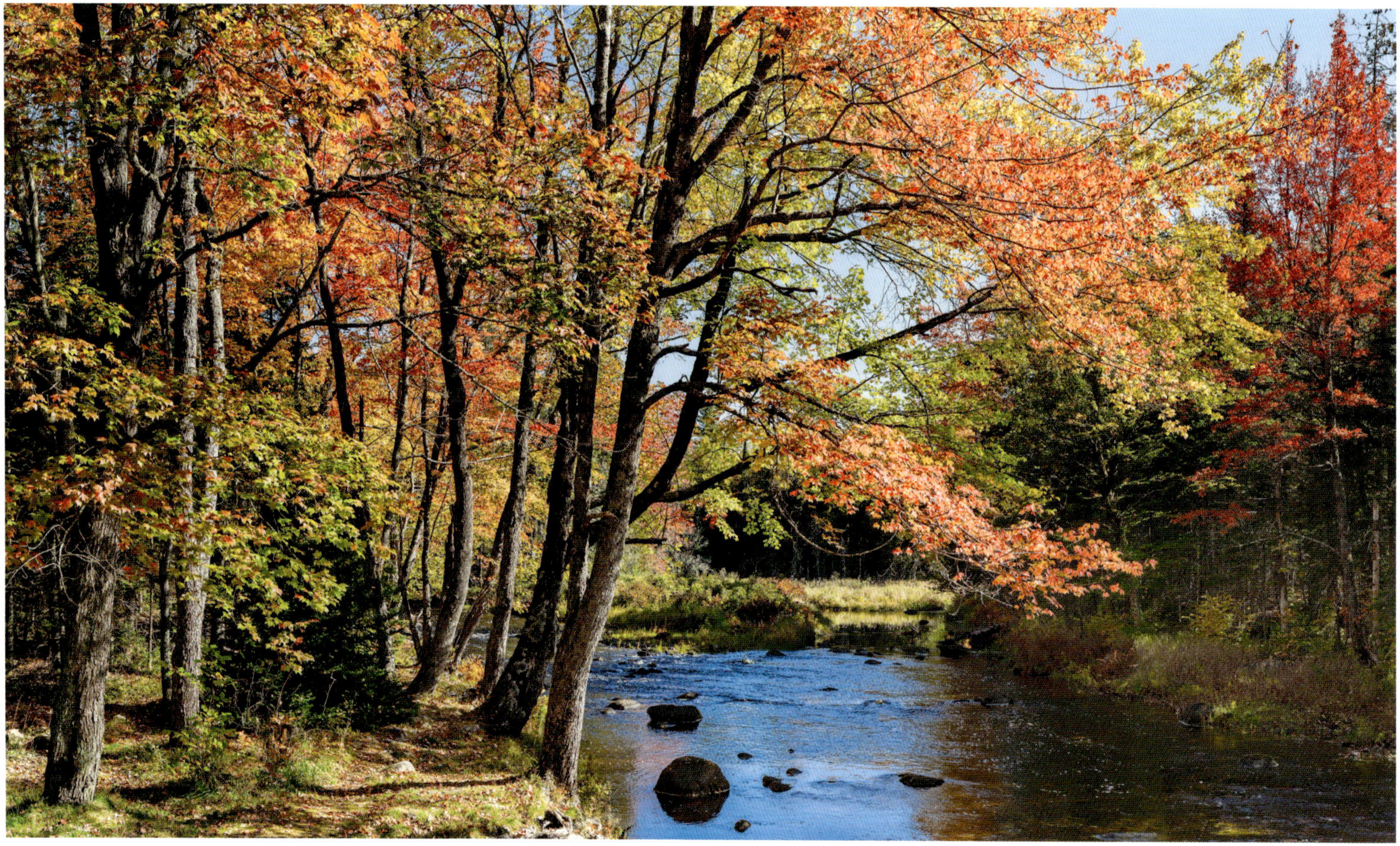

Red maple trees and Crawford Stream, Maine

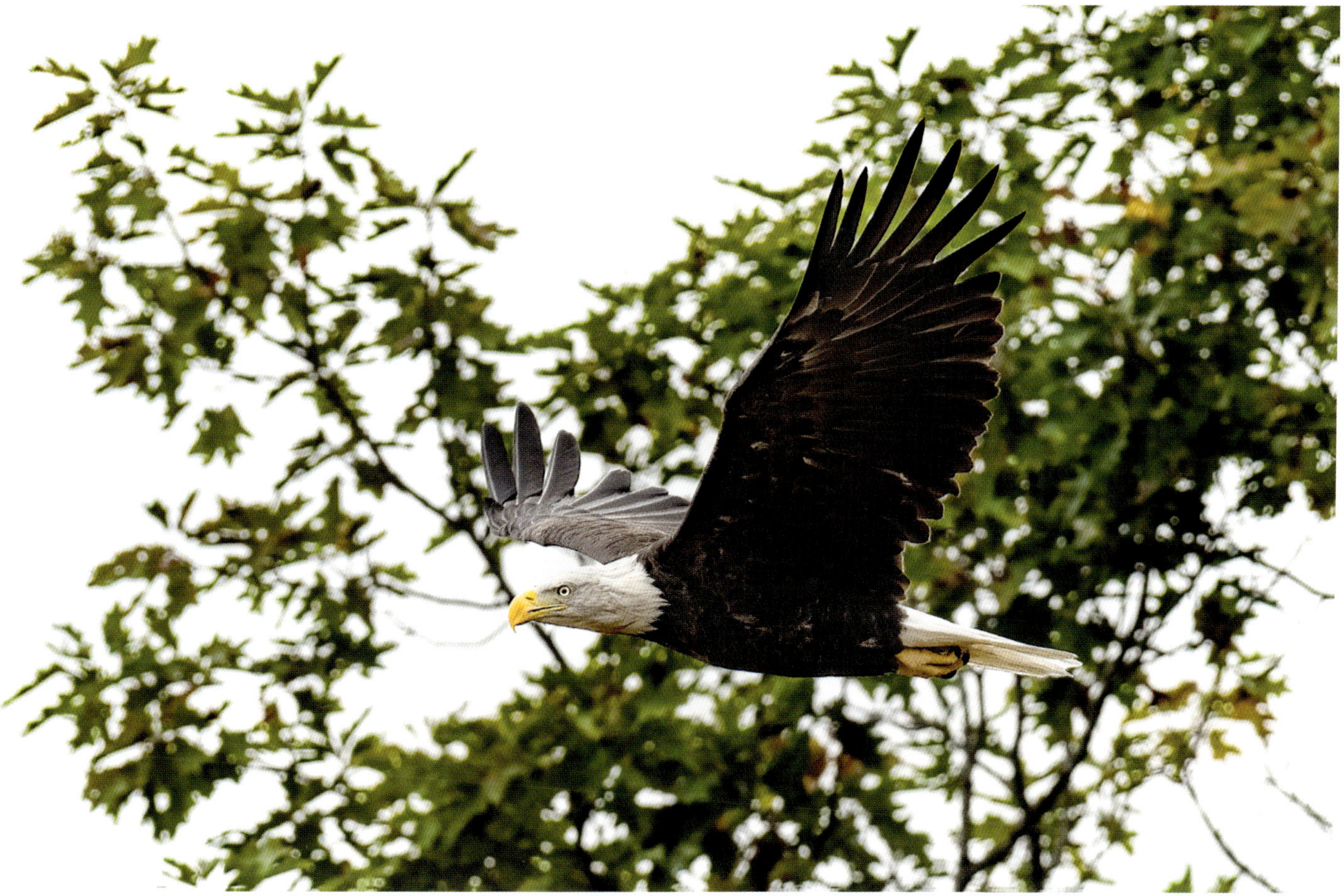

Bald eagle, Telus Lake, Maine

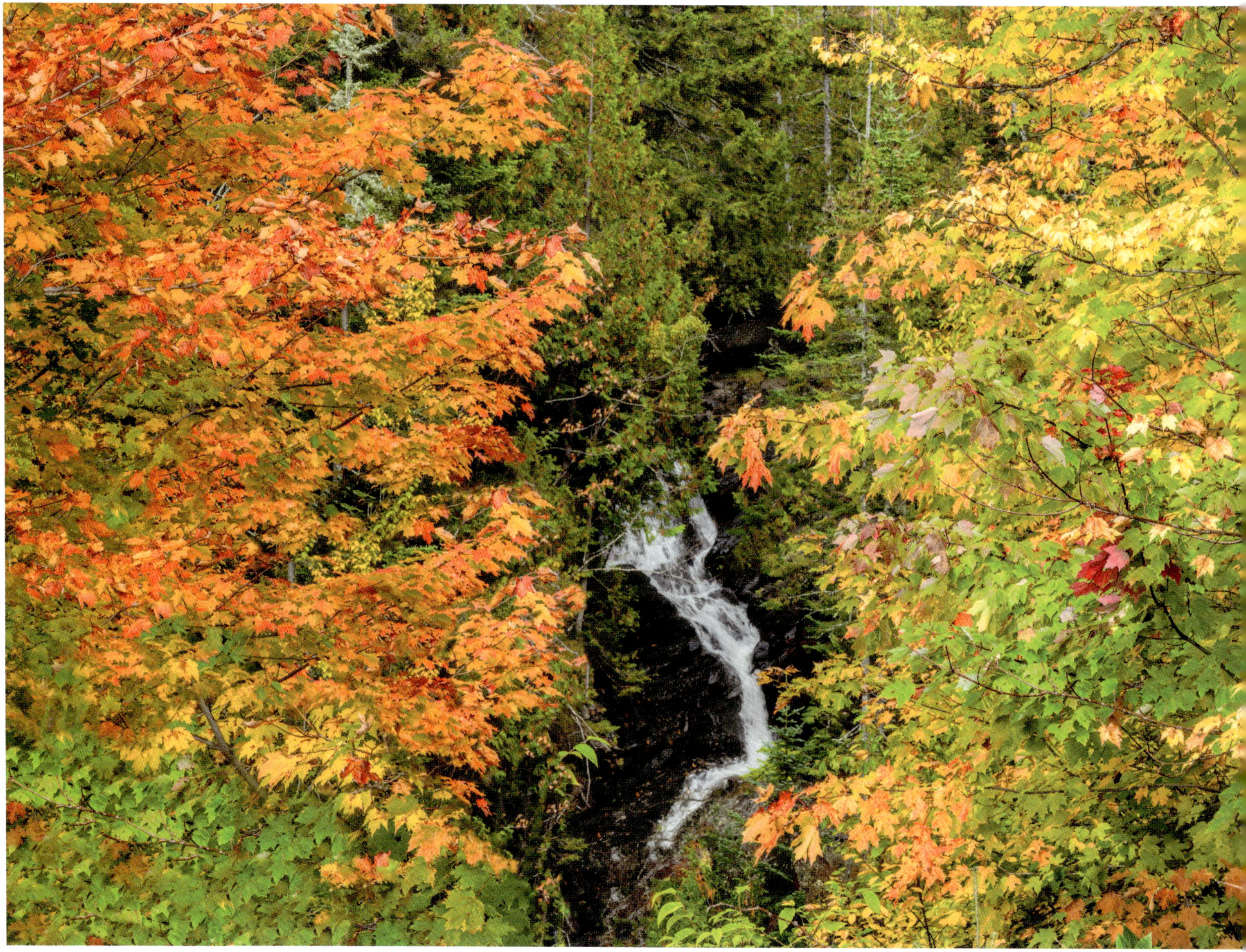

Jim Mac Falls through sugar maple trees, Maine

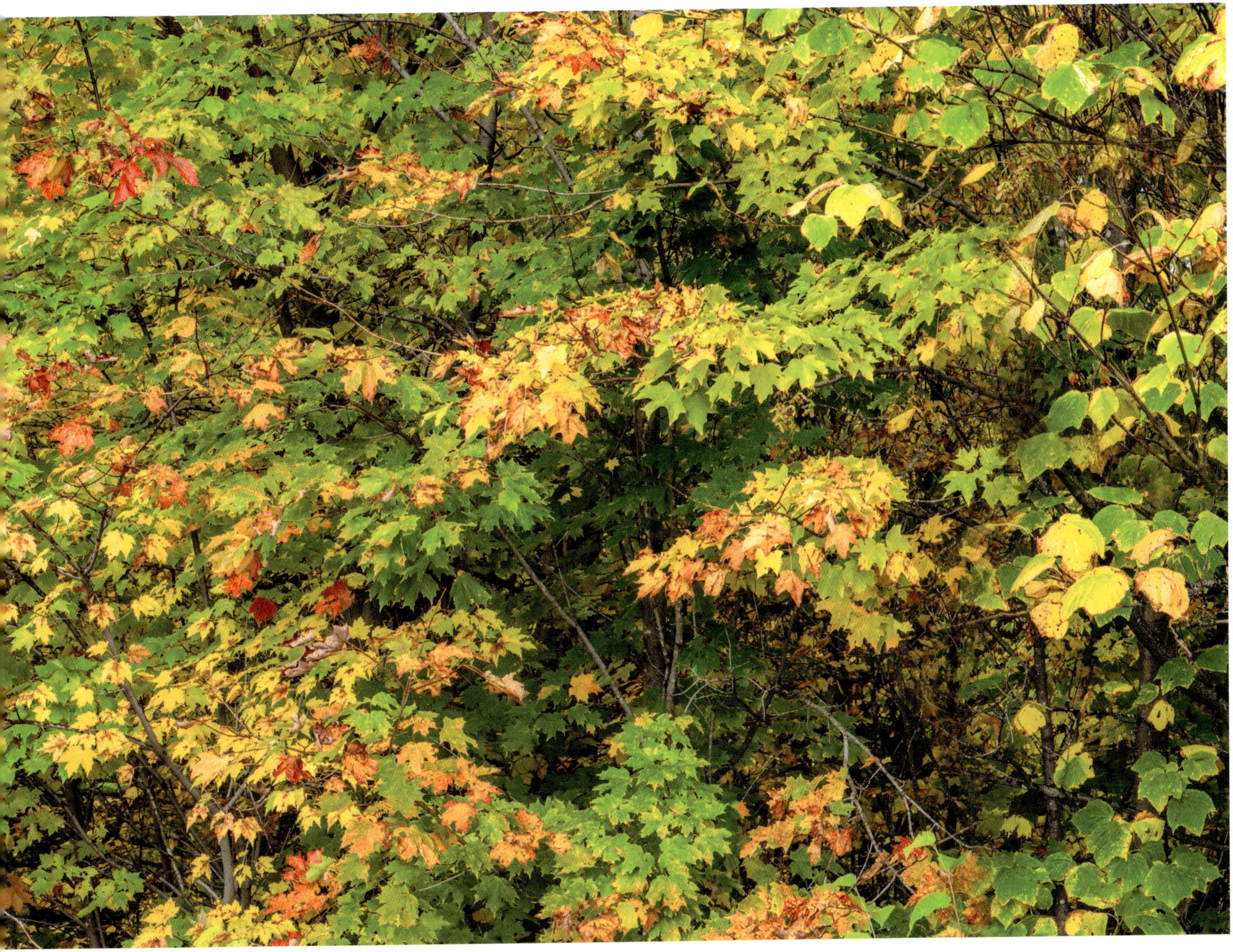

I pulled over to look at a map and spotted this waterfall by chance. There was no way to get closer, so I stood on top of Bob the Truck to get the best angle I could.

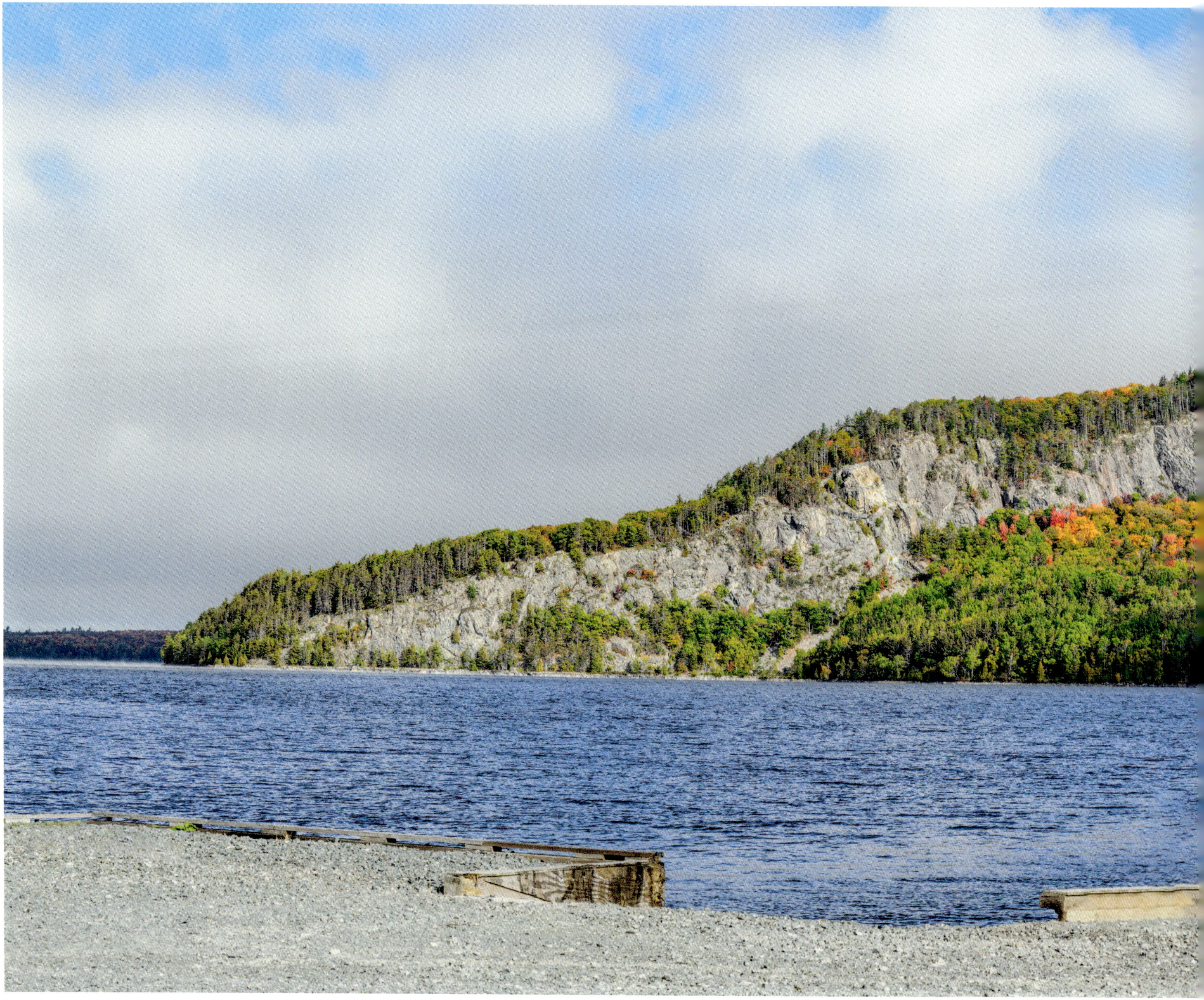

Mount Kineo, Maine

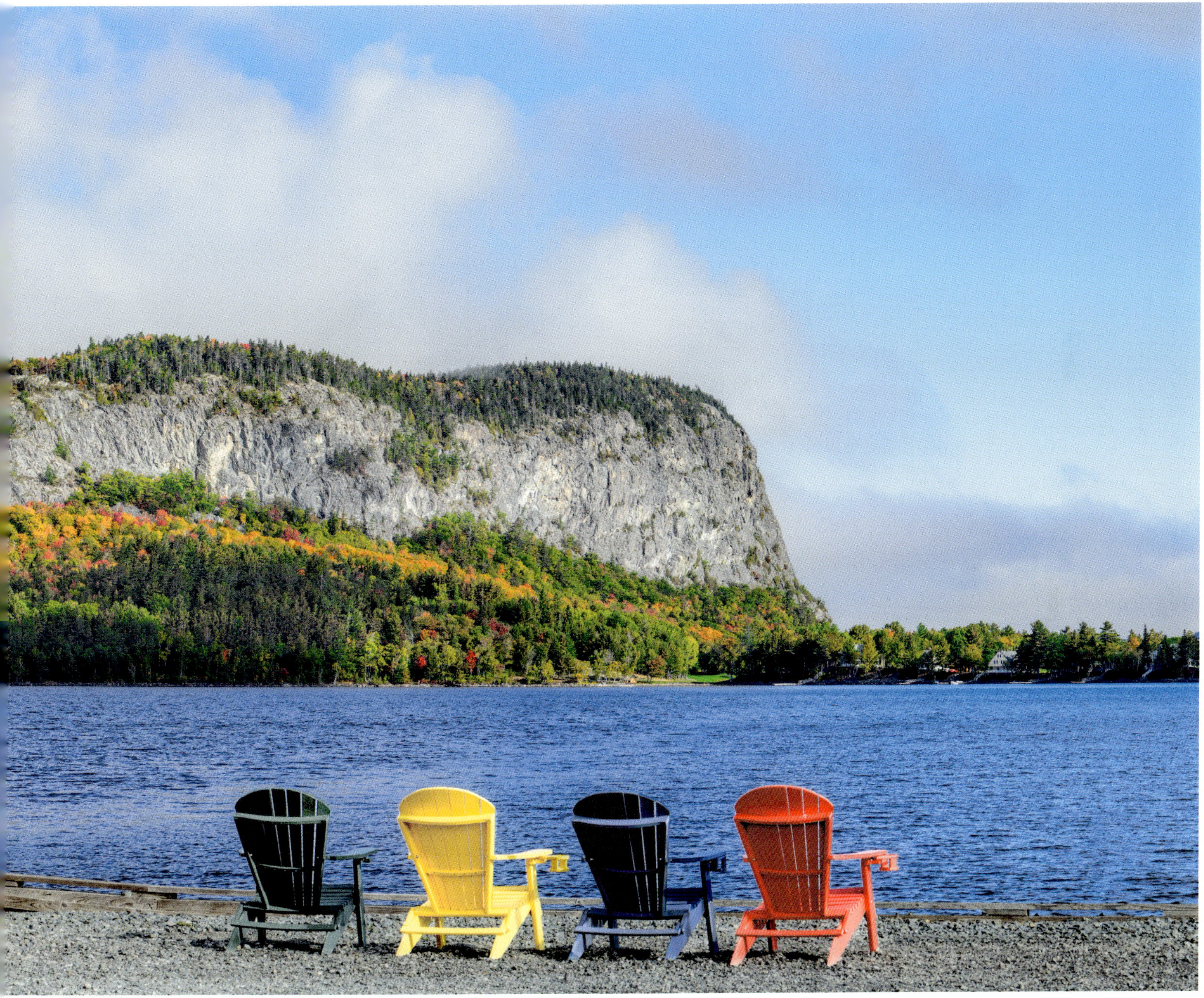

I sat there for a while after taking this photo. I invite you to do the same. It is a nice way to say goodbye.

APPENDIX

For all of the photographers out there who love to have all the tech information, I have included this appendix. May the geeks like me enjoy!

Image Number	Image Name	Camera	Lens	F/Stop	Shutter Speed	ISO	Pano Image Count	Pano Levels	Native Dimensions in Inches
01	Cape Neddick Lighthouse	Nikon D700	Nikkor 35mm f/1.4	f/16	1/320	100	11	1	34x11
02	Land's End Road	Nikon D750	Nikkor 85mm f/1.8	f/13	1/20	100	7	1	48x17
03	Wood Island Harbor	Nikon D810	Nikkor 50mm f/1.4	f/11	1/400	64	8	1	42x19
04	Town of Biddeford Pool	Nikon D810	Nikkor 50mm f/1.4	f/10	1/125	64	10	1	42x19
05	Under the boardwalk	Nikon D700	Nikkor 35mm f/1.4	f/22	1/250	100	10	1	45x17
06	The Pier	Nikon D700	Nikkor 105mm f/2.8	f/16	1/80	100	10	1	48x17
07A	Bug Light	Nikon D750	Nikkor 85mm f/1.8	f/10	1/400	400	17	2	43x26
07B	Strutting seagulls	Nikon D500	Nikkor 200–500mm f/5.6	f/5.6	1/2000	160	n/a	n/a	24x16
08	Knubble Bay	Nikon D810	Nikkor 50mm f/1.4	f/11	1/200	200	13	1	55x21
09	Doubling Point Light	Nikon D700	Nikkor 35mm f/1.4	f/9.3	1/125	100	9	1	41x16
10	Ocean Point	Nikon D750	Nikkor 85mm f/1.8	f/11	1/125	1600	8	1	54x19
11	Hendricks Head Light	Nikon D810	Zeiss 135mm f/2.0	f/13	6"	64	5	1	35x14
12	Granite Hall store	Nikon D750	Nikkor 35mm f/1.4	f/11	1"	100	11	1	36x14
13	Pemaquid Point Lighthouse	Nikon D750	Nikkor 85mm f/1.8	f/16	1/80	100	30	3	73x29
14A	Maine coastline	Nikon D700	Nikkor 35mm f/1.4	f/14	½	100	8	1	32x23
14B	Morning fog	Nikon D750	Nikkor 85mm f/1.8	f/10	1/60	100	3	1	24x19
15	Rowboat	Nikon D750	Nikkor 85mm f/1.8	f/11	1/100	100	6	1	36x14
16	Harbor Cemetery	Nikon D810	Nikkor 85mm f/1.8	f/13	1/125	64	12	1	64x20
17	Damariscotta River	Nikon D700	Nikkor 105mm f/2.8	f/11	1/160	100	13	1	34x12
18	Lawn display	Nikon D750	Nikkor 85mm f/1.8	f/14	1/40	100	8	1	59x19
19	Port Clyde Harbor	Nikon D750	Nikkor 85mm f/1.8	f/11	1/40	100	10	1	50x16
20	Shack and lobster traps	Nikon D810	Nikkor 85mm f/1.8	f/11	1/60	64	9	1	47x18
21	Marshall Point Light	Nikon D700	Nikkor 35mm f/1.4	f/16	1/50	100	15	1	60x20
22	Penobscot Bay and Camden	Nikon D810	Zeiss 135mm f/2.0	f/8	1/60	64	22	2	65X20
23	Belfast Harbor	Nikon D700	Nikkor 50mm f/1.4	f/10	1/160	100	12	1	56x17
24A	Pumpkin Island Light	Nikon D810	Nikkor 50mm f/1.4	f/16	1/15	64	7	1	41x21
24B	Wildcat Creek	Nikon D810	Nikkor 50mm f/1.4	f/13	1/10	64	22	2	68x36
25	The Love Barn	Nikon D750	Nikkor 35mm f/1.4	f/8	1/200	100	7	1	56x20

26	Sedgwick Harbor	Nikon D810	Nikkor 50mm f/1.4	f/11	1/640	200	10	1	65x20
27	R.L. Greenlaw's office	Nikon D750	Nikkor 85mm f/1.8	f/13	1/60	100	10	1	51x16
28	Stonington Harbor	Nikon D750	Nikkor 85mm f/1.8	f/11	1/50	100	9	1	52x19
29	Sunset Harbor	Nikon D810	Nikkor 50mm f/1.4	f/11	1/250	64	10	1	51x19
30	School Street Pier	Nikon D700	Nikkor 35mm f/1.4	f/16	1/400	100	9	1	47x19
31	Stonington, Maine	Nikon D810	Nikkor 200–500mm f/5.6	f/11	1/100	64	8	1	70x21
32	Blue Hill Bay	Nikon D750	Nikkor 85mm f/1.8	f/10	1/400	400	8	1	60x20
33	Thomas Bay	Nikon D810	Nikkor 50mm f/1.4	f/11	1/60	64	8	1	48x19
34	Twin Hills Cottages	Nikon D810	Nikkor 50mm f/1.4	f/11	1/60	64	10	1	45x17
35	Red maple, Little Long Pond	Nikon D850	Nikkor 50mm F1.4	f/14	1/40	80	20	2	66x31
36	Edenbrook Motel	Nikon D850	Nikkor 50mm f/1.4	f/11	1/100	80	9	1	65x21
37	Somes Sound	Nikon D850	Nikkor 50mm f/1.4	f/11	1/80	64	22	2	72x26
38	Sunset at Tremont Wharf	Nikon D850	Nikkor 50mm f/1.4	f/9.0	1/6	80	8	1	48x20
39	Champlain Mountain	Nikon D810	Nikkor 50mm f/1.4	f/16	1/80	64	9	1	48x19
40	Red barn and spindle trees	Nikon D850	Nikkor 50mm f/1.4	f/14	1/100	64	24	2	81x26
41	Eagle Lake	Nikon D810	Nikkor 50mm f/1.4	f/10	1/60	64	8	1	50x18
42	The Happy Clam Shack	Nikon D850	Nikkor 50mm f/1.4	f/11	1/100	64	7	1	53x22
43	Lobster Co-Op	Nikon D750	Nikkor 85mm f/1.8	f/11	1/100	100	8	1	67x23
44A	Fort Point Light	Nikon D300	Nikkor 10.5mm f/2.8	f/2.8	1/350	2500	n/a	n/a	24x16
44B	Schoodic Point	Nikon D300	Nikkor 105mm f/2.8	f/16	1"	100	n/a	n/a	24x16
45	Abandoned house	Nikon D850	Nikkor 85mm f/1.8	f/8	1/60	64	8	1	52x22
46	Destiny Cove	Nikon D750	Nikkor 85mm f/1.8	f/10	1/30	100	8	1	48x17
47	Donovan Cove	Nikon D850	Zeiss 135mm f/2.0	f/10	1/25	64	5	1	48x18
48	Millpond	Nikon D850	Zeiss 135mm f/2.0	f/14	1/15	64	10	1	51x18
49A	Posing gull	Nikon D300	Nikkor 80–400mm	f/5.6	1/1000	500	n/a	n/a	24x16
49B	West Quoddy Head Lighthouse	Nikon D750	Nikkor 35mm f/1.4	F11	1/25	100	18	2	44x30
50	Long Cove	Nikon D810	Nikkor 85mm f/1.8	f/14	1/15	64	9	1	53x18
51A	Pier at Eastport	Nikon D750	Nikkor 35mm f/1.4	f/11	1/80	100	10	1	47X32
51B	Lobster trap floats	Nikon D300	Nikkor 105mm f/2.8	f/16	1/20	200	n/a	n/a	24x16
52	Lubec, Maine	Nikon D750	Nikkor 85mm f/1.8	11	1/80	100	6	1	48x19
53A	Railroad bridge	Nikon D850	Nikkor 50mm f/1.4	f/11	1/100	64	16	2	47x28
53B	Penobscot Narrows Bridge	Nikon D810	Nikkor 50mm f/1.4	f/10	1/500	64	18	2	57x32
54A	Little Long Pond Road	Nikon D850	Nikkor 50mm f/1.4	f/11	1/30	80	7	1	45x21
54B	Sugar maples	Nikon D850	Zeiss 135mm f/2.0	f/9	¼	64	7	1	44x22
55	Barn and pumpkins	Nikon D810	Nikkor 50mm f/1.4	f/10	1/500	64	8	1	48x18
56	Fences, fog, and fall	Nikon D850	Nikkor 85mm f/1.8	f/13	1/40	64	11	1	59x21
57	Giant windmills	Nikon D810	Zeiss 135mm f/2.0	f/10	1/200	64	9	1	65x20

58	Paradise apples	Nikon D750	Nikkor 35mm f/1.4	f/11	1/250	100	10	1	36x15
59	Hayfield, Mexico, Maine	Nikon D810	Nikkor 50mm f/2.0	f/13	1/160	64	11	1	57x20
60	View From Quill Hill	Nikon D810	Nikkor 50mm f/1.4	f/13	1/50	64	7	1	48x19
61	Mooselookmeguntic Lake	Nikon D810	Nikkor 50mm f/1.4	f/13	1/50	64	9	1	60x22
62A	Gold Brook Road	Nikon D810	Nikkor 50mm f/1.4	f/13	1/125	64	5	1	27x21
62B	Logging road	Nikon D810	Nikkor 50mm f/1.4	f/13	1/60	64	16	2	48x38
63	Flagstaff Lake	Nikon D810	Nikkor 50mm f/1.4	f/13	1/200	64	9	1	61x20
64	Sunset over Rangeley Lake	Nikon D810	Nikkor 50mm f/1.4	f/10	1/15	64	10	1	74x24
65A	Moose	Nikon D500	Nikkor 200–500mm f/5.6	f/7.1	1/3200	3600	n/a	n/a	24x22
65B	Red maple tree and boats	Nikon D850	Nikkor 50mm f/1.4	f/11	1/13	64	5	1	48x44
66	Fall reflection	Nikon D850	Zeiss 135mm f/2.0	f/11	1/160	64	7	1	52x21
67	Birch and sugar maple trees	Nikon D850	Zeiss 135mm f/2.0	f/11	1/5	64	7	1	56x23
68	Double Top Mountain	Nikon D850	Nikkor 50mm f/1.4	f/11	1/100	64	11	1	57x22
69	Blue spruce trees	Nikon D850	Zeiss 135mm f/2.0	f/2.0	1/40	64	12	1	47x18
70	Pond and birch trunks	Nikon D810	Nikkor 50mm f/1.4	f/13	1/125	64	7	1	53x21
71	Morning mist on First Roach Pond	Nikon D850	Zeiss 135mm f/2.0	f/10	1/400	64	9	1	50x22
72	Otter Pond	Nikon D850	Nikkor 50mm f/1.4	f/11	1/100	64	6	1	37x16
73	Currier's Flying Service	Nikon D850	Nikkor 50mm f/1.4	f/11	1/50	64	10	1	56x21
74A	Mount Katahdin and Abol Stream	Nikon D850	Nikkor 50mm f/1.4	f/11	1/160	64	18	2	58x37
74B	White-breasted nuthatch	Nikon D500	Nikkor 200–500mm f/5.6	f/8	1/3200	8000	n/a	n/a	24x15
75	Mount Katahdin and Rainbow Lake	Nikon D850	Nikkor 50mm f/1.4	f/14	1/80	64	11	1	63x22
76	Big Squaw Mountain	Nikon D850	Zeiss 135mm f/2.0	f/13	1/10	64	16	2	70x30
77	Mountain View Pond	Nikon D850	Nikkor 50mm f/1.4	f/10	1/80	64	28	2	88x33
78	Parlin Stream	Nikon D850	Nikkor 50mm f/1.4	f/10	1/50	64	7	1	46x19
79	Sumerset Junction Road	Nikon D850	Zeiss 135mm f/2.0	f/11	¼	64	12	1	75x22
80	Wild blueberries	Nikon D850	Zeiss 135mm f/2.0	f/10	1/40	64	22	2	96x35
81	Railroad bridge, Brownville Junction	Nikon D850	Zeiss 135mm f/2.0	f/14	1/60	64	8	1	53x22
82A	Red maple trees and Crawford Stream	Nikon D850	Nikkor 50mm f/1.4	f/11	1/40	64	6	1	35x20
82B	Bald eagle	Nikon D500	Nikkor 200–500mm f/5.6	f/8	1/2500	1250	n/a	n/a	24x14
83	Jim Mac Falls	D850	Nikkor 50mm f/1.4	f/11	1/30	64	9	1	62x24
84	Mount Kineo	Nikon D850	Nikkor 85mm f/1.8	f/11	1/60	64	7	1	43x18

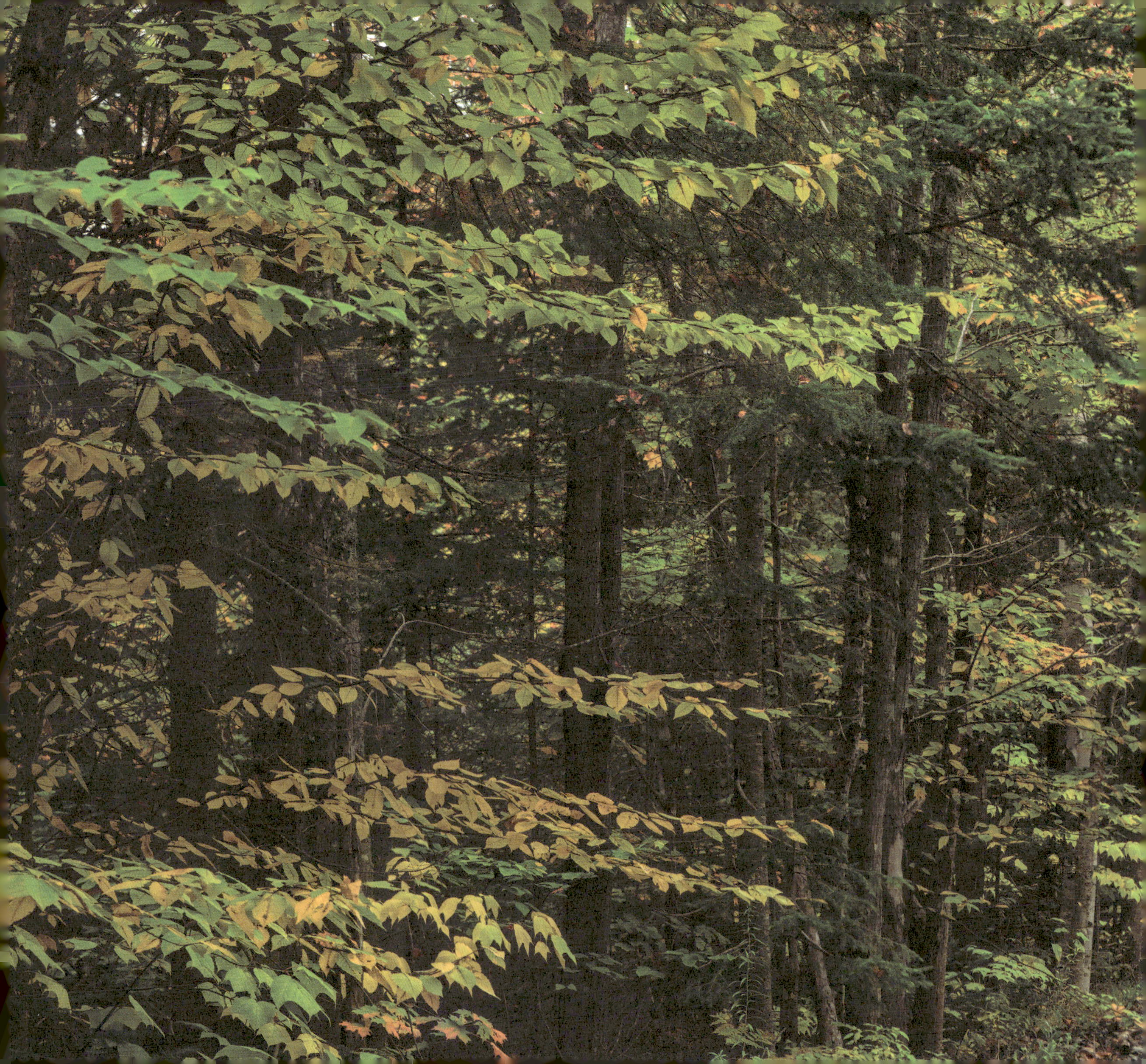